ASSEMBLIES

ASSY. REF. Nº	PART Nº	DESCRIPTION	ASSY. REF. Nº	PART Nº	DESCRIPTION
1	S4 1/J CR1553A	LEVER LOCKING RETURN SPRING CAP. 1-OFF.	3	S4 8/A. CR1363	BLOCK BREECH. 1-OFF
2	S4 6/V	BUTT ASSY. 1-OFF.	4	S4 12 CR112A	TRIGGER ASSY. 1-OFF.

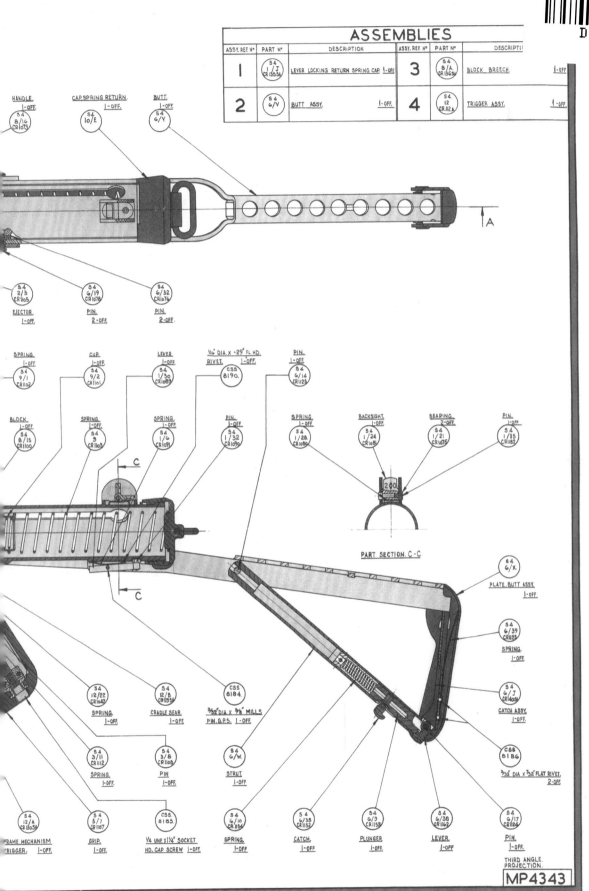

HANDLE.
1-OFF.
S4 8/16 CR1073

CAP SPRING RETURN.
1-OFF.
S4 10/E

BUTT.
1-OFF.
S4 6/Y

A

S4 2/3 CR1105
EJECTOR
1-OFF.

S4 6/19 CR1078
PIN.
2-OFF.

S4 6/32 CR1076
PIN.
2-OFF.

SPRING.
1-OFF.
S4 9/1 CR1102

CUP.
1-OFF.
S4 9/2 CR1101

LEVER
1-OFF.
S4 1/30 CR1083

1/16" DIA. X .29" FL HD.
RIVET. 1-OFF.
CSS 8190.

PIN.
1-OFF.
S4 6/14 CR1125

BLOCK.
1-OFF.
S4 8/15 CR1100

SPRING.
1-OFF.
S4 9 CR1103

SPRING.
1-OFF.
S4 1/6 CR1091

PIN.
1-OFF.
S4 1/32 CR1099

SPRING.
1-OFF.
S4 1/28 CR1080

BACKSIGHT.
1-OFF.
S4 1/24 CR1081

BEARING.
2-OFF.
S4 1/21 CR1079

PIN.
1-OFF.
S4 1/35 CR1182

C

C

2.00

PART SECTION. C-C.

S4 6/X.

PLATE, BUTT ASSY.
1-OFF.

S4 6/39 CR1123
SPRING.
1-OFF.

S4 6/J CR1403
CATCH ASSY.
1-OFF.

CSS 8186

3/32" DIA X 7/32" FLAT RIVET.
2-OFF.

S4 12/22 CR1042
SPRING.
1-OFF.

S4 12/B CR1041
CRADLE SEAR
1-OFF.

CSS 8184
3/32" DIA X 3/8" MILLS
PIN. G.P.S. 1-OFF.

S4 6/W.

S4 3/11 CR1113
SPRING.
1-OFF.

S4 3/8 CR1108
PIN
1-OFF.

STRUT
1-OFF.

S4 6/17 CR1162
PIN.
1-OFF.

S4 12/A CR1303A
FRAME MECHANISM
TRIGGER. 1-OFF.

S4 5/7 CR1107
GRIP.
1-OFF.

CSS 8185
1/4 UNF. X 1 1/4" SOCKET
HD. CAP SCREW 1-OFF.

S4 6/10 CR854
SPRING.
1-OFF.

S4 6/35 CR1152
CATCH.
1-OFF.

S4 6/5 CR1155
PLUNGER
1-OFF.

S4 6/38 CR1162
LEVER
1-OFF.

S4 6/17
PIN.
1-OFF.

THIRD ANGLE.
PROJECTION.

MP4343

A History of the Small Arms made by the Sterling Armament Company

A History of the Small Arms made by the Sterling Armament Company

Excellence in Adversity

Peter Laidler, David Howroyd and James Edmiston

Pen & Sword
MILITARY

First published in Great Britain in 2020 by
Pen & Sword Military
An imprint of
Pen & Sword Books Ltd
Yorkshire – Philadelphia

ISBN 978 1 52677 330 2

A CIP catalogue record for this book is
available from the British Library.

Typeset by Mac Style
Printed and bound by Printworks Global Ltd

Pen & Sword Books Limited incorporates the imprints of Atlas, Archaeology, Aviation, Discovery,
Family History, Fiction, History, Maritime, Military, Military Classics, Politics, Select, Transport,
True Crime, Air World, Frontline Publishing, Leo Cooper, Remember When, Seaforth Publishing,
The Praetorian Press, Wharncliffe Local History, Wharncliffe Transport, Wharncliffe True Crime
and White Owl.

For a complete list of Pen & Sword titles please contact

PEN & SWORD BOOKS LIMITED
47 Church Street, Barnsley, South Yorkshire, S70 2AS, England
E-mail: enquiries@pen-and-sword.co.uk
Website: www.pen-and-sword.co.uk

Or

PEN AND SWORD BOOKS
1950 Lawrence Rd, Havertown, PA 19083, USA
E-mail: Uspen-and-sword@casematepublishers.com
Website: www.penandswordbooks.com

Contents

Prologue

Being a manufacturer of something consumable had its appeal. The trouble with the Sterling was that it was built to last forever.

James Edmiston, *The Sterling Years*

My father Francis (Frank) Laidler was a long-serving and senior Warrant Officer in the British Army, and as a result I got used to seeing him carrying and using guns. When I was in my early teens, I used to go on the rifle ranges with him and, between details, one of his soldiers would inevitably give me enough basic instruction, and stay with me so I could fill any vacant range detail. By the time I joined the Army, as an Armourer Apprentice at Carlisle, in the Royal Electrical and Mechanical Engineers (REME) in 1963, I had fired most of the weapons in current service, including the 3.5″ rocket launcher.

To me, what eventually emerged as the Sterling Sub-Machine Gun was always referred to by my father as the "Patchett". We didn't know about the genius of George Patchett then, or of David Howroyd, Frank Waters, Bert List and the rest of the company who got the gun going.

As Armourer Apprentices at Hadrian's Camp in Carlisle, we learned about sub-machine guns in our 6th term. That was the last term of our second year. During this period we were instructed on the Pistol, Browning, 9mm HP, No1 and 2 Mk1 and No2 Mk1* [stocks of which had been supplied to the UK Military from Canadian production at the John Inglis Co Ltd, Toronto, in 1944–1945]. We also learned inside-out the Pistol, Signal 1″ and the Pistol, Signal 1.5″. And lastly, the Sterling Sub-Machine Gun. From that date, in September 1964, the terms 'Sten', 'Patchett', 'Sterling', 'SMG', 'Tommy Gun' or anything else that even remotely referred to a sub-machine gun gave way to the correct Army nomenclature "Gun, Submachine,

The unkindest cut: a skeletonised Mk4/L2A3 trigger mechanism.

Skeletonising/sectioning is a practice undertaken by generations of Armourer-apprentices, to test their mechanical aptitude, understanding of instructions, and ability to work together as a team.

This was Peter Laidler's work during his third year trade test phase. Such apprentice 'art' was graded, and the best examples usually presented to visiting dignitaries or other local worthies, presumably for use as paperweights. Fortunately, or unfortunately, depending on your point of view, the author's work rarely merited presentation to others, and was usually left in a pile with the other also-rans, until being liberated by him!

The government label on this piece reads, "L2A3 UF57A 15307 (gun details) A/T (apprentice tradesman) LAIDLER, 63A (intake group). (Courtesy Peter Laidler)

9mm L2A3". Even today, to me and every other Armourer who has ever served, this gun is referred to as simply the "L2".

We were instructed under the eagle eye of our affable civilian instructor·, the late Edward"Eddie"Stone, who was assisted by REME Armourer Staff-Sergeant instructor Stan Etchells. I wonder how many other Ex-Carlisle Armourer apprentices recall Eddie Stone's impromptu rendition of *God Save the Queen* played penny-whistle fashion on the Vickers MMG steam tube. We used the steam tube wrapped with old rags to clean out the L2A3 gun casings. The L2s we used during our classroom instruction were all well-used examples, having been stripped and assembled literally hundreds of times by apprentices. But, more to the point, there were differences between some of the guns. It was then that I learned from Eddie Stone and Stan Etchells of the origins of the "Patchett". 'I'm sure that there's a MkI among these somewhere", Eddie Stone remarked. And sure enough, there was. Also among our training examples was an L2Al (a MkII), and an L2A2 (a MkIII).

The idea for *The Guns of Dagenham* was a result of a conversation I had with a group of Armourers after an hour of range testing an old and tired Sten gun. David Lines, the examiner, commented that whatever else was said about the Sten, it reeked of nostalgia and he doubted whether the current gun, the L2A3 Sterling, could ever command such respect in the future. I thought about what he said. After all, the Sten was in service for about 25 years, from 1941 to 1967, and was produced in 8 Marks. On the other hand, the Sterling L2 series has lasted from 1951 (or thereabouts) to 1994 in UK Military service, and beyond with other Military Forces. During that time it has also been produced in 8 Marks, although not all of these saw military service. As REME Armourer Roger Smith put it, "the L2 is so reliable that it'll probably just fade away, and be remembered like a Morris Minor. Given a bit of care, something that would probably last forever."

While I was gathering information together, I wrote a letter to the Editor of the *Dagenham Post*, a local newspaper, telling him of my project with the request that any former Sterling employees write to me.

The authors, David Howroyd (left) and Peter Laidler, in the SMG and Pistol Room at the MoD Pattern Room, Nottingham. (Courtesy David Howroyd)

Many did, with messages of encouragement. Good though they were, the linchpin seemed to be missing. Then, several weeks later, I had a letter from Bert List suggesting that I contact David Howroyd, the last Engineering Director of the Sterling Company. I did, and found the missing linchpin. David had seen my letter and decided that sooner or later, if I was serious, I would find him. David had already written a lot about his life at Sterling, others involved with the guns, and the company's history. What we both needed was a meeting of minds. The maker had met the user.

David and I hope that this book will be referred to as the definitive history of the trusty Sterling series of sub-machine guns. We of course have been helped by the fact that not a lot has been written previously about these guns.

For those technically-minded readers, we hope that what is written is compromisingly technical enough to be understood by all. We would like to think that every question ever asked about these tough little guns is answered in this book, as between David and myself, our first-hand experience covers every aspect of the Sterling, including (on his part) design, development, troubleshooting, manufacture, assembly, and sale, and (on my part) use under the most atrocious active service conditions, maintenance, repair and finally, deactivation or destruction, usually after an extremely arduous life.

We make no apology for including sizeable references to the Lanchester, the older brother of the Patchett/Sterling. We both feel that this solid Lanchester foundation was important: indeed, if the Lanchester had not been developed and produced at the Sterling works, the Patchett/Sterling might never have evolved there.

We trust that when the L2 Sterling sub-machine gun has been obsolete for 25 years, people will still speak of it with affection. Certainly thousands will still be out there, in every part of the globe, still giving 'sterling' service.

Peter Laidler
Marcham, Abingdon
Oxfordshire
August, 1995

Foreword

By Lieutenant Colonel (Ret'd) 'Tug' Wilson, MBE, Small Arms School Corps

My first contact with Peter Laidler was through his previous publications. I had taken over the appointment of Curator [of the Infantry and Small Arms School Corps Weapons Museum, at the Infantry Training Centre, Warminster] in 1992, and was deter mined to improve my knowledge regarding the history and the development of weapons, particularly small-arms. Having been an engineer prior to joining the Army and spending my entire service in weapon related jobs, I had already accumulated a modest knowledge about weapons design and their use in operations. However, I realised that if I was to be successful in my new venture, I required a little bit extra. To that end I spent many a happy hour browsing through what was on offer in the museum's comprehensive reference library. During my research I found that many publications failed to provide me with that "little bit extra", but not so Peter's endeavours.

I have since had the pleasure of talking to Peter in person and know why his books are so full of the information I sought. A pragmatic person with an eye for detail and more than a fair share of enthusiasm.

This time he has joined forces with David Howroyd, and I have thoroughly enjoyed this well researched and presented book on the history of a weapon that has always been present throughout my 33 years in the service: the SMG. I have no hesitation in recommending it to anyone who has an interest in the weapon or just about the history of weapons in general.

Peter and David state in the Prologue that they hope that this book will be referred to as "the definitive history of the trusty Sterling series of sub-machine guns". Peter and David, I am sure it will. Thank you for the excellent read.

'Tug' Wilson
Curator,
The Infantry and Small Arms School Corps
Weapons Museum,
The Infantry Training Centre,
Warminster, Wiltshire

Foreword of 13th April 2019

By James Edmiston

When I was proposed for the Worshipful Company of Gunmakers by the late Harry Lawrence a director of James Purdey in February 1978, Mr. Lawrence took great delight in showing me a gorgeous pair of Purdey shotguns in which every part of one was interchangeable with the other. Philistine to the core, I pointed out that Sterling made 2,500 pairs of guns per annum where each part of not only each pair was completely interchangeable, but every pair and every sub-machine gun had all parts which were universally interchangeable. In a way, this illustrates the diverging paths of fine production engineering and traditional gun-making. At the same time Sterling was intensely proud of the achievements of two of its employees who had established some highly technical engineering processes after coming from Purdey to work at Sterling after the war.

There is little detail that I can add to the earlier history of Sterling that the late David Howroyd has told so well. There is also little I can add to the encyclopaedic content of Peter Laidler who was totally immersed in the gun during his years serving with REME.

There is however a hidden theme that has dogged the company since George Patchett won the machine carbine trials at Pendine, and that is the hostility of the Government and some of its agencies toward the company over many decades, even to the extent of supporting foreign commercial rivals. This has probably been caused by the quicker and more efficient ability to operate as a private company although limited by funding, in contrast to a department of government that is answerable to controllers at every step it takes, but it does not excuse it.

The original book "The Guns of Dagenham" for which we have purchased the rights, was published by Collector Grade Publications in Ontario, Canada in 1995.

I have taken the liberty of making a few additions probably gleaned in the main from the late Major Bevan Keen who was so helpful to me when curbing my enthusiastic exuberance in the early days of my involvement with the company. One always learns, and one always should continue to learn, and more importantly, listen.

A friend of Keen's was Bob Jennings who owned a gun shop in Fareham and had served eighteen years in the Royal Navy. The odd part was that he had spent less than eighteen months of that time at sea. Rumour had it that he had been sent out during the Malaysian Emergency to "pot" wanted Communist terrorists. Along with his Dayak tracker, they were required to behead their victims and bring back those heads in sacks to the base for purposes of identification. I asked him about the effect of the tropical heat during such an operation. He admitted that the main problem was the smell, but was happy in the fact that it wasn't too often the wrong head.

Behind the shop in Fareham was a factory where he made special pieces of equipment to the order of the Ministry of Defence. I am also most grateful to him for his patient instruction when he accompanied me on my first sales tour of the Far East. Tuan Bob was the representative also of Scotos night vision sights which were made in Leesburg Virginia. That was a marriage made in heaven between a silenced Sterling and a night scope to the extent that when we exhibited together at a Farnborough Air Show as an enhancement to airfield security, the British Press erupted with the headline "Horror Gun at Show". The American boss of the company, one Q. Johnston, was unfortunately killed by a truck when coming out of his works and the company ceased trading. Not long after that sad event, the British Company Pilkington P.E. started making excellent second generation night vision products and so we were able to continue the remarkable combination.

Colonel Hugh MacWhinnie (US) and British Brigadier David Wilson not only represented Scotos, but also The Military Armament Corporation of Powder Springs, Georgia who were making Gordon Ingram's MAC-10 sub-machine gun. The SBS (Royal Marines) had bought some of these as they were very compact and could be carried easily by frogmen. I admit to being open to making the MAC-10 in UK, as it was compact and had the hand to hand ease of magazine location in darkness. It would have been very cheap to produce as Sterling already possessed a good range of heavy mechanical presses, and the gun, within its limitations could have given us an entrée to the lower end of the market. (We lost a large order for the Peruvian Police to the Spanish Star smg, purely on price.) Unfortunately the then boss of MAC wanted some huge down payment as a licence fee and an equally high fee to teach us how to make sub-machine guns which I politely declined as being a trifle superfluous. Later, we did have a requirement from a Middle Eastern country for 10,000 Ingrams/ MAC-10's for which we could obtain a British export licence, but the American Government refused one, so we could not even 'deal'. It did however, spawn a last ditch hurried attempt to produce something to offer in the shape of the Sterling Mark 7, which perfectionists like ourselves could only describe honestly as a "lash up".

In the twenty-five years since the original book was written, there have been so many changes, although most of the armed forces of the West are equipped with assault rifles and smg derivations that emanate from the AR-15/M-16/AR-18. There is undoubtedly a police requirement for a small but reliable and accurate sub-machine gun, but the designs that are poised have to await decision on calibre. Sterling with all the production engineering drawings of such small-arms and more, thus doth keenly await the outcome.

JSME.
London W1.

Tribute to Robert Blake Stevens

Blake Stevens was born in Toronto, Ontario, Canada in October 1938, and died at his home in Gores Landing, Ontario, Canada in April 2018.

After finishing school, he had a 10-year career in systems analysis and computer programming within the financial industry, General Motors, and the Department of National Defence in Canada. At the same time, outside of his corporate commitments, as well as being an avid gun collector, he ran his own mail order gun parts business called "Collector Grade Parts & Accessories" for several years – hence the name "Collector Grade Publications" when he started his own publishing company.

After leaving the corporate world Blake studied for two years at the Toronto New School of Art, and for the rest of his life maintained his lifelong passion for music and high fidelity sound and the arts. As an aside he played the trumpet and flugelhorn in his high school dance band.

His first foray into gun book writing was when he wrote a small four page pamphlet on the Canadian Inglis "High Power" pistol for another publisher in 1974. This whetted his appetite to enter the publishing business for himself, and as an expert wordsmith, he was fortunate to be able to marry together his hobby for guns and writing, and form what has now become one of the world's renowned gun book publishers "Collector Grade Publications" in 1979.

Over the past forty years, Blake has edited and produced a series of over sixty critically-acclaimed books on modern small-arms, twelve of which he wrote or co-authored himself.

Blake was a charming and generous man whom I had the pleasure of meeting on a couple of occasions in London. I possess some of the Collector Grade Books and they are characteristically informative and magnificently illustrated in every way, and hence were an unqualified source of pride for Blake. It never crossed my mind to produce a book so detailed about Sterling when I was "in harness", and I feel both honoured and privileged to have been asked by Peter Laidler to join in the update. I will make sure that it continues in Blake's strong tradition, in spite of the change of name and change of publishing house.

I also take this opportunity of thanking Susan Fraser, Blake's wife, for all her help and co-operation in setting up this arrangement with such ease. I wish that all my life's dealings had been thus.

James Edmiston
13th. April 2019

P.S. I used to play the trumpet in my school band!

A Potted History, 1901–1939

First Armsmaking Use of the North River Thames Bank, Dagenham, Essex

The land upon which the later Sterling Engineering Company was to be situated was formerly known as Wantz Farm in Rainham Road (South) in Dagenham. Prior to 1901 the land had been farmed by the local Gray family. In 1901, the land was purchased by the Morris Aiming Tube and Ammunition Company.

Those familiar with small-arms will immediately recognise this name. Morris tubes were rifled tubes inserted into the barrels of .303″ SMLE (later, the Rifle .303″ No1). The tubes were chambered and bored to use a low-velocity .25″ cartridge, for use on indoor ranges.

The Morris Tube company went into liquidation in 1909 and the four-acre site was purchased by the Sterling Telephone and Electric company under the direction of the Managing Director, Guy Burney.

Electricity and radio were comparatively new and the Sterling Company was quick to jump upon the bandwagon, so to speak. They manufactured crystal receivers, but without amplifiers. These, of course, needed headphones, which Sterling also manufactured, calling them "radio head telephones". They also made a combination valve and crystal receiver for use with a loudspeaker. The separate loudspeakers made by Sterling were named "Baby", "Primax" and "Magnavox".

In the years between 1922 and 1925, the four-acre site had grown first to ten acres, then to eighteen acres. The factory also built its own power station, gasworks, printing shop, fire station, first-aid room, canteens for the staff, a recreation hall and parking for up to 700 staff bicycles. It is difficult to believe that this enlightened regard for staff welfare took place in the 1920's, although in later years, and under different managers, staff welfare and the obvious

spin-off of good labour relations remained a hallmark of the Sterling Company.

One feature that was remarkable up to the day the Sterling factory closed was the "Family Circle". This is a uniquely British phenomenon where, in spite of there being many large local employers all paying good wages, the Sterling factory employed many complete families, from grandfathers to fathers and sons including mothers and daughters. This is a distinct bonus for employer and employee as the company becomes part of the family and the family becomes part of the company. It breeds good relations, but, more importantly, it builds up a trusting bond.

An aerial view of the works taken in 1920 shows that the site also had its own in-house cabinetmaking shop, assembly works, fire-proof paint and tool stores, switchboard, coil winding shop, garages, millwrights section, metal finishing shop, an enamelling works and many, many more facilities.

In 1929 the overall holding company of which Sterling was a part was incorporated as John Ismay & Sons, Ltd. In 1932 the Sterling company itself became known as Sterling Works (Dagenham) Ltd. Products of the period were incandescent electric lights and other lighting apparatus, including lighting produced by gas, spirit and oil. This also included accessories such as lamp mantles, globes, fittings, chemicals and most other substances connected with lighting.

On April 5, 1933 the holding company's name was changed to Sterling Electric Holdings Ltd, under the authority of a Board of Trade certificate number 274738. This was confirmed by a Special Resolution passed at an extraordinary general meeting of the company on January 5, 1939.

The Companies Act 1929
AND
The Companies Act 1948.

COMPANY LIMITED BY SHARES.

Memorandum

AND

Articles of Association

OF

STERLING ELECTRIC HOLDINGS LIMITED

Incorporated the 5th day of April 1933.

COSMO CRAN & CO.,
39 LOMBARD STREET,
LONDON, E.C.3.

1. The title page from the record book of Sterling Electric Holdings Ltd, the parent holding company of Sterling Engineering Co Ltd from 1939 until 1972. (Courtesy David Howroyd)

World War II Creates a Society of Direction

From today's vantage point, after 50 years of relative worldwide peace, modem society understandably takes certain freedoms for granted. But during World War II, Britain lived in a society of *direction*.

When the war broke out, the men were called up for the defence of their country. Skilled professionals were directed to jobs wherever they were needed. Young boys, called "Bevin Boys", were ordered to work in the coalmines; women were called up for service in the Forces, and were also directed to work in factories or other suitable venues such as the Land Army. No one escaped.

This was also true of the factories. Sterling, who in peacetime had been happily manufacturing the newly-invented wireless and a variety of other harmless devices such as gas mantles and chemical toilets, were *told* what they would manufacture. Thus, as described in this book, Sterling became a hub of small arms development, and successfully manufactured the Lanchester Sub-Machine Gun, the De Lisle Silent Carbine, and the Patchett Machine Carbine, which, after a protracted period of arduous trial and improvement, became the world-famous Mk4 Sterling, adopted by the UK Military as the SMG, L2A3. One powerful instigator of the now commonly accepted practice of a private company manufacturing military equipment had been none other than Winston Churchill, who just prior to the outbreak of the war had ordered that Mr George Patchett and his wife be spirited out of Occupied Europe and installed at Sterling.

However, the fact that an ex-wireless and vacuum cleaner company beat out all comers, even the Royal Ordnance Factories and established British gunmakers such as BSA, to become Supplier of sub-machine guns to the British Forces after WWII, made Sterling's success a very controversial topic.

Initial War Work for Sterling

A small selection of Sterling's war-related work included 25-pounder field gun recoil assemblies, submarine valve equipment, Sterling bomber bomb slips and control equipment, and Sten gun magazines.

Also, by what appears to have been the merest of chances, Sterling were also awarded a contract to develop and produce what became the Lanchester Sub-Machine Gun, and it is at this point that we pick up the story in detail.

Part I

The Military Sterling

Chapter One

The Lanchester Sub-Machine Gun

First contract:		June 13, 1941
Last contract:		October 9, 1943
Obsolescent in Royal Navy:		1972
Obsolte in UK Military:		1979
Quantity Produced:	Sterling (two factories; codes S109 and M619) at least:	64,580
	Greener (code M94):	16,990
	Boss (code S156):	3,900
	Total unknown; at least:	74,579

Introduction: Britain in Dire Straits

When Britain went to war in 1939, there were no sub-machine guns of any sort in her Order of Battle. In fact, the armouries were bare. It was not until early in 1940 that the British Purchasing Commission in New York was instructed to buy all the Thompson sub-machine guns that it could lay its hands on. In all, orders were placed for 300,000 Thompson sub-machine guns and a staggering 249 million rounds of .45″ ammunition. The priority for Thompson guns came second only to Hudson antisubmarine aircraft. Things were that desperate.

Sadly, shipping losses meant that only 100,000 of these guns ever reached Britain. Initially these guns were supplied on a "cash–and–carry" basis, but by the end of 1940 Britain had lost about one-third of its war-like stores, and British cash and gold reserves within the US had been cleaned out. We had no "cash", and how we got around the "carry" problem is another story that will be told when full details of "Lend-Lease" are released.

In the census of August, 1940 as the Military were finalising their plans to defend the UK against the forthcoming invasion, it was established that of the 30,000 (approx) Bren guns made up to that date, only 2,300 were available for service. The remainder had been lost in action. Desperate needs called for desperate action.

Home Production a Must

Once the gold reserves were gone it was a case of necessity that Britain, in desperation, just had to manufacture her own sub-machine gun. In a report marked Secret and dated 1 January, 1940, the Chief Inspector of Small Arms (CISA) was given two commercial German: MP28 (II) "machine carbines", one in 7.63mm calibre and another in 9mm calibre, to evaluate. These guns, designed by Hugo Schmeisser in the later 1920s and produced by the C G Haenel *Waffenfabrik* of Suhl, Germany, had been "obtained" by the British Consul General in Addis Ababa.

Functioning was poor with frequent misfires. Certain modifications were undertaken with the extractor, which was causing friction. The functioning improved-until the extractor broke. The extractor from the 9mm gun was substituted and from then on, the functioning was excellent, providing captured German ammunition was used. The ICI batch was considered to be underpowered, as it caused a runaway gun.

All in all, CISA concluded, the gun was a satisfactory weapon from a functioning point of view, and gave

2. Right side view of a typical German MP28 (II), a rudimentary blowback 9mm side-feeding, box-magazine sub-machine gun designed by Hugo Schmeisser and manufactured for commercial sale by the CG Haenel *Waffenfabrik* of Suhl, Germany. An improvement over the original Bergmann MP18 design, which had utilised modified 8″ Artillery Luger barrels and 32-round Artillery Luger snail drum magazines.
The gun that became the Lanchester was, by direct order, as close a copy as possible of the German MP28 (II).

MoD Army, RMCS Shrivenharn

accurate shooting up to and including 200 yards. He also added that there was little to choose between the Schmeisser, the Bergmann, the Solothurn and the Oerlikon. It appears that from then onwards, the stage was set for what became the Lanchester.

On 12 August, 1940 a meeting was held to decide upon a home produced sub-machine gun. It was decided there and then that any gun Britain was to manufacture would be in 9mm calibre, although there was talk that "our" gun would be better suited in .380″ calibre, as ammunition supplies would be more readily available. This notion was quickly abandoned after an officer of the Ordnance Board explained that a 9mm bullet would penetrate seven thicknesses of 1″ deal board at 100 yards, and 5 thicknesses at 200 yards. The .380″ bullet fired from a similar barrel would only penetrate two thicknesses of 1″ deal board at 50 yards!

Holding the wooden fore-end with the left hand meant that it was uncomfortably close to the right hand holding the small of the butt: the trigger finger was only 4″ from the left hand. The Board considered that if this did cause a problem, the left hand could hold the barrel casing or that it would be a simple enough matter to add a vertical grip for the left hand. The Board considered that there should be no difficulty in manufacturing the gun, as it only contained 75 parts, but would possibly take up to

six months to put in production. It was simple to teach and use, and accurate up to 200 yards. It was therefore quite suitable for aerodrome defence. They also added that a 32-round magazine was preferable to a 50-round magazine.

Co-ordinating the Requirements for the "9mm Schmeisser Carbine"

On 26 August 1940 a meeting was held to co-ordinate the requirements of the Services for the "9mm Schmeisser Carbine". The following were present:

- Col F Gibson, Chairman
- Col C Chipster, CISA
- Col J Icke, Ord Board (who later got the No4 T sniper riflegoing)
- Gp Capt G Pidcock, RAF, Ord Board
- Cdr G Oswald, RN, Director, Naval Ordnance
- Cdr W Redman, RN, Chief Insp., Naval Ordnance
- Major J Lugard, Deputy Asst, Director (smallarms)
- Major R Shepherd, Chief Superintendent of Design (who later designed the Sten)
- Major J Evatt
- Mr A Jackson, Ministry of Supply
- Mr E Parmenter, Ministry of Supply
- Mr J Morgan, Directorate of Armament Procurement

The purpose of the meeting was "to co-ordinate service requirements and home production of the new [sub-] machine gun."

It transpired that British Army requirements were then being satisfied by the Thompson. The Royal Navy had ordered 2,000 9mm Smith &Wesson carbines, and also required a further 10,000 of the new "Schmeisser Carbines". The RAF required 10,000 of the new Schmeissers but wanted a lightened version based upon the "parachutist's model", presumably the MP38.

The production of each type was then reviewed. Drawings were already in hand for the [MP28(II)] "Schmeisser", and it was estimated that deliveries, based on a 50,000 requirement, could start in 4 months.

As rapid production was a primary consideration, it was agreed that there was no time to investigate the possibility of modifications or improvements. Any deviation from the laid-down design would only be to assist production, and not functioning. This meant of course that the RAF could not have their lightened "Schmeisser".

The wood stock was an essential Navy requirement, as was the sword bayonet attachment, with the possibility of fitting the No4 bayonet at a later date. Similarly, it was only the Navy who required 50-round magazines: the RAF suggested that 32-round magazines would suffice for them. (Wise fellows those RAF lads!)

The Board concluded the meeting by stating that production of the "Schmeisser Carbine" would proceed with an initial order of 50,000 guns, and that anticipated delivery times would be available on 2 September. All deliveries would be pooled, and the Navy and the RAF would receive 25,000 each.

Introducing George Lanchester

3. George Lanchester (centre, in light suit), shown with members of his design team in front of an Alvis light tank in 1939, before becoming involved with the gun that later bore his name.

Courtesy Chris Clark

George Herbert Lanchester was born on December 11, 1874 at Hove, in Sussex. When the Lanchester Motor Company was formed in 1904, he became Chief Assistant to his brother Frederick. In 1910 he became Chief Designer.

During World War I George Lanchester designed and built 38-horsepower armoured cars, which were soon operating in Europe. After the war, his 1927 model was the first-ever armoured car built from a purpose-made chassis. This model equipped the 11th Hussars and the 12th Lancers, the first mechanised regiments in the British Army.

Another of his inventions was the crownwheel-and-pinion axle differential.

George Lanchester was an engineer, not a gun-maker, but he carried a lot of influence. He was the youngest of three, including brother Frank, who owned the Lanchester Car Company. King George VI would use nothing but Lanchester cars in all State functions.

Upon the outbreak of World War II, George Lanchester had been seconded to the Sterling Engineering Company as a technical adviser, employed in the production of six squadrons of sound-ranging vehicles for the Dutch Government. These were all lost during the fall of Java.

The Sterling Connection–by the Merest of Chances

The decision to place the manufacture of the British "Schmeisser" with Sterling Engineering Co Ltd at Dagenham was undecided until the very last minute.

Originally, the gun was to have been produced by another engineering company, Alfred Mann & Co of nearby Romford, and Sterling was to have produced Bren Gun Carrier bogie wheels.

For reasons best known to the Ministry of Supply, George Lanchester at Sterling was given a mandate to develop the "9mm Schmeisser Carbine". (Just who got lumbered with the Bren Gun Carrier wheels must remain one of life's unknowns!)

At Sterling, it was reported that the two Georges – Lanchester and Patchett – never got on well together. However, Lanchester's brief with the Sterling Company was simply to put into production and manufacture a copy of the German MP28II 9mm sub-machine gun. This was to be done as quickly and as cheaply as possible.

Although they do not appear to have undertaken any other small-arms related work, Alfred Mann & Co later produced large quantities of Lanchester barrel blanks and casings for Sterling, marking these casings close to the foresight protectors with their wartime code 'S230'.

The Pilot Project the "Sterling Automatic Carbine"

Several problems needed to be ironed out. The back sight spring needed to be stronger to prevent the cursor (range) slide moving during firing, and the strength of the return spring had to be increased.

Contract number P1908 dated 18 October, 1940, which authorised the pilot study into the completion

4. "PG" (Pilot Gun) No 4, then known as the "Sterling Automatic Carbine". This gun fired 5,205 rounds with only 26 stoppages on November 28, 1940. With a few slight modifications, this pattern was adopted as the Lanchester Sub-Machine Gun in June ,1941.

Note (from front) the fabricated foresight protector and bayonet lug, and the rivetted bayonet standard, incorporating the front sling swivel, both hurriedly added. Along with the 50-round magazine, these were Royal Navy requirements not found on the earliest guns (PG 1–PG 3).

MoD Pattern Room collection

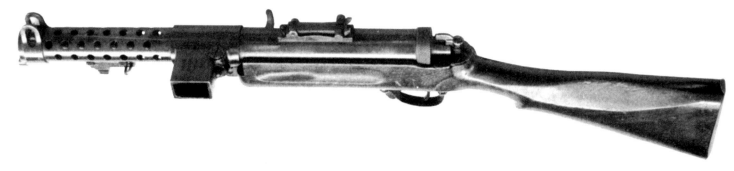

5. Closeup of top of receiver of Pilot Gun no 4, showing "Sterling Automatic Carbine" markings. The gun was not called the 'Lanchester' until after the initial contract was signed in June, 1941. (MoD Pattern Room collection)

of the drawings, production and firing trials, was costed at £3,615.

PG (pilot guns) 1 and PG2 were first test fired on 8 November, 1940. These guns, described in the Public Records Office archives as "British Schmeisser MGs", were tested again with different ammunition, including British ICI, US Winchester, captured Beretta, Bergmann and c.1936 German stocks.

This successful firing trial was completed on 28 November, 1940 when gun PG4, marked "Sterling Automatic Carbine", fired 5,205 rounds with only 26 stoppages. It was stressed that these "only 26" stoppages were due principally to the ammunition, and not the design of the gun.

Certain features were agreed upon to simplify production and additionally, the change lever positions were to be marked 'A' and 'R' to indicate "Automatic" and "Repetition". The gun would also have sling loops fitted.

50,000 Lanchesters: (Nearly) All for the Royal Navy

An initial contract order was placed for 50,000 guns on 13 June, 1941, the complete gun being costed at about £14 each. The operation to put the gun into production being under the control of George Lanchester, the gun then took on his name.

To compound the problems of initial production, Britain did not have sufficient 9mm ammunition production facilities. A swift order for 110 million rounds from the United States was placed, to feed the forthcoming demand, both from the Lanchester and the later Sten, then under secret first development at RSAF Enfield.

It emerged that the gun was neither cheap nor quick to produce. Production over 28 months averaged 3,410 Lanchesters per month. Consider that in one week in 1943, the BSA plant at Tysley assembled 47,000 Mk2 Stens!

This first order for 50,000 guns was to be split 50-50 between the Royal Navy and the Royal Air Force. By this time the British Army had supplies of the Thompson, and they made it quite clear that the Thompson was what they wanted, so the Army kept the Thompson.

The Royal Air Force would immediately receive the 2,000 newly-acquired Smith & Wesson 9mm carbines, for the defence of aerodromes and airfields now springing up around the country. (Ironically, the RAF had originally requested a copy of the MP38).

Thus, all the Lanchesters would go to the Royal Navy. That the Lanchester was the exclusive preserve of the Royal (British, Canadian, New Zealand, Indian, Australian, etc etc) Navy is not strictly correct. The Sterling archives contained a photograph of a company of soldiers marching with Lanchesters. Peter Laidler also spoke to an ex-Royal Artillery Bombardier (a Corporal) whose unit had Lanchesters issued while they were in India.

The Lanchester was used in action in India/Burma, and is clearly seen on Archive film in the hands of sailors during the defence and fall of Hong Kong. Not quite the gun to have at hand when the going gets really tough, but marginally better than the Japanese SMG of the time.

Post-WWII, the Kenya Police had quantities of Lanchesters, including SN 23273A, issued during the Mau-Mau campaign.

Trying to Take the Lanchester to the Navy Tailors

Once it was clear that the Navy would have all (but see above?) Lanchester production, the Chief Inspector of Naval Ordnance (CINO) was obliged to ask some searching questions concerning its intended use in Naval service. In November, 1940 he asked for information on:

• the number of rounds that could be fired without undue heating
• probable barrel life
• components and quantity required for usual maintenance purposes
• maintenance required for the gun as a whole

• performance with different ammunition
• accuracy at varying states of barrel life
• greatest range at which reasonable accuracy could be expected
• functioning of the gun at temperatures down to –5°C.

Although many of these excellent questions would be answered later, initially there was a problem! In March, 1941 the Ordnance Board told CINO that they could not begin trials to ascertain the answers to CINO's questions, because there were no production guns available. It was a case of "don't call us, we'll call you."

Describing the Original Mk1 Lanchester

The original Mk1 Lanchester came fitted with a Single and Automatic selective-fire facility, and a tangent rear sight.

In reality, the selective-fire trigger mechanism of the Mk1 Lanchester was a pig-in-a-poke. Correct functioning depended on far too many variables. The tripping lever (8), hinged about the sear stop screw

(9), had a small, spring-loaded disconnector (10) at the rear end that would trip the spring-loaded extension on the trigger bar (2) when the change lever was in the 'R' position. It goes on and on, getting worse!

None of the Mk1 trigger mechanisms Peter Laidler has examined have functioned correctly, even under classroom conditions. Quite how they fared with a

6. An early official photo of the Mk1 Lanchester, disassembled into major groups. This wartime photo is stamped on the back 'SECRET-NOT TO BE PRINTED' and a pencilled line of disinformation reads, "Suomi Finnish Carbine 9mm". (Courtesy James Alley)

7. Closeup, left side view, showing features of the Lanchester Mk1 selective-fire trigger mechanism.

Note the rotating tripping lever. At the rear of the tripping lever is the spring-loaded disconnector.

Apart from the dubious protection of the ill-fitting wooden buttstock (not shown; another Navy requirement), the mechanism was open to a hostile salt-water environment. (MoD Army, RMCS Shrivenham)

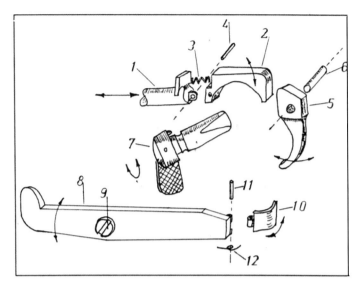

9. Components of the Mk1 Lanchester trigger mechanism (representative only; not to scale):

1. Bar
2. Extension, trigger bar
3. Spring, trigger bar extension
4. Pin, axis, trigger bar extension
5. Trigger
6. Pin, axis, trigger
7. Lever, change
8. Lever, tripping
9. Screw, sear stop
10. Disconnector
11. Pin, axis, disconnector
12. Spring, disconnector. (Drawing by Peter Laidler)

8. Closeup, right side view. The disconnector can be seen, under the arched, articulating trigger bar extension. The change lever at the front of the trigger guard is shown in the 'S' (single shot) position. When rotated to 'A' (automatic), an internal cam pushes the disconnector clear of the trigger bar.

Note the receiver is slotted all the way to the rear, so that the bolt, to which the cocking handle is screwed, can be removed. (MoD Army, RMCS Shrivenham)

had to be formed and machined. Due to production difficulties it was decided to use a machined brass or bronze casting instead.

First Relaxation of Standards

The first relaxation in standards was announced in June, 1941 (just days after the first Lanchester production contract had been awarded), when two-groove barrels were authorised in order to utilise Sten barrel production facilities. Although Peter Laidler has examined only a couple of hundred Lanchesters for this study, he confesses to never having seen a "two-groover".

The Remarkable "Sten Chamber"

Later, in December, 1941 the Ordnance Board were asked to look into the possibility of fabricating

Naval boarding party, contaminated with salt water and grit or sand, is anyone's guess!

Later the tangent rearsight was replaced by a simple and cheap 100–200 yard flip-over rearsight that was originally suggested in July, 1940, although it was not implemented until some time later.

The stock was made of beech, with a brass (but later pressed steel and still later an alloy) butt plate. The original (approx) 120 Mk1 guns were produced with a heavy fabricated steel magazine housing, which

Lanchester barrels by using drawn 9mm rifled tube, Sten gun fashion, and shrinking/brazing the breech and muzzle flanges in place. These flanges were very accurately machined in normal production, because the breech flange affected feed, and the muzzle flange determined the accuracy. The strength of the brazing was questioned, but it was agreed that there was never a possibility that a Lanchester barrel would reach 400°C.

Two barrels were fabricated to specification DD(E) 2980 and 2981, but it appears that these trials did not materialise. The chamber specification was to be the same, that of design number DD(E)2653.

This remarkable chamber specification has been described elsewhere as the "Sten Chamber". This is not quite correct. As there was only a loose specification standard for the European 9×19mm cartridge, the Lanchester was engineered and manufactured to function correctly with a vast number of ammunition variables that were or might be available. The result was that the Lanchester could and would digest virtually anything.

The Sten, later Patchett and still later Sterling guns also inherited this chamber. In fact, it was only during the 1960s that a true 9mm NATO standard chamber was specified. Apart from the Patchett/Sterling having the depth increased by .012″, it remains the same as Lanchester specification DD(E)2653.

Introducing the Mk1* Lanchester

10. Left side view of a typical Lanchester Machine Carbine, Mk1*. Note the absence of the change lever, and the stamped, 100–200 yard flip-over rearsight, welded to the receiver.

The Simplified Trigger Mechanism

Quite quickly we see a major relaxation, and the later Mk1* version was produced with an automatic fire facility only.

In January, 1942 trials were undertaken with a redesigned trigger mechanism that incorporated "… only a compression spring and solid trigger bar." This Automatic Trigger Mechanism was tested on Lanchester Mk1 no 19, when rounds were fired in short bursts. There was only one stoppage, due to an ammunition fault, but concern was expressed about manufacturing tolerances within this gun.

The Ordnance Board suggested that this trigger mechanism should be adopted forthwith, although quality control was deemed so bad that the manufacturers were urged to "check dimensions of components against the drawings."

The design of the trigger was also improved, the finger contact surface being rounded instead of flat.

Also on the Mk1* the sculptured cocking handle was replaced with one machined from round bar stock. It has been suggested that some of the riveted bayonet brackets were also cast with a longer mounting standard, in order that some Lanchesters would accept the P14/Mod17 bayonets. In short, there were many variables.

The Early-Production Steel Safety Slide

The steel safety slide (fig 19, item 27A) is fixed to and rotates about the sear stop screw. Being spring steel,

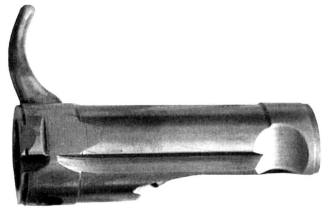

11. (Left) The two types of Lanchester breech blocks.
Above: Mk1, showing longitudinal slot for disconnector, and curved cocking handle.
Below: Mk1*. The cocking handle is now plain bar stock, machined to size.
   Both cocking handles were threaded into the side of the bolt, necessitating a slot completely through the rear of the housing. (MoD Army, RMCS Shrivenham)

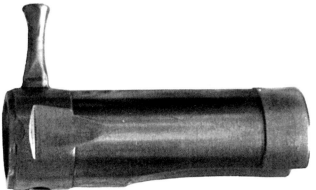

12. (Below) Right side closeup of a Mk1* Lanchester with stock removed, showing rare safety lever (fig 19 no 27A).
   This device hinged about the sear stop screw and nut (fig 24 no 59). When raised, it blocked the cocking handle from being accidentally pulled back. Not mentioned in the production or Ordnance Board records, nor the RN User Handbook, it is shown as a later addition in the 1943 Parts List.
   Note the rear sight and trigger housing are both welded to the casing. (MoD Army, RMCS Shrivenham)

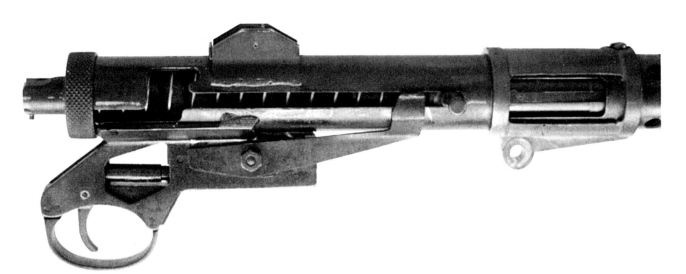

it could be raised and locked into the "safe" position behind the cocking handle when the breech block was fully forward, thus preventing the gun being accidentally fired should it be dropped butt-first with a magazine in place. This feature was omitted from later production.

Converting the Mk1 Lanchester to Mk1*

The conversion from Mk1 to Mk1* specification was easily achieved by simply removing the select fire lever in front of the trigger guard, and the tripping lever fixed to the left side of the trigger frame. By doing so, the disconnecter fixed to the Mk1 trigger bar could not articulate to trip the sear each time the trigger was squeezed.

Some converted guns also have the articulating Mk1 trigger bar replaced with the solid Mk1* type. One sure sign of an original but converted Mk1 gun is the presence of a 1/4″ diameter hole in the front solid part of the trigger guard, close to where it meets the wooden fore-end.

The Proposed "Mk2" Lanchester

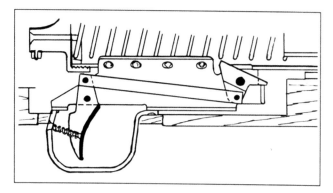

13. Drawing no DD(E) 3161 dated 5 May, 1942, formulated by the Cheshunt Design Office, shows plans for a proposed "Mk2" Lanchester fabricated trigger mechanism. (Drawing by Peter Laidler)

Drawing no DD(E) 3161 dated 5 May, 1942, formulated by the Cheshunt Design Office, shows plans for a proposed Mk2 version of the trusty Lanchester. This gun is the usual Mk1* type but has fabricated trigger mechanism side plates, formed at the front to provide a stop for the simplified sear, and a stamped trigger guard. Internally, the trigger mechanism is all that was changed. In the proposed Mk2, the trigger is fabricated (stamped) and pinned to the sear by means of a stamped trigger bar. Once released, the trigger returned by means of a simple captive spring seated behind it.

The Mk2 trigger did away with the following Lanchester parts (numbered from the parts list in fig 24): machined trigger bar (53), trigger bar spring (54), trigger plunger (58), sear stop screw and nut (59).

The drawings do specify that the straight cocking handle screwed to the bolts of both the Mk1* and proposed Mk2 Lanchesters is the "Handle, cocking, Mk2", which presumes that the beautifully curved original handle was the Mk1.

The new trigger mechanism would have made the Lanchester marginally lighter and cheaper to manufacture, but, fortunately or unfortunately, depending on your point of view, the Mk2 never reached fruition.

Mk1* Lanchester Endurance Trials in 1942

Between September and October 1942, three Mk1* Lanchesters, numbered SA-3061A, SA-3082A, and SA-3145A, were tested at Pendine to ascertain:

- accuracy, with and without bayonet
- penetration into wood
- function under sand, mud and arctic conditions
- probable barrel life and endurance of mechanism
- trials of old and new extractors
- reliability of 50-round magazines.

Quite early on, Lanchester extractors were found to be snapping off at the locating boss. Four experimental extractors, made of different material and to different specifications, were available for the trials. The requirement was that any new extractor should be capable of lasting at least 15,000 rounds. The scientists concluded that an extractor with an undercut boss, with the grain running longitudinally, as manufactured by Monotype Ltd was satisfactory.

Those remaining stocks were modified by Holland and Holland and marked with a letter 'M' on the outside of the boss. The undercut boss is clearly shown in the parts list, item 60.

Gun 3061 suffered a bulged barrel at 10,415 rounds.

Gun 3082 gave broad-side-on and "tippers" at 11,590 rounds. A new barrel was fitted and a further 13,800 rounds were fired. It gave "tippers" at 12,000 rounds but was still reasonably accurate at 13,800 rounds.

Gun 3145 fired the full 15,000 rounds unscathed. The fitting of a bayonet did not affect accuracy at all.

The magazines on trial did not fare well. The Ordnance Board suggested that they needed improvement in manufacture. They also suggested that it might be worth investigating the insertion of an auxiliary spring down the front. This had recently been approved for the Bren and was proving to be successful.

Trials Results

The Mk1* guns operated perfectly at temperatures down to –20°F. Breakages were not numerous, and could generally be attributed to fair wear and tear.

Insofar as the mud and sand test was concerned, the report stated "… the carbine will function, but the trigger mechanism is liable to become jammed. Magazines are not likely to be useable."

Thus this trial effectively answered those questions asked by CINO in November, 1940.

Improved Barrel Locating and Retention

One other modification was introduced at about the same time. The barrel was originally secured within the casing by a screw which entered the front flange while the head of the screw locked against the casing. This was not successful for a number of reasons.

Future production was altered so that the barrel was located and prevented from rotating by a shouldered screw (no 11), which went down through the magazine housing and locked into a slot in the top of the rear barrel flange. A far more successful idea, clearly shown in the photographs and Parts List.

First Whiff of the N.O.T. 40/1 (the Sten), and the Patchett

Simultaneously, the RSAF Enfield design staff at Kelman Road in Cheshunt, Hertfordshire were adding the final touches to the next sub-machine gun, code numbered N.O.T. 40/1. It was cheap, cheerful and deadly, and, after all, you can only kill a man so dead. The Sten gun was on its way.

In the meantime, George Patchett was busy in another part of the Sterling factory. Not just busy, but very busy …

The Three "Light Lanchesters"

George Lanchester produced three known versions of a lightened Lanchester gun. When Sterling was closed in 1989 these three guns formed part of the historic company collection, and are now housed in the MoD Pattern Room in Nottingham.

These guns must be regarded as the fruits of a small, in-house project that had no official sanction. Indeed, Lanchester was prevented from pursuing these ideas when the Ministry of Supply became aware of them.

A General Description

All three Light Lanchesters are very early Mk1 guns, fitted with the very early wrapped steel magazine housing. This may seem surprising in view of the known unreliabilty of the Mk1 trigger mechanism, but quite likely these early obsolete guns were all that could be spared for Lanchester's experiments.

These "lightened" Lanchesters are all unmarked, and none has a wooden butt. All three guns show efforts to seal the trigger mechanism's internal parts.

The First Light Lanchester

The first gun has the trigger mechanism sealed with two bolted-on side plates. A moulded pistol grip is fixed to the rear of the trigger mechanism frame. Into the rear of this grip a simple detachable 'T-shaped Sten gun butt (identical to that shown on the second

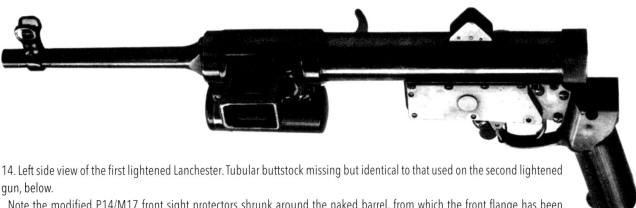

14. Left side view of the first lightened Lanchester. Tubular buttstock missing but identical to that used on the second lightened gun, below.

Note the modified P14/M17 front sight protectors shrunk around the naked barrel, from which the front flange has been removed. The unusually shaped wooden foregrip was added because there was nowhere else to grip the front end of the gun. (MoD Pattern Room collection)

gun) could be fitted, and locked into place with a modified magazine catch screw. The dual-range rear sight was taken directly from a production Mk1* Lanchester.

The barrel has been reversed, with the chamber machined into the threaded muzzle flange, which now threads into the shortened receiver casing. A P14 rifle front sight assembly has been shrunk onto the muzzle end. The casing has been further lightened by machining away surplus material from the magazine housing. Due to the absence of a forestock and/or a perforated barrel jacket, an unusual horizontal grooved wooden foregrip is fitted under the magazine housing.

The Second Light Lanchester

The second gun is almost identical to the first, but has a slightly redesigned and simplified change (or fire-select) lever, which simply moves a Sten-gun type tripping lever to the left or right for auto or single-shot fire. Lanchester mated this with a Sten breech block but, because of the impossible geometry of the Sten block within the lightened casing, the (horizontal) cocking handle was relocated on the left side, where it was protected by the magazine housing.

Although these guns are lighter than the Mk1 Lanchester, they are still heavy compared with the Patchett and Sten.

15. Left side view of the second lightened Lanchester. Very similar to the first gun, but utilising a modified Sten breech block with the cocking handle fitted to the left side.

There was a slight internal change to the fire select lever, but the trigger mechanism was still based on the unreliable Mk1 Lanchester. (MoD Pattern Room collection)

The Third Light Lanchester. First Combination of Selector and Safety

16. Right side view of the third lightened Lanchester. It is easy to see how this gun in particular could be mistaken for an early Patchett prototype.

This third gun incorporated a number of important advances, while retaining the barrel casing, an important feature obviously worth its extra weight. The 'Paxolin' (impregnated linen) grip and trigger mechanism are mounted near the point of balance, and the distinctive Lanchester change lever, at the front of the trigger guard, controls a redesigned trigger/sear arrangement which does away with the connecting rod. The double-hinged folding butt idea proved to be light and strong, and was later used on the one-off S11 "stamped Sterling" (Chapter Fourteen). (MoD Pattern Room collection)

The third Light Lanchester is quite similar to the Patchett. Whether this was due to pure evolution or a sneak preview of George Patchett's first prototypes is a moot point, although this gun has been described elsewhere as "a prototype Patchett".

The pistol grip is positioned almost at the point of balance, and the sear, which releases the breech block, is mounted within the trigger mechanism itself, unlike the normal Lanchester, where it is connected to the trigger by a rod.

Also, on the original Mk1 Lanchester, the change lever was a separate component, situated at the front of the trigger guard. It affected the mode of fire only, and had nothing to do with putting the gun on safe. On the third light Lanchester, these functions were all combined in one unit. The change lever had three positions; "Auto", "Repetition", and "Safe". If that sounds familiar, it should, for this three-position trigger safety (in a self-contained unit) was carried over into the Patchett.

This whole gun has been professionally converted, once again from an early Mk1 Lanchester, and retains the full-length perforated casing.

The folding butt was similar to the Patchett. Similar, but different enough to avoid a patent quarrel with George Patchett! The Lanchester folding butt proved quite robust, thanks to its TWO attachment points through the rear of the trigger mechanism side plates. Interestingly, this idea was later carried over into the one-off stamped Sterling S11 prototype discussed in Chapter Fourteen.

Ministry of Supply Prevents Further Development

However well these lightened guns answered some of the criticisms being levelled at the production Lanchester, they were not found to be within George Lanchester's original mandate. The Ministry of Supply thus prevented further development of these lightened prototypes, which were successfully test fired, on the grounds that they offered no significant advantages over the Mk2 Sten.

Summing Up Lanchester Production

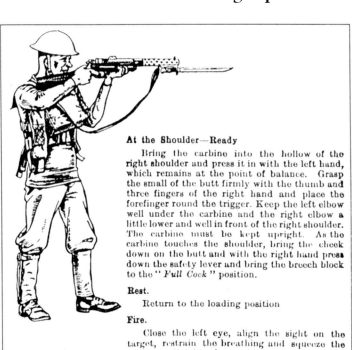

At the Shoulder—Ready

Bring the carbine into the hollow of the right shoulder and press it in with the left hand, which remains at the point of balance. Grasp the small of the butt firmly with the thumb and three fingers of the right hand and place the forefinger round the trigger. Keep the left elbow well under the carbine and the right elbow a little lower and well in front of the right shoulder. The carbine must be kept upright. As the carbine touches the shoulder, bring the cheek down on the butt and with the right hand press down the safety lever and bring the breech block to the "*Full Cock*" position.

Rest.

Return to the loading position

Fire.

Close the left eye, align the sight on the target, restrain the breathing and squeeze the trigger. Release the trigger immediately the carbine fires. After a pause bring the carbine to the "*Rest*" position.

17. From Admiralty Ordnance Manual BR832, dated 17 June, 1943: "Firing the Lanchester 9mm Carbine". This officially produced Lanchester User Handbook replaced the July, 1941 "unofficial" Lanchester handbook, locally produced at the Royal Navy Gunnery School, HMS *Excellent*, at Portsmouth, England. The handbook states that for balance and instant readiness, the bayonet will always be fixed during firing.

The sailor carries two ammunition pouches which each carry three 50 round magazines, a total of 300 rounds. The small wallet on the front of his right-hand pouch (shown hatched) is to carry the cleaning kit, magazine loading tool and gun stripping/combination tool.

These guns were well made and as one might expect, little used. As a result they were still on Royal Navy Service until declared obsolete in 1972. Many are still in service with users of ex-Royal Navy ships. (MoD Royal Navy)

The first contract for the Lanchester was dated 13 June, 1941 and the last contract was dated 9 October, 1943. Officially, a total of 79,790 service Lanchesters plus 1,000 Drill Purpose guns were manufactured. They were neither cheap, at £14 each, nor were they quick to produce.

By this time Britain had long since been divided into three geographical districts: North, Midlands and South, and every firm in the length and breadth of the realm with any manufacturing capacity whatever had been investigated, logged and given a code number with a 'N', 'M' or 'S' prefix. Virtually every firm, large and small, was given war work.

Sterling was granted the original (undated) contract for 20,000 Lanchesters and the initial assembly contract for 19,990 dated 13 June, 1941. They immediately set about sub-contracting most of the manufacturing work to over 70 sub-contractors, including W & T Avery (previously a manufacturer of kitchen scales and equipment, who supplied Lanchester butt plates and butt plate assemblies); Lines Bros (now Tri-Ang toys) who heat-treated sears and magazines, and P Llster (a diesel engine manufacturer who supplied Lanchester cocking handles).

The Four Lanchester Assemblers

Lanchester assembly contracts were actually awarded to three firms: Sterling (two plants), W W Greener, and Boss & Co. By the time the last guns were produced in October, 1943, production was: Sterling: 58,990; Greener: 16,990; and Boss & Co: 3,900. These are the production figures held at the Public Records Libraiy, but the true figures are far greater than these.

Sterling assembly of the Lanchester was split between the Sterling Engineering Co Ltd in Dagenham (code marked S109) and the "Sterling Armaments Company" satellite factory in Northampton (code marked M619). Some early guns do not appear to be code marked at all except by serial number prefix of 'S', 'A', or 'SA'.

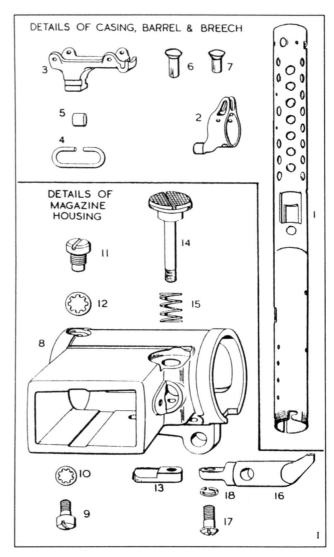

18. Sheet I from the official List of Components for the Mk1* Lanchester Machine Carbine: Details of Casing, Barrel and Breech (above), and Details of Magazine Housing (not to scale). The nomenclature of the parts is as follows:

1. Casing, barrel and breech
2. Protector, foresight
3. Bracket, bayonet
4. Swivel, sling
5. Peg, sling swivel
6. Rivet, bayonet bracket (4)
7. Rivet, foresight protector (3)
8. Housing, magazine
9. Screw, magazine housing (2)
10. Washer, magazine housing screw (2)
11. Screw, barrel Mk2
12. Washer, barrel screw
13. Catch, magazine
14. Screw, magazine catch
15. Spring, magazine catch
16. Ejector
17. Screw, ejector
18. Washer, ejector screw. (MoD Royal Navy)

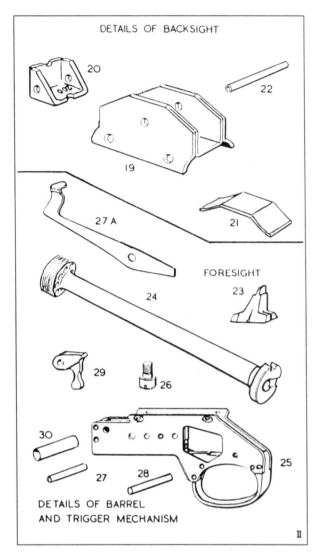

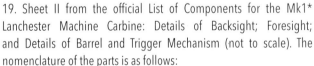

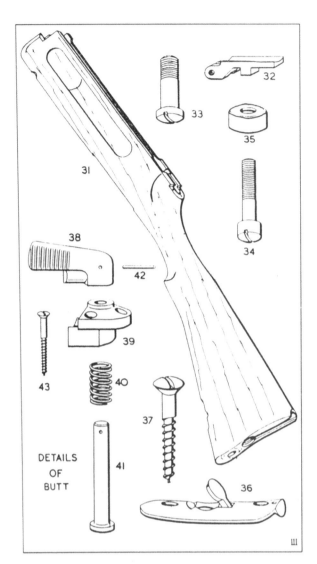

19. Sheet II from the official List of Components for the Mk1* Lanchester Machine Carbine: Details of Backsight; Foresight; and Details of Barrel and Trigger Mechanism (not to scale). The nomenclature of the parts is as follows:

19. Bed, backsight, Mk2
20. Leaf, backsight, Mk2
21. Spring, backsight leaf, Mlc2
22. Pin, leaf backsight
23. Blade, foresight
24. Barrel
25. Block, trigger assembly
26. Screw, trigger mechanism block (4; replaced by welding in 'A'-suffix guns)
27. Dowel, axis trigger
27. A Lever, safety
28. Rivet, trigger block (9)
29. Sear
30. Pin, axis sear. (MoD Royal Navy)

20. Sheet III from the official List of Components for the Mk1* Lanchester Machine Carbine: Details of Butt (not to scale). The nomenclature of the parts is as follows:

31. Butt
32. Hinge piece
33. Screw, hinge
34. Screw, hinge retaining piece
35. Cup, hinge retaining screw
36. Plate, butt assembly
37. Screw, butt plate (2)
38. Catch, breech casing
39. Bracket, breech casing
40. Spring, catch breech casing 41 Pin, axis breech casing catch
42. Pin, securing breech casing catch
43. Screw, catch breech casing (3). (MoD Royal Navy)

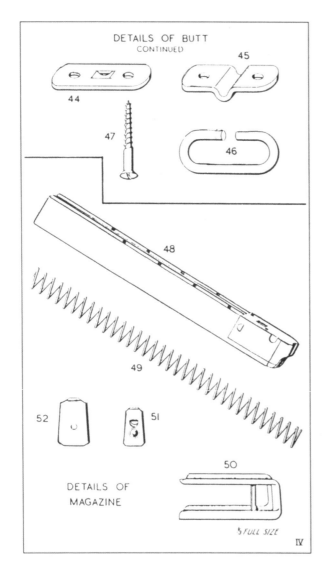

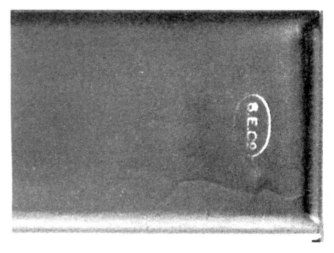

22. Closeup of the side and bottom plate of a 50-round Lanchester magazine made by Sterling Engineering Co Ltd. Note the small oval containing the initials 'S.E.Co.'
Other makers were Lines Bros (marked 'L.B.') and Accles & Pollock.

21. Sheet IV from the official List of Components for the Mk1 * Lanchester Machine Carbine: Details of Butt, continued, and Details of Magazine (not to scale). The nomenclature of the parts is as follows:

44. Plate, rear sling swivel 45 Bracket, rear sling swivel 46 Swivel, sling rear
47. Screw, rear sling swivel(2)
48. Magazine
49. Spring, magazine platform
50. Platform, magazine
51. Retainer, bottom plate
52. Plate, bottom. (MoD Royal Navy)

According to the contract records, Sterling was to have made guns serially numbered from 1 to 9999, then A1 to A9999 and then B1 to B9999, and so on. For reasons lost in the fog of the war this did not happen, and Sterling guns were initially numbered from 1 to 9999 then (S)A1 consecutively to about A64580.

The same happened to Greener (code marked M94), who should have numbered from G1 to G9999 but instead numbered consecutively from G1 to G16990.

Boss guns (code marked S156) are numbered from H1 to H3900.

We cannot ascertain true production figures for no reason to believe the figures of 16,990 and 3,900 respectively are incorrect. The last (?) Sterling-made Lanchester was numbered in the region of A64580. So while playing the numbers game, not in itself an accurate method, the 64,580 total plus the 9,999 un-prefixed guns makes the Sterling total at least 74,579.

These are the recorded data, but the true facts differ. While Greener and Boss made guns are relatively scarce, one Greener gun, clearly marked with the M94 code and fired by the author, was serially numbered 50162. It does not have the 'G' prefix, and numerically is well in excess of the 16,990 manufactured by them. On the other hand many more certainly do carry 'G' and 'H' prefixed serial numbers. The theories as to why this should be seem to be endless.

The only true way to ascertain the maker of a particular Lanchester is by the code letters of S109 (Sterling Dagenham), M619 (Sterling Northampton), M94 (Greener), or S156 (Boss).

23. The Lanchester in action with the 19th Motor Gun Boat (MGB) Flotilla, Vahti Bay, Turkey, 1943.

   The boarding party of MGB 643, armed with Lanchesters, M1917 Enfields and pistols. The names of this smiling crew are (rear row, from left): AB 'Yorkie' Warren; PO Cox'n Benny Lynch; Captain of boat (name unknown but a Belgian). Front row, from left: AB Campbell; Mechanic Peter Reeves; John 'Sparks' Hargreaves.

   In addition to the personal weapons, MGBs were heavily armed with a 6-pounder gun, multiple .50" Vickers (water jackets and flash hiders visible at left), 2-pounder MG and 20mm Oerlikon cannons in powered mountings. The enemy nicknamed these boats 'ants', because they could never get rid of the bloody things!

   The 19th Flotilla were active in striking enemy shipping around the Greek and Turkish islands of Leros, Somo and Kos, where few of today's holidaymakers are aware of the wartime past. (Courtesy John Hargreaves)

   One feature, pointed out to us during this research, is that if Greener and Boss guns were subsequently allocated serial number batches within the general Lanchester numbers, then this could reduce the number of Lanchesters made to a grand total of 74,579, instead of this figure being the total for Sterling alone.

Lax Standards During Late Production

Where gun numbers are quoted as a change point, there must be a degree of fluidity in the actual number due to the overlap between the phasing out of the old and phasing in of the new parts.

   Towards the end of production, quality standards reached an all-time low. Guns numbered from (approx) SA 35500 were built to the cheapest and most basic of all the configurations. Rough and sharp edges appear to be the norm. Certainly, some guns seen recently have component parts and wooden stocks the quality of which simply beggars belief. Times were tough in 1843!

   The records that related to Lanchester production were removed from the manufacturers by Department S6 of the Ministry of Supply after production ceased. Those records that remain are the scant details that found their way into Public Archives after the war, or were retained on closure of the Sterling factory in 1989.

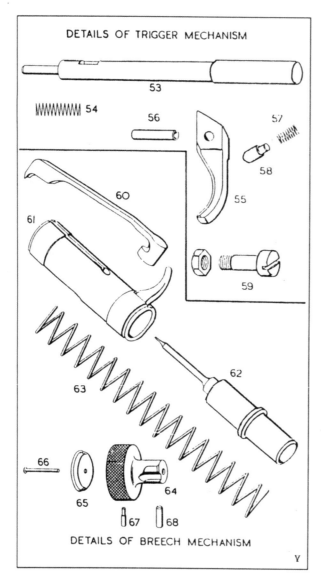

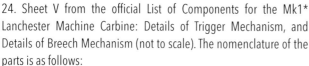

24. Sheet V from the official List of Components for the Mk1* Lanchester Machine Carbine: Details of Trigger Mechanism, and Details of Breech Mechanism (not to scale). The nomenclature of the parts is as follows:

53. Bar, trigger, Mk2
54. Spring, trigger bar
55. Trigger
56. Pin, axis trigger
57. Spring, trigger
58. Plunger, trigger
59. Screw, sear stop,(with nut)
60. Extractor
61. Block, breech with (early) cocking handle
62. Pin, firing assembly
63. Spring, return (main spring)
64. Cap, end, breech
65. Housing, return spring
66. Rivet, end cap
67. Peg, locking breech end cap
68. Pin, positioning breech end cap. (MoD Royal Navy)

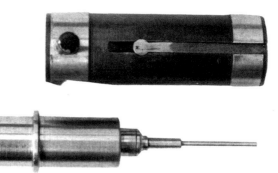

25. The Lanchester breech block, and separate firing pin assembly. The majority of Lanchester firing pins resemble no 62 in fig 24, above, but the thin, stepped shank of this particular firing pin is one of several minor variations seen.

Although pinned in place, the firing pin was a press fit in the return spring block, and was not supplied separately.

Note the small, sideways letter 'M' on the rear of the extractor, signifying that this is an original item, modified. Original extractors were prone to snapping across the rear. (MoD Army, RMCS Shrivenham)

Markings

Sterling-made Mk1 Lanchester guns are marked on the top of the magazine hoousing:

LANCHESTER
MK.1.
SA.
['S' indicates Sterling manufacture and 'A' indicates serial number prefix]
9877
C.F.
[Unknown code followed by small numbers].

Sterling-made Mk1 Lanchesters converted to Mk1* at Admiralty workshops (Gosport) and 2 Base Workshop REME, Tel-El-Kabir, Egypt:

LANCHESTER
MK.1.
SA
*14838 A
C.F. 42

(The 'A' serial number suffix is explained below.)

Or in the case of Sterling guns manufactured as Mk1*s:

LANCHESTER
MK.1*
SA M619
35537
C.F. 73

As notes, 'M619' was the Ministry of Supply Contractor code for "Sterling Armaments Co, Northampton".

Boss-made Lanchesters are marked:

LANCHESTER
Mk1* (only Mk1* manufactured)
BOSS (in very small letters)
H---
CF 60 (various code numbers seen).

Some later guns have the code 'S 156' in place of the name 'BOSS'.

Lanchesters made by Greener are marked:

LANCHESTER
Mk1* (only Mk1* manufactured)
M 94
G---
CF 54 (several variables of this code have been noted).

Markings on Ex-Royal Navy Lanchesters

After service with foreign forces, ex-Royal Navy Lanchesters have appeared on the international market recently. These are marked with two broad arrows, point-to-point, stamped just before the serial number. The point-to-point arrows, which appear as a six-pointed star, are sometimes accompanied by the letter 'S'. This series of marks authenticates these guns as former UK Goverment ordnance stores sold to foreign governments.

The actual year of manufacture of any particular Lanchester can be found stamped in small, almost military proof mark on top of the rearmost magazine housing flange that encompasses the casing.

A Critique of the Lanchester

Quite what the German High Command thought of Britain's plight when we took steps to manufacture an obsolete 1920s model German sub-machine gun is not recorded, especially as they went to war with the MP38, but no doubt their peals of laughter took on quite a hollow ring when their Intelligence chiefs reported favourably on the first of the deadly MkII Stens that were captured at Dieppe.

There were several drawbacks with the Lanchester. The first was that it was very expensive. The second was to plague its later and younger brothers, the Sten and Patchett: the magazines; and 50-round ones at that!

The 50-round Lanchester magazine was not a good idea. Once the magazine got anywhere close to being fully loaded, the base-plate would come away from the magazine case, due to the excess spring pressure. The result was chaos, as the base-plate and spring flew one way and the rounds another. Thoughtfully, each Lanchester was supplied with a much-needed magazine loading tool.

The Sten and Patchett magazines were only of 32-round capacity, but even 32 rounds were impossible to hand-load through the lips of a single-feed magazine!

It would be unfair to blame the various short-comings of the gun on George Lanchester. It was clear from the start that he was not a gun designer nor an Armourer, but an engineer. Nevertheless, several points were completely overlooked.

For example, a gunmaker would have known from experience that a firing pin retained within the breech block only by pressure from the return spring will immediately spell trouble for the user, who will probably experience ruptured primer caps or misfires. True to form, misfires were a feature of the Lanchester.

Small BA screws were initially used to retain the magazine housing, the trigger mechanism block, and the backsight body, to the casing. An Armourer would have known that firing vibration would soon loosen these screws. However, when George Lanchester set about designing out these and other faults, he was told that this was not in his mandate, and that his ideas were not needed. Later Lanchesters had the backsight bed and trigger block welded in place.

Another valid criticism was that the 9mm Lanchester weighed more than the .303″ service rifle! It was built like a battleship. Even the body casing tube had an incredible .10″ (one-tenth of an inch) wall thickness. Compare that with the .065″ (sixty-five thousandths of an inch) wall thickness of the Sten and Sterling, then add a cast-brass magazine housing, a wood stock, a buttplate, and a 50-round magazine: no wonder the Lanchester was heavy!

The Lanchester was not all bad, and some of its best features survived in the Sterling. Those that spring to mind include the perforated air-cooled casing which in the authors' experience is (virtually) impossible to overheat, and the superb design of the chamber. The flip-over 100–200 yard backsight leaf idea and foresight blade and protectors are also reminders of the Sterling Mk4/L2A3's Lanchester heritage.

Whichever way one looks at it, the Lanchester was simply an expensive way of using up strategic raw material and valuable machine-tool time. It was even manufactured to accept the then-current 17″ No1 rifle bayonet!

A recent magazine article published in England reported on "… the Lanchester, which many today regard as the finest SMG ever built." Unfortunately, it seems that hindsight and rose-tinted spectacles have diminished its many shortcomings. Let's just use a phrase and say that it filled a hole.

26. A Lanchester on duty with the Royal Navy, Suez, 1956.

British occupying forces in Suez were always armed. Here (from left) Leading Patrolmen 'Nobby' Clarke, 'Junior' Bulford, and another with a Lanchester gun, ashore at Port Said with their mothership, HMS *Maidstone*, in the background.

Note the long magazine pouches, worn across the chest by the rightmost sailor, especially made for the Navy's 50-round Lanchester magazines. (Courtesy 'Nobby' Clarke)

The Fifty-Round Magazine: More Show than Go

Peter Laidler recently spoke to a very senior Training Warrant Officer, who as a young soldier, took part in the 1956 de-nationalisation of the Suez Canal. His platoon had come across an armoury in a deserted Egyptian barracks near Port Said. With the aid of their old Bedford QL troop carrier and nosing bar (a polite Army term for a battering ram) they smashed their way in, to find the armoury lined with racks of virtually new Lanchesters. They quickly found that the 50-round Lanchester magazines fitted their Mk5 Stens.

Lanchester Variations

The Lanchester was produced with a whole host of variables, and can be found in the following configurations:

- earliest Mk1s with wrapped steel magazine housing
- later Mk1s and all Mk1*s with cast-and-machined brass magazine housing
- Mk1 with single and automatic fire facility
- Mk1 modified to Mk1* specification
- Mk1* automatic fire only
- breech bolt slotted underneath (Mk1)
- breech block plain (Mk1)
- curved cocking handle
- straight cocking handle
- wooden fore-end with or without finger grooves
- wooden fore-end with or without safety lever slot
- wooden fore-end with or without butt-trap oil bottle hole
- tangent backsight
- tangent sight base screwed to casing
- tangent sight base welded to casing
- flip-over dual range backsight
- barrel secured with muzzle screw at top
- barrel secured by stepped screw at breech flange
- any one of three types of rear sling loop
- brass, pressed steel or alloy butt plate
- with or without pressed steel safety lever
- trigger block screwed to casing
- trigger block welded to casing
- flat finger part on trigger
- rounded finger part on trigger
- Patt17/M17 bayonet standard (rare).

The Admiralty User Handbook Explains:

The 'A' Suffix, Applied to "Non-Interchangeable" Guns

Up to gun A14832, the trigger block and tangent sight bed were attached to the casing with screws, but from gun number A14833, the trigger block and tangent sight bed were welded to the casing. Others in this serial number range have the screw holes drilled in place but welded over. The implications of this are that thenceforth, it would be impossible to remove the magazine or sight housings from the gun casing.

Thus, although the Lanchester was made to be fully dismantled and therefore carry interchangeable parts, it subsequently wasn't, due to the fact that the backsight bed and trigger housing were welded into place and could no longer be removed. Paragraph 108 of Admiralty Ordnance Manual BR832, the official Admiralty User Handbook on the Lanchester, dated 17 June, 1943, states that:

A number of carbines in which the component parts are not strictly interchangeable have been accepted into Naval Service. Such carbines are stamped with a letter 'A' after the serial number.

It is interesting to note from the production records that gun number 14833, mentioned above, was manufactured as an Mk1 but released to the Admiralty as serial number A 14833-A-, indicating that some parts were not interchangeable because they were welded in place. A good example of an 'A'-suffix gun.

The Admiralty User Handbook also states that all Mk1 carbines were to be modified to Mk1* specification. Accordingly, the parts list does not include any of the obsolete Mk1 trigger mechanism parts. It is for this reason that original and unmodified Mk1 Lanchesters are extremely rare.

27. Closeup of the cast-brass or bronze magazine housing of an ex-Australian Navy Lanchester, Mk1*, No 20780 A, marked (2nd line) as a Mk1, although manufactured as a Mk1*. The 'A' serial number suffix indicates non-interchangeable (welded-on) parts (see text).

Note the production code (M619, left centre), indicating manufacture by the satellite "Sterling Armaments Co" factory in Northampton.

The magazine release button and the ejector at the rear of the housing are clearly shown, as well as the later style of barrel retention screw (top right). (Bruce Gorton collection)

Ruptured Primers and Misfires Become "Premature or Weak Cartridges"

As noted, the separate firing pin design meant that the Lanchester was vulnerable to light strikes causing misfires, and firing pin over-protrusion causing ruptured primers. An interesting approach to these phenomena was to blame them on the ammunition! Paragraph 66 of the Admiralty Handbook stated:

Premature or weak charges are comparatively common and will leave a bullet stuck in the bore which will be bulged if another shot is fired without clearing the bore. Accordingly, whenever a stoppage occurs, the bore must be examined to make sure that it is clear, before opening fire a gain. Carbines of later manufacture contain a length of mild steel rod in the butt for the purposes of clearing such stoppages.

We pass no comment on the obvious here beyond the question, "How do you know if there is a bullet stuck in the bore, especially during automatic fire?" A "weak charge" does not necessarily cause a stoppage!

28. Lanchesters in use on the Frigate HMS *Cardigan Bay*, 1961. This photo shows Rating Colin Noden firing a Lanchester from the fo'c'sle of *Cardigan Bay*, while the Gunnery Officer looks on. Behind and between these two men, another rating is firing a Lanchester from the waist, while crouched behind him (in white hat) the Gunnery Instructor oversees others firing from the prone position. In the left foreground, two more Lanchesters, their magazines and the all-important magazine loading tool are lying on the deck matting. (Courtesy Colin Noden)

The safety implications of this suggestion beggar belief, as does the notion that any user would put up with a bar of steel rattling around in the butt trap!

Indeed, where would the hapless sailor stick the steel rod if his gun was of later production, made after the butt-trap oil bottle hole had been omitted?

Phasing Out the Lanchester

Although the Lanchester was built to last (many were still serving on Royal Navy ships into the early 1970s), production did not and the last guns were produced in October, 1943. Spare part production ceased at the same time and thereafter spares, especially Mk1 trigger parts, were always hard to obtain. It was for this reason, and to standardise user training, that where necessary, Mk1 guns were converted to Mk1* specification.

The first full-scale deployment of Lanchester guns was to the Battle Cruiser HMS *Renown*. The last time they featured in the inventory of the British Navy was in 1978, when the last mobilisation/war reserve store Lanchesters were withdrawn and subsequently destroyed at Yeovilton in Somerset. Not that they were all destroyed – in fact, several escaped! Even so, 37 years of service quite an achievement, even if the last eight or so were spent in grease.

Lanchester Carbines formed part of the Complete Equipment Schedule of many ex-Royal Navy ships sold during the 1950s and 1960s. As a result, it was quite common for those nations (Chile being one that springs to mind) to request spare parts from the Sterling Company up until the mid 1970s. Alas, by that time all of the Lanchester spares had been used up. But, never one to miss an opportunity, Sterling would then offer to sell them new Mk4 Sterlings!

The Latter-Day History of George Lanchester

After production of the Lanchester carbine ceased in 1943 George Lanchester remained at the Sterling company as a technical adviser, organising production of other war-related equipment.

He also later designed a 7.62mm delayed-action heavy machine gun for use with armoured cars. A tool-room sample was manufactured, but constant trigger mechanism failure saw the demise of the project.

After the war he took a sideways move to become technical adviser to the Russell Newberry Company, one of the subsidiaries of Sterling Engineering. After his 87th birthday in December, 1961 he commented, "I was given the sack in June, 1961 as being too old …"

George Lanchester died at his North Devon home in February, 1970 at the age of 95.

The Lanchester Legacy: Barrels for the First 4,000 Patchett/Sterlin

The end of Lanchester production in October, 1943 found Sterling sitting on a stockpile of 4,000 Lanchester barrels. As further discussed in later chapters, these were modified and used in the first ten years' worth of production, and thus Sterling did not acquire its own barrelmaking facility until 1953.

There were also many Lanchester body casing/magazine housing assemblies left at the factory after the war. These were sold off for their scrap brass/bronze value.

Authors' Limited Experience with RN Lanchesters

Both authors' experience with the Lanchester is very limited. As a young Armourer in New Zealand, Peter Laidler went to collect a couple from the New Zealand Navy at its Devonport Naval Base, both of which were to be restored and preserved. These Lanchesters had been removed from the ships HMNZS *Royalist* and *Blackpool*, and later used on the frigates *Otago* and *Wiakato*.

All but one of the remainder were destroyed by Armourers at Papakura. One was set aside and hidden, and later restored to firing condition for display in the Instructional Museum at the New Zealand Northern Ordnance Depot, Ngaruawahia.

Chapter Two

The Prototype Patchetts

Introducing George Patchett

George William Patchett was a tall thin man, originally from Nottingham. Before the war he had been a successful motorcyclist, and at one time held the world two-wheel speed record. Alas, a motorcycle accident left him with a slight limp.

He worked for FN in Herstal, Belgium, who, as well as being armsmakers, were motorcycle manufacturers, too. It was at FN where he met Val Browning and thus George gathered his knowledge of guns. From FN he went to work in Crechoslovakia, for Jamacek and was living there when the Sudetenland was invaded by the Germans.

Just prior to war breaking out in 1939, orders for his hasty removal from Czechoslovakia came from Winston Churchill himself. George was spirited out, complete with microfilm drawings of all then-current prototypes and inventions. George's French wife was also spirited out of France, and they both met up again in England. They lived at Homchurch

in Essex during the war and afterwards, while he was employed by Sterling.

George Patchett was a workaholic who could be found in the Sterling works from early in the morning till late at night, working on his designs. He would also take the time to speak personally to those who were charged with working on his components or designs, asking questions about machining methods in order to evaluate the difficulty or ease of their manufacture.

The First Firing Prototype

We do not know the exact date of completion of the first prototype Patchett gun, but it was mid-1942. Similarly, the exact date the last prototype Patchett was made is also unknown, but it was around the end of 1943. We do know that a total of 24 prototypes were made.

George Patchett's earliest experimental guns, incorporating his own ideas for a sub-machine carbine are thus very few in number, and while speaking of

29. Right side view of the very first Patchett. Date of manufacture unknown, but this gun, without butt or sights, was first submitted for Ordnance Board trials on 25 September, 1942, where it fired 412 rounds.

The folding butt and (primitive) sights were fitted for the later February, 1943 trial: close examination clearly shows that the butt and backsight have been brazed in place after the gun was originally blackened. The foresight is an adjustable-for-height screw.

The trigger mechanism is retained by a split screw. The breech block is a modified Lanchester item, with cocking handle installed in a new 50° cocking handle slot above the (Lanchester) extractor. (MoD School of Infantry, Warminster)

30. Top closeup of the first Patchett prototype fired, showing hand-stamped markings on the magazine housing, reading "PATCHETT/ MACHINE CARBINE".

There is no serial number present on this gun, nor is one visible on any of the components. The letters are all individually stamped, none too straight or square. (MoD School of Infantry, Warminster)

numbers, some of the very earliest have no serial numbers.

Numbered or not, all of these Patchett prototypes have a magazine housing set at 90° to the casing, Sten gun fashion, and accept only Lanchester and Sten magazines.

A Debt to the Lanchester and the Sten

As noted in Chapter One the two 'Georges', Lanchester and Patchett, did not get along. This was perhaps a pity, because both saw the value of features in each other's designs, and it is interesting to conjecture what they might have come up with a team. If George Lanchester was not above "adapting" folding butt ideas just enough so they would not infringe on Patchett's patents, it is clear that the basis upon which George Patchett started his work was the Lanchester.

Or, more to the point, he began with what the Lanchester *lacked* in the way of refinements, such as a central, balanced pistol grip and a folding butt; and to correct its faults, such as its impossible weight.

Patchett took a good long hard look at the Lanchester. Indeed, some of the best features of the

Lanchester are evident on the very early Patchett guns, and some remained throughout Sterling production: the perforated casing; the foresight protectors; the flip-over backsight; and the magazine catch/ejector configuration are items that spring to mind.

George Patchett took a long hard look at the later well, although, apart from the fact that the Sten and the Patchett are both 9mm calibre and share the same .065″ tube thickness, 1.5″-diameter casing and 50° cocking handle angle, right from the start the Patchett was a far superior design.

Describing the First Firing Prototype

Let us look at the earliest firing prototype known, the unnumbered, handstamped "Patchett Machine Carbine" now held at the School of Infantry.

The casing is 1.5″ diameter, the same the Sten, but perforated Lanchester-fashion with a series of 9/16″ holes, drilled down the length of the casing from the muzzle to the breech.

At the muzzle a sleeve is threaded internally, and into it a standard MkI Lanchester barrel is screwed. The barrel is retained by the normal Mk1 Lanchester keeper screw.

On firing, the muzzle blast acts an open venturi, effectively drawing ambient air forward through the eight holes in the front barrel flange, pulling cool air in through the holes in the casing and over the barrel. In the authors' opinion, it must be (virtually) impossible to overheat the casing while firing a gun equipped with this method of cooling, a feature taken straight from the Lanchester (and its German antecedents).

The foresight consists of a hexagonal-headed screw with a bead-type foresight that could be adjusted for height but not laterally.

Coming down vertically to the centre of the gun, the magazine housing is square-on to the casing, giving away its Lanchester/Sten origins. The ejector and magazine catch configurations have been taken straight from the Lanchester; after all, they were both designed to take the same magazine.

The magazine catch, release button and ejector all function identically to the later production Sterlings, although the style was changed a little. The exact changes are fully detailed in the following chapters.

Also in the centre of the gun we find the pistol grip, and patented trigger mechanism. The pistol grip is made in two separate halves from brown Tufnol (Paxolin), held together with an upper and lower male/female screw and nut This material can be readily identified by the linen/cloth weave visible within it: a more recent example of its use is in the hand-grips of UK-manufactured No7 Mk1 bayonets.

The earliest Patchett breech blocks are simply standard Lanchester items converted for this purpose, and can be identified by the 2½" long by ³/₁₆" wide extractor, visible through the ejection port.

The firing pin is separate and enters through the rear, another point taken straight from the Lanchester. However, on the Lanchester, the cocking handle was more-or-less permanently screwed into the right side of the breech block, and the casing thus had to be slotted right through to the rear end.

Some early Patchett prototypes have the cocking handle protruding from the body at a 90° angle to the pistol grip, thus highlighting their use of unmodified, ex-Lanchester breech blocks.

Others have a shouldered cocking handle which sits in a new hole drilled in the right side of the (Converted Lanchester) breech block, positioned

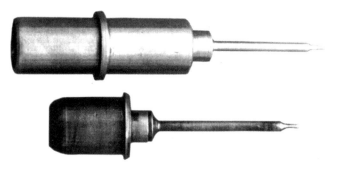

31. Separate firing pins.
Above: Lanchester.
Below: early Patchett type.
This type is the most commonly depicted in factory drawings, although as we shall see, later Patchett protoypes featured a number of variations of the separate firing pin idea, some retained in the block by the cocking handle, and some vice-versa! (MoD Army, RMCS Shrivenham)

above and forward of the original hole, at an angle of 50° from the horizontal. This cocking handle is removed through an enlarged portion at the rear of its slot.

The return spring, also a standard Lanchester item, seats onto the positioning ring of the firing pin extension, within the hollowed rear of the breech block.

All of the early Patchett prototypes use either converted Lanchester or Sten breech blocks. Those using Sten breech blocks have a 1¾" long by ³/₁₆" extractor slot visible, while true Patchett (and later Sterling) breech blocks have a very short, ⅞" by ³/₁₆" extractor slot.

The earliest rear sight consists of a No1 rifle type square-notched block, brazed to the top of the casing. In fact it looks suspiciously like one taken directly from a Lanchester. There was no provision for lateral adjustment on these first guns.

The First Patchett/Sterling Patent (August, 1942): "Change Fire Mechanism"

On most selective-fire sub-machine guns, the Thompson and Mk1 Lanchester, for example, single-shot fire is obtained by means of a tripping lever which intrudes into the boltway. The bolt trips the tripping lever, which releases the sear, which snaps up to catch and hold the bolt in the cocked position. Tripping levers are notoriously fickle: too hard, and they snap; but too soft, and they bend. Either way the result is an unserviceable gun.

Patchett's trigger mechanism eliminated the bolt-operated tripping lever. During single-shot fire with a Patchett or Sterling, the sear is released by the precisely-timed tripping lever (called the "sear locking lever" in Patchett's patent drawing), which is actuated by the inner change lever (the "selector finger").

In his first patent with Sterling, George Patchett described his celebrated trigger mechanism as follows: **559,469. Automatic firearms. Patchett, G W, and Sterling engineering Co Ltd. Aug 17, 1942, No 11520 [Classes 92(ii) and 119]**

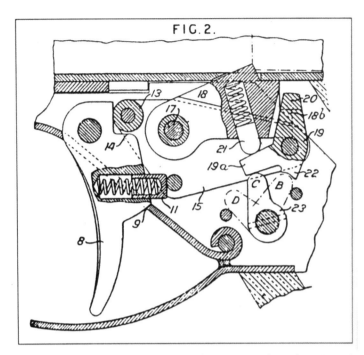

FIG. 2.

32. Fig 2 from George Patchett's first patent with Sterling. Several pins and components, as well as the location of the three sear positions auto ('D' in drawing) semi ('C') and safe ('B') remained the same throughout Sterling production. Taken from the patent, the nomenclature of the components of this earliest known Patchett trigger mechanism is as follows:

8   trigger
11   trigger/sear carrier spring and plunger
13   sear carrier roller
14   trigger shoulder
15   sear carrier (later the sear cradle)
17   sear/sear carrier pivot
18   sear
18b sear tail, forked
19   sear locking lever
19a sear locking lever arm
20   'T' headed arm
21   sear spring plunger
22   sear locking lever arm
23   selector finger (later the inner change lever). (Courtesy British Patents Office)

... Relates to change fire mechanism applicable particularly to recoiling breech-bolt guns of the blowback type. The sear (18) is mounted on the same pivot (17) as the trigger-operated sear-carrier (15) and has a forked tail (18b) which receives the

'T' headed arm (20) or a sear locking lever (19) pivoted on the carrier (15). The lever (19) has arms (19a, 22) which co-act with the finger (23) of a selector device, which may be set in positions, B. C.D for safety, single shots or automatic firing. The trigger (8) rocks the carrier by contact of a shoulder (14) with a roller (13) on the carrier. When the selector finger is in position B it engages the locking-lever arm (22) and prevents movement of the sear carrier and sear. In position C, when the trigger is pulled, the carrier is rocked clockwise and the finger (23) engages the arm (19a) thereby rocking the lever (19) and disengaging its 'T' head from the sear tail. The sear is thus released and is urged upwards to re-cocking position by a spring plunger device (21) which acts also upon the locking lever. Upon release of the trigger, the carrier (15), together with the lever (19), is returned to cocked position, the former by a spring (11) and the latter by the spring plunger (21). In position D, the selector finger (23) cannot engage the locking lever which therefore holds the sear locked to the carrier (15) so that the sear remains depressed as long as the trigger pull is maintnined. The sear is operative to hold the breech bolt in open or closed positions, and when the mechanism is dosed and set for "Safety" the bolt cannot be jolted to open position. The trigger is shaped at (9) so as to fit closely in the trigger plate opening.

First Firing Trials

On 25th September, 1942, George Patchett's unnumbered gun was first shown and demonstrated to the Ordnance Board. This original gun did not have sights fitted (although there was provision for a "primitive" sighting arrangement), nor was there a butt. Clearly it was meant to be fired from the waist.

In Ordnance Board Proceeding (OB Proc) 19,930 of 12th October, 1942, the Board described their initial experience with the Patchett Machine Carbine as follows:

Report of Firing Trial 25-09-42

Mr Patchett demonstrated his carbine, which from a short examination was seen to have the following features:

1. *Essentially, with the exception of the trigger mechanism, the weapon is a Lanchester without butt or sights.*
2. *The trigger mechanism is self-contained and incorporates a change lever giving single, automatic or safety when operated by the thumb of the right hand. In the safe position the breech block is locked in the forward position. The trigger mechanism and pistol grip are situated approximately half way along the casing near the "point of balance".*

The carbine was functioned satisfactorily, and during a rough test for accuracy, on a screen at 15 yards it was noticed that there was a distinct tendency to pull to the right.

Number of rounds fired – 412.

Stoppages – one misfire due to low cap.

Comments – this weapon is intended for firing from the hip only. The only novel feature in a weapon of this type, apart from the trigger mechanism, appears to be the locking of the breech block in the forward position …

The Ordnance Board expressed reservations about the strength of the return spring cap in the event of a blowout, and indeed this early (ringless) retaining method was soon changed.

As noted, the unnumbered first firing prototype fired 412 rounds with only one misfire, and that was due to ammunition and not the gun. Quite an achievement, first time around!

Further Improvement the Removable Trigger Unit

As reported by the Ordnance Board in OB Proc 21,596 of 8 February, 1943, by December, 1942 George Patchett had added a further improvement to his patented trigger whereby the complete mechanism could be removed, cleaned and replaced as one assembly. This operated just as it does today: a coin (or the rim of a 9mm cartridge) rotates the retaining pin through 90°, the pin is pushed out with the bullet end of a cartridge, and the trigger mechanism unit is removed.

Due to its being described as "… a Lanchester without butt or sights", the Director of Naval Ordnance (ONO) was asked for his comments on the gun. He replied that the trigger mechanism "has advantages over the present Mk1[*] Lanchester trigger gear in that when the safety catch is on, the bolt can be locked in the forward position and that it can fire single shots." However, it was judged extremely complicated and "impossible to make by the firms working to Lanchester standards"!

Curiously, the ONO also stated that if the safety were applied with the bolt partially cocked, then the whole (trigger) mechanism would break. Quite how he reached this conclusion is not clear. On the understanding that the trigger mechanism fitted to this gun is still the original, then the gun CANNOT be partially cocked with the safety applied to 'S' (Safe). If it were in the 'A' (Auto) or 'SA' (Semi-Auto) position and the gun were partially cocked, moving the change lever to 'S' (Safe) would simply rotate the inner change lever which would bear down hard against the sides of the sear cradle. It would take a feat of strength, but the only item that would be damaged would be the detent pin, which would shear. One could argue that making the smallest and cheapest part the weak link in the chain is sound engineering practice.

Clearly nothing was done about this perceived "fault", because it remained in the Sterling design throughout production. Peter Laidler has seen many loose inner/outer change levers, but never a sheared detent pin.

George Patchett also made his trigger unit side plates, and trigger and buttstock axis pins, from stainless steel, so that they could never rust or otherwise seize in place, a feature which stands the Sterling in good stead to this day.

Another feature retained throughout production of the military Patchett and later Sterling is the order of the change lever positions, from left to right 'A' (automatic) 'SA' (on initial prototypes only; later 'R' for Repetition or single-shot) and 'S' (safe).

Fitting the First (Primitive) Sights and Folding Butt

A folding butt and (primitive) sights were first fitted in 1943, and, as a result of further firing tests the War Office took up considerable interest in Patchett's designs. After all, that's what they spirited him out of Czechoslovakia for, and his wife out of France! They suggested that the Patchett gun be trialled against other sub-machine guns.

The Second Patchett/Stirling Patent (August, 1942): "Change Fire Mechanism"

In his second patent with Sterling, George Patchett described his folding butt as follows:

> **566,875. automatic firearms. Patchett, GW, and Sterling engineering Co, Ltd. May 26, 1943. No 8445. [Class 119]**
> *… A machine carbine or other automatic firearm has a collapsible butt which folds under the weapon when not in use, but which forms a rigid triangular assembly when swung into operative position. The butt, which is shown in full lines in the collapsed position, and in broken lines in the operative position,*

comprises a forked main member (F) pivoted at (10) on the underside of the spring casing (1), a strut (G) pivoted at (15) to the main member and a butt plate (H) which is pivoted at (21) to the strut and has ears (26) adapted to engage frictionally over the end of the member (F). The butt plate having a positioning step engaged by the member (F). The butt plate is urged into contact with the end of the member (F) by a longitudinal spring plunger in the strut (G), the spring plunger acting on a lug (22) on the butt plate and having a catch (19) which secures the butt assembly to the barrel casing when collapsed. The main member (F) is retained in operative position by lugs which engage a pair of longitudinal grooves in a block on the underside of the recoil spring end cap (6). A pivoted spring-held locking member (40), when pressed at (43) permits the end of the cap (6) to be pressed forward slightly to release the member (F), whereupon by straightening the strut (G) and butt plate (H) into alignment with the member (F), the butt assembly maybe swung to the underside of the barrel casing, in whichposition the catch (19) is able to enter a slot therein. The butt plate is then swung back onto the full-line position shown, this movement allowing the catch (19) to move into locking engagement with the barrel casing.

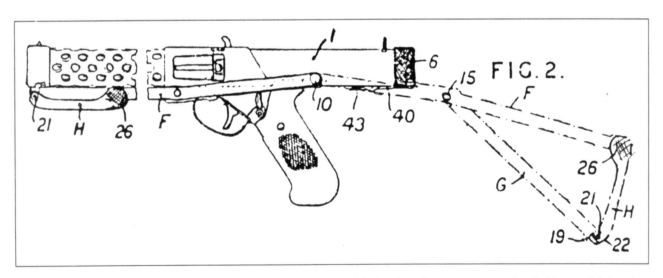

33. Fig 2 from Patchett's second patent with Sterling, covering his design of folding butt. The components as identified here and their actions are described in the text. (Courtesy British Patents Office)

First Competition for the Patchett

As reported in OB Proc 22,349 of 26 March, 1943, the first comparative trial of the unnumbered Patchett, now fitted with a folding butt and primitive sights, took place in February, 1943 against three 9mm Welguns (numbered 3, 5 and 6), and three 9mm Mk4 Stens (numbered 2, 3 and 5). The Welgun was not being trialled as a replacement for the Sten, but was being tested at the request of SOE at Welwyn City (hence the names WELgun and WELrod).

This first comparative trial was conducted using Lanchester Mk1* (SN 21900A) and Mk2 Sten (SN E30621A) as control samples.

The trial report contained in OB Proc 22,349 stated that "… At 150 yards[!] the accuracy of the Patchett falls off rapidly. Its failure to diagram, with a fixed tripod box, at 175 yards and beyond is conspicuous".

Although it survived the sand and heat tests, the Patchett came last in this first competitive trial, as it was a complete failure in the mud test.

However, in summation the Board considered that the Patchett machine carbine "is as yet in the early stages of development and capable of much improvement …"

The First "MkI"

Still a Long Way to Go to the "True" Mark I

It appears that there is no such thing as a "typical" Patchett prototype. Confusingly, with the appearance of a gun very similar to the unnumbered first firing prototype featured above, George Patchett was already stamping in the designation 'MkI'.

This and its quick successor 'MARK I' appear on most if not all the developmental and trials Patchetts, but as we shall see, the perfected "Mark I" version that Patchett himself took to market in the early postwar years was still several long years, and many painstaking improvements, away.

However, even though the configurations of some components could (and did) change dramatically from one prototype to the next, the main concepts of Patchett's brilliant design remained: the balanced grip; the central, side-mounted magazine; and the patented, compact trigger mechanism, the only one of its kind that could REALLY be put on 'safe', with the bolt secured forward.

Describing Patchett Machine Carbine MkI No EXP1

The 90° magazine housing and the pistol grip and trigger housing are still welded to a drawn steel sleeve,

34. Right side view of Patchett Machine Carbine MkI No EXP1, still featuring the earliest known method of attachment of the magazine housing/ pistol grip and trigger housing, which are welded to a separate sleeve; the distinctive front barrel housing (enclosing a stock Lanchester barrel), and the rudimentary sights.

Note the Lanchester bolt, with cocking handle in a horizontal slot in the casing. (MoD Pattern Room collection)

35. Top closeup view of the magazine housing of prototype MkI No EXP1, showing markings. (MoD Pattern Room collection)

As with the first firing prototype, the trigger mechanism and housing are deeply sculpted above and forward of the trigger, to provide room for inserting a gloved finger.

From left to right, the change lever markings on this gun are 'A' (Auto), 'SA' (Semi-auto), and 'S' (Safe).

The pistol grip is made in two halves of Tufnol, diagonally hand-chequered, with a keeper plate screwed into the bottom of the grip base as a support for the grip plate retaining screw, inserted from below. The trigger mechanism screw-headed retaining pin, which bears against an internal flat spring retained between two waisted pins, is slotted along its length to assist in its retention.

Also at the centre of the gunare the folding butt trunnions. The butt struts have curved sides to aid rigidity. The butt plate top wings are not chequered. The very early prototype butts look and operate exactly the same as those on the early production guns. Although they were undeniably weak and flimsy, the fact remains that the same principles, with a slight change of geometry, still operate today.

cut vertically on its front face and angled like the pistol grip at the rear, which is itself welded to the casing, just like the first firing prototype. This example has been enhanced by the addition of a projecting finger stop fitted to the forward edge of the ejection port.

The barrel is still a stock Lanchester item, screwed into a separate housing at the front of the casing. The sights are rudimentary: the foresight a post and the rear sight a non-adjustable aperture. These features identify this gun as one of the very earliest prototypes, and yet it's already a 'MkI'!

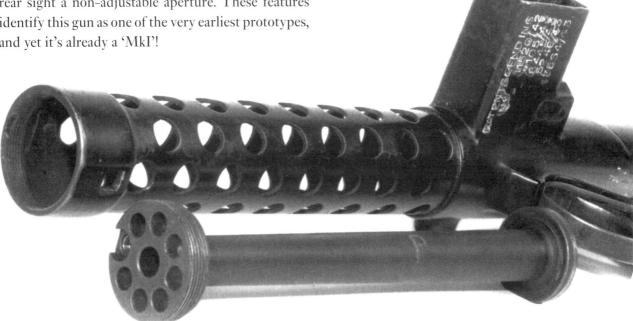

36. Front three-quarter view of the muzzle end of Patchett MkI No EXPI, with a-holed MkI Lanchester barrel unscrewed from the reinforced muzzle end of the casing, showing thumbnail locking recess for MkI Lanchester muzzle keeper screw.
Note pending wartime patent numbers, stamped into bottom of magazine housing. (MoD Pattern Room collection)

37. Closeup of selector lever markings 'A', 'SA', 'S' as found on prototype EXP1. While the *order* of the three positions remained the same throughout Sterling production (except for George Patchett's one-off experimental "Machine Pistol", discussed below), 'SA' (Semi Automatic) soon gave way to 'R' (Repetition). (MoD Pattern Room collection)

As we shall see, later improvements included the addition of a butt plate retaining spring to positively hold the butt plate open, and chequering of the ears (fig 33 no 26) to make assembly and folding easier. As discussed in Chapter Eight, an early Patchett folding butt such as this was fitted to a single, experimental "airborne" version of the Sterling-produced .45 calibre De Lisle silenced carbine during the fall of 1943.

At the rear end, the return spring cap rotates directly on the casing. The three male locking lugs for the back cap are pinned and brazed to the rear of the casing, while the corresponding female recesses are formed within the cap. The back cap itself is cylindrical, with no serrations or chequering.

As noted, comments had been raised about the strength of this return spring cap arrangement, especially should a cartridge blow back. The Lanchester cap used an interrupted screw thread, and the Sten a steel ring within a top housing with lower flange.

The method of retention used on the Patchett was quickly changed to the arrangement now in use.

Early Modifications Stay the Course

Prototype Extraction Problems

One night, during the course of one of George Patchett's 'good hard looks', he made a serious slip. There was a problem with difficult extraction being encountered with the prototype Patchett gun. George was sitting in his office late one night with a gun not fitted with a trigger mechanism. He was slowly feeding live rounds from the magazine, observing their oscillating path from the feed lips into the chamber as he gently closed the bolt. Once while pulling back the bolt his finger slipped from the cocking handle, and the remainder of the live rounds in the magazine fired, putting bullets all over the office and into his filing cabinet. It was a blessing that the office was otherwise unoccupied.

This prompted him to change the design of the cocking handle, so that thereafter it was unable to rotate in the casing, as it did on the Sten and on his own earliest prototype. Stan Wingrove eventually solved the extractor problem.

The Non-Rotating Cocking Handle in the First of Many Guises

On prototype MkI No EXP1 the breechblock again a modified Lanchester item, with the fixed Lanchester cocking handle removed and the hole in the hollowed bolt opened up through both sides to accommodate an interesting if short-lived design of non-rotating cocking handle.

The rear extension of the Lanchester firing pin has been shortened, and lateral keyhole slots drilled through forward of the mainspring stop ring.

A tubular spring guide slides over the block, locating against the mainspring stop ring on the firing pin extension.

The forward-curving cocking handle has a waisted shaft, with a longitudinal rib brazed on to prevent over-rotation.

The horizontal cocking handle slot in the casing extends forward just slightly into the casing sleeve, and terminates at the rear in a circular hole near the

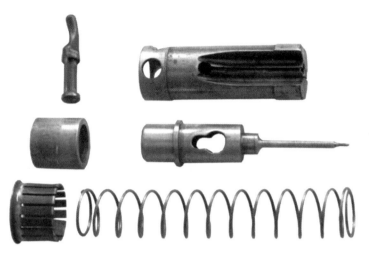

38. The earliest drawings of the Patchett Machine Carbine all depict the firing pin shown in fig 31 (below). However, after shooting up his office and filing cabinet one night George became dissatisfied with this basic design, and developed several different apparent 'one-offs' of cocking handle/firing of which featured a non-rotating cocking handle.

The casing of MkI No EXP1 is slotted horizontally, the non-rotating cocking handle removable through a circular hole at the rear, which is normally covered by the return spring cap. When assembled, the keyhole slot in the firing pin extension engages with the waisted stem of the cocking handle to prevent withdrawal. Note the (short-lived) splined return spring cup. (MoD Pattern Room collection)

rear face of the casing, for cocking handle insertion. This hole is covered by the rear cap when it is assembled.

To assemble, the breech assembly lined up with the cocking handle insertion hole in the rear of the casing, and then the firing pin block is pulled slightly rearward, until the large holes of the keyhole slot are lined up with those of the breech block. The cocking handle is then inserted and the firing pin block pushed forward to prevent withdrawal.

A splined mainspring guide sleeve with 15 slots, a push fit into the rear of the casing, centralises the return spring.

Early Changes to the Trigger Mechanism

The trigger mechanism shown in the patent drawing (fig 32) soon underwent a series of small improvements, all of which were apparently aimed at increasing the spring power available to the sear

carrier (later termed the sear cradle), and the trigger, thus leading to more positive sear action.

The trigger/sear carrier spring and plunger (fig 32 no 11) which in the prototype pushed the trigger *forward* were deleted, and another similar spring and plunger were positioned within the trigger mechanism frame, above and in front of the trigger, where they pushed *back* on a flat added to the upper portion of the trigger. This eliminated the need for the pin on which the spring and plunger (11) seated.

There was also a change in the shape of the sear carrier (15). The new sear cradle was powered by a separate spring and guide, which pivoted at its rear end to provide maximum thrust to the sear cradle and sear.

These changes only improved the sound basic principles of Patchett's patented trigger mechanism. The sear, tripping lever and selector finger (inner change lever) fitted to his earliest experimental guns operate identically to those in later models. In fact, given that the trigger mechanisms fitted to these experimental guns were generally hand–made and fitted, most parts are interchangeable with the trigger components in the later MkII Patchett, first adopted

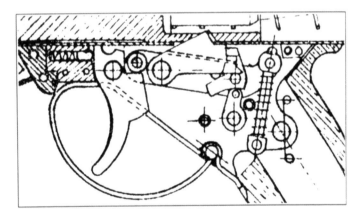

39. A closeup of the earliest post-patent trigger mechanism, taken from George Patchett's original mimeographed brochure entitled *Patchett Machine Carbine*, tentatively dated summer, 1943 (fig 42).

Note that the bolt is forward, and the safety is on. As stated in the brochure, "The Patchett Machine Carbine is the only weapon of this kind fitted with a safety device which operates with the bolt in the forward or closed position and/or in the cocked position." (Courtesy MoD Pattern Room, Nottingham)

as the L2A1 by the British Army a decade later in 1953. Technically-minded readers may compare the patent drawings with the exploded view of the Mk4 trigger mechanism (fig 155). Yes, the Mk4-the original design was that good!

The Patchett in Further Comparative Trials

As reported in OB Proc Q 1,775 of 20 December, 1943, the next trial of the Patchett against serious competition took place between 22 September and 5 October, 1943. This time the competition was between 9mm Welgun number 1, Patchett prototype "No 001", a modified "special" Mk4B Sten, an Australian Austen MkII number 2 and Owen MkII number 43, and an un-numbered private entrant, the 9mm Andrews. The Patchett came second overall, behind the MkII Owen. In 1943, you had to be good to beat the Owen!

Remarks concerning the Patchett following the trials were as follows:

a. *The foresight, while suitably robust, is very thick for accurate shooting, and the dome reflects light.*
b. *The method of locking the butt is not positive.*
c. *The length of the butt is much improved since last tested, but is still too short even for short firers.*
d. *The attachment of the front barrel housing to the front of the barrel casing is not sufficiently strong, this was found to be fractured at the end of the trial.*

e. *Apart from (c) above, the gun is comfortable to hold and has a workmanlike appearance.*

The Third Patchett/Sterling Patent (October, 1943): the Helically Ribbed Bolt

579,660. Automatic small arms. Patchett, GW, and Sterling Engineering Co, Ltd. Oct 25, 1943, No 17564. [Class 119]
Later breech blocks follow the patented design that incorporated George Patchett's simple but effective helical ribs, patent number 579660 of 25 October, 1943. In this patent, George Patchett described the advantages of the ribbed bolt as follows:

… Obstruction of the action of a machine-Carbine of the blow-back type by mud or dirt deposited in the bolt-way (5) is prevented by providing longitudinal or helical ribs (2) on the bolt (1); the ends (8) of the ribs are pointed or chisel-shaped and the ribs may be continuous or interrupted. The ribs provide clearance spaces (3) between the bolt and the bolt-way to receive the loosened deposits.

Not mentioned in the patent description is the fact that these ribs also reduce friction. This idea is so simple that it begs the question why it wasn't ever thought of before. So simple, and in Peter Laidler's experience as an Armourer, so effective too. Well done, Mr Patchett!

40. Right side view of the top-feeding Australian Owen gun. The MkII Owen provided very serious competition for the prototype MkI Patchetts. Thirteen years later, in 1956, the Australians took a commercial Mk4 Sterling and several more military L2A3s for evaluation, but the Owen had proven itself to the complete satisfaction of the Australian Army.

As late as 1968 Peter Laidler and fellow Battalion Armourers Johnny Cottrell, John Dudley and Lauri Taggart were armed with Owens while serving with the 8th Royal Australian Regiment. courtesy Australian Army (London)

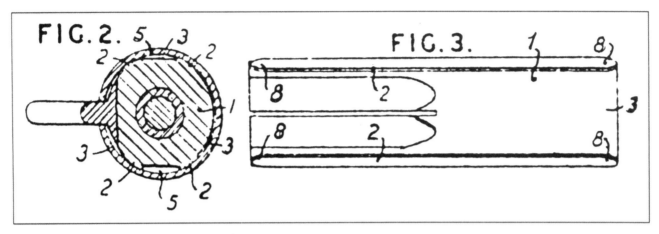

41. Figs 2 and 3 from George Patchett's ribbed bolt patent, dated October 25, 1943.

These drawings, which clearly show a Lanchester bolt with the cocking handle in the horizontal position, also show the longitudinal ribs and grooves as being in the horizontal plane, and not helical. (Courtesy British Patents Office)

Earliest Patchett Literature

In what was to be the forerunner of a latter-day cornucopia of company-produced literature on the Patchett and later Sterling, the first-ever 'Handbook' on the Patchett was an undated set of six typed-and-mimeographed pages, hand-titled simply *Patchett Machine Carbine*, probably produced in the summer of 1943. In all likelihood the text was written by George Patchett himself.

This rare, A4-size handbook is bound within stiff, plain brown cardboard, and features on the inner cover a montage of poorly reproduced photographs depicting the unnumbered first firing prototype (fig 29).

The following excerpts describe some of the many well-thought-out but subtle advantages of the Patchett, along with some interesting insights into

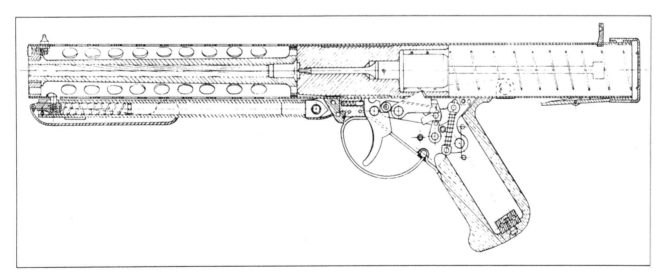

42. A drawing from George Patchett's first mimeographed wartime handbook entitled Patchett Machine Carbine, excerpted below and tentatively dated mid-1943.

Note the (folded) butt, the (rudimentary) sights, the ribbed (Lanchester) bolt, and the horizontal cocking handle slot ending in a square notch (such as featured on Patchett "MARK I No 001" described below). The early trigger mechanism is remarkably similar to the final Mk4 type.

The Lanchester barrel has been modified (front flange removed and muzzle diameter threaded), and the casing no longer incorporates the distinctive front barrel housing. (Courtesy MoD Pattern Room, Nottingham)

George Patchett's previous career. In the process, George Patchett cannot resist a few snide remarks aimed at the ageing Lanchester and its forebear, the German "Schmeisser":

General Description of the Patchett Machine Carbine

This weapon has been specially designed for modern warfare and is a machine carbine fitted with a folding butt enabling it to be used either as a folded weapon fired from the hip or, with the butt extended, fired from the shoulder. The overall length of the carbine is 27 inches and when folded it measures only 18 inches. The blowback principle has been adopted and the performance of the weapon is similar to the well known "Schmeisser" which has been in use on the Continent since 1917. In spite of the small dimensions of 18 inches the length of the barrel is the same as that of the "Schmeisser" as is also the weight of the bolt and firing pin. The main springs of the two weapons are interchangeable and the distance for the bolt to recoil is the same in both cases. Given the same ammunition both weapons should have the same penetrating power, range and rate of fire. The Patchett Machine Carbine however, weighs only 5½ lbs complete against the "Schmeisser's" 9½ lbs. This advantage in conjunction with the overall dimensions, whilst retaining the same fire power and ballistic characteristics, is an achievement of considerable importance in mobile fighting and a further examination of this new weapon will show other advantages.

The sample weapons submitted for trial have been produced by the Sterling Engineering Co Ltd who were responsible for the development and design of a modified "Schmeisser", the Lanchester Machine Carbine, some three years ago. [PG (Pilot Gun) no 1 was completed in November, 1940: Ed.] The designer of the Patchett Machine Carbine has been connected with Continental Armament manufacturers over a long period and was for three years in charge of the Banc d'Essai *at Fabrique Nationale d'Armes de Guerre, Liège, Belgium (1928–1930) and for nine years engaged as Chief Designer to the National*

Arms Factory, Zbrojovka Ing FJanacek, Prague, Czechoslovakia (1930–1939).

The Patchett Machine Carbine is the only weapon of this kind fitted with a safety device which operates with the bolt in the forward or closed position and / or in the cocked position. Other weapons not 'so fitted can be accidentally discharged by dropping them or shock, such as could be produced when leaping from a lorry, train, boat or wall. Some weapons have a means of locking the bolt back in its rearward position, but this has the disadvantage that the ejection slot is uncovered and the entry of foreign matter leading to stoppage is possible.

The sear of the Patchett Machine Carbine acts on a bent formed on the bolt face and is in permanent contact with the underside of the bolt during its forward run from the cocked position. A great advantage is claimed for this feature in that the sear being in its depressed position offers little or no resistance to the bolt's movement, whereas in other weapons having the bent at the rear of the bolt sufficient energy maybe required to depress the sear, at a critical point of the recoil, that, with a weak charge, the bent may not be engaged by the sear and uncontrollable automatic fire initiated or double taps registered with the weapon set for single shot.

The trigger mechanism in the Patchett Machine Carbine is of unit construction and a complete entity. There are no push rods or tie rods interposed between the trigger and the sear which, under extreme temperatures, could lead to erratic operations. The trigger pivot is less than ¾ inch from the sear pivot …

The trigger mechanism comprises a means of obtaining, by thumb control, safety setting, single shot setting or fully automatic setting. When set for automatic fire, the rate is approximately 600 rounds per minute and on single shot setting, shots can be fired at the rate of 120–140 rounds per minute. The safety setting as previously described gives safety with the bolt in any position …

… the weapon is completely stripped into 7 parts or units. The main unit consists of barrel casing – barrel – butt assembly – pistol grip – end cap

lock – sights – magazine housing with magazine catch and ejector. [The other six units are] the trigger assembly; the end cap; the main spring; the firing pin; the cocking handle; the breech bolt and extractor.

To carry out the above stripping, no tools of any description are required and the stripping can be performed in 15 seconds. The assembling of the weapon can be carried out in 20 to 30 seconds …

Either the Lanchester 50rd magazine or the Sten 32rd magazine can be used in the Patchett Machine Caibine …

The barrel is unscrewed from the back A locking screw at the front of the barrel must be removed as well as the ejector before attempting to remove the barrel …

The trigger return spring and plunger are not essential for the functioning of the mechanism and may be dispensed with if the locking lever spring has been lost and the trigger return spring used as a replacement …

The "Second-Stage" Prototypes

Describing Patchett Prototype MARK I No 001

This is the first Patchett prototype depicted herein to be constructed without the forward and central sleeves. Notwithstanding George Patchett's description in the first wartime handbook, the stock Lanchester barrel still threads in from the front, but the rear flange now resembles the front flange in that it has been drilled with eight lightening holes around its circumference. The front sight is a vertical tapered post.

As with prototype MkI No EXP,1 a curved finger guard has been fitted to the forward radius of the ejection slot, but here the cocking handle slot terminates in a square notch to allow the base of the cocking handle to slide vertically in and out of 'T' slots in the breech block.

A three-lug, bayonet-catch sleeve is pinned and brazed to the rear of the casing, to provide better support for the end cap.

The rear sight is a fixed vertical aperture.

The trigger housing is still deeply radiused above the trigger to allow maximum clearance for a gloved finger, but the trigger mechanism itself has a less

43. Right side view of Patchett prototype 'MARK I No 001', showing differences in construction from earliest prototypes.

Compare with fig 34: note the absence of the front barrel housing and wraparound central sleeve. The magazine housing and trigger housing/grip plate assembly are now welded directly to the casing. The horizontal cocking handle is also positioned further forward.

Note the square notch at the rear of the (closed) cocking handle slot: as shown below, this gun featured yet another interesting but short-lived cocking handle retention system.

This gun featured in the first successful trials of George Patchett's patented ribbed bolt in October, 1943. (MoD Pattern Room collection)

44. Top closeup view of the magazine housing of Patchett prototype 'MARK I No 001'. This gun featured in the first, successful ribbed bolt firing trials at the Pendine Experimental Establishment on 20 October, 1943. (MoD Pattern Room collection)

45. Closeup view of the right rear of the casing of Patchett prototype MARK I No 001 with end cap removed, showing the end cap sleeve. The square notch in the cocking handle slot resembles that shown in the drawing in *Patchett Machine Carbine* (fig 42). (MoD Pattern Room collection)

46. Closeup of the right rear of the casing of Patchett prototype 'MARK I No 001', showing how the unique square-bodied cocking handle is removed or replaced through the square slot.

Flanges machined on the front and rear of the handle body enter the 'T'-slots undercut in the breech block. (MoD Pattern Room collection)

47. Closeup of the ribbed breech block and cocking handle from Patchett prototype 'MARK I No 001' A spring-loaded detent in the cocking handle body enters the depression in the centre of the slot in the breech block, to ensure proper positioning. (MoD Pattern Room collection)

pronounced undercut and does not match this deep radius.

The grip plates are made in two halves of Tufnol, retained to the grip plates by two screws per grip. The trigger mechanism retaining pin is still a split screw, as on prototype MKI No EXP 1.

The breech block features four raised, sharpedged helical ribs for scraping out fouling, the block being bored out centrally from the rear to accept the firing pin and spring guide block. The front face of the block is flat, with no angled extractor side.

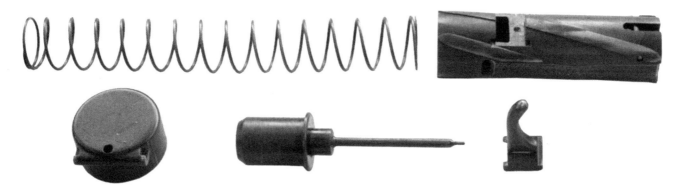

48. Right side view of the breech mechanism of Patchett Prototype 'MARK I No 001'. Note the firing pin extension, which resembles that depicted in fig 42. (MoD Pattern Room collection)

The cocking handle slides vertically on 'T' slots in the breech block, and is located centrally by a spring and ball detent corresponding with a recess in the breech block. The underside of the cocking handle plate has a radius undercut for half its length at the rear, corresponding to the outside diameter of the main spring guideblock on the firing pin. This means that the cocking handle must be assembled *before* the firing pin/spring guide.

The side wings of the butt plate are finely chequered, to assist in pulling the plate away from the strut to fold the assembly.

Favourable Ribbed Bolt Trials at Pendine

As also reported in OB Proc Q1,755 of 20 December, 1943, a special comparison trial was held at Pendine Experimental Establishment on 20th October, 1943 featuring Patchett MARK I No 001, with the special ribbed bolt compared against the 'normal' item.

The Board concluded that the lighter "sandmud-proof" ribbed bolt gave a marked improvement under conditions of sand and mud, although further tests would be needed to check its endurance.

They also raised questions as to why the Patchett delivered more than its fair share of "lightly struck detonator caps" and "caps not struck", especially when using captured German 9mm ammunition. George was working on this, though!

Catch 22: the Patchett "Likely", but Production "Precluded"

In November, 1943 the weapons under test were all fired again at Bisley by the Small Arms School, along with a new entry, the experimental Vesley V43.

This time the trials report concluded that "not *one* of the designs in question rigidly meets the specification in its present form, although the Patchett shows most promise of doing so." Indeed, the Patchett (virtually) satisfied the General Staff requirement for a new SMG, soon to be issued on 7th January, 1944 (Chapter Three). Things were certainly taking shape!

The Board reported that the result was as they expected (with first place going to the Mk II Owen), due to the fact that the Owen gun was already in service while the others were simply on trial. The Australians had long since discovered that the Austen was no match for the Owen!

However, the Board concluded somewhat ambiguously that "… the limitations of production capacity preclude any new requirement for this type of weapon being stated as a short-term policy, except so far as improvements to an existing Service design are concerned".

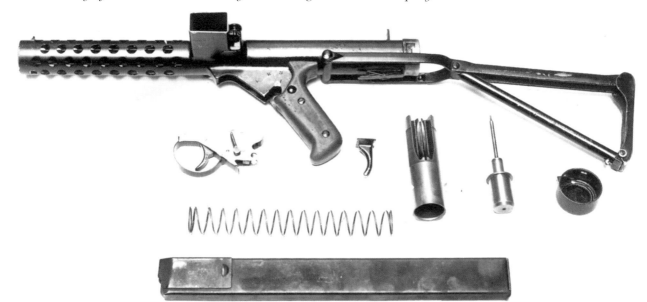

49. Patchett prototype MARK I No 001 photographed to accompany OB Proc 24,647 dated 10 September, 1943, one month before the successful firing trials at Pendine. Note the 50-round Lanchester magazine. (Courtesy MoD Pattern Room, Nottingham)

The Front-Flange Barrel Retaining System: a Lasting Change for the Better

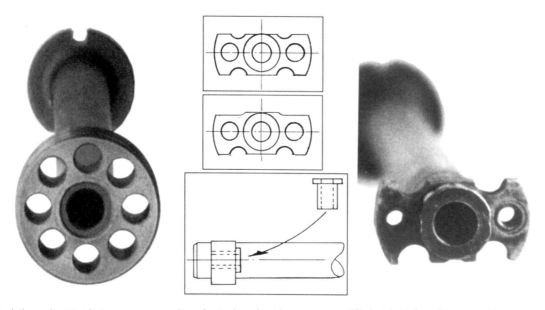

50. As noted, the earliest Patchett prototypes used Lanchester barrels, either as is or modified with the front flange machined away completely and the barrel diameter threaded, the barrel then being screwed in from the rear.

A new method of barrel retention was soon devised, which remained in use throughout Sterling production. (Ex-Lanchester barrels were used in approximately the first 4,000 Patchett/Sterling SMGs.)

Left: front view of stock Lanchester barrel, showing locating slot (top rear) and the 20TPI (Whit)-threaded, 8-holed front flange. (MoD Royal Navy)

Centre, top: front view of a modified Lanchester barrel, wherein the top and bottom edges of the front flange have been machined away (unequally, to ensure a one-way fit in the front barrel support). Two of the original 8 circumferential holes remain, plus the vestiges of four others.

Centre, middle: a variation of this process, with the vestiges of top two circumferential holes machined away completely.

Centre, below: left side view of barrel, showing front flange reduced in thickness (to allow muzzle to protrude). Two OBA screw-threaded inserts are brazed into the two remaining horizontal holes from the rear, and the muzzle is chamfered. (Drawings by Peter Laidler)

Right: the conversion, complete. (MoD Army, RMCS Shrivenham)

Chapter Three

"Pilot" and "User" Trials Patchetts

The Pilot Model – the "Trials Twenty"

In January, 1944 the General Staff of the War Office approved a new specification (long-term policy) for the next generation of small arms weapons, described as follows:

1. a .303-inch light rifle
2. a 7.92mm light automatic gun
3. a 7.92mm sniper's rifle with telescopic sight
4. a 7.92mm self loading rifle
5. a 9mm machine carbine
6. a 7.92mm medium machine gun.

The new long-term specification stated that the machine carbine should be 9mm calibre, weigh 6 lbs, be capable of putting 5 singly aimed shots into a 12″ × 12″ square at 100 yards with a cyclic rate of fire of about 500rds/min.

In OB Proc Q 1,810 of 12 January, 1944 the Ordnance Board reported that the Patchett, with its patented ribbed bolt, was well on its way to meeting these requirements. The success of Patchett MARK I No 001 in October, 1943 (Chapter Two) was recorded in the following Remarks by the Board:

1. *The special "breech bolt" … was fitted to the Patchett carbine as the result of its [earlier] failure in sand and mud tests at Pendine. It was fitted to the weapon when tested at Bisley (see Proc No Q 1,755). The incidents of "lightly struck caps" and "caps not struck" are being investigated.*
2. *As the result of the promise shown by the Patchett machine carbine, towards meeting the Generol Staff specification … an order has been initiated for the supply of 20 weapons, with the Sterling Engineering Co Ltd. This order has as its objects*

(i) a test of production for the weapon and (ii) further trials to substantiate the design, which is basically of Schmeisser origin. Assembly of the weapons ordered will take place towards the close of January, 1944 …

We know from the contract records held at the Public Records Library that on 12 January, 1944, Sterling Engineering were contracted to manufacture these 20 guns, at a contract price of £4,464. This price did not include any funds for further design and development, as this was considered to have been already completed by George Patchett.

Describing the Trials Twenty

OB Proc Q 2,320 of 21 June, 1944 reports that these twenty pilot guns, which we call the "Trials Twenty" (nos 053 to 072 inclusive), were delivered to the Ordnance Board by George Patchett personally on April 28, 1944.

Most of the component parts on these pilot guns are individually numbered to the serial number of the gun, to aid in identifying them and returning them after the interchangeability trials. The serial number can be found on the butt assembly, return spring cap, the alloy pistol grip and the barrel, to name a few locations.

The Family Resemblance Grows

The first thing that any Armourer or another who is used to working with guns will note is that the Trials Twenty guns are beginning to look remarkably like their later brother, thc Mk4/L2A3. To be sure, the magazine is still square-on, Sten gun fashion, and like the prototypes, they will only function with Sten/Lanchester magazines.

51. Right side view of perhaps the most famous of the Trials Twenty Patchetts, still owned by the Ministry of Defence, serial no 054, with butt extended. Note the cast metal alloy pistol grip.

On 21 June, 1944 this gun, together with gun no 053, each fired a record 10,700 rounds, virtually non-stop.

These two guns went on to feature in many other tests and comparisons. During later trials, the Small Arms School Corps examiners could only hazard 250,000 as a guess at the total number of rounds each had really fired, and so instructions were issued that the accuracy of these two guns should not be judged against the competition.

Both nos 053 and 054 were eventually retired to the Royal Military College of Science in Shrivenham where more trials, some of a scientific nature, took place. (MoD Army, RMCS Shrivenham)

The magazine housings and finger guards are still edge-welded to the casing and the joints filed into a smooth radius, a tedious task with the glass-hard weld. The finished body casings were Parkerised and then sprayed with black paint.

New (and Better-Protected) Sights

The sighting arrangements on the Trials Twenty were radically altered and improved. Heavy, solid foresight protectors were taken straight from the Lanchester, while early versions of the current fabricated type were also introduced on some guns. The foresight blade is the solid type, taken straight from the Lanchester and adjustable for height only by changing the blade, but for deflection by moving it left or right within the friction-fit housing. There were seven sizes of blade, ranging from 1.530″ above the centre line of the bore, in .020″ increments up to 1.650″.

The rearsight idea also appears to have been taken straight from the late Mk1 and Mk1* Lanchester, except it utilises the Mk2 flick-over dual range aperture leaf from the No4 rifle, a sight leaf very close to the later Sterling production style.

What was apparent with the pilot guns, and featured as a positive fault during its trials, was that the upright rearsight protectors were only .45″

apart. In conditions of half light and poor visibility, the close proximity of the backsight protecting ears blocked out any residual light that would assist in fast target acquisition. On some of the later user trials guns the distance between the ears was increased to .55″, which appears to have solved the problem, as the distance remained .55″ throughout all subsequent Sterling production.

52. Closeup of the magazine housing of Trials Twenty Patchett No 057, showing pantographed markings. Note the paint-over-Parkerising finish.

In January, 1945 this gun was sent to the Small Arms School for further trials. (MoD Pattern Room collection)

First Use of the Converted Lanchester Barrel

The muzzle cap resembles the 8-holed Lanchester barrel's front flange, but is now a separate component fixed within the casing, and has only seven holes in a pitched circle around the muzzle. The barrels used on the Trials Twenty guns (and indeed for some time to come) were converted from ex-Lanchester stock as shown in fig 50, and retained by two OBA screws through the horizontally opposed holes in the endcap, threading into the reworked front barrel flange. The early screws were cheese-headed with screwdriver slots, while Allen bolts were used in later production.

To cater for the Sten left-hand, single-feed position, the breech face of the barrel was throated to allow bullets to feed properly. Throating the breech was not a new idea and once again, this process owes its ancestry to the Lanchester.

The Trials Twenty guns represent the first general appearance of Patchett's patented helical ribbed bolt, discussed in Chapter Two.

Some of these guns appear to have pistol grips made of cast alloy material, while later examples have black bakelite pistol grips, showing slight modifications to be described later.

The magazine catch and ejector configurations are conventional Lanchester, with the ejector retaining screw threaded into a thick anti-rotation plate. In

53. Front closeup view of a Trials Twenty Patchett, showing the seven holes in the circumference of the heavy nose cap.

Note the two slot-headed screws which secure the converted Lanchester barrel (fig 50) in the casing, and the solid Lanchester front sight protectors. (MoD Pattern Room collection)

fact the magazine catch, screw, spring and ejector of the MkI Patchett (but not the MkII or later) are interchangeable with the Lanchester.

Initially there was no provision for a bayonet on the pilot model guns, because the specification did not require a bayonet.

Further Modifications to Cocking Handle and Firing Pin

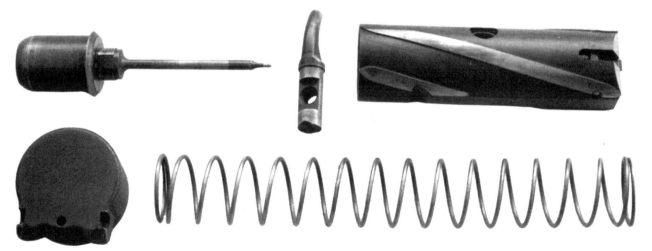

54. The further-modified cocking handle and firing pin arrangement supplied with the Trials Twenty Patchetts.

In this model the firing pin passed through a round hole in the elongated cocking handle shaft. (MoD Pattern Room collection)

55. Closeup of the non-rotating cocking handle in a typical Trials Twenty gun (no 063), showing round hole through which the firing pin passed.

Note the rounded 'cartridge rim' screwdriver on the bottom (left). (MoD Pattern Room collection)

In the Trials Twenty Patchetts the firing pin/cocking handle interface was the subject of a further modification. The thin front portion of the firing pin now passed through a round hole drilled in the elongated cocking handle shaft, thus maintaining the non-rotating cocking handle principle. While completely different from the methods employed in the prototypes, this still meant that, in order to strip the gun, the firing pin had to be withdrawn before the cocking handle.

Successful Initial Trials of the "Trials Twenty"

OB Proc Q 2,320 of 21 June, 1944, which reported the delivery of the twenty pilot guns by George Patchett on April 28, 1944, continued with a description of the initial trials to which the pilot guns had been subjected, as follows:

CIA W, 18 May 44 to Sec OB:

Twenty weapons, nos 053 to 072 (both inclusive) supplied by Mr Patchett on 28 Apr 44 have now all been subjected to brief trial, agreed by Ordnance Board, as follows:

Stage A: Functioning
1. *One magazine single shot*
2. *One magazine short bursts.*
3. *One magazine continuous auto.*
4. *One magazine at 80° elevation (10 rds SS, 10 rds SB [Short bursts], 10 rds continuous auto).*
5. *One magazine at 80° depression (10 rds SS, 10 rds SB, 10 rds continuous auto).*
6. *Three magazines continuous auto: each magazine timed: the average of the three being recorded as the rate of fire for the given carbine.*

Stage B: Accuracy
1. *At 100 feet, two 10-round diagrams SS*
2. *At 100 feet, two 10-round diagrams SB*
3. *At 50 feet, two 10-round diagrams SS*
4. *At 50 feet, two 10-round diagrams SB*
5. *At 100 yards, two 10-round diagrams SS*
6. *At 100 yards, two 10-round diagrams SB*
7. *At 200 yards, two 10-round diagrams SS*

Results

All carbines functioned correctly throughout the trial except that during Stage A (1) carbine no 060 gave three double taps and carbine no 062 gave one double tap. But this fault did not occur at any subsequent time during the trial with these Carbines and it is thought that the fault was probably due t.o the internal friction in the reciprocating parts due to slight "burrs" which disappeared as the weapon "bedded down".

Early in Stage A it was noticed that in the majority of the carbines (14 out of 20) the tip of the strike – approximately 3/8 inch of reduced portion – was becoming bent to an extent that would inevitably prejudice functioning later. The fact was reported by telephone to Mr Patchett He investigated immediately and supplied twenty fresh strikers and had returned to him the twenty old ones. No recurrence of the fault occurred with any of the twenty fresh strikers during the remainder of the trial.

It appears that a mistake (which will not be repeated) had occurred during the production operation of hardening the striker tip.

Speed – The maximum speed was given by weapon no 056 at 613 rounds per minute. The minimum speed was given by weapon no 063 at 568 rounds per minute.

The average speed of the twenty carbines was 583 rounds per minute.

Accuracy – The standard of accuracy in general falls within CIA W acceptance limits for 9mm carbines.

The mechanical finish in general was very good, judged by usual production standards; we would however like to see the "blacking" of the external finish made a little more permanent if possible. It tends to rub off rather badly, especially in the presence of oil, and this was most noticeable under the barrel casing where subject to much rubbing by the firer's left hand.

All the twenty weapons passed our acceptance trials satisfactorily and we consider, and recommend, that they are fit to go for " user" trials.

Remarks by the Board

1. *The military and technical objects for the 20 pilot weapons are defined in Procs Q1,755 and Q1,810.*
2. *The Board are informed that a special production order has been satisfied for 100 Patchett carbines,* *and that these have been issued to troops, while the technical development of the design proceeds.*
3. *The average weight of the pilot weapon is 6 lb +/- ½ oz. Interchangeability of the component parts is reported to be satisfactory for these pilots.*

   The average rate of fire for the new weapons is 583 rounds per minute. This rate is rather higher than that given by the prototype model when worn (545 rpm). It is expected, however, that the rates of fire for the pilot models will be lower when using Mark II ammunition and when the barrels have been subjected to wear.
4. *The external finish of the pilot weapons, although "Parkerised" initially, is capable of improvement. This matter is being investigated.*

The First Printed Handbook

As described in Chapter Two, George Patchett first issued an undated, mimeographed, 8-page brochure hand-titled *Patchett Machine Carbine*, probably during the summer of 1943.

The first *printed* Patchett Handbook appeared in the autumn of that year: a small (4½″ × 8″) 16-page green-covered brochure with several pages of photographic illustrations (reproduced below).

The printed text is basically abridged from the original mimeographed version (Chapter Two), with the snide remarks about the "Schmeisser, which has been used· on the Continent since 1917" watered down considerably, and the details of George Patchett's decade of experience with Continental armsmakers skipped over entirely.

(Belatedly) Heralding the New Barrel

The transformation from the first prototype Patchett Machine Carbine into the Sterling Sub-Machine Gun may be seen as an admirable series of improvements to a basically good idea, made by a tenacious and determined man who also just happened to be a genius at machine-design and production. However, it appears that George Patchett was far happier in the shop or on the range than at his writing desk, updating instructions.

56. The (green) cover of *Patchett Machine Carbine 1943*, the first printed Patchett Handbook. (MoD Pattern Room collection)

We have noted that Patchett's mimeographed *Patchett Machine Carbine* was the first of what would become (especially after 1972) a veritable flood of literature, produced by the Sterling company in support of its products. In the printed *Patchett Machine Carbine 1943* we confront the first of many "lags" in Sterling literature, between the actual date of introduction of a change, and the update of the drawing and/or the printed description. This is quite understandable, as presumably updated handbooks would not be printed until most (if not all) copies of the earlier edition had been given out, whether obsolete or not.

In the printed text of *Patchett Machine Carbine 1943*, a small slip of paper has been tipped in over the original barrel removal instructions. A judicious peek underneath reveals the following documented change:

Original:
The barrel is unscrewed from the back. The ejector must be removed before attempting to remove the barrel. The barrel has a left-hand thread.

Tipped In on Slip of Paper:
To remove the barrel, unscrew two fixing screws on the front face and press out the barrel from the front towards the rear. The ejector and trigger should be removed first.

Introducing the Patchett "Carrying Equipment"

In the second (undated) printed handbook *Patchett Machine Carbine* (discussed below), this device was described (but not pictured), as follows:

Carrying Equipment
A carrying equipment has been designed to enable the weapon to be carried with the greatest ease and at the same time to be instantly available when needed.
*   This consists of a metallic nosepiece which fits into a webbing container and having a strap with a 'D' to enable it to be connected to the standard magazine pouch strap. The carbine is clipped onto*

57. The short-lived Patchett "Carrying Equipment", pictured (but not described) in *Patchett Machine Carbine 1943* and described (but not depicted) in the later (undated) *Patchett Machine Carbine*. (MoD Pattern Room collection)

the metallic nosepiece and locked into position by the magazine catch. To remove the carbine it is necessary to disengage the magazine lock catch, upon which the weapon is free for removal from its support.

The Carrying Equipment first appeared in a small montage of blurry photographs on the title page of George Patchett's mimeographed *Patchett Machine Carbine*, although the equipment is not mentioned in the 8-page text. Curiously, all the illustrations in the first printed *Patchett Machine Carbine 1943* also depict the Carrying Equipment, but no printed description is included: indeed, the name of the device itself is not mentioned.

It appears the Carrying Equipment lived largely in George Patchett's dreams. Even though it is invariably depicted as being worn by men in uniform, it was never adopted.

58. From *Patchett Machine Carbine 1943*, the "Carrying Equipment" as worn.

The main web section was securely hooked over the issue web belt, and the front casing support tab (shown here at top) added to the right shoulder strap. Note the Sten magazine pouch. (MoD Pattern Room collection)

Serious Endurance Trials

As noted, the Trials Twenty were all built and assembled to the specification of January, 1944, and were to compete in trials scheduled to begin with the initial acceptance tests (recorded above) on 21st June, 1944.

Nobody knew at the time quite what the full trial series would entail, and what the guns would ultimately be subjected to, and thus nobody could realise that these rugged guns would shrug off most of what was eventually to choke the opposition.

Following the successful initial trials with the pilot models, a total of 48,000 rounds of selected British Mk1Z, Mk2Z, Canadian, American, captured German brass-cased, captured German steel-cased, and Italian 9mm ammunition was procured for a series of serious endurance trials at Pendine. Six Trials Twenty guns were selected at random, two of which were required to fire 10,000 rounds each and the others to fire up to 5,000 rounds each, as follows:

Gun No	No of Rounds Fired
053	10,700
054	10,700
055	4,950
056	5,930
068	4,970
069	4,970

The guns were minutely examined afterward, and although there was a degree of wear, this was declared as "… no more pronounced than we would expect due to fair wear and tear."

Gun no 056 had a defective return spring but as this was a Lanchester item which had come from an

59. The Patchett Machine Carbine, as worn on the Carrying Equipment. The alloy grip can clearly be seen.

Note the hook on the end of the casing support strap, hooked into a cooling hole in the front end of the casing and adjusted to add vertical support to the gun. (From *Patchett Machine Carbine, 1943*, MoD Pattern Room collection)

outside contractor, the fault was beyond the control of George Patchett and the Sterling company.

Most of these guns were returned to Pendine for disposal at the end of these exhaustive trials, but those that remained with the trials team still featured in later trials and, as a result, many have been noted with all manner of slight modifications.

As noted in OB Proc Q 2,320,above, it was the success of the Trials Twenty guns that saw the next batch, which we call the Troop Trials 101, ordered for extended user trials in September, 1944.

The One-Off Patchett "Machine Pistol"

60. Left side view of George Patchett's experimental 9mm "Machine Pistol", basically a short, folding-butt sub-machine gun fitted with an ingenious collapsible casing. (Here the casing and butt are both shown extended, ready for firing.)
     Note George Patchett's patented folding bayonet (left), discussed in Chapter Four. (MoD Pattern Room collection)

61. Top closeup view of the magazine housing of the Patchett Machine Pistol, showing markings.
     The Patchett Machine Pistol featured some innovative ideas, but was not built to any War Office or Ordnance Board requirement, and was thus largely ignored by the military. Only this one example was ever built. (MoD Pattern Room collection)

62 (right). The Patchett Machine Pistol in the Patchett "Carrying Equipment", worn by an officer of the Home Guard. (Patchett himself!)
     Compare with fig 59: note the remarkable compactness of the Patchett Machine Pistol. (Courtesy MoD Pattern Room)

63. Left side view of the 9mm Patchett Machine Pistol with casing telescoped and butt folded over the top, showing Patchett's patented folding, spring-loaded bayonet (discussed in Chapter Four). Note change lever positions 'R', 'S'. 'A', unique in all Patchett/Sterling production to this one experimental model. (MoD Pattern Room collection)

At the same time he was developing his MkI Machine Carbine, George Patchett also produced a one-off example of an elegant, telescoping "Machine Pistol", which the Ordnance Board christened the Patchett "Carbinette". It is not strictly one of Patchett's submachine guns, and was not built to any specific order, but it is one of the most interesting guns he ever built.

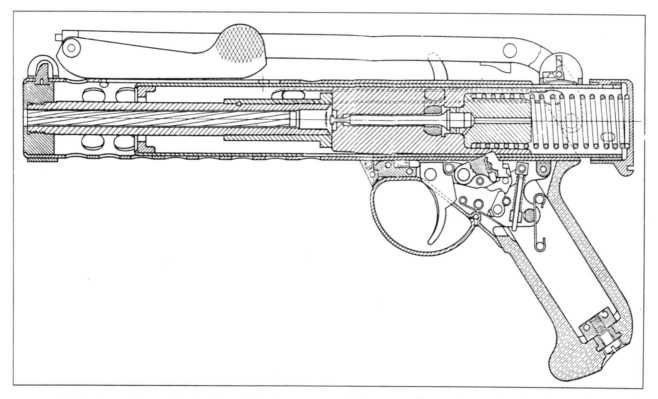

64. From a Sterling factory drawing dated 7.12.43, a left side cutaway view of the 9mm Patchett Machine Pistol. In this (telescoped) position the gun is exactly 12$\frac{7}{8}$" long overall.

Note the barrel is still screwed into the heavy nose cap. The separate firing pin passes through a hole in the (50°) cocking handle, as in fig 54. (MoD Pattern Room collection)

This pistol, now resident in the Ministry of Defence Pattern Room, is all the more remarkable in that it was Patchett's only attempt at such a project.

It was subject to a trial of sorts later in the war, the results of which were inconclusive; but in any case there was no expressed need for such a gun.

The Patchett Machine Pistol incorporates an ingenious telescoping casing. When the breech block is in the fired position, the rearmost part of the casing can be closed up a further 4″. To fire the gun, the cocking handle is pulled to the rear, cocking the gun and extending the casing. Because of this telescoping casing configuration, the folding butt closes over the top of the gun.

Quite unusually, due to a slightly different tripping lever and inner change lever combination, the change lever markings on the Patchett Machine Pistol show from left to right 'R' (repetition) 'S' (safe) and 'A' (automatic). This differs from the arrangement on every other Patchett or Sterling SMG examined, which is 'A'-'R'-'S'.

The Patchett Machine Pistol also marked the first appearance of George Patchett's patented folding bayonet, further discussed in Chapter Four.

Fitting the No5 Rifle Bayonet

65. Left side view of Trials Twenty Patchett no 062, the only one known to remain of the four guns initially fitted by Sterling with No5 Rifle bayonets in June, 1944. (MoD Pattern Room collection)

66. Left side closeup view of the front of the casing of Trials Twenty Patchett no 062, the only one remaining of the four returned to Sterling in June, 1944 to have bayonets experimentally fitted, and returned again in October to have the bayonet standards repaired.

The rivetted plate covers and reinforces the earlier damage. The bayonet standard is located further to the rear than on later production.

Note the heavy Lanchester foresight protectors. (MoD Pattern Room collection)

67. Top closeup view of magazine housing of Trials Twenty Patchett no 062, showing markings. (MoD Pattern Room collection)

Four of the Trials Twenty guns, Nos 060, 062, 064 and 065, were subsequently returned to Sterling on 24 June, 1944 to investigate the feasibility of fitting the No5 rifle bayonet.

The project was undertaken, and the modified guns were fitted with bayonets (which makes them look like later Troop Trials 101 guns to the untrained eye), and returned to Pendine. There was a problem. The Sterling engineers had completed the task as a feasibility study, not a trials study where bayonets fitted to these modified guns were to be put through a series of punishing tests. The bayonet standards proved to be weak and vulnerable, and, as a result of damage sustained during the trials, the four modified guns were returned to George Patchett at Sterling for repair in October, 1944.

This time the project was undertaken as a trials study. Later tests were successful, due to a strengthened bayonet standard. Throughout Sterling production the bayonet standard remained strengthened at the base, inside the casing, by a reinforcing plate.

The success of this project saw to it that the next guns ordered, the Troop Trials 101, had Nos rifle bayonets fitted as standard.

Introducing the 'Crackle' Finish

As discussed in Chapter Seven, the induction brazing process, latterly used with great success in permanently attaching the components of the gun's casing assembly, was not introduced until series production of the Sterling began in the mid-1950s. Prior to that, production of the relatively few numbers of guns required relied much more intensively on hand-work.

Early magazine housings were butt-welded to the casings, a process that left an unsightly bead of glass-hard weld around the joint. This was laboriously ground to approximate a smooth radius from casing to housing (with greater or lesser success, as examination of the closeup photos of these early guns will reveal).

In response to Ordnance Board complaints about the durability of the Parkerised-and-painted finish in use up to that time, a process was developed whereby a wood resin was added to a tough black paint which, when sprayed on the completed casing and oven-baked, set up into a random, non-slip surface of tiny, hard wrinkles on a dullish black background, rather like Parkerising in reverse! *Voilà*, the crackle finish, which as David Howroyd points out, had the happy secondary advantage of hiding "a multitude of sins", especially in smoothing over the residual grind marks on the welded joint between the casing and magazine housing.

The later switch to induction brazing solved this problem, as it was a much more controllable process and left a far neater join. However, by that time the crackle finish had established itself as entirely satisfactory, and it was thus maintained throughout all commercial Sterling production, only the UK Military usually opting for matt black paint.

68. Left side view of Trials Twenty Patchett no 063, the first Patchett seen bearing the "Rivell" or 'crackle' finish. This process was developed by Sterling as an acceptably tough military finish that, in the words of David Howroyd, hid "a multitude of sins". Used throughout Sterling production. (The bayonet standard was a later retrofit, in the style of the later production guns.) (MoD Pattern Room collection)

69. Top closeup view of magazine housing of Trials Twenty Patchett no 063, showing markings.

Compare with fig 67: this appears to be the first appearance of the successful "Rivell" ('crackle') finish. (MoD Pattern Room collection)

Were Patchetts Used at Arnhem?

The controversy over whether any Patchett guns were involved in the mighty airborne forces battle at Arnhem in September, 1944 may never be fully resolved.

To date, in spite of much research, there has been no *documentary* proof that Patchett guns were used in action at Arnhem or the crossing of the Rhine by the 1st or 6th Airborne Divisions. There is certainly no sight of a Patchett in any of the 2,000 photographs taken during the run-up to, or during, the battle. No remains of a Patchett have ever been recovered from the battlefield.

However, it has been reported elsewhere that a quantity of early Patchetts were used in action by paratroopers of 1st Airborne Division at Arnhem. George Patchett himself stated in the first postwar handbook entitled *Patchett Machine Carbine* (Chapter Four) that during the war the gun "… was used by British commando units after exhaustive tests had been made."

Years later, during the run-up to the (almost) certain adoption of the slightly modified MkIII/L2A2 gun, later called the Mk4/L2A3 (Chapter Seven), a press day was organised on 19 February, 1955. The Sterling press release reported that "… a

few early models were brought into service just before the end of World War II."

This assertation was affirmed even more specifically in the January, 1973 edition of the Sterling User 'Handbook for the Mk4/L2A3A: "Limited quantities [of Patchetts] saw service in Europe before the end of World War II."

… and If So, How Many Went?

Quite how many Patchetts might have been used at Arnhem is a matter of conjecture, but Peter Laidler was reliably told many years ago by Tommy Fitch, a wartime paratrooper and survivor of Arnhem and the original curator of the Airborne Forces Museum at Aldershot, that he (Tommy) believed it was six. Whatever the number, it cannot have been more than 20, and none returned.

Certainly, from the hardware side, the remotest possibility does exist. Of the four guns sent to the Airborne Forces Development Centre (AFDC) for evaluation, only one can be accounted for and three, known by serial number, never featured in another trial. If this is correct, then without doubt, it would have been Trials Twenty guns Nos 067, 070 and 072 that blooded their teeth in anger, as these were submitted for trial on 28th April, 1944 and as at 31st January, 1945 they were the only guns not available for disposal. Gun No 062, listed as "held at AFDC", was returned to the Sterling company in October, 1944 for repairs and rests today in the MoD Pattern Room collection, so clearly it cannot have gone to Arnhem in September, 1944, whence none returned.

Could it be that just three went? Maybe Tommy Fitch was NEARLY correct after all!

The Sterling Family Compact in Action

Throughout the war Sterling was in the forefront of good employee relations. Because of the long hours, sometimes 12 hours a day for seven days a week, for many weeks on end, there was even an on-site hairdresser. Sport also played its part and, like most large establishments, and the Army is no exception, those members of successful sports teams inevitably seemed to find that time was made available for sports practice or important company matches while, remarkably, pay was not docked for this"company absence", as it was described on the time cards. By 1944, there were 1,600 employees at the Sterling company, many of whom were hastily trained but extremely skilled female toolmakers. These highly skilled persons were to form the backbone of the company workforce in the immediate postwar and later years.

The factory had its own fire brigade, with a mobile high-capacity water pump. Selected factory personnel were authorised to switch off and isolate the electricity and gas supply in case of enemy action. Enemy action did arrive at the factory on two occasions when a V1 flying bomb, then a V2 rocket, blew half the roofs off, took out 90% of the window glass, and, as noted below, destroyed many company records.

There was a fire-watching rota, where all members of the staff were assigned rotating duty shifts to listen for enemy aircraft from a specially built tower. This high tower, situated in the centre of the factory complex, was a vantage point from which many romancing couples were discreetly observed "doing what comes naturally" to coin a phrase!

User Trials with the "Troop Trials 101"

70. Left side view of a "Troop Trials 101" Patchett, showing butt extended. (Courtesy David Howroyd)

71. Left side closeup of a "Troop Trials 101" Patchett, showing bayonet standard screwed in place through a steel reinforcing plate, fitted on the inner side of the casing wall. Note the first appearance of the Sterling stamped foresight guards. (MoD Pattern Room collection)

72. Right side closeup of Troop Trials 101 Patchett, showing sling loop retrofitted. The sling loop also acted as a front finger guard.

There were many variations on the sling loop idea, but the best, which eventually emerged, was to forget the loop entirely and put a brass closing hook on the end of the sling. (MoD Pattern Room collection)

As noted in OB Proc 2,320 of 21 June, 1944, the success of the Trials Twenty in initial and endurance trials had prompted the Ordnance Board to order a further 100 Patchett machine carbines for extended user trials. These guns are referred to as the "Troop Trials 101" because while an even 100 were ordered, it appears a total of 101 were delivered. They were numbered from 080 to 180, leaving of course the unanswered question where are the guns numbered 074 to 079 inclusive? (For that matter, where are all the MkI guns numbered after 001 and before 053?)

All the Troop Trials 101 guns were built to the same specification, which followed the general pattern of the earlier Trials Twenty form, except the Troop Trials 101s could take the No5 rifle bayonet.

The specification did not spell out that it was to be the No5 rifle bayonet per se, but merely stated that ' it should be a bayonet "… of the type fitted to the No5 rifle". In the Accessories Chapter we will see how this caused the Sterling engineers a great deal of head-scratching.

A Triumphant Delivery

The Sterling company gun registers were destroyed by fire following enemy flying bomb action on 21 March, 1945. Nevertheless, Sterling carried on with the aid of a small flip–open notepad.

Although the OB Proc states that only 100 user-trials guns were ordered, a handwritten page torn from the notepad, dated 26 March, 1945, the next document held in the Sterling company records at the Public Records Office, indicates that 101 guns were delivered (right).

Once again we must accept that many of these guns were subsequently modified, albeit very slightly in most cases, as a result of lessons learned and requirements dictated by the tests and trials, but they certainly started out as being identical.

One of this batch, SN124, featured in later trials. It was these later trials guns that went to British troops around the world for evaluation.

73 (right). During a near-disastrous fire at Sterling caused by last-ditch enemy flying bomb action in March, 1945, the Sterling gun registry books were destroyed. This is the first page of the hastily-introduced 'new' register, a simple flip open notepad. Dated 26 March, 1945. Its content is self-explanatory.

The note is signed by Mr Trevillian, Sterling's Security Officer, and countersigned by Inspector Sage of the East Ham Police Station. (Courtesy David Howroyd)

Disposal of the Trials Twenty Patchetts

In January, 1945 the Ordnance Board instructed that the Trials Twenty Patchetts be disposed of in the following manner:

Director of Armaments:	058, 064[†]
Assistant Chief Inspector of Armaments Design:	059, 065[†]
Experimental Establishment Pendine:	061, 063, 068, 069

Small Arms School: 055, 056, 057, 060[†]
Royal Military College of
Science: 053, 054
Chief Inspector of
Armaments: 062[†*], 066, 067*,
070*, 071, 072*

Those four marked [†] were the ones experimentally fitted with No5 rifle bayonets at Dagenham in June, 1944, and returned to Sterling for repairs in October, 1944.

As noted, those four marked * had been sent for evaluation to the Airborne Forces Development Centre (AFDC), whence guns SNs 067, 070 and 072 might possibly have been taken to Arnhem. Certainly as at 31 January, 1945 these three were the only guns not available for disposal per the Ordnance Board's instructions.

Guns 061, 063, 068 and 069 later featured in trials of 9mm ammunition to a special sk3371B specification with a bullet weight of 106 grains against standard 9mm MkIIZ ball (with a bullet weight of 115 grains).

Just where most of these historic guns are now is anyone's guess, but some still exist. We know that Patchett SN 046 found its way to the Airborne Forces Museum, intact and in perfect running order after a mysterious forty-four year hiatus between 1944 and 1988. It was handed into a Buckinghamshire Police station during an arms amnesty, where rumour has it that its rarity was noticed by a certain PC Frank Grover, who immediately diverted it from a furnace like Valhalla. Its future existence is now assured.

Of the four Trials Twenty guns returned to Sterling to be fitted with No5 bayonets, only no 062 is now known to exist.

74. After an estimated 250,000 rounds or more fired during the summer of 1944, Trials Twenty Patchett no 054 was brought out of retirement for a final outing in the careful hands of four experienced Armourers (and two very lucky Armourer apprentices!) on 22 September, 1994 (fig 324), a few months over fifty years after the original trials.

Once again, it ran like a well-oiled sewing machine, never missing a beat, here in the expert hands of Armourer Warrant Officer Ray Davies REME, another ex-Carlisle apprentice. (Photo by Peter Laidler)

Chapter Four

From MkI to Production

75. From the May, 1948 handbook *Patchett Machine Carbine*, discussed below: a right side view of the "standard" commercial model MkI Patchett, shown with buttstock extended.

Note there is provision for neither bayonet nor sling. (Courtesy David Howroyd)

OB Proc 30171, dated 31 January, 1945, included the following concluding remarks from the test team at Pendine regarding the Trials Twenty Patchetts:

> ... *The accuracy of these weapons appears satisfactory ... Functioning under normal, Arctic and Sudan conditions, using British, American, Canadian, German (brass and steel) and Italian ammunition, is satisfactory ... Functioning under standard sand conditions is comparatively good. The functioning under standard mud conditions compares favourably with its contemporaries at present in Service ... Endurance was beyond reproach.*
>
> *Conclusion – With regard to accuracy, functioning, endurance and penetration, it is considered that the Patchett machine carbine is suitable for Service.*

The Proc continued with the Ordnance Board's summation of the endurance trials of the pilot model Patchetts, and reported on the success of user trials with the "Troop Trials 101", as follows:

Remarks by the Board
The trials reported [in Chapter Three] conclude the Board's endurance trials of the Patchett design of 9mm machine carbine. Parallel small scale trials (not reported in Proceedings) have also been carried out by the Board with the following:

a. *9mm Patchett machine carbine fitted with the No5 rifle bayonet.*
b. *9mm Patchett machine carbinette.*

These latter projects have shown promise and are available for extended trial if required.
    The Board are informed that –

a. *User trials of the weapons made to a special production order have proved satisfactory.*
b. *The designer has applied for his carbine to be released from the Secret List with a view to export. It is understood that this application has been granted.*
c. *Proposals have been made by the designer for reducing the cyclic rate of fire of his weapon to*

a rate below 500 rpm when using Mark IIZ ammunition.

These proposals, neither of which it is claimed affect the weight of the weapon, involve

  i. *The incorporation of a retail brake, which entails a modification to the breech block; or*

  ii. *A modified breech block/recoil spring combination.*

d. *The Standing Committee on Infantry Weapon Development decided at a meeting in the War Office on 19 Jan 45 to modify the General Staff specification for a machine carbine … to the effect that –*

  i. *The provision of a bayonet is preferred and that it should, if possible, be of the same pattern as that used with the No5 rifle.*

  ii. *Cyclic rate of fire not more than 600 rpm instead of 500 rpm.*

… The Board, who were present at the above trials, concur in the conclusions of S of E (Pendine). They note that the weapons under trial meet the amended GS Specification … in all respects.

It should have been downhill all the way for George Patchett and the Sterling Engineering Company after this, but events were to ensure that the next few years remained an uphill struggle.

The Trials Patchetts had been recommended as "suitable for Service", but there were no big Government orders, and the official UK Military SMGs were still the Mk2 and Mks Stens.

The General Staff issued guidelines for the next generation of postwar sub-machine carbine in April, 1945. Llttle had changed from the Troop Trials 101: the Nos bayonet was a requirement; and magazine capacity was to be between 30 and 60 rounds.

In the meantime, it was a case of "hurry up and wait", as the extended troop trials continued. With the Patchett taken off the Secret List, George was naturally keen to market it wherever he could. After all, there was money to be made in the postwar arms industry.

76. From the May, 1948 Patchett handbook, left side view of the "standard" model MkI Patchett, showing butt folded.
   Note the absence of bayonet mounting or sling swivel. (Courtesy David Howroyd)

The Trials Patchetts Today

Over the course of the extensive pilot model and user trials a number of unofficial modifications were incorporated into the Trials Patchetts, starting with the fitting of a loop to the return spring cap to enable a sling to be fitted. We have seen one ex-UK military trials gun with a No4 rifle type butt sling loop brazed

to the return spring cap. Initially the sling loop was set in the vertical position, but this was changed in later production to lie horizontally.

One other modification was to screw, and later braze, an identical sling loop to the front casing. Other guns have a wire sling loop brazed to the front

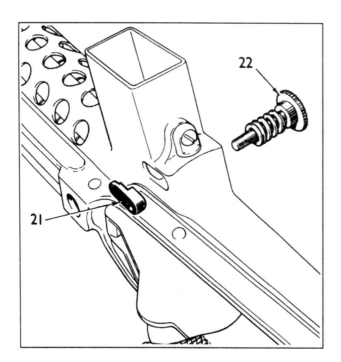

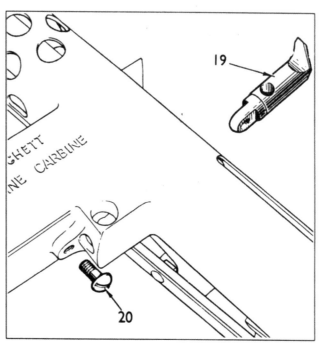

77. The first UK Military *User Handbook* (*Provisional*) for the *Carbine, Machine Patchett, 9mm, EX* was not published by the Inspectorate of Armaments, Woolwich until 1952 (fig 107). While it was intended to support the MkII pattern gun (82° magazine housing), two anachronistic drawings depict the 90° magazine housing of the MkI.

This figure: Removal of Magazine Catch and Spring, Patchett MkI. (Courtesy MoD Pattern Room, Nottingham)

78. From the 1952 *User Handbook* (*Provisional*) *for the Carbine, Machine Patchett, 9mm, EX*: Removal of Ejector and Screw, Patchett MkI. Note the markings on the 90° magazine housing, which will only accept Sten or Lanchester magazines.

The use of anachronistic material was a common phenomenon throughout the lifetime of the Patchett/Sterling, both in UK Military and in Sterling commercial literature. (Courtesy MoD Pattern Room, Nottingham)

of the casing, which looks suspiciously like a length of $^1/_8''$ welding rod bent to shape and brazed into place! The MkI sling loop configurations have been seen mounted on theleft and right sides of thecasing, where they also served as front finger guards.

No doubt there were other small modifications carried out by Armourers, the Small Arms School Corps instructors who were on the trials evaluation teams, and indeed by Sterling themselves.

It is also clear that some repairs took place, in addition to these local modifications. As well as showing signs of extensive use, some of these guns have been hastily repainted. Others have retaining pins hammered over for tightness, foresight protectors re-shaped with pliers, and bent butt frames roughly realigned with a mallet.

As noted, these guns finished the trials in many different guises. One that does deserve mention:

some of these guns appear to have been fitted with the MkII type cocking handle and pistol grip screws, which together can be used as stripping tools (further discussed in Chapter Five).

By and large, the main variation within these later trials guns is the fitting of different sling loops.

The extractor followed the stepped prototype design, but was now rounded. The design of this extractor gave the Sterling designers nightmares. If the bullet presentation angle was just a degree or so out, the bullet would concertina into the rear face of the barrel. This was highlighted while a MkI was being used as a test-bed for the later curved magazines, and it was established that the extractor was the cause of the problem. While George Patchett was away, the problem was identified and to this day, extractors have a small, almost indiscernible, flat surface at the very end of the claw.

The heavy rear portion of the firing pin, shaped to accept the inner end of the single return spring, was thus referred to as the "return spring block". This, together with a shaped recess within the return spring cap, kept the return spring central within the casing.

The butt fitted to the MkI gun followed the prototype shape and form, manufactured to patent number 566875 dated 5 May, 1943. It was certainly not soldier-proof, but very few things are! Due to a design fault the butt plate was retained in place by a . shaped step, which, while later corrected, could, and frequently did, snap shut during the troop trials – Ouch!

The main problem was that the top part of the fabricated-and-brazed inverted 'U'-shaped main frame was open for 90% of its length and, although slightly strengthened by the inclusion of a corrugated groove down the butt main frame, it was still very weak and fragile.

The MkI return spring cap also differed from the prototype pattern in allowing a small amount of forward movement to the cap in order to release the butt.

Some MkIs use the early cast alloy pistol grip but others, made for commercial purposes, have grips made from black bakelite.

Comments from the trials teams suggested that it was difficult to operate the change lever with the right thumb because there was no recess in the grip to allow the thumb to operate the change lever. Later bakelite (and still later plastic) grips have a slot recessed into the left side. This recessing of a thumb slot was a new idea that had just been successfully applied to the .380″ No2 revolver, in order to allow the thumb more room to operate the barrel catch. One of the Trials Patchetts examined during this study has had its alloy grip modified in this way.

The First Postwar Handbook

The first two Patchett handbooks, the undated, 8-page mimeograph entitled *Patchett Machine Carbine* and the first printed, green-covered *Patchett Machine Carbine 1943* have already been described.

Three years after the war a second small green covered, 22-page typeset brochure was printed up, again entitled *Patchett Machine Carbine*. Basically an expanded edition of *Patchett Machine Carbine 1943*, the postwar edition was published in May, 1948, although it was cannily left undated to delay its obsolescence as long as possible.

Excerpts from this interesting document reveal the eager-to-please George Patchett offering his commercial MkI Machine Carbine with or without sling swivels, and with a choice of bayonets-none; folding; or detachable (No5 rifle):

9mm Patchett Machine Carbine

This weapon was produced during the World War 1939–1945 and was used by British Commando Units after exhaustive tests had been made by the War Office to determine the most efficient machine carbine.

The weight of the carbine is 6 lbs (2.75kg) and the folded length is 18 inches (45cm). With the butt extended the overall length, less bayonet, is 28 inches (70cm). The weapon can be fired with the butt extended or folded.

The carbines can be supplied with or without bayonets …

Notes on the description of the gun, its functioning and disassembly in the May, 1948 handbook are repeated from the earlier wartime handbooks. However, further sections of interest concern the use of the Patchett, as follows:

Using the Carbine

The weapon should be clean and free from oil or grease.

Open the butt into the extended position.

Check the action and single shot functioning by setting the control lever to 'R' and verifying that the sear is tripped during the recoil of the bolt. Cock the action and apply the safety catch.

Insert a magazine into the mouthpiece and push home until locked by the magazine catch.

The weapon is now cocked and ready for use.

"PATCHETT
MACHINE CARBINE"

STERLING ENGINEERING CO., LIMITED
STERLING WORKS · DAGENHAM · ESSEX

79. The title page of the May, 1948 *Patchett Machine Carbine*. (Courtesy David Howroyd)

Components of the MkI Patchett Machine Carbine

1. foresight protectors
2. foresight
3. front barrel support
4. gun casing
5. barrel
6. breech block
7. firing pin
8. rocking handle
9. return spring block
10. return spring
11. rear sight
12. rear sight protector
13. return spring cap
14. catch, return spring cap
15. pistol grip
16. screw, retaining, pistol grip
17. butt catch
18. strut, butt catch
19. butt plate
20. magazine catch
21. ejector
22. trigger guard
23. change lever
24. pin, retaining. trigger mechanism. (Courtesy David Howroyd)

Firing from the Hip

For preference, stand about 30 paces from a sand or earth bank so that the strikes can be easily seen.

Put a target (a piece of paper or cardboard, or an empty cigarette packet will do) on the bank. Get the feel of the weapon. The butt plate should be held by the elbow into the side, the forearm pressing the butt triangle round the haunch bone. In this manner the weapon can be rigidly held by one hand. For greater control, hold the barrel casing with the left hand, the magazine resting on the lower forearm and the left elbow pressed into the groin. Lean slightly forward, as this position will enable effective automatic fire to be held on a small target, and having got the feel of the weapon, set the control lever to 'R' (single shot setting), press the trigger keeping your eye on the target and watch your strike. The advantage of firing into a bank may now be seen. If you have missed the target, as shown by your strike, raise or lower the muzzle slightly, or move it left or right, as may be required. Any movement should be preferably slight and another shot fired to check whether further correction is necessruy. With practice it will be found possible to hit a playing card in three shots at 20 to 30 paces.

Having got the feel and control of the carbine with single shots, set the control lever to 'A' (full automatic setting) and tiny short bursts. When

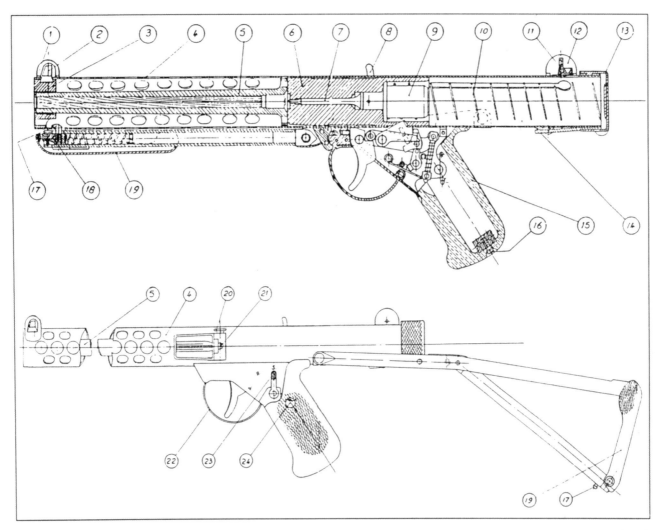

80. From the May, 1948 *Patchett Machine Carbine*: drawings of the "Standard" MkI Patchett Machine Carbine, with main components numbered.

Above: left side sectioned view of Carbine with butt folded. Numerous anomalous features, many of them by this time superseded, still appear. Compare with fig 42: note the variant threaded barrel retention system, with no abutment flange; the improved (and protected) sights; the Patchett (50°) cocking handle slot; and the detent and spring added to the inner change lever. The cocking handle appears to be the earliest style, retained in the right hand side of the bolt only.

Below: left side view of Carbine with butt extended.

firing the burst over a wide target, it is preferable to swing the burst to the left as this will counteract any tendency of the weapon to run to the right.

Accurate Shoulder Firing

When firing from the shoulder, the form of the butt will be found an advantage; the cheek can be rested on the butt as with a rifle. For firing from the

shoulder no special advice will be necessary to most users, but it has been found an advantage to get the left hand well forward to give the maximum control.

At 100 yards, firing 10 single shots, 6-inch groups can be achieved, at 200 yards range 12-inch groups are possible, and at 300 yards 18-inch groups have been registered from the prone position.

Options Available on the Commercial MkI Patchett

81. MkI Patchett return spring caps (end-caps) were offered either plain (left) or fitted with a sling loop (centre), rivetted in place with the loop in the vertical plane (right).

The idea of screwing/rivetting sling loops onto the casing and return spring cap was intended to allow a user/buyer to upgrade his standard no-sling guns to sling-fitted guns, as and when funds permitted. (MoD Pattern Room collection)

As noted, it was George Patchett's idea to offer the MkI gun on the commercial market with either his patented folding 'spike' bayonet (the folding blade had already been largely withdrawn), or a detachable No5 rifle bayonet, at extra cost.

Even though the "standard" (and presumably cheapest) MkI gun did not have bayonet or sling loop facilities, optional rivetted/screwed bayonet standards and swivels were available which, together with the separate nose cap, allowed a user/buyer the option of upgrading his standard guns.

The Fourth Patchett/Sterling Patent (December, 1946): the Folding Bayonet

The folding bayonet was not one of George Patchett's better ideas. Although the patent was registered in March, 1944, it was not perfected until December, 1946. There were periodic on-going tests with the folding bayonet, but the UK Military authorities were not interested.

Patent number 583092, dated 13thMarch, 1944 gives full details of the "Folding bayonet for small arms" as registered by the Sterling Engineering Company. The design of the folding bayonet was

described by George Patchett, in this, his fourth patent with Sterling, as follows:

583,092. Folding bayonets for small-arms. Patchett, GW, and Sterling Engineering Co Ltd. March 13, 1944. No 4639 [Class 119]. Complete specification accepted December 9, 1946.

… This invention relates to a new or improved folding bayonet and bayonet attachment for firearms. It has in combination a clip, collar or a like support (6) fixable about the muzzle of said firearm. A bayonet (8) hinged within said clip and a spring loaded plunger (11 & 12) housed in the shoulder of said bayonet adjacent to the hinge. There is a recess in the [casing] to receive and hold the plunger so as to secure the bayonet in an operatively fixed condition. A resilient catch [Fig 1, item 24] means to lock said bayonet in a folded condition and instantly releases same therefrom at will.

Note the use of the words "new or improved". There was nothing new about folding bayonets, but George Patchett's idea was certainly an improvement on an existing theme.

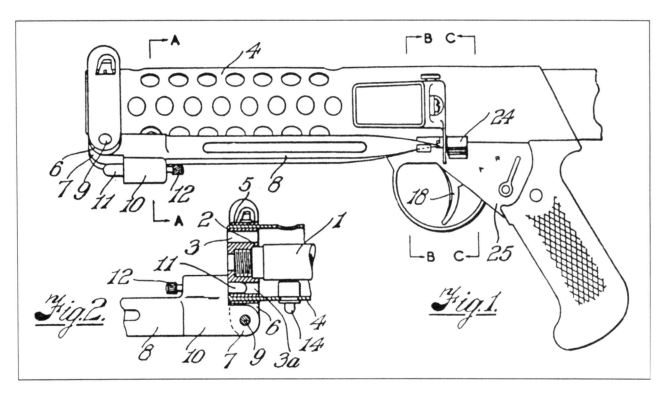

82. Figs 1 and 2 from George Patchett's fourth patent with Sterling, no 583,092 of December 9, 1946. The numbers are referred to in the text, below.

Note the gun depicted appears to be the Patchett Machine Pistol, but with standard SMG change lever markings! (Courtesy British Patents Office)

Quite how nobody detected that this folding bayonet method had been used elsewhere and probably/possibly had a foreign patent attached to it, remains one of life's little mysteries. An exact copy of the Sterling patented folding method also appeared later on Chinese and other carbines and rifles.

Different Blade Styles Used in Trials

It would appear that four styles of blades were tested: the first was similar to the No5 bayonet; the second was a very long and narrow version of the first; the third, today in the Pattern Room collection at Nottingham, is a stubby version without the top 'Bowie'-shaped cutting edge; while the fourth was a fluted spike, not unlike those fitted to the No4 rifle.

In operation, according to the May, 1948 edition of *Patchett Machine Carbine*, the spring-loaded bayonet "… swings into the forward position and is automatically locked ready for use. This action is too fast to be followed by the human eye." The movement was indeed fast – the blades cut more operators' hands than its designer intended!

These folding bayonets were only used experimentally, between 1943 and 1946. Thereafter,

83. The (extremely rare) origins of the Patchett folding bayonet: a converted Nos rifle bayonet blade has been flexibly mounted to a variant, 8-holed Patchett front barrel support.

This was the first of four variations in blade shape used over the course of this project. (MoD Pattern Room collection)

84. From the May, 1948 *Patchett Machine Carbine*: left side view of a MkI Machine Carbine equipped with the fourth variation of Patchett's patented spring-loaded folding bayonet. The fluted spike is shown folded and retained by the catch, the stud of which is just visible under magazine mouthpiece. The catch could only be operated with the butt opened.

   According to the handbook, this safety catch when pressed "releases the bayonet which, impelled by a strong spring, swings into the forward position and is automatically locked ready for use. The action of this engagement is too fast to be followed by the human eye." (Courtesy David Howroyd)

the Patchett carried the bayonet we have come to accept with the MkII/L2A1 onwards, namely, the distinctively large-ringed No5 MkI, named after its original use on the .303" No5 "jungle carbine".

Weaknesses of the Folding Bayonet

The principal inherent weakness with the folding bayonet did not lie at the hinge point, but with the retaining plunger (11 and 12, fig 82) that retains the bayonet in the extended position.

   Regretfully we have to say that bayonet fighting is not a clinical business. A bayonet (or a pistol perhaps?) is the last means of mechanical defiance before one engages in hand–to–hand fighting with the enemy. Bayonet fighting does not only include thrusting the bayonet, but hacking, slashing, twisting and anything

85. From the May, 1948 *Patchett Machine Carbine*: top view of a MkI Patchett, showing butt and spike-bladed bayonet extended.

   Note 90° magazine housing, the 32-round Sten magazine in place, and the flimsy, open-topped butt frame. (Courtesy David Howroyd)

else more or less macabre that you can imagine. It was during this series of tests that the weakness of the retaining plunger and the corresponding hole in the nose-cap came to light. None of the folding bayonet plungers on test survived. Additionally, the small catch used to retain the bayonet in the closed position was frequently tripped by the sling, allowing the bayonet to slash open.

One other positive disadvantage pointed out in contemporary reports was that while the bayonet was fixed to the gun, it could not be utilised for its secondary purpose, as a knife, even for opening tins of food. It was whimsically remarked that it could, provided you only wanted half a tin, because while one side of the tin was being punctured with the bayonet it invariably fell over! An important point for soldiers fending for themselves.

It would appear that by the time the MkI gun was offered for commercial sale, the folding blade type bayonet was already obsolete. In any case, none appear to have been sold on MkI guns.

The May, 1948 *Patchett Machine Carbine* also shows the gun fitted with a detachable No5 bayonet, utilising the optional nose cap with built-in bayonet boss and the add-on bayonet standard.

86. The optional nose cap which, in conjunction with a bolt-on or rivetted bayonet standard, was offered to potential buyers of the "standard" MkI Patchett to enable them to upgrade their guns to take the Nos rifle bayonet. (Courtesy David Howroyd)

87. From the May, 1948 *Patchett Machine Carbine*: left side view of the MkI Patchett fitted with the optional bayonet standard and nose cap. No5 rifle bayonet in place.
 Note also the (vertical) rear sling swivel, another option for buyers of the "standard" MkI. (Courtesy David Howroyd)

No Sale – Options or No

The Sterling Company certainly devoted a lot of time and effort looking into these buyer-specific options, but it appears that very few, if any, commercial buyers purchased the MkI Patchett, options or no. In fact, the authors were unable to find details of *any* commercial sales of the MkI gun. David Howroyd cannot recall

any, and those documents that list early sales do not contain details of any MkIs. Once it became common knowledge that the UK Military were seriously looking at another of George's offerings, perhaps other government buyers also sat and waited. It was as if they knew the MkII was in the wings.

Key Magazine Improvements

The Fifth Patchett/Sterling Patent (May, 1946): the Roller Magazine Follower

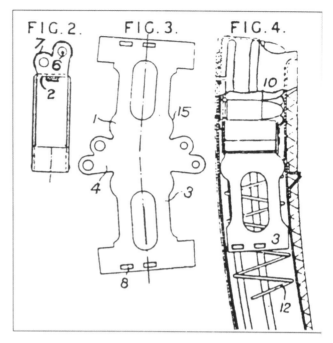

88 (right). Figs 2, 3 and 4 from George Patchett's Fifth Patent with Sterling, described in the text. (Courtesy British Patents Office)

615,471. Cartridge magazines. Patchett, GW, and Sterling Engineering Co Ltd. May 9, 1946. No 14059 [Class 119]

Described as follows:

… A spring impelled platform for use with a box magazine of the type described in specification 615,466 has an elongated skirted body provided with lands and a roller or rollers adapted to engage rails formed on the sides of the magazine, said roller or rollers being in rolling engagement with the lowest cartridge in the magazine. A stamping (1) of sheet metal is bent into the rectangular form shown in Fig 2, lugs (4) being pressed up to carry stub shafts (6) of two tapered rollers (7). Stamped up lands (8) provided on the side walls (3) are adapted to engaged impressed rolls in the sides of the magazine (10), and the said walls (3) have rounded shoulders (15) providing line contact with the end walls of the magazine. A spiral spring (12) is attached at its upper end to a spring abutment platform (2) below said rollers and at its lower end to a base abutment member resting on the closure plate of the magazine …

This masterstroke, together with Patchett's round-section magazine spring (discussed below; patent not granted until 1952) were both incorporated in the production Sterling magazines.

The First Six Hybrid MkII Patchetts

Up until October, 1946, Patchett guns were not factory-fitted with sling swivels but the Ordnance Board asked that six "improved" Patchetts be supplied, modified as follows:

• rearsight to have a 100–200 yard change-over lever
• redesigned grip to allow easier control of change lever
• attachment of sling swivels to allow use of Sten sling
• redesigned bayonet boss and making bayonet standard permanent
• finish of guns to be 'Rivell' (crackle) paint.

Last but not least, the guns were to have the "new type of magazine mouth piece, to enable the use of Patchett's special patented magazines".

This last improvement was important because it is the first time that the now familiar 82° angled magazine housing is mentioned.

89. Two views of the one of the first six MkII Patchetts produced, serial no 05.

Above: top view with butt extended and breech block closed. Note the 82° forward angle of the magazine "mouthpiece".

Below: left side view with butt extended and breech block cocked, magazine removed. Note the first use of the external lever (no 22, fig 91) on the dual-range, flip-over rear sight.

These first six MkIIs were basically just MkI casings with new magazine housings attached.

Note the continued use of the ex-Lanchester heavy foresight protectors, and the cylindrical MkI end cap, now factory-fitted with vertical sling swivel.

The top of the (bakelite) pistol grip has been recessed to permit better control of the change lever. (Courtesy MoD Pattern Room, Nottingham)

90. Front closeup view of the special detachable muzzle cap/bayonet boss featured on the hybrid Patchett MkIIs Nos)1–06. The hole at 12 o'clock was used in co junction with the two square openings in the front sides of the casing (visible in figs 89 and 91) to affix George Patchett's experimental detachable silencer (Chapter Eight). (Courtesy MoD Pattern Room, Nottingham)

91. Two views of Patchett machine carbine MkII no 05, with butt folded and breech block cocked.

   Above: right side view. Note the words 'LOCK' and 'FREE' moulded into the bakelite grip around the trigger mechanism retaining pin.

   Below: bottom view with hand-made curved magazine inserted. (Courtesy MoD Pattern Room, Nottingham)

92. Patchett MkII No 05, disassembled to show general layout of components.

   Note the dual return springs (14, 12), the subject of Patchett's sixth patent with Sterling (discussed below), and the truncated return spring block (11) and absence of a separate firing pin. These six initial MkIIs featured the first attempt at an integral firing pin machined into the face of the breech block. Note also the detachable muzzle cap (4); the barrel (2) is still a converted Lanchester item. (Courtesy MoD Pattern Room, Nottingham)

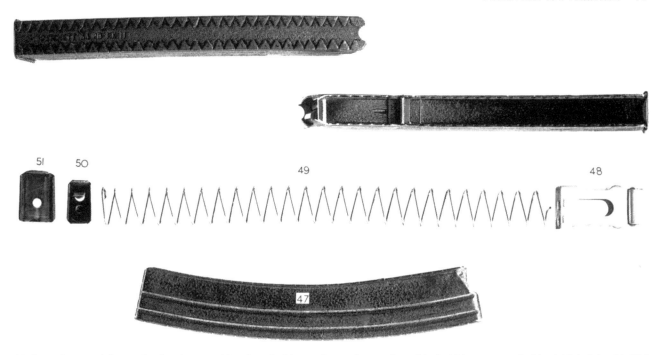

93. Several views of George Patchett's original hand-made 34-round curved magazines, 24 of which were supplied for initial trials with MkII machine carbines nos 01 through 06.

Note the distinctive saw-tooth rear edges, and markings on back (top): 'PATCHETT 34 RD MKII'.

Although already fitted with Patchett's soon-to-be patented roller magazine follower (no 48 above), these first curved magazines still utilised the Sten-pattern oval-plan spring (no 49, above). (Courtesy MoD Pattern Room, Nottingham)

First Appearance of the 82° Magazine "Mouthpiece"

OB Proc Q 4,702 of 25 October, 1946 confirms that six "improved model" Patchett machine carbines, plus 24 hand-made curved magazines, were to be made available from George Patchett at Sterling. These guns were marked 'Patchett/Machine Carbine/MkII No' (01 through 06).

Seven of our old friends were also provided for comparison trials: Trials Twenty guns 060, 064, 065, (bayonets fitted) plus 057, 068, 069 and 071, all with 90° magazine housings.

Unexpectedly, during these trials, using these first MkII–pattern guns with curved magazines (albeit only hand made tool-room examples) the guns gave poor results. George investigated and stated in a letter that this was due to fouling between the ejectors and breech blocks, which was reducing the breech block energy. After consultation, the Board disagreed! They stated that it was due to low return spring force. Whatever the cause, it was quickly resolved.

BSA Horns In

Meanwhile, a challenge had come from the Birmingham Small Arms Company, which like Sterling, was also a diversified private company involved in armsmaking. Four BSA sub-machine guns, numbered 4, 6, 7 and 9 were first subjected to a long series of trials in October, 1945, in which several of these first-pattern BSAs were damaged.

The next BSA trials were held in June, 1947, but this time, the BSAs were so-called "second-pattern" guns, (in reality refurbished and modified first-pattern guns that had been damaged in the initial trials), fitted with curved, 30-round 9mm magazines.

BSA were not new to curved 9mm magazine development, as they had manufactured similar magazines for trials 9mm Thompson guns, but George Patchett had already patented his roller platform with ample clearance to allow mud and dirt' space to dissipate.

94. Left side view of the 9mm BSA Sub-Machine Gun, serial no 6. This is a second-pattern gun, fitted with a sliding barrel sleeve onto which a No4, No7 (shown) or No9 bayonet would fit.

    The BSA had no cocking handle *per se*, and was cocked by turning and pumping the handguard, known as the "cocking sleeve".

    The second-pattern BSAs were in reality refurbished and modified first-pattern guns which had been damaged during the initial trials. The attrition rate was high, with poor welding and flimsy parts the principal culprits. (MoD Army, RMCS Shrivenham)

The First Comparative Trial (September, 1947)

The first comparative trial between the prototype MkII Patchetts and the second-pattern BSA with curved magazine had taken place at Pendine between 8th and 16th September, 1947. The BSA gun had also been modified in order to take a No4 rifle bayonet.

The Patchetts were slightly over the 6-pound weight limit, but performed well due to their low automatic rate of fire of 530 rds/min.

Other guns trialled were Patchett Mk I's nos 071 and 124, Patchett MkII number 001 (Chapter Five), the short-lived MCEM 3 experimental carbine number 2, and a modified BSA.

The BSA possessed faults that could not be ironed out. These included trigger mechanism weaknesses, stiffness in cocking, and fracture of the cocking sleeve mechanism.

The main problem with the Patchett was the trigger mechanism. The OB Proc stated that each time the breech block contacted the sear, which kept the breech block 'cocked' and to the rear, the force was felt on the firer's finger, which became bruised.

It could have been that the continued hammering of the breech block onto the sear during the long

periods of heavy unrelenting use these trials Patchetts had seen, had elongated the sear axis pin holes in the cradle and frame: suffice it to say that the same trigger mechanism design was used throughout Sterling production.

Patchett's Sixth Patent (December, 1950): Doubling Up the Return Springs

As mentioned, problems were experienced during trials with the first curved-magazine Patchetts, whether due to fouling of the ejector on the breech block, as claimed by George Patchett, or by low return spring force, as asserted by the Ordnance Board.

George Patchett's sixth patent for Sterling covered the double return springs as featured on the six hybrid MkIIs (fig 92):

686,628 Automatic fireanns. Patchett, GW, and Sterling Engineering Co Ltd. Dec 51950. No 29763/50. Gass 92(ii).

… To increase the energy imparted to the bolt (2) and firing pin (6) of an automatic firearm, two springs (12, 13) of differing compression values are provided, these springs being coaxially and

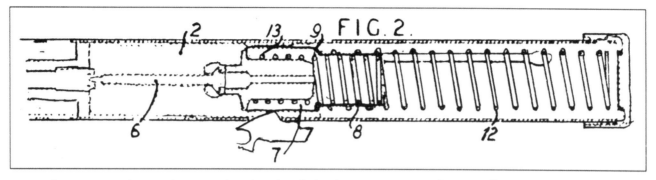

95. Fig 2 from George Patchett's sixth patent with Sterling, described in the text. (Courtesy British Patents Office)

telescopically mounted and being combined with a coaxial abutment cap (8) slideable in a recess (7) of the bolt. The cap provides an abutment for the rear end of the inner spring (13) and for the forward end of the outer spring (12), and in the construction shown has a flange (9) which lightly engages the cylindrical wall of the recess (7) and forms the abutment for the spring (12). In a modification the firing pin is integral with the bolt (2).

Engineers' opinions will differ as to the true value of springs of differing compressive value when used in this context. Certainly some later Sterling guns did not use the inner spring (nor did the Canadians; Chapter Nine)!

The Patchett on Top in Further Comparative Trials (January, 1951)

In January, 1951, the Patchett was subject to further comparative trials, this time against the improved BSA, the MCEM 3 experimental carbine and a newcomer whose reliability and simplicity was to shake both BSA and Sterling, the Madsen Model 50!

The Sterling company informed the Board that they were tooling–up to produce the MkII Patchett and magazines in quantity, and later submitted MkII guns 011 and 012 to the trials. Poor old BSA could only supply 6 rebuilt guns, numbered W1001 to W1006 inclusive, although four others in the process of being refurbished, W1007 to W1010, were made available later.

The Madsen performed extremely well, but was let down by its vertical magazines, which did not

allow the mud and sand to drain away. However, these Madsen magazine faults were not insurmountable, as both BSA and Patchett had discovered when they developed their curved offerings.

This time the Patchett was the best all–round performer. During the accuracy tests, the conducting officers were unable to state how many rounds the Patchetts had fired, but because it was probably in excess of 15,000 rounds, Patchett accuracy diagrams were to be treated with reserve when compared with others. The Board also stated of the Patchetts on trial,

… these weapons are identical to those previously tested in September, 1944 during which trial two carbines fired 10,000 rounds without any stoppages attributable to the weapons. These two carbines have been in use and in your trials since they were made on 28th April, 1944 .

The BSA was incapable of operating in a sandy environment, which really caused its demise. It was also subject to stress fractures. BSA lodged a strong protest which attributed these stress fractures to the method by which they were clamped (to an adapted Vickers MkIVB tripod incidentally) during the accuracy tests. In OB Proc Q6,767, one of the conducting officers saw fit to qualify BSA's objections by commenting, "… the representative of Sterling Engineering Company Ltd, however, made no such protest." That says it all, really!

The Ordnance Board Evaluates the Four Contending Machine Carbines

OB Procs Q 6,975 and Q 7,058 were dated respectively 27th July and 16th October, 1951.

Following the watershed trials at Pendine in July, 1951, the Ordnance Board in OB Proc Q 6,975 described the status of the four contending machine carbines as follows:

MCEM (Australian) No 2 Machine Carbine

The MCEM (Australian) No 2 machine carbine requires further development There were, for instance, many failures to eject, and CIA reports faults which necessitate modification to the design. As the present functioning of this weapon is of a lower standard than the others tested, points have not been given …

Madsen Machine Carbine

The Madsen machine carbine is obviously designed for mass production as it is made from pressings with very little machining or finishing. Its performance is nevertheless good except in sand and mud, where it fails mainly due to the design of the magazine. This machine Carbine, however, fails to comply with many War Office requirements and considerable development would be necessary to make it acceptable. One feature of its design, the forward grip safety, is a novel and effective method of preventing the accidental firing of a round by jolting the weapon, but in its present form it would probably be unacceptable to the user because a firm grip with the left hand is necessary to fire as well as trigger pressure from the right The reduction in weight of the lighter model is not considered warranted, as it entails a decrease in robustness and wearing surfaces.

BSA Machine Carbine

The BSA machine Carbine is … not yet fully developed. In functioning and reliability it appears now to be nearly up to the standard of the Patchett, *except for the cocking mechanism which fails badly under certain conditions and is being completely redesigned. No forecast can be made as to whether the redesign will be successful.*

Patchett Machine Carbine

The Patchett machine carbine is now fully developed. It conforms to War Office requirements more nearly than any other machine Carbine, the points of noncompliance being only 3 oz excess weight and a slightly high rate of fire. Its performance is excellent, being easily the best of all machine carbines tested in spite of a disadvantage due to hand-made magazines. The Mark II magazines are of pressed steel, not tube, and on the present hand-made ones the fullering is carried too high, the front section is sloped too much, and the mouth too easily damaged. These faults are likely to cause mal-feeds and light strikes, but should not be present in machine-made magazines, a prototype of which has been seen by a member of the Board.

The Board are of the opinion that the Patchett machine Carbine is suitable for immediate adoption and introduction into the Service. The Mark I Patchett was found satisfactory in user trials in 1945 (Proc No 30,171) and no further user trials would be required.

The President of the Ordnance Board has been informed verbally by DG of A that a recommendation is required as to which of the machine Carbines under review is best suited for immediate approval by him. The Board, having considered the foregoing evidence, recommend the Patchett.

In the circumstances, the Board will await further instructions from DG of A before dealing with the projected modifications to the BSA machine Carbine. The Board, however, consider it unlikely that a fully· modified BSA would be superior to the Patchett.

The Ordnance Board thus concluded by again recommending the Patchett for adoption by the British Army.

However, BSA asked for a brief respite in order to carry out some modifications, due to the fact that some specification changes that had taken place might have prejudiced their somewhat slim chances. This stay of execution was granted until 1952.

This delay was to be the double-edged sword upon which BSA would fall.

The Nail-Biting Two-Year Prelude to Adoption

Following the Ordnance Board's 1951 recommendation that the latest Patchett gun be adopted, Sterling began to manufacture its improved production model, the MkII "EX", for widespread evaluation within the British Army.

George Patchett used to tell the story that while all these trials were taking place, the heads of the BSA team would entertain the officers conducting the trials in the plush surroundings of the Officers' Mess, while wise old George stood the Small Arms School Corps (SASC) Senior NCOs, the men actually doing the work, to a few beers in their mess. You could have saved your money, George! Men transferring into the SASC are all long-serving and experienced weapons experts in their own right, and carry a minimum rank of Sergeant. Most are Warrant Officers who don't mince their words. If THEY said the Patchett was the best, then it was. If they said the Patchett won, then it won fairly in a straight fight.

All was not quite that simple, however. There was to be a further nail-biting period for Patchett and the Sterling company between July, 1951 and 18th September, 1953 as trials continued, against the finest contenders that could be found.

Further Trials of Improved Production Patchetts (1952)

The next trial was between an improved production Patchett and an improved Madsen. The Madsen came back into the fight with redesigned magazines which operated perfectly. So did the Patchett, with magazines that incorporated the second of Patchett's two magazine patents.

This time the BSA could not compete against the Patchett, and it was finally withdrawn on the orders of the Director of Infantry. In 1943 you had to be good to beat an Owen, but by 1952 you had to be VERY good to beat a Patchett!

The Seventh Patchett/Sterling Patent (March 6, 1952): Curvilinear Side Wall Ribs and Round-Section Compression Magazine Spring

692,768. Cartridge magazines. Patchett, GW, and Sterling Engineering Co Ltd. March 6, 1952. No 5911/52. Class 92(ii) and 119.

During this time, strengthening ribs were added to the magazine's curved sides, which, among other things, reduced the friction of the magazine platform to virtually nil as it moves up and down. Front-to-rear friction was reduced by the use of two small nibs on the front and rear of the platform. The two follower rollers are slightly tapered, not to cater for the 18.5″ radius, or the taper of the cartridges, but to allow the platform to move freely up the magazine tube which is tapered from rear to front.

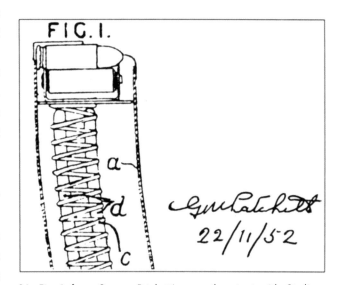

96. Fig 1 from George Patchett's seventh patent with Sterling, discussed in the text. (Courtesy British Patents Office)

Bottom right: signature of George W Patchett (dated 22 November, 1952). (Courtesy David Howroyd)

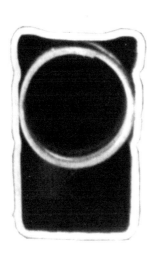

97. End elevation of two magazines, both cut away at 90° to show the distinct end profiles and springs.
     Left: Patchett/Sterling. Note how the four grooves in the curvilinear sides form a box to guide the round magazine spring.
     Right: Sten. The spring appears to have plenty of room, but when it is compressed it buckles unpredictably against the sides of the casing, creating friction. (MoD Army)

This innovation was registered with patent number 692,768 dated 6 March, 1952. Unlike the roller patent, number 615,471 (fig 88), which used an oval plan-view spring, this patent utilised these four deeply pressed strengthening ribs to act as the four equidistant corners of a curved, internal box.

This allowed the use of a helical compression spring, hitherto unknown in a magazine of this capacity, which cannot distort in its travel up and down the magazine.

George Patchett explained these further examples of his remarkable mechanical acumen in the patent disclosure, as follows:

… A cartridge magazine (a) [fig 96] having cuevilinear side walls tapering slightly towards one another and united by curved front and back plates, is characterised by the provision of guide elements (d) along the side walls for maintaining a helical compression spring (c) in the arcuate form corresponding with the contour of the magazine. In the form shown the magazine is of sheet metal suitably pressed to provide the elements (d), and in a modification the elements are welded on the inner surfaces of the side walls.

The Trials Years: a Wrapup

A remarkably rugged and extended series of trials took place with pilot and user trials models of the Patchett machine carbine between 1946 and 1953, in every theatre of operations where British Forces were stationed. These included steaming hot and swampy Malayan jungles, the dust and sands of the Libyan desert, the bitter frozen winter of Korea and north-west European winters, down to the mud of Salisbury Plain and Soltau ranges.

In comparison trials with other contenders, where two guns performed similarly the criteria were slowly tightened up so that one contender would inevitably be squeezed out, leaving the other to emerge as the winner. Thus it was that the simplicity and reliability of the Patchett won through every test that could be devised, including the ultimate trial: combat under atrocious conditions.

Of course, these trials did not indicate that the Patchett could not be improved. During the course of its life, the gun was subjected to many more trials and tests to see whether certain items could be improved upon. These tests and their results are discussed in the chapters ahead.

The Final Tally: Sterling. Fair and Square

The Patchett came out on top of all the other guns on test Contrary to reports of another close contender nearly making the grade, the Sterling was followed in an ironic second place by the control sample, the Mk5 Sten gun it was to replace, and in third place by an outsider, a variant Madsen SMG later called the Model 53 (fig 99). Well done and a round of applause for George Patchett, Reginald Shepherd and Harold Turpin!

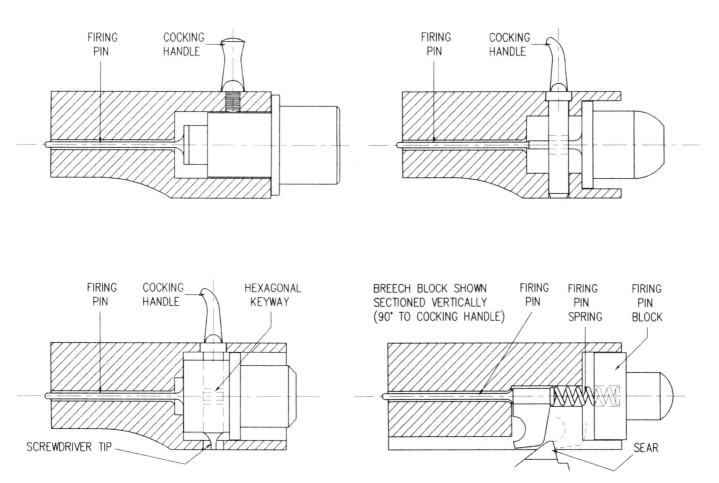

FIRING PIN   COCKING HANDLE

FIRING PIN   COCKING HANDLE

FIRING PIN   COCKING HANDLE   HEXAGONAL KEYWAY

SCREWDRIVER TIP

BREECH BLOCK SHOWN SECTIONED VERTICALLY (90° TO COCKING HANDLE)   FIRING PIN   FIRING PIN SPRING   FIRING PIN BLOCK

SEAR

Stories abound about the competition from BSA. However, at the last fence, the Sterling won. Let no one tell you anything different, the Sterling won hands-down. In fact in one series of tests it was described as "unstoppable".

A Cat Amongst the Pigeons: the "Rifle, 7mm No 10 MkI"

During this period, another gun was also the subject of extensive trials with the UK Military. The controversial Enfield-designed "bullpup" .280″ EM-2 Self Loading Rifle appeared to be winning out over the FN FAL as the next British shoulder rifle; indeed, the EM-2 was on the point of being adopted as the short-lived "Rifle, 7mm No10 MkI". This time, however, the politicians from both sides of the Atlantic were having their say!

Unfortunately, as far as machine carbine procurement was concerned, this introduced yet another snag. One of the advantages seen in the EM-2 rifle was that it was compact enough to "double-up" as a machine carbine. Thus, if the EM-2 remained, the smaller quantity of MCs required would be Madsens. On the other hand, the 7.62mm FAL could NOT double-up: if it was adopted, the much larger quantity of machine carbines needed to augment this rifle would be the Patchett.

In OB Proc Q7,058 of 16 October, 1951, the following correspondence was recorded:

DG of A, 5 Oct51,to Sec OB (re No Q 6,975).
We have recommended to the War Office that the Patchett machine carbine should be adopted if the 7mm EM-2 rifle cannot efficiently fill the role of the

Sten in the "teeth" arms. If, on the other hand, it is decided that the 7mm EM-2 rifle should replace the Sten in "teeth" arms, we have recommended that the Madsen, modified to take a double column magazine, should be adopted with the proviso that time to develop and prove the modification is necessary. The reliability of the Madsen is considered sufficiently good for L of C troops, where the weapon is kept under better conditions. This latter recommendation was also made on the grounds of cost of production.

The War Office are going to carry out trials with the BSA, Patchett and Madsen machine carbines and the 7mm EM-2 rifle, from which it is hoped that a decision can be made as to the suitability of the rifle in the machine carbine role.

In conjunction with these trials we wish you to carry out trials of the Madsen modification of the double column magazine and to confirm or otherwise the superiority of the Patchett over the BSA in view of the recent modifications to the latter weapon. Three modified weapons of each type of machine carbine are being put through their acceptance tests at CIA Testing Section, Enfield, and will remain there pending your despatch instructions.

It is requested that these further trials should be completed before the end of November, 1951, if possible.

Action–Address to DG of A

… [The Board] do not consider it necessaiy to include the Patchett machine carbines as a control since the trials arranged are identical with those recently held and reported in Proc No Q 6,975.

As it happened, an inch-measurement version of the FN FAL was adopted, in conjunction with Canada and Australia, as the the superb Rifle, 7.62mm L1A1 (known as the C1 and later the C1A1 in Canada).[*]

On 18th September, 1953, almost 11 years after his first machine carbine had been fired, George Patchett's perseverance paid off in full. The MkII Patchett Machine Carbine was adopted for British Military service as the L2A1.

Interchangeability So Far

On the question of interchangeability of parts among the prototype and Trials MkI guns with the most common production model, the later Mk4/L2A3, it is quite likely that, except for the magazines, parts from the Mk4 guns can, in most cases, be used in the MkI guns, certainly as assemblies.

With the earliest prototypes, given that the basic shapes of most parts are very similar, it would not be beyond the wit of a good bench fitter or Armourer to adapt. In short, there is no need for an early gun to be non-operational for lack of parts.

As an example, while Peter Laidler was examining a trials gun for this study, he noticed that one of the two sear steps (which is engaged by the tripping lever in the fire mode) had broken off. A current Mk4/L2A3 sear was a direct replacement.

---

[*] This story is told in Collector Grade Publications The FAL Rifle.

The Two Runners-Up

98. The best of the postwar competition for the Patchett was the 9mm Mk5 Sten, shown here in right side view.

The Mk5 Sten first saw action in the hands of paratroopers of the British 1st Airborne Division at Arnhem. It was a tough and reliable gun, built to higher standards than the Mk2.

This example is still fitted with the (quite) rare front pistol grip, a short-lived component that was screwed to a steel band around the barrel nut. When it worked loose it could be screwed tighter, but this simply crushed the wood further, then the thin sides split. All were removed from UK Military service after May, 1947. (Courtesy Rod Venners)

98. A Madsen Model 1950 with curved magazine, in the capable hands of Armourer WO Ray Davies, REME, a colleague of Peter Laidler 's for 30 years.

This gun was the first to be fitted with a curved, doublefeed magazine, developed especially by Madsen for the UK trials and later standardised on the Madsen Model 1953.

Also at the insistence of the UK Military, these last trials guns were not equipped with the grip-safety (usually located behind the magazine housing).

The reliability and 'useability' of the Madsen gun shook Patchett and impressed the trials team, but nevertheless the Patchett was the out-and-out winner, being officially described as "unstoppable". (MoD Army, RMCS Shrivenham)

Chapter Five

Mr Patchett's Gun Gets Called Up

Patchett 9mm Machine Carbine MkII
(Gun, Sub-Machine, 9mm L2A1)

Date introduced:	Sterling:	May, 1953
	UK Govt:	18th September, 1953
Date deleted:		February, 1955
Obsolescent in UK Military:		April, 1955
Quantity produced:	Sterling commercial	3,730
	MkII Patchetts for UK Military	2,800
	L2A1 SMGs for UK Military	6
	Total production:	6,536

As discussed in Chapter Four, the FIRST Patchetts fitted with the 82° magazine housing were manufactured for trials of the then-newly patented curved magazine with roller follower, several years before the L2A1 was adopted. These guns were basically late MkIs with 82° magazine housings welded on, and featured a further interesting variety of internal bolt components, notably the first, short-lived attempt at an integral firing pin.

MkII No 001: the Most Curious Patchett of All?

100. Right side view of Patchett MkII No 001, also delivered for trials some time before the MkII was officially adopted.
Note the MkII-style tapered return spring cap, but the continued use of the heavy ex-Lanchester front sight protectors.
Aside from the lengthy extractor slot this gun appears normal enough, but inside it represents yet another complete, and complex, redesign.
David Howroyd describes it as "a one-off Ministry Official's dream". (MoD Pattern Room collection)

First mentioned in a CIA (Chief Inspector, Armaments) trials report dated 5 October, 1950, MkII No 001 easily qualifies as the most curious example of the MkII, and possibly of any Patchett ever constructed. David Howroyd even suggests that it is in fact a combination of several sets of experimental parts, and that it may never have featured in trials as it is now constructed.

The end cap is the tapered MkII type, and the front sight protectors are still the heavy ex-Lanchester type. However, it is the complex modifications within the trigger/bolt mechanism that put this gun quite apart from the normal run of MkII Patchetts. It would appear that the purpose of this modification was to prevent hangups with the base of a cartridge sliding across the breech block face, and to possibly delay the normal advanced primer ignition.

The trigger has a secondary sear bent filed into its upper face. The front block of the trigger housing has a recess milled into it to accommodate a secondary

101. Top closeup of magazine housing of MkII Patchett machine carbine No 001, showing markings.

Note the 'crackle' finish covering the welded radius between the magazine housing and casing. (MoD Pattern Room collection)

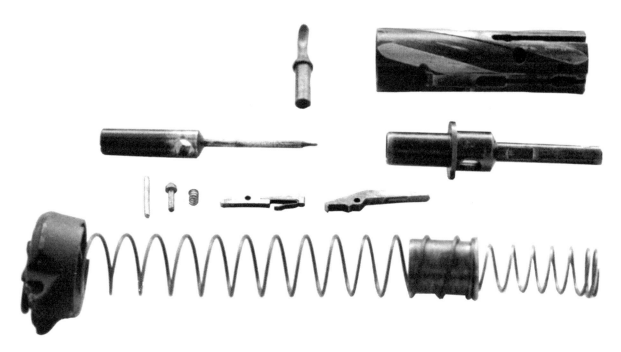

102. The unusual bored-through breech block of Patchett MkII No 001, stripped to show internal components as described in the text. From left to right:

Top row: ribbed-shanked cocking handle; breech block. Note the wider helical ribs, the elongated extractor slot and the 3-step slot in the underside for the secondary sear.

Second row: separate firing pin; central sleeve.

Third row: extractor axis pin; large-headed axis pin for trip lever; extractor coil spring; elongated extractor.

Bottom row: recoil spring cap with outer return spring, inner return spring cup, and inner return spring. (MoD Pattern Room collection)

front sear, sear detent and spring. The notched sear bent on the trigger contacts the secondary sear, and rotates the sear nose down out of contact with the central sleeve trip lever housed in the breech block.

The breech block assembly itself (fig 102) consists of three major components. On the outer breech block the helical ribs are much wider than normal. The centre of the block is bored through to the diameter of a 9mm cartridge rim, to accept a hollowed central sleeve, itself bored through to accept a separate firing pin/recoil spring block.

An elongated ($2\frac{1}{8}''$ overall length) extractor fits into the elongated slot on the side of the breech block, activated by a small coil spring.

In addition to the normal flat and sear safety notch on the underside of the breech block, there are two further sear locations for the secondary sear housed in the modified trigger housing. A three-step slot runs from the front face at normal sear bent depth, stepping down to approximately $\frac{3}{8}''$ deep about $\frac{5}{16}''$ from the front face and stepping down again approximately $1\frac{1}{4}''$ from the front face. A sear with flat 'V' spring rotates about a transverse large headed axis pin, the 'V' spring bearing on the second step.

The 9mm-diameter central sleeve slides through the hole in the centre of the breech block, the stepped-up rear diameter of the sleeve filling the normal inner diameter of the breech block, the cocking handle hole in the sleeve being elongated so that the face of the sleeve is either level with the front of the breech block or pushed back against the front of the cocking handle shank, to give the normal recessed bolt face. A large-diameter collar on the sleeve fits the large inside diameter at the rear of the breech block, and provides support and location for the buffer spring. A smaller diameter rear section is both a guide for the buffer spring and location for the separate firing pin and block, which is drilled with a transverse hole for a sliding fit with the shaft of the cocking handle. The rear face of the firing pin block has a screwdriver slot for rotary location.

This complex mechanism is completed by a unique double-fingered ejector, one finger or the other of which is selected depending on whether the cartridge is fed from the top or bottom feed position of the magazine.

When assembled, the action of the buffer spring against the inner sleeve puts forward pressure on the sleeve. If the secondary sear is holding the sleeve back, the face of the breechblock is recessed in the normal way with the firing pin projecting normally. If the secondary sear is tripped, the inner sleeve is pushed forward, under the influence of the return springs, almost level with the front face of the breech block, shielding the firing pin.

103. Left side view of an early experimental MkII Patchett machine carbine, shown with buttstock extended.
Note (from front) the stamped foresight protectors; the standard production pattern cocking handle, machined from ½″ bar stock and bent slightly forward; the cutout in the moulded plastic grip (for ease of manipulation of the change lever); the angled rear sight adjusting lever set between the 100- and 200-yard blades; the ribbed butt strut for lateral strength; and the unusual lengthened return spring cap with added rear 'step' with vertical sling swivel fitted. (Courtesy MoD Pattern Room, Nottingham)

Complex or not, this gun (or a version of it) featured in several late trials against BSAs, the Australian MCEMs, and early MkI Patchetts, and according to the trials results it survived all tests with little or no adverse comment, unlike the other contenders. Nevertheless, MkII No 001 remains unique: no further action was taken to amalgamate the unusual secondary sear, double ejector, and three-piece breech block with wider helical grooves into further production.

Examining Another 'Pre-Adoption' MkII Patchett

104. Right side view of a further MkII Trials Patchett, serial no 18, shown with buttstock extended.
    Note (from rear) the ribbed butt strut and the tapered body cap with vertical sling swivel. (MoD Pattern Room collection)

Several further examples of the early MkII pattern were made up for trials before the design was adopted by the Ministry of Defence in September, 1953. One such MkII held in the MoD Pattern Room collection, serial no 18, embodies numerous features which were standardised on the UK Military MkII.

The butt strut is grooved for lateral strength (but still open on the top). This was an undeniably weak

105. Two views of the magazine housing of Patchett Machine Carbine MkII No 18, showing markings.
    Left: top view. Note how the butt-welding and crackle paint have obliterated the final 'E' in 'CARBINE'.
Right: bottom view, showing the British patent numbers under which Sterling claimed exclusive rights to the various features of the Patchett design. (MoD Pattern Room collection)

feature of the early production guns, and many required replacement during trials and while in limited service. The vertical sling loop on the tapered return spring cap is retained by a pressed plate secured to the cap by two countersunk rivets.

The pistol grip is of brittle black plastic, with a steel insert for the retaining screw support. As further described below, the slot-headed pistolgrip retaining screw has a lengthened hexagonal shank which mates with a hexagonal hole in the cocking handle to form a 'T'-shaped tool for removal of the Allen headed barrel screws. The cocking handle has a screwdriver blade on the bottom end of its shank. The breechblock has an angled front edge to assist clearance of ejected cases, and the helical ribs feature sharp front and rear faces to cut through fouling. The ejector has a convex outer edge, slotted for lightness.

Also, as described below, the firing pin/cocking handle system of the first 300 or so MkIIs is different again, and features a fixed, shouldered firing pin.

For the first time, the barrel features a clearance slot under the breech flange to allow fouling pushed forward by the breech block to be ejected through the cooling holes in the bottom of the casing.

First Militaty Contract the "Patchett 9mm M/C EX"

The first MoD contract for quantities of the MkII Patchett, dated 8 July, 1953, was for "9mm EX" machine carbines, numbered 01 to 300.

The First (Provisional) Military User Handbook

The first military User Handbook for the Patchett was produced during the changeover to the 82° magazine housing, and issued in 1952 to support ongoing troop trials. In this Provisional Handbook the "Carbine, Machine, Patchett, 9mm, EX" was introduced to the troops as follows:

Section I – General
Introduction
This carbine provides the soldier with a light and easily-handled weapon which is capable of producing a volume of automatic fire at short notice.

It is a short-range weapon used to engage the enemy at ranges up to 100 yards. It may be used with effect at longer ranges, according to the degree of skill of the firer, but the penetrative power of the

106. Top closeup view of the magazine housing of Patchett 'EX' serial number 251. Note the matt black finish.
    As noted, the first 300 UK Military MkIIs were marked this way. (MoD Pattern Room collection)

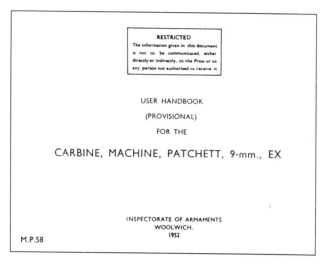

RESTRICTED
The information given in this document is not to be communicated, either directly or indirectly, to the Press or to any person not authorised to receive it.

USER HANDBOOK

(PROVISIONAL)

FOR THE

CARBINE, MACHINE, PATCHETT, 9-mm., EX

INSPECTORATE OF ARMAMENTS
WOOLWICH.
1952

M.P.58

107. The cover/title page of the first MoD Provisional Handbook, entitled *Patchett Machine Carbine 9mm EX*. (Courtesy MoD Pattern Room, Nottingham)

bullet seldom will justify fire at ranges in excess of 100 yards.

The carbine is particularly suitable for street fighting, wood clearing, patrols, and any other conditions when the enemy may appear suddenly at close quarters and from different directions.

It is an automatic weapon, operated by case projection, or blow back action, and can be fired in single rounds or in bursts. Normally it may be fired in bursts of two or three rounds, but on occasions the aimed single shot will be found effective.

Technical Details

Calibre	9mm
Length: butt folded	18 inches
butt extended	28 inches
Weight: carbine only	6 lbs (approx)
w/full mag (34 rds)	7 lbs 10 oz (approx)
w/full mag & bayonet	8 lbs 4 oz (approx)
Length of barrel	7.8 inches
Number of grooves	6
Pitch of rifling	1 turn in 9.84 inches
Twist of rifling	right hand
Sight radius	16.379 inches
Sights: rear	aperture
fore	blade
Sight range	100 and 200 yards
Cyclic rate of fire	550 rpm (approx)

The "Last Gasp" for the Patchett Folding Bayonet

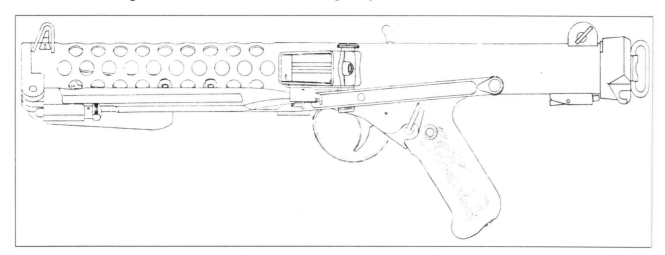

108. From an undated Sterling factory blueprint marked "Patchett Machine Carbine MkII Flip Bayonet".

George Patchett's folding bayonets had not fared well in earlier trials, and a major re-think had resulted in the detachable No5 MkI bayonet being adopted for use with the L2A1 . According to David Howroyd, only one MkII, no KR 1730, was produced with the Patchett patented folding bayonet.

This gun was sent to Kenya. (Courtesy MoD Pattern Room, Nottingham)

Ordering Further Quantities of Military MkII Patchetts

The MkII Patchett was adopted for limited UK Military Service in September, 1953 and allocated a Vocabulary of Army Ordnance Stores reference number of B3/CR 47 GA.

Two follow-ons to the initial 300-gun "9mm EX" contract added Patchett machine carbines marked simply "Patchett 9 m/m MIC" nos 301 to 2100, then 2101 to 2600. A final 200 (nos 2601 to 2800) were added by a further contract dated 9 January, 1954. Patchett MkII No 2772, today retained at RMCS

109. Top closeup view of Patchett 9m/m MIC No 8930, showing markings.

This is the highest number seen of several inexplicably high-numbered guns bearing these markings. (MoD Pattern Room collection)

Shrivenham, was militarily proofed in 1954 and was sent for UK Military user trials on 9th January, 1954.

Notwithstanding this, guns marked "Patchett 9m/m MIC" have been seen bearing inexplicably high numbers, as high as 8930.

"SMG No 800" Presented to the Secretary of State

An entry from the MoD Contracts/Serial Numbers Record Book reads as follows:

NOTE: Carbine (SMG) No 800 issued to Sec of State by Sterling Eng Co, was not completely inspected or finally accepted by DI/ARM. No 800 A allotted in lieu.

The British Army Adopts the 'L' Series of Designations

The "Last Patchett"

In July or early August, 1954, the Ministry of Defence contracted for additional MkII guns with military markings: at first three, to be numbered 02, 03 and 04, but soon raised to a grand total of six, nos 02 through 07.

L2A1 number 01, manufactured in March, 1953, was retained by the Sterling company, and is now held in the MoD Pattern Room. This was the last gun to be marked with Patchett's name.

110. Top closeup view of the magazine housing of L2A1 No 01, the "Last Patchett". This appears to be the last example of the laborious butt-weld-and-grind-smooth method of attaching the magazine housing.

Until the company was closed by British Aerospace in 1989, this gun was retained by Sterling as part of their collection. (MoD Pattern Room collection)

111. Top closeup view of the magazine housing of L2A1 No 07, showing markings. This was the last of only seven guns produced with L2A1 markings.

Note the first appearance of the induction-brazed maga- zine housing. (MoD Pattern Room collection)

The Last of the (Magnificent) Seven

The remaining six examples of the L2A1 were marked "GUN/SUB-MACHINE/9mm L2A1/No" (02 through 07).

L2A1 No 06, examined for this study, was supplied to the Ministry of Defence in September, 1954 which confirms that use of the 'L' series of designations (the L1A1 rifle, the L2A1 SMG, L3A1 Browning, L4A4 LMG; etc) commenced at that time. Apart from the different markings, the commercial and military MkIIs are identical to the L2A1.

The 'M/C' on the earlier MkIIs stood for "Machine Carbine". The term "Gun, Sub-Machine" was also not adopted by the UK Military until 1954, as can be seen from the markings on L2A1 no 07. Some of the earlier guns marked 'M/C' have had the 'M/C' lined through and 'GUN SUB-MACHINE' engraved in its place.

Describing the Patchett MkII (L2A1)

Looking at the gun as a whole, certain things immediately become apparent to the experienced eye. The first thing that strikes one is the fact that unlike the earlier Patchetts, this gun just LOOKS like the Sterling guns we now recognise. The first and most obvious departure is that the MkII/L2A1 is the first production gun to incorporate the new magazine housing, angled forward at 82° to accept the superbly designed curved magazines which incorporate George Patchett and Sterling patents 615471 of 9th May, 1946 (the roller platform) and 692768 of 6th March, 1952 (the curvilinear ribs and round-section coil mainspring).

As a result of the adoption of the curved magazine with its superior double feed positions, the breech face of the barrel was modified by machining the shallow double-angle bullet feed ramp into the breech identical throughout 360°. The half-round single finger guard was retained, attached to the casing ahead of the ejection port.

The butt (part no CR 7 MA, Parts List) was fabricated by brazing the four parts of the top frame together. This was a direct but (somewhat) stronger copy of the butt featured on the MkI Patchetts. The butt frame sides are narrow in width and thickness. The top, inverted squared-off 'U' section was still virtually topless throughout 90% of its length, which just asked for trouble. However, the production butt plate was secured to the frame in the firing position by a spring that asserted itself under the frame. Another improvement over the MkI butt frame was that the frame sides have a strengthening corrugated rib down their length. Additionally, in the folded position the butt plate is secured to the butt frame by a dimple punched in each side ear mating with a corresponding recess in the butt frame sides-'.-a point forgotten about later on in the first Mk4s!

It should have been obvious for all to see that this light and fabricated butt frame was destined to suffer. Indeed, on two of the guns examined during this research, the accompanying trials paperwork states that after suffering irreparable damage, the original butts were replaced with the later MkIII/L2A2 pattern butt. Indeed, on the 1955 series, marked '9mm L2A1', it is clear that the later, MkIII/L2A2 butt was fitted at the factory! It must be assumed that the stronger MkIII butts were fitted to earlier guns as part of Sterling's ongoing improvement process. In any case, the better and stronger MkIII butt, while still not as strong as the ultimate Mk4/L2A3 type, was a direct replacement onto the MkII.

The First (Brittle) Plastic Grip

On the MkII gun the early cast alloy pistol grip was replaced by the now familiar black plastic pattern made by Helix Plastics, complete with clearance cut to allow the left thumb more room to operate the change lever. Early black plastic pistol grips were made from brittle bakelite, the sort that old 78 rpm gramophone records were made from, and like the 78s, broke just as easily. The slightest obstruction, and the last tweak of the grip screw would see a chunk fly off.

Dual Return Springs and Factory-Fitted Sling Loop

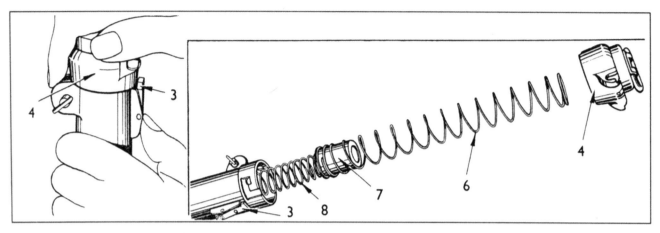

112. From the Provisional Handbook for the MkII "EX" Machine Carbine: the return spring cap (4) has been removed by pressing in the front of the butt catch (3), pushing the cap forward, and rotating it anti-clockwise until locking lugs on the cap have disengaged from the locking recesses on the casing, allowing disassembly of the outer (6) and inner (8) return springs, together with the inner return spring cup (7). (Courtesy James Alley)

The MkII/L2A1 incorporated the inner and outer return springs (the subject of George Patchett's sixth patent with Sterling, number 686628 dated 5th December, 1950, discussed in Chapter Four), held together none too successfully by the return spring cup.

The return spring cap, now flared out towards the rear, and a rear sling loop with a retaining plate was riveted to the rear of the cap. The original MkII sling loop was in the vertical position, in order that the sling would clear the butt as it was folded or extended, although many MkII (vertical) loops were later replaced with the MkIII (horizontal) pattern. To help centre the outer return spring in the casing, early MkII return spring caps were fitted with a round spring locator held in place by the sling loop retaining plate rivets.

Securing the Separate Firing Pin

The principal reason for a separate firing pin was to eliminate waste in service caused by chipped, broken or otherwise distorted firing pins, which, with the Sten, necessitated complete replacement of the breech block.

However, it is clear from the numerous experimental firing pin/cocking handle interfaces discussed above that George Patchett was not happy with the Lanchester idea of the separate firing pin.

From an Armourer's point of view, this was a potential nightmare. As noted, if firing pin protrusion (FPP; ideally between .040″ and .048″) is too great, primers are ruptured; too little protrusion, and misfires occur. FPP in a breech face utilising a separate firing pin was dependent on far too many variables.

114. Front closeup view of MkII breech block face showing shouldered firing pin partially removed.
Note the slotted extractor. (MoD Pattern Room collection)

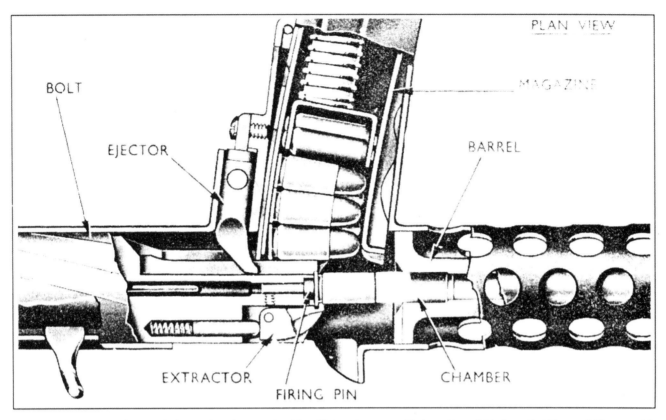

113. Top cutaway view of a typical MkII Patchett showing shouldered firing pin mounted in face of breech block, and held by small "Screw, grub" (part no MC 8814, Parts List) located behind the extractor. (MoD Army, REME)

The double return spring patent (no 686628, dated 5 December, 1950) goes on to say that "… In a modification, the firing pin is integral with the bolt (face)". As we have seen (Chapter Four), the integral firing pin was introduced in the first six 'MkIIs' supplied in 1946 for comparison trials of the then newly developed curved magazine.

The integral firing pin was re-introduced somewhere during the switchover from the MkII to the later MkIII breech block (Ministry of Supply part number CR 998). Initially, however, about 200 military MkIIs were fitted with a modified MkI-type breech block (CR 866) which incorporated a shouldered, removable firing pin (CR 869), held in place by a small grub screw (MC 8814) located behind the extractor.

The advantages of this removable firing pin were three-fold. First, the headspace problems inherent in the separate, spring-driven Lanchester-type firing pin were obviated once and for all; second, it

allowed Sterling to use up all the drilled-through breech blocks still in stock; and third, in those days of somewhat unperfected heat-treating procedures, a replaceable firing pin could be separately hardened and, if it did become broken or chipped, it could be replaced without scrapping the entire breech block. Hardening techniques were soon improved, and later firing pins were machined into, and hardened integrally with, the breech face.

Certainly from an Armourer's point of view, the change to a breech block fitted with either of these fixed firing pins was a sound move.

The Firing Pin Extension Becomes the "Centre Pin"

Within the CR 998 breech block (L2A1 parts list) the erstwhile firing pin extension (CR 910) has been shortened to remove the firing pin tip, and renamed the "centre pin". It now acts only as a locating pin within the centre of the breech block.

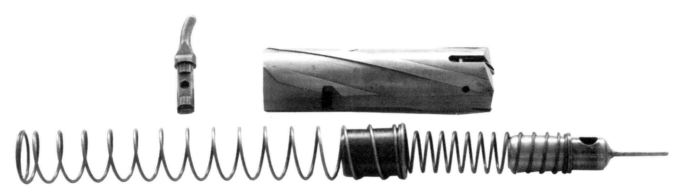

115. Breech components of a typical MkII Patchett Machine Carbine (later 'Gun, Sub-Machine, L2A1').
   Top row, from left: cocking handle, breech block (CR 866) with separate, removable firing pin.
   Bottom row: outer return spring; return spring cup; inner return spring; "centre pin" with shortened locating pin. (MoD Pattern Room collection)

The half-length extension at the front of the MkII/L2A1 "centre pin" was deliberately left intact so that it would be impossible to assemble the breech block and return spring assembly incorrectly. The centre pin and recoil springs had to be fully home in the rear of the breech block first, and then the cocking handle. If the cocking handle was seated in the breech block first, it barred the centre pin from entering its seat.

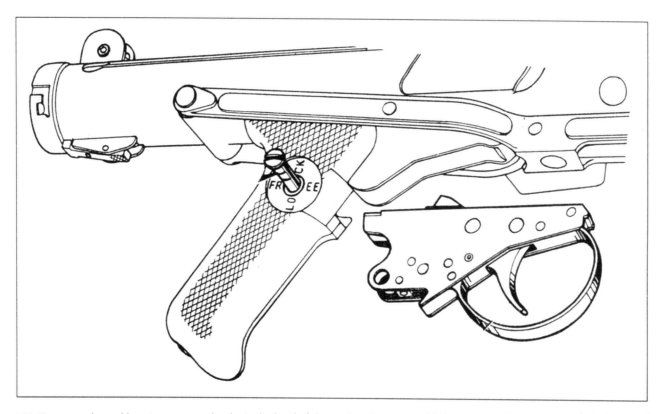

116. To remove the en bloc trigger group, the slot in the head of the captive trigger assembly locating pin (CR911) is turned (by the rim of a 9mm cartridge or the screwdriver tip of the cocking handle) into line with the word 'FREE' on the right side of the pistol grip, and pushed outwards (with the blunt end of the cocking handle or bullet of cartridge). The trigger is then pressed and the trigger group pulled outwards to remove from casing.
   Internally, this mechanism is virtually identical to the later (Mk4/L2A3) trigger assembly. The trigger guard is not detachable, and the trigger is a different shape, but basically the projections on the front lower edge of the trigger frame are all that prevent interchangeability of trigger assemblies. Not an insurmountable problem, as witness the many early guns now fitted with Mk4 trigger mechanisms. (Courtesy MoD Pattern Room, Nottingham)

It was mentioned at the time that this pin could be used as a drift to remove the extractor axis pin. As it transpired, this was only half correct. The extension pin could be used to START removing the extractor axis pin, but soon became tight in the axis pin hole. And a good thing too, for as soon as the extractor was removed, the spring and plunger followed it into the grass or sand, to be lost forever. Most soldiers would be reluctant to report the loss, and the gun would go back into the armoury incomplete.

The Chief Inspector of Armaments looked into the question of whether this extension on the centre pin served any real purpose. The report concluded that it did not. He suggested that if one was damaged, then it could be simply removed without detriment to the operation of the gun. In later Marks a spring and plunger achieved the same aim of preventing incorrect assembly of the gun.

Like the MkI Patchett (and the Stens, of course), the weight of the breech block assembly was finely balanced to give the guns the cyclic rate of fire of 540 rpm. Any change in the weight of the reciprocating parts would cause a problem with the mathematics and/or physics of the gun.

Experiments with Precision-Cast Breech Blocks

In June, 1954 some MkII guns were fitted with precision-cast breech blocks. Precision casting then was obviously not up to today's standards, because the trials report stated that some machining still had to be completed, and that there was nothing to be gained over the then-current machined and hardened breech blocks, which were in fact retained throughout Sterling production.

Other MkII Design Features

First Arctic Trigger Experiments

During the troop trials with the King's Shropshire Light Infantry in Korea, the question of an arctic trigger mechanism adaptor had been raised.

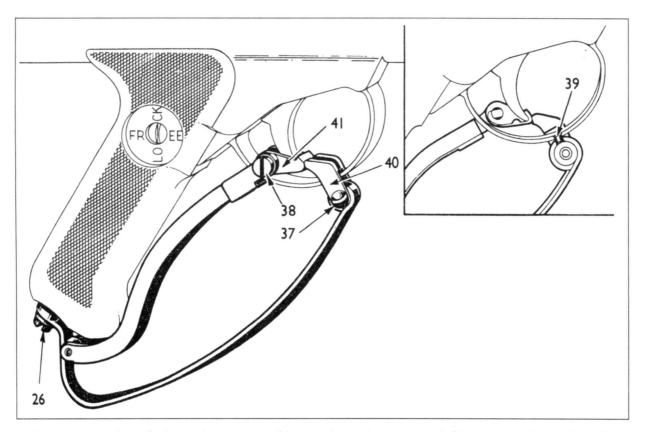

117. The arctic trigger adaptor for the MkII/L2A1. Not one of Sterling's better ideas, as a perusal of the instructions (quoted below from the military Provisional Handbook) will indicate.
Imagine trying to follow these instructions in a slit trench during a winter's night in Korea! (Courtesy MoD Pattern Room, Nottingham)

There is no facility to remove the trigger guard from the MkII/L2A1 for use in arctic climates, but MkII and MkIII trigger guards have a hole (shown at item 39 above) in the bow. Sterling developed a rather complicated arctic trigger attachment which screwed to the base of the pistol grip and contacted the trigger through this hole. When properly adjusted, this allowed the trigger to be pulled while wearing thick mittens.

Instructions concerning the installation of this device were printed in the Provisional User handbook, as follows:

To Fit Arctic Trigger

To Fit:

Remove pistol grip screw (26). Release the side plate screw (37) of the arctic trigger, and remove the cross pin (38) by turning it and pushing it out. Fit the guard to the bottom of the pistol grip and position the locating peg (39) into the hole in the standard trigger guard.

Tighten the side plate (40) to the guard by the screw (37), using the cocking handle and pistol grip screw as screwdriver and tommy bar. Replace pistol grip screw and hook the link (40) of the arctic trigger onto the standard trigger. Connect the link of the arctic trigger by the cross pin (38). This pin is locked by a spring similar to that of the trigger bolt and the slot should be vertical when finally positioned.

To Remove:

Reverse the order of assembly.

A true detachable arctic trigger guard for the SMG did not come about until the introduction of the Mk4/L2A3 in 1956.

Foresight Protector Variables

The last of the fully-machined ex-Lanchester foresight protectors of the MkI gun were utilised, along with the now familiar folded sheet steel pattern. But, some MkII guns on trial (L2A1s No 5 and No 6 for example) have small rounded foresight protectors, housing a block that accepts one of eight incrementally sized No4 rifle style foresight blades. From a sales standpoint the idea of eight foresight blades was most laudable, but with the advent of the adjustable-for-height Sterling foresight, which was soon to emerge, the idea was short-lived.

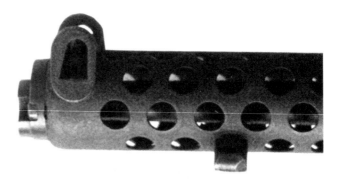

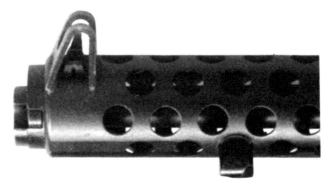

118. Two different foresight protectors used on the MkII Patchett.

Above: the last of the leftover, machined-from-solid Lanchester protectors, converted. In use only through (very) early MkII production. Note that this early MkII does not have the distinctive flat machined on the casing forward of the bayonet standard: it would be very difficult to fit a bayonet to this gun.

Below: earliest pattern of stamped-and-folded foresight protectors. Later (Mk4) protectors have a distinct dog-leg or 'kink' across the front, making the front and rear parallel for about half their height. (MoD Pattern Room collection)

120. A further view of the muzzle end of Patchett 9m/m M/C No 8760 (fig 119), showing details of the adjustable front sight and bayonet standard. (MoD Pattern Room collection)

119 (Left). Two more different foresight protectors used on the MkII Patchett.

Above: designed in order that other user countries might purchase a selection of eight different No4 rifle foresight blades, instead of the seven different sizes of Lanchester type blades previously used. A short-lived idea, as the protectors themselves proved weak, and the introduction of the single, adjustable foresight blade made the idea redundant.

Below: Patchett MIC bearing the impossibly high serial number 8760, with a set of flared foresight protectors similar to the No5 rifle. On this gun, the No4 rifle-style foresight blade is laterally adjustable by means of left and right zeroing screws, located on each side of the protectors. adjusted laterally by means of a threaded screw. (MoD Pattern Room collection)

This lever formed a 'V' shape when rotated between its forward and rear positions. When the lever was forward, the backsight was set for 200 yards, and when back, 100 yards.

Still Utilising Surplus Lanchester Barrels

The barrels (CR 865) fitted to the MkII/L2A1s (and some early MkIII/L2A2s) were still modified Lanchester items, converted from surplus WWII stock. These can be identified by the small recess (the Lanchester locating and locking mark) at the top of the rear flange, seen by looking through the ejection port These barrels also show vestiges of the multiholed front flange, although this feature is only visible when the gun is fully stripped.

As noted, the front barrel flange is purposely offset top-to-bottom, to ensure fool-proof assembly at all times. When the barrel seats in its locating recess within the barrel support at the front of the casing, the extractor slot is perfectly aligned with the extractor in the breech block. The rear end of the barrel is not fixed in any way, except by its position within the circumference of the casing.

It was suggested that MkII/L2A1 barrels were more likely to bulge than those of a Sten. This was said to be due to the different wall thickness. One gun, number 251, now resident at the Pattern Room, was subject to intensive tests whereby the barrels were deliberately bulged, after which the report concluded that there was no significant difference between the MkII/L2A1 converted Lanchester barrel and a Sten barrel.

Backsight Modifications

The distance between the upright ears of the backsight had already been widened from .45″ to .55″, to overcome the difficulty experienced with the MkI gun of changing the backsight over between 100 and 200 yards. For good measure a small lever, similar in style to the trigger mechanism change lever, was fitted to the left side of the backsight on the MkII.

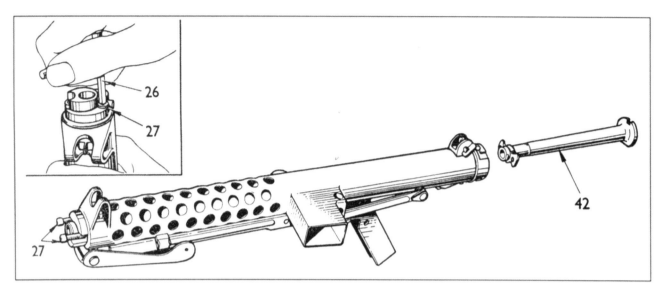

121. From the 1952 Provisional Handbook: removing the barrel from the MkII Patchett.

At upper left: the two Allen-headed "screws, retaining, barrel and grip" (CR 912) are removed, using the hexagonal extension of the grip retaining screw as the key and the cocking handle as the tommy bar.

Note the telltale vestigial holes in the thin front flange of the converted Lanchester barrel, and the distinctive Lanchester locating notch in the top of the rear flange. (Courtesy MoD Pattern Room, Nottingham)

Foolproof Assembly – with One Exception

From the MkII/L2A1 gun onwards, with one minor exception, it is impossible to assemble a Sterling gun incorrectly. The exception to the rule of foolproof assembly is the cocking handle, which can be assembled 180° out.

George Patchett's cocking handle was deliberately designed with opposing flats which run within the cocking handle slot in the casing, so that rotation was impossible. This was to design out a fault with the Sten (and first Patchett prototypes) where in the cold and wet, the cocking handle could (and frequently did) rotate and roll out of the hand, to accidentally fire the gun. A point that George Patchett found out to his cost one evening!

Any soldier, or former soldier, will confirm that accidentally firing a sub-machine gun (or any other type of gun for that matter), does not endear one to one's comrades, and is appreciated to an even lesser extent by one's Platoon Sergeant!

Field Servicing: a Two-Edged Sword

122. Closeup of the cocking handle of a typical MkII Patchett.

Compare with fig 55: the hole in the shaft is now a hexagon rather than plain round, and serves a different function. (MoD Pattern Room collection)

One of the selling points of the A1 was that it was fully serviceable by the user in the field. It is correct that the user could fully strip this gun, without the need for any special tools other that a coin or a 9mm cartridge (except for the butt assembly, which is secured with a button-headed pin and a smaller cross pin on each side).

To strip the gun it was first necessary to use the rim of a 9mm case or a small coin; (an old sixpence was suggested: "Sixpence was almost a week's pay!" commented one ex-National Serviceman of the era) to rotate the trigger mechanism retaining pin to the 'FREE' position, and then push it out with the

123. The short-lived stripping tools built into the MkII Patchett. An ingenious idea in theory but, as explained in the text, not a practical one.

The hexagonal Allen key on the extended shaft of the grip screw fits through the hexagonal hole in the cocking handle, which is provided with a screwdriver tip. Each component acts as the tommy bar for the other. (Courtesy REME Sgt Roger Smith)

nose of a 9mm bullet. Once this had been done, the same coin (or cartridge rim) could be used to undo the pistol grip retaining screw (CR 913). This screw had an extended shaft in the shape of a hexagonal $^3/_{16}''$ Allen key. The cocking handle (CR 909) had a screwdriver head machined onto the inner end and, halfway down the shank, a $^3/_{16}''$ hexagonal hole. One then slid the hexagonal pistol grip screw extension into the corresponding hole in the cocking handle and *voilà*, a 'T'-shaped tool.

It was then possible to unscrew the magazine catch and ejector screw with the screwdriver end of the cocking handle, using the pistol grip screw as the tommy bar, and then remove the two barrel retaining Allen bolts, using the Allen key end of the pistol grip screw with the cocking handle as the tommy bar.

However laudable this idea was in theory, in practice it spelled disaster. The first things to go missing in the sand or long grass were the springs, followed by the screws, followed by —. Suffice it to say that the idea of field-servicing was short-lived, and did not survive beyond the MkII/L2A1.

Fully stripping a gun by the user was not a new idea. It was a feature of the Mk1 Bren. Significantly, by the time the Mk3 and 4 Brens had emerged, the user was only permitted to strip the gun down to its five major assemblies. Now, without being unkind to the more technically-minded soldier-users, Armourers all agree that 'field stripping' should mean just that: stripping in the field sufficient to clean the gun.

The Experimental Malayan Shotgun-Style Sight Rib

124. Right side view of MkII Patchett no 2772, showing the experimental Malayan shotgun-style sighting rib running the full length of the casing. The foresight blade and backsight have been removed, and the rib is held securely between the foresight slot and the remains of the backsight ears.

At least three MkIIs were so modified.

Note the rear sling swivel: the original (vertical) MkII loop has been replaced with the MIcIII (horizontal) type. Many MIcIIs still exist that have been retrofitted with various modifications, particularly the stronger MkIII butt. (MoD Army, RMCS Shrivenham)

Three of the MkII guns now preserved by the UK Military at RMCS, Shrivenham; the School of Infantry, Warminster; and SAS, Hereford have had the foresight blades and backsights removed and replaced by a shotgun-style sighting rib, running the full length of the casing. These guns were trialled in the Malayan jungles against guns fitted with Singlepoint sights to see whether a shotgun-type rib sight offered any 'first-shot-hit' improvement.

This idea was short-lived, because the wider (.55″) backsight ears had already virtually solved the problem of aiming and shooting at fleeting targets in conditions of poor visibility. Reports document that shooting in pouring rain or monsoon conditions are as difficult as in near darkness in the deepest impenetrable jungle, and Malaya has plenty of both. Subsequent Malayan guns were supplied with oversized 100-yard apertures to cater for this problem.

Barrel Length Experiments

One other experiment carried out during the same period was to lengthen the barrel for increased accuracy. There was an inevitable price to pay, in the increased length and weight of the gun. This project did not proceed past the experimental stage due to technical difficulties. However, these experiments did pave the way for the longer Mk6 gun barrels (Chapter Eleven).

Holding-Open Devices

The Sterling company were asked by a potential buyer whether a Holding Open Device (HOD) could be inserted into the boltway of the gun, to hold the breech bolt to the rear after the last round had been fired from the magazine. One gun was modified with a small HOD incorporated into an ingenious articulating ejector. Although it worked, George Patchett realised that it was so intricate that it would soon fail in dusty or muddy conditions.

From the purely practical point of view, holding open devices are notoriously fickle and prone to damage (as was that fitted to the original 7.62mm L4 Bren, which was quickly deleted). As a result, they were not regularly used on UK Military weapons.

This experimental gun also incorporated a small device within the breech block and trigger mechanism whereby even if the gun were only partially cocked, the breech block would be held to the rear, and a small internal safety sleeve would withdraw the firing pin from the face of the breech block.

George also tried a magazine-operated holding open device, similar to those of the Bren and the FAL rifle. This was slightly more successful, but required special magazines. By the time full trials were over, the buyer had opted for standard guns. Once you have used a gun in action, when you hear the metallic ring of the bolt hitting the breech face, you just KNOW the gun is empty!

MkII/L2A1 Variations

To sum up, MkII/L2A1 guns will be seen with the following variables:

- fully open (MkII) or partially open (MkIII) top butt frame.
- conventional leaf and blade sights, or experimental shotgun sight rail
- No4 foresight blades in narrow protectors, or folded-and-wrapped (standard-width) foresight protectors
- fixed, or later adjustable-for-height, foresight blades

- Allen key tool-type pistol grip screw, or standard Allen screw
- screwdriver-tipped cocking handle, or later type with tool capability deleted
- early guns without second (front) finger guard, late guns with front finger guard
- earliest guns with separate MkI-type firing pin; some (approx 200) guns with removable firing pin held in face of breech block by small grub screw; later guns with firing pin integral with breech block.

Kenton Redgrave Enshrined in the First Commercial Serial Number Prefix

Commercial MkII guns made between May and November, 1953 had serial numbers beginning simply 'No'.

The SN prefix 'KR' (the initials of Sterling's Managing Director, Kenton Redgrave) was first applied to the commercial MkII on November 2, 1953, beginning with SN KR 1000, which was part of an order sent to Kuwait.

The 'KR'-prefix MkIIs correlate as follows:

Serial Number	Date of Manufacture
KR 1000	2 November, 1953
KR 1500	July, 1954
KR 2000	November, 1954
KR 2500	January, 1955
KR 2730 (the last MkII)	29 March, 1955

125. Top closeup view of magazine housing of Sterling MkII no KR 2722, showing markings. Note the first appearance of the distinctive boxed STERLING logo, which appears on all later Sterling guns and literature.

Produced early in 1955, this was the eighth-to-last MkII made (the last was no KR 2730). (MoD Pattern Room collection)

'KR'-prefix MkIIs were sold to a number of countries, including Bermuda, Botswana, Brunei, Hong Kong, Kenya, Kuwait, Singapore, Sudan, Syria, Tanzania and Tripolitania (later Libya). All were obviously impressed as, with the exception of Syria, they went on to purchase later marks of Sterling guns.

Retrofitting the MkII/L2A1 with Later Parts

The MkII/L2A1 only served for a couple of years until it was superseded by the even shorter-lived MkIII/L2A2 in 1955. Then those MkII/L2A1 guns still in service were modified, using MkIII parts where necessary. Certainly the weak butt assemblies were widely replaced, as were the cocking handles, pistol grip screws and converted Lanchester barrels.

Components of the MkII/L2A1 Patchett are fully interchangeable with those of the later Mk4/L2A3 Sterling, with the following exceptions:

- the Mk4/L2A3 trigger mechanism is interchangeable as a complete assembly. But if Mk4/L2A3 trigger mechanism is fitted, the MkII/L2A1 pistol grip must be slightly modified at front to allow side plates clearance (or use Mk4/L2A3 grip).
- the Mk4/L2A3 pattern ejector can be filed to fit the MkII.
- the Mk4/L2A3 butt assembly is totally non-interchangeable, due to its geometric redesign.
- the Mk4/L2A3 barrel will fit, IF barrel screw holes in casing are reamed out to accept shank diameter of the ¼″ UNF threaded Allen screws used with Mk4/L2A3 barrel.
- the Mk4/L2A3 return spring cap will fit ONLY if used in conjunction with the Mk4/L2A3 locking lever. The same applies for the lever, locking, return spring cap.

Parts List for Gun, Sub-Machine, 9mm, L2A1

The Parts List for the MkII/L2A1 gun was not issued by the War Office's Director of Ordnance Services until 1956, when a combined listing was published for both the L2A1 and L2A2 guns.

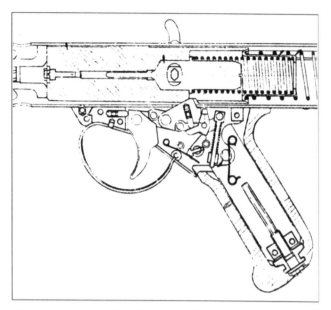

126. From an undated Sterling factory blueprint, a cutaway view of the trigger and breech block assemblies of a MkII (L2A1) Patchett.

Note the shouldered removable firing pin (CR 869), the shortened shank on the "centre pin", and the Allen key extension on the pistol grip retaining screw. (Courtesy MoD Pattern Room, Nottingham)

Neither of these early military Parts Lists was illustrated, and we have therefore inserted a column after the 'Qty' (quantity per gun) column, which references the nearest equivalent part in the Mk4/L2A3 illustrated Parts List (Chapter Seven). For example, a MkII/L2A1 part suffixed with 'C 31' will indicate part number 31 in the Mk4/L2A3 'C' (casing) section; in this case, the magazine catch. A 'T' suffix will indicate the trigger mechanism section and 'B' the butt section.

Note the two breech blocks specified: the earlier assembly (CR 111 SA) is the one fitted with the shouldered firing pin (CR 869; fig 125), while in the later assembly (CR 122 SA) the firing pin is integral. Note also the seven different-sized (Lanchester style) foresight blades (next page). These were identified by being numbered –3, –2, –1, 0, +1, +2, and +3, and their selective use allowed the mean point of impact to be raised or lowered by 4.5″ at 100 yards (1″ at 25 yards).

Catalogue No	Designation	Qty	Mk4/l2A3 Equiv
CR 47 GA	Gun, Sub-Machine, 9mm, L2A1	1	
CR 894	Backsight	1	C 8
CR 865	Barrel	1	C 15
CR 111 SA	Block, breech	1	C 16
CR 866	Block	1	C 17
CR 867	Extractor	1	C 18
CR 868	Pin, extractor	1	C 19
CR869	Pin, firing	1	–
CR870	Plunger, extractor	1	C 21
MC 8814	Screw, grub, BA, steel, cup pt, socket hd, No 6	1	–
CR 871	Spring, extractor plunger	1	C 20
	OR		
CR 122 SA	Block, breech	1	C 16
CR 998	Block	1	C 17
CR 867	Extractor	1	C 18
CR 868	Pin, extractor	1	C 19
CR 870	Plunger, extractor	1	C 21
CR 871	Spring, extractor plunger	1	C 20
CR 892	Bush, retaining, backsight lever	1	C 6
CR 7 MA	Butt, assembly	1	B 1
CR 876	Bush	1	–
CR 113 SA	Catch, butt	1	B 8
CR 877	Catch	1	B 9

Catalogue No	Designation	Qty	Mk4/l2A3 Equiv
CR 878	Rivet	1	B 11
CR 879	Spring	1	B 10
CR 880	Pin, catch, butt	1	–
CR 881	Pin, tube, butt	1	–
CR 882	Pin, butt plate and tube	1	B 14–17
CR 883	Plate, butt, rear	1	B 7
CR 884	Plate, butt, side	1	–
CR 106 A	Tube, butt, assembly	1	B 2
CR 885	Catch	1	B 6
CR 887	Pin, catch	1	B 5
CR 889	Spring	1	B 4
CR 114 SA	Tube, butt	1	B 2–3
CR 886	Pin, spring, retaining ring .	1	
CR 888	Ring, retaining, spring	1	–
CR 890	Tube	1	–
CR 891	Washer, butt plate and tube pin	2	–
CR 112 SA	Cap, return spring	1	C 27
CR 999	Cap	1	C 27
CR 1000	Locator, outer return spring .	1	–
CR 1001	Plate, swivel	1	–
CR 875	Swivel, sling	1	–
CR 893	Casing	1	C 3–4
CR 902	Catch, magazine	1	C 31
CR 903	Cup, inner return spring	1	C 25
CR 904	Ejector	1	C 30
CR 972	Foresight, 0.530	1	C 35
CR 973	Foresight, 0.550	1	C 35
CR 907	Foresight, 0.570	1	C 35
CR 906	Foresight, 0.590	1	C 35
CR 905	Foresight, 0.610	1	C 35
CR 974	Foresight, 0.630	1	C 35
CR 975	Foresight, 0.650	1	C 35
CR 908	Grip	1	T 32
CR 909	Handle, cocking	1	C 28
CR 897	Lever, backsight	1	–
CR 115 SA	Lever, locking, return spring cap	1	C 10
CR 895	Lever	1	C 11
CR 879	Spring	1	C 13
CR 1002	Pin, axis, return spring cap lever	1	C 14
CR 910	Pin, centre	1	C 23
CR 911	Pin, locating, trigger assembly	1	T 33
CR 898	Pin, locking, butt retaining pin	2	B 19
CR 899	Pin, retaining, butt	2	B 18
CR 915	Screw, ejector	1	–
CR 913	Screw, grip	1	T 34
CR 914	Screw, magazine catch	1	C 33
CR 912	Screw, retaining, barrel and grip	2	C – T 39
CR 900	Spring, backsight	1	C 7

Catalogue No	Designation	Qty	Mk4/l2A3 Equiv
CR 901	Spring, locating pin	1	–
CR 916	Spring, catch, magazine	1	C 32
CR 917	Spring, return, inner	1	C 24
CR 918	Spring, return, outer	1	C 26
CR 102 A	Trigger assembly	1	–
CR 116 A	Cradle, sear	1	T 15
CR 919	Guide, spring, main	1	T 18
CR 920	Pin, distance, side plates	3	T 17
CR 921	Plate, side	2	T 16
CR 922	Roller	1	T 19
CR 117 A	Guard, trigger	1	T 30
CR 923	Block, spring, main	1	T 14
CR 924	Block, thrust	1	T 4
CR 925	Guard	1	T 11 – 12
CR 1003	Lever, change, part 1	1	T 6
	OR		
CR 926	Lever, change, part 1	1	T 6
CR 927	Lever, change, part 2	1	T 8
CR 928	Pin, axis, spring detent	1	T 5
CR 960	Pin, detent	1	T 9
CR 929	Pin, stop, part 2 change lever	2	T 13
CR 970	Pin, thrust	1	–
CR 930	Plate, side	2	T 3
CR 931	Rivet, plate, side . . .	3	T 5
CR 932	Spring, pin, detent .	1	T 10
CR 933	Lever, tripping	1	T 20
CR 934	Pin, sear and trigger . . .	2	T 23
CR 935	Pin, tripping lever	1	T 21
CR 936	Plunger, sear and trigger .	1	T 25
CR 937	Sear	1	T 22
CR 939	Spring, sear cradle . . .	1	T 26
CR 938	Spring, sear and trigger	2	T 24
CR 940	Trigger	1 .	T 27 – 28
CR 103 A	Magazine, 9mm, L1A1		
CR 1004	Case	1	
CR 1137	Pin, retaining spring .	1	
CR 1010	Plate, bottom	1	
CR 124 SA	Spring, assembly	1	
CR 1006	Pin	1	
CR 1007	Plate, retaining	1	
CR 1005	Platform	1	
CR 1008	Roller	2	
CR 1009	Spring	1	
CR 1011	Spring, plate, bottom	1	

Chapter Six

The First Sterling

Sterling SMG 9mm MkIII (Gun, Sub-Machine, 9mm L2A2)

Date adopted:		February, 1955
Date declared obsolescent:		March, 1956
Quantity produced:	Sterling commercial (KR prefix):	1,570
	Sterling L2A2s for UK Military:	2,879
	Total:	4,449

Describing the MkIII

127. Left side view of a typical MkIII, the first of the Patchetts to bear the Sterling name, with butt extended and magazine removed. The MkIII was a fine gun that won many friends for Sterling around the world.

Note the reinforced (ribbed) butt, and the rear sight lever, which now describes an 'L' rather than a 'V' when flipped from 100 to 200 yds. (Courtesy Mike Harrison)

The introduction of the MkIII saw the name of the gun officially changed in Sterling literature from "Patchett Machine Carbine" to "Sterling Sub Machine Gun".

However, Sterling engineers admit that many early MkIII guns were in reality leftover MkII casings upgraded with some (if not all) of the MkIII features. Serial number KR 2807 was one such, manufactured as a MkII and upgraded to MkIII/L2A2 specifications.

Those early MkIII guns that started life as had the '9mm MkII' corrected with the aid of a small chisel to read '9mm MkIII', KR 2817 being another recently-seen example.

Because of this overlap between the MkII/L2A1, hybrid MkII–MkIII and MkIII/L2A2, the MkIII came with a host of small and largely insignificant variables.

The Official Description

The Electrical and Mechanical Engineering Regulations (EMER's), the Armourer's Bible, stated the principal differences between the MkIII/L2A2 and the previous MkII/L2A1 as follows:

a. *CASING. An additional HANDGUARD is provided just below the foresight housing.*

 The BACKSIGHT LEVER has been repositioned so that when horizontal the backsight is set at 100 yards and when vertical is set to 200 yards. The distance between the backsight leaves has been increased. The diameter of the 100 yard aperture has been made larger.

 The LEVER,LOCKING, RETURN SPRING CAP has been provided with a small pin on the rear underside.

 The RETURN SPRING CAP has been recessed to receive this pin and modified so that the sling swivel is now horizontal although the swivel retaining strop is still rivetted in place.

b. *BUTT ASSEMBLY. The main member has been strengthened and drilled for lightness with $5 \times {}^{7}/_{16}$" holes along the top edge.*

c. *RETURN SPRING CUP has been provided with a small nib to retain the outer return spring.*

d. *The firing pin (or extension) has been omitted from the CENTRE PIN, hereafter called the COCKING HANDLE BLOCK*

e. *The BREECH BOLT has been re-designated the BREECH BLOCK*

 To prevent incorrect assembly of the cocking handle, a plunger and spring has been – fitted into the central hole of the breech block (formerly occupied by the separate firing pin or the extension on the centre pin. See 'd' for details). This prevents the cocking handle being inserted before the cocking handle block (formerly the Centre pin) is in position.

 The FIRING PIN is now integral with the breech block/ace.

f. *COCKING HANDLE has been re-designed and there is no provision to use it as a tool for stripping the gun.*

128. Top closeup of magazine housing of an early, unserialled MkIII Sterling, showing markings.
 Compare with fig 125: note 'II' converted to 'III'. (MoD Pattern Room collection)

g. *THE BARREL The recess in the (top of the) rear end of the flange has been omitted. The front flange has been strengthened.*

h. *The screw end of the MAGAZINE CATCH SCREW has been drilled to allow it to be secured by expansion*

j. *The PISTOL GRIP SCREW has been redesigned and is now interchangeable with the barrel retaining screws. There is no provision to use this grip screw as a tool.*

We can see that many of these changes are definite improvements over the former MkII/L2A1, and what is evolving is the ultimate Mk4/L2A3.

A Detailed Comparison: MkIII/L2A2 vs the MkII/L2A1

Further comment on the above official descriptions will provide a detailed look at the components described and compare them with those from the MkII Patchett.

 The additional hand guard (or "finger-guard" according to the Sterling literature) positioned

129. The lion at bay-Kenton Redgrave in his office, affably demonstrating the ideal paperweight: an early MkIII Sterling. By the time of this official press release photo, dated February 8, 1955, Sterling was aware that their gun had been chosen as the next British general issue SMG. The caption reads as follows: "Mr Kenton Redgrave, Managing Director of Sterling Engineering Co Ltd, Dagenham, England, the firm responsible for the design and development of Britain's latest weapon – the Sterling Sub-Machine Gun – which has recently been adopted by the British Army to replace the Sten Gun, and which is now in production."

Note the front finger guard, and the alternative pattern front sight protectors. (Courtesy David Howroyd)

Inset, upper right: signature of Kenton Redgrave.

just below the foresight protector, was added in the interests of safety. It was accepted that during training and instruction in camps there was no real danger, but whilst in action, hot, sweaty, sticky and wet hands might slide forward over the muzzle. This hand (or finger) guard was the same shape as the rear hand guard, but back to front.

The enlarged 100-yard aperture now permitted the use of the sight in conditions of half light or poor visibility.

Increasing the distance between the upright ears of the backsight from .45″ to .55″ was a good idea, and .55″ it was to remain throughout Sterling production.

The repositioned MkII backsight lever provides an easy point of recognition over the MkII, because instead of forming a 'V' it forms an 'L' when flipped from 100 to 200 yards.

The small pin added to the underside of the Lever, Locking, Return Spring Cap ensured that the lever now acted as a three-way lock. Fully closed against its spring, the lever fully locks the return spring cap in position. The FIRST part of opening only allows the cap to be pushed forward, to fold the butt. The SECOND part of its opening lifts this pin clear of the cap, allowing the cap tobe fully depressed AND rotated through 120°, to strip the gun.

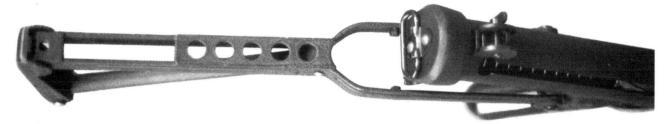

130. Top view of the strengthened, fabricated butt of the MkIII Sterling. A definite improvement over (and interchangeable with) the MkII/L2A1, but still not strong enough for the job at hand. (MoD School of Infantry, Warminster)

This modified locking lever could be used on the earlier MkII/L2A1 guns, providing a small slot was cut in the MkII return spring cap OR if a later . MkIII or Mk4 cap was fitted. Some of the return spring caps fitted to MkIII/L2A2 guns were clearly former MkII caps with the VERTICAL sling loop strap rivets drilled out, the sling loop and plate rotated through 90°, the cap re-drilled and the loop and plate re-rivetted to become HORIZONTAL. Waste not, want not, as they say!

The parts list indicates that some MkIII/L2A2 return spring caps retain the circular internal return spring centraliser retained in place by the two ling loop rivets. In later production this centraliser plate was integrally machined into the casting.

Additional Strengthening of Butt Frame

The MkIII/L2A2 butt frame was still a brazed composite part, featuring additional strengthening of the main-frame. It was stronger than the MkII/L2A1, although still not quite strong enough.

The strengthened mainframe was the only part that differed to any degree from the MkII/L2A1 butt, and both are fully interchangeable as assemblies. Many MkII/L2A1 guns were subsequently modified with this stronger butt frame (NATO part number B3/CR. 8 MA; Sterling manufacturer's number P 108/G/L).

The return spring cup was modified to aid assembly of the gun. The last coil of the INNER return spring is increased in diameter to become a spring loaded friction fit within the inside of the cup . This is not possible with the OUTER spring. As a result, assembly was difficult because the cocking handle block, inner return spring and return spring cup easily become detached from the outer return spring. A small nib was added to ensure that the last coil of the outer spring was held to the return spring cup. As the inner spring is held in place by friction, the whole return spring assembly of the outer spring, cup, inner spring and cocking handle block remains together, therefore easing assembly of the working parts.

131. Left and centre: rear views of two return spring caps: MkII Patchett (left) and MkIII/L2A2 Sterling (centre). Both contain identical parts, but the loop has been repositioned from horizontal to vertical.

Some MkIII caps are seen with the former horizontal rivets drilled out and the bracket and loop rotated through 90° and re-rivetted. A case of waste not, want not, as they say!

Right: Inside view of MkIII/L2A2 Sterling return spring cap, showing two rivets holding the sling loop bracket in place.

Some caps were machined without the internal round locator for the outer return spring. When this was the case, a separate locator was rivetted in place. (MoD Army, REME)

A Missed Opportunity: the Controversial "Block Cocking Handle"

As discussed in Chapter Five, the front of the separate firing pin was initially cut off, and the extension renamed the "Centre Pin" in the parts list. MkII/L2A1s, hybrid upgraded commercial MkII/MkIIIs and early MkIII/L2A2s retain this facility.

In later MkIIIs (and in the Mk4), the vestiges of the firing pin were removed completely, and the centre pin was renamed by the military as the "Block, Cocking Handle" (Sterling still called it the "Centre Pin"). The blind central hole in the breech block now contained a spring and plunger (interchangeable with the extractor spring and plunger).

The main function of the cocking handle block was to serve as a collar for the inner return spring and therefore centralise the return springs. However, the Canadian engineers at Long Branch did not take one bit of notice of the need for a cocking handle block in their C1 gun. With a little thought, the deletion of the separate firing pin could have included the elimination of this costly frill from the MkIII/L2A2 and Mk4/L2A3 Sterlings, saving both weight and expense. It was not beyond the wit of man, as subsequent guns proved.

Thus, two distinct cocking handle blocks may be encountered on MkIII/L2A2 guns: ex-MkII "centre pins" with shortened firing pin extensions, and the later "block, cocking handle" with the nose of the flushed-off block supported by a spring-loaded plunger mounted within the breech block.

Although the MkIII/L2A2 and Mk4/L2A3 breech blocks were given different part numbers, they are interchangeable in all but number.

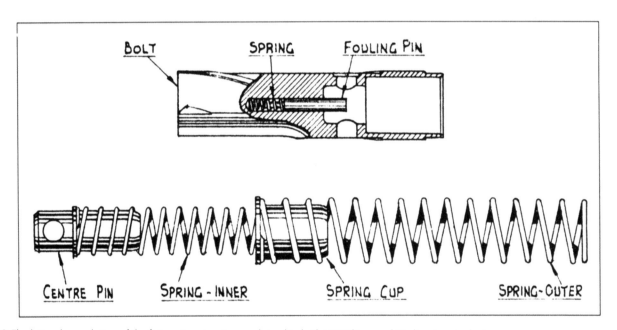

132. The latter-day evolution of the firing pin extension, explained in both UK Military and Sterling terminologies.

Above: left side view of the late MkIII and Mk4 breech block (bolt) sectioned to show block plunger (fouling pin) and spring.

Below: late MkIII and Mk4 recoil spring assembly. From left: block, cocking handle (centre pin); inner return spring; inner return spring cup; outer return spring.

The purpose of the block plunger (fouling pin) and spring (which were interchangeable with the extractor spring and plunger) was to prevent misassembly, by keeping the cocking handle from going fully home unless the cocking handle block (centre pin) was in place first.

Following the switch to the controversial "block cocking handle" the Sterling MkIII User Handbook was amended by tipping in the above illustration (over an earlier drawing of the long-obsolete single return spring).

The instructions were also amended by tipping in a hand printed, mimeographed slip, which read:

"… the spring-loaded fouling pin will prevent mis-assembly since the cocking handle cannot be inserted until this pin is pushed forward by the centre pin on the spring assembly. This ensures that the cocking handle must pass through the hole in the centre pin." (Courtesy James Alley)

Early Proofing Procedures

All SMGs were 100% checked by the Sterling Inspection Department after assembly. Those destined for British Service were proofed by the UK Military, while commercial guns were sent to the proofmaster of the London Proof House, which is an Independent Worshipful Company of Gunmakers set up by Royal charter.

Up to early MkIII production, the barrel, breech block and casing were all proofed, and this is the reason early guns show proof marks on the return spring cap locking ring at the rear of the casing as well as on the barrel and breech block.

It was quickly established that proofing the casing was not required, although the guns continued to be proofed assembled, as this was a convenient way of holding the barrel and breech block together during the proofing operation.

Getting Rid of User-Strippability

The screwdriver tip on the inner end, and the hexagonal hole in the shaft, were eliminated in the MkIII cocking handle. At the same time, the pistol grip retaining screw with the Allen key extension was deleted, and replaced with a standard 0 BA hexagonal recessed-headed Allen bolt, that was to be interchangeable with the two barrel retaining screws. This did away with the two ingenious tools built into the MkII/L2A1.

As result of this change in the MkIII/L2A2 pistol grip screw, the screw hole in the base of the MkIII/L2A2 plastic pistol grip has a smaller diameter. The MkII/L2A1 grip will fit a MkIII/L2A2 gun, but not vice versa.

As mentioned, however laudable the idea of the user being able to fully strip his gun in the field, in practice it inevitably meant that parts got lost and then the guns failed to operate. These modifications to the MkIII/L2A2 ensured that henceforth, userstripping the gun meant just FIELD STRIPPING and no more.

In conjunction with these two modifications, the magazine catch screw was recessed at the end to allow Armourers to stake the hollowed end, thereby fully securing the magazine catch, screw and spring, as well as the ejector, to the gun.

The Problematic Early Ejector Assembly Soldiers On

Like the MkII/L2A1, the MkIII/L2A2 ejector was still retained in place by the button-headed bolt with its tenuous thread within the anti-rotation block. The threaded portion of the block was really insufficient, and the threads could strip quite easily. Once this thread had stripped, it could not be re-welded due to the fact that the housing itself was only brazed to the casing.

New Zealand Armourers with whom Peter Laidler served evolved a simple repair for this problem. This entailed filing or machining the anti-rotation plate to the thickness of the later Mk4/L2A3 plate, then simply using the tvfic4/L2A3 ejector and shouldered-stepped Allen screw.

One other method was to simply eliminate the ejector screw, leaving the ejector locked in position by the magazine catch screw.

The First Purpose-Built Sterling Barrels

As further discussed in Chapter Seven, in the words of David Howroyd, "until midway through MkIII/L2A2 production the Sterling Company were using the approximately 4,000 production Lanchester barrels that remained in stock after Lanchester production ceased."

Barrels specially manufactured by (and for) Sterling do not have the small recess on the top of the rear locating flange. Also the front flange of the MkIII/L2A2 production barrel was strengthened by making it thicker, thus giving the barrel retaining screws more engagement and thereby making the barrel more secure. The MkIII/L2A2 barrel can be identified by the Ministry of Supply reference number CR 1113 stamped on the front flange.

Flange Modifications

There was a period of head-scratching by the Sterling engineers after one particular batch of guns fitted with early, purpose-built barrels failed to zero. On investigation, it was discovered that some residual brass had seeped inside the edges of the front barrel support during the induction brazing of that component to the casing.

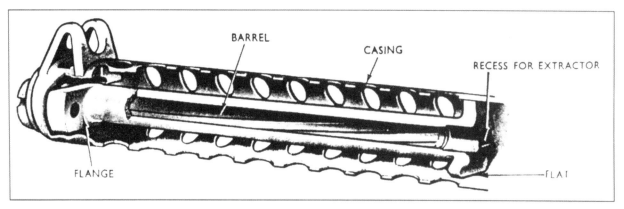

133. Diagrammatic right side view of the Sterling-made barrel, shown installed in the casing and partially cut away. Note the thicker front flange.

   The front flange was purposely offset more to the bottom than the top, to ensure fool-proof assembly and also to ensure the recess for the extractor was perfectly aligned with the extractor in the breech block.

   The flat shown at the bottom of the breech end of the barrel was to allow dirt, sand and other debris, dislodged by the helical ribs of the breech block, to be pushed into the front casing and cleared. (MoD Army, REME)

Subsequently, the front top edge of the front barrel flange was chamfered to clear excess braze that might weep into the nose cap during the induction brazing process (and which was impossible to remove!).

Standardising the Sten/Lanchester Chamber

At the same time the barrel chamber dimensions were finalised and the Sten/Lanchester form was standardised.

Until 1954, Sterling sub-machine gun production was undertaken alongside many other items being manufactured at the Sterling factory. Only in 1954 did David Howroyd move production into a separate gun-shop, set up to concentrate exclusively on the manufacture of the MkIII/L2A2.

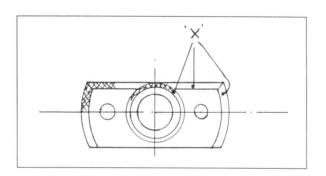

134. Front view of Sterling-made barrel. showing front flange offset top to bottom to prevent incorrect assembly. The chamfers 'X', shown partially cross-hatched, were added after inital production, to clear any residual brass that might have wept into the front barrel support during induction brazing of the casing. (Drawing by Peter Laidler)

135. A view, taken from Rainham Road South, Dagenham, of one of the original circa-1920s buildings on the substantial Sterling site. During WWII Sterling manufactured Sten gun magazines, Sterling bomb slips for the Sterling bomber, and other products in this low, single-storey building. When James Edmiston purchased the Sterling Armament Company in 1972, David Howroyd moved all production of the Mk4 Sterling back into this building, where it was to remain until everything was sold to British Aerospace in 1989. ·

   Note the sign (centre), "Sterling Works". (Courtesy David Howroyd)

The L2A2: History and Markings

A total of 2,879 MkIII Sterling sub-machine guns were contracted for on 10 December, 1954, and first supplied to the Ministry of Defence on 19th December,1954.In 1955 the MkIII was adopted as the L2A2, an improvement over the L2A1. In the UK Military Order of Battle, it was allocated a Vocabulary of Army Ordnance Stores reference number of B3/ CR 54 GA. MkIII Sterlings designated L2A2 for UK Military issue were given the distinctive new serial number prefix 'US55A' (1955 being the only year of their manufacture), with serial numbers running from US55A 1 to US55A 2879. UK Military L2A2s were marked:

GUN

SUB-MACHINE

9mm L2A2

No. US55A – (number 1501 examined in detail)

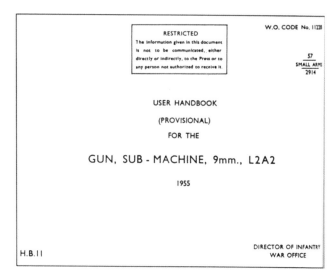

137. The cover/title page of the 1955 MoD Provisional User Handbook for the "Gun, Sub-Machine, 9mm, L2A2". (Courtesy MoD Pattern Room, Nottingham)

136. Top closeup view of magazine housing of UK Military L2A2, showing markings. (MoD Pattern Room collection)

Officially, the MkIII/L2A2 had a UK Military service life of only a very few months before the announcement came in. September, 1955 of the adoption of the Mk4 as the general–issue L2A3.

The L2A2 was declared obsolescent in March, 1956 due to the anticipated arrival in large numbers of the L2A3, the design of which was then being "perfected" at ROF Fazakerley. This meant that L2A2s were still authorised for use until individually worn out and declared 'ZF (condemned), or until all L2A2 spares ran out.

The L2A2s in British Service were not declared obsolete until 1959, at which time all stocks were (supposed to have been) withdrawn.

Marketing the Commercial MkIII

The Sterling MkIII was also available commercially, to approved governments and their agents.

Introduction of the MkIII saw a continuation of the later MkII 'KR' serial number range, using the initials of Sterling's Managing Director, Kenton Redgrave. Commercial MkIII Sterlings were marked:

STERLING
S.M.G.
9mm MkIII
No. KR – (number 4145 examined)

Commercial MkIII Serial Number Ranges

As noted, the last commercial MkII was produced on 29 March, 1955, numbered KR 2730. Officially, the commercial MkIII range ran as follows:

138. Top closeup view of a commercial MkIII Sterling magazine housing showing rolled markings and heavily pantographed serial number (KR 4145), the latter making it difficult to grind out a number or engrave another over top.

From the moment the serial number was applied, the gun became a classified and strictly controlled item. Other markings were rolled on, including the Patchett/Sterling patent numbers underneath the magazine housing. (Courtesy Roy Wade)

Serial Number	Date of Manufacture
KR 2731	8 April, 1955
KR 3000	July, 1955
KR3500	November, 1955
KR4000	February, 1955
KR 4301 (the last MkIII)	13 June, 1956

The last MkIII, no KR 4301, was sold as part of a batch to Hong Kong in November, 1956.

MkIII Sterling Users

User countries of the commercial MkIII Sterling include Bahrain, Bermuda, Botswana, Brazil, Burma, Cyprus, Cuba, Egypt, France, Germany, Hong Kong, Iraq, Israel, Jordan, Kenya, Lebanon, Lesotho, Libya, Malaya, Nicaragua, Qatar, Rhodesia, Singapore, South Africa, Sudan, Sweden, Tripolitania, Uganda, USA and Venezuela.

Most were obviously happy with the product as, with the exception of Bermuda, Brazil, Egypt, Israel, Nicaragua, the USA and Venezuela, all went on to buy large quantities of the later Mk4. Canada and New Zealand also had small quantities of this gun, probably supplied by the UK Government for evaluation purposes. ·

139. Cover/title page of the commercial User Handbook produced by Sterling to support the MkIII. Issued one per gun.

This was the first such Handbook (approx 8" wide × 5½" high). This style and format stayed the course and remained in use throughout Sterling production.

For many years, users of MkII and MkIII guns obtained their replacement spares through the Sterling Company or the Crown Agents. In the later years, as supplies of the early butt assemblies and ejectors became scarce (most of the remainder of the components being generally interchangeable), the Sterling company would offer to buy back the obsolescent guns AT THE PURCHASE PRICE, in a part exchange for brand-new Mk4 guns. There were no takers.

Summing Up the MkIII

Mostly Improvements, but One Backward Step

The MkIII Sterling was basically a series of retrofittable improvements over the MkII. In fact, all the MkIII modifications could quite easily be, and often were, incorporated into the MkII/L2A1s that were by this time in limited but worldwide service.

However, there was one retrograde 'improvement' incorporated into certain MkIIIs. As mentioned in the previous chapter, certain later MkIIs had been fitted with small and ineffective foresight protectors, housing one of eight adjustable No4 rifle-style foresight blades. Use of these was carried over into some MkIII guns. The 'No4 rifle' foresight system was NOT a good idea, and soon showed itself to be weak and ineffective. Fortunately, common sense prevailed, and this modification was short-lived on the MkIII, although those customers unfortunate enough to have purchased guns so equipped soon demanded a return to the tough and easily repaired MkII foresight protectors.

MkIII/L2A2 Variants

We cannot list *every* variant of the MkIII gun, but here is an abridged list:

- fabricated/folded foresight protectors with Sterling foresight, or small rounded foresight protectors with No4 rifle-type foresight
- breech block with empty hole in rear to accept "centre pin" extension, or breech block with spring and plunger in rear with flushed-off "cocking handle block"
- ex-Lanchester barrels with thin flange and locating recess, or Sterling-manufactured barrels marked CR 1113
- unmodified return spring cup which allows springs to separate,.or later cup with nib
- modified ex-MkII return spring cap (with rivet holes partially showing) or MkIII/L2A2 cap.

The L2A2 Soldiers On (and On ...)

Although the MkIII/L2A2 SMG was declared obsolete in 1959 and quickly phased out of service, some soldiered on, unseen. In 1994, when the new UK Military SA80/L85A1 rifle had replaced both the L1A1 rifle AND the L2A3 sub-machine gun in Military service, and all remaining Sterling guns had supposedly been withdrawn, TEN mint and eminently serviceable L2A2 guns were discovered in service with a rear echelon unit based near Winchester, 40 years after they had been introduced. A big hand for George Patchett and the engineers at Dagenham!

140. Left side closeup of a MkIII Sterling fitted with alternative pattern foresight protectors, designed to accept one of eight incrementally sized No4 rifle-type foresight blades. The adjustable-for-height foresight blade was introduced shortly afterwards, making the use of the widely available No4 rifle blades redundant. (MoD School of Infantry, Warminster)

141. Range-testing the MkIII Sterling: Major Robert Turp supervises Mrs Tyrell, a machine shop operator (centre, kneeling) and Miss Jesse Butts, a member of the office staff (right) test-firing early MkIII Sterling SMGs. (Note the rounded foresight protectors).

Captured by a remote camera, this test was to illustrate that the gun has no appreciable recoil, and could easily be handled and fired by a woman or man of small stature. The later Police Carbine, manufactured with civilian use in mind, was used by many women in areas of civil unrest, such as Malaya, Kenya and Rhodesia.

Note the ejected shell cases: one from Miss Butts' gun is passing her right lapel, and one from Mrs Tyrill's gun is just passing Major Turp's left lapel, below his British Legion pin. None of the participants is wearing ear protection, as such devices were considered mere fripperies until about 1967 .

Miss Butts' gun is smoking well … savour the moment, ladies! (Courtesy David Howroyd)

Towards the Mk4

It is true to say that the MkIII gun was used as a yardstick upon which to base the next gun, which became the Mk4/L2A3. Many tests were carried out on the MkIII/L2A2 by the Chief Inspector of Armaments and his staff at Enfield.

In April, 1955 tests were carried out to ascertain the strength of the punched and folded foresight

protectors. Guns were dropped from increasing heights onto a concrete slab and the distortion of the protectors measured. Each time the gun was dropped it was range tested. Each time the zero was

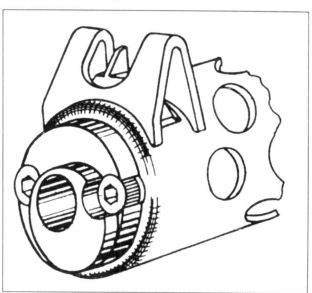

142 (right). Another hand-tipped-in illustration added to the Sterling MkIII User Handbook, illustrates the later type of 'dog-legged' stamped foresight protectors, with the notice:

Foresight (see para 9.11 and Section 4):

The weapon is now fitted with the L2A2 type foresight and guard as illustrated. This is different in design but the general instructions in Section 4 apply, except that the seven sizes of foresight blades are available instead of three, thereby avoiding the necessity of using the No4 rifle foresight blades for the extremes … (Courtesy James Alley)

maintained and the foresight was protected. Once the drop-height reached 4', the tests were abandoned.

In March, 1956 the MkIII/L2A2 gun was used for trials into the suitability of using the then-current adjustable foresight. The trials were a success and the adjustable foresight became standard on the Mk4/L2A3 gun. The same adjustable foresight can be used on the Lanchester and MkII Patchett.

Interchangeability: MkIII/L2A2 with the Mk4/L2A3

As with the MkII, the parts list for the MkIII/L2A2 was not illustrated. We have therefore inserted a number immediately to the left of the 'QTY' (quantity per gun) column. This number illustrates the nearest equivalent part in the Mk4/L2A3 illustrated parts list. Therefore a MkIII/L2A2 part, suffixed with 'T 22' will indicate part number 22 in the Mk4/L2A3 trigger mechanism section. 'C' will indicate the casing, and 'B' will indicate the butt section.

All the components of the later Mk4/L2A3 will fit the MkIII/L2A2, with the following exceptions:

- barrel: Mk4/L2A3 barrels will fit PROVIDING the front barrel screw holes in the MkIII casing are reamed out to accept ¼" UNIFIED (UNF) Allen bolt shank diameters. ¼" UNF Allen bolts are used, because the Mk4/L2A3 barrel is threaded for this size.
- butt assembly, which was geometrically re-designed on Mk4/L2A3.
- ejector, although the Mk4/L2A3 ejector could be filed to fit (or the MkIII/L2A2 casing could be filed to take the better Mk4/L2A3 ejector).
- trigger parts, but Mk4/L2A3 can be fitted as a COMPLETE ASSEMBLY to MkIII/L2A2 guns. Modify MkIII/L2A2 pistol grip to clear front of trigger mechanism side frames, or fit Mk4/L2A3 grip as well.

Production of MkIII spares ended with production of the last MkIII gun in June, 1956, and further spares for earlier guns were supplied from Mk4 stock. The only exception to this was a small run of replacement MkIII stocks, made up to satisfy customers in 1964-1965.

The authors enlisted the aid of computer drawing facilities to investigate whether it would be possible to retro-modify a currently available Mk4/L2A3 butt assembly to MkIII/L2A2 specification. Due to the total geometrical and physical redesign, it was not considered possible. *C'est la vie.*

Parts List for Gun, Sub-Machine, 9mm, L2A2

As noted, a combined Parts List for the L2A1 and L2A2 SMGs was issued by the War Office's Director of Ordnance Services in 1956. The L2A1 Parts List is included in Chapter Five.

Neither of these early military Parts Lists was illustrated, and so we have again inserted a column after the 'Qty' (quantity per gun) column, which references the nearest equivalent part in the Mk4/L2A3 illustrated Parts List (Chapter Seven).

Catalogue No	Designation	Qty	Mk4/l2A3 Equiv
CR 54 GA	Gun, Sub-Machine, 9mm, L2A2	1	C 8
CR 1012	Backsight	1	C 15
CR 1113	Barrel	1	C 16
CR 125 SA	Block, breech	1	C 17
CR 1013	Block	1	C 18
CR 1117	Extractor	1	C 19
CR 868	Pin, extractor	1	C 21

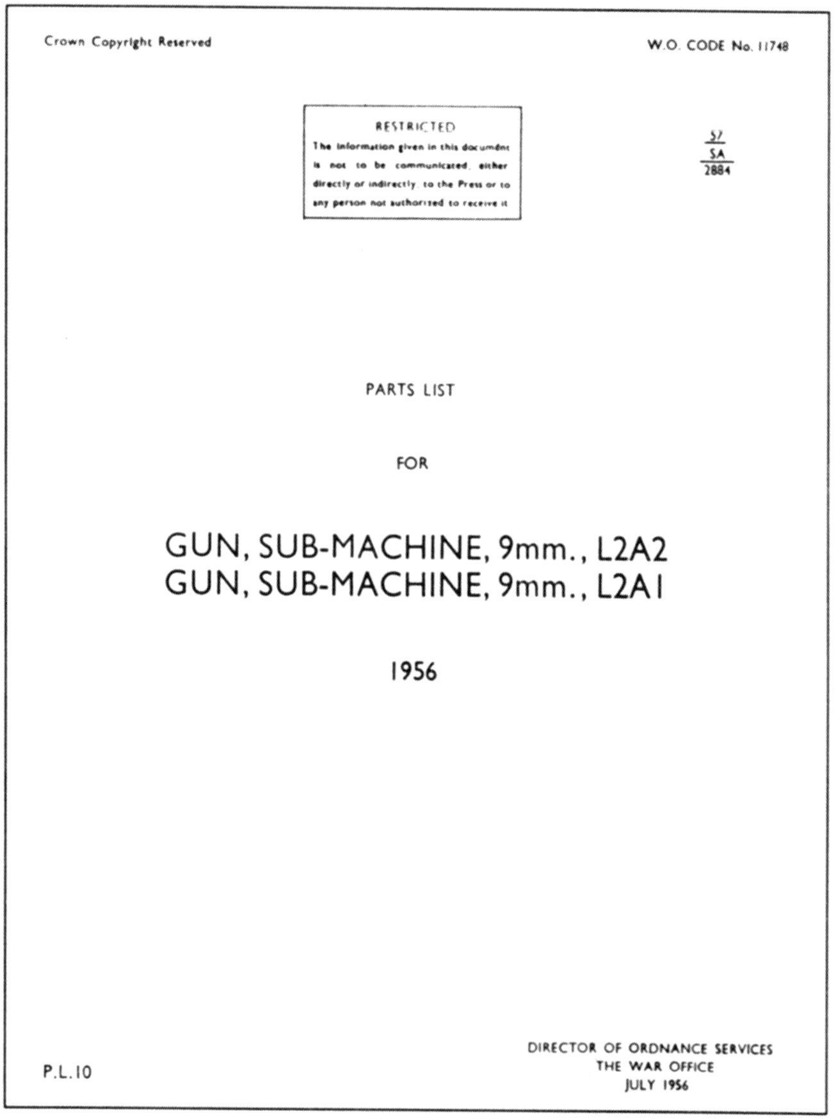
Crown Copyright Reserved

W.O. CODE No. 11748

RESTRICTED
The information given in this document is not to be communicated, either directly or indirectly, to the Press or to any person not authorised to receive it

57
SA
2884

PARTS LIST

FOR

GUN, SUB-MACHINE, 9mm., L2A2
GUN, SUB-MACHINE, 9mm., L2A1

1956

P.L.10

DIRECTOR OF ORDNANCE SERVICES
THE WAR OFFICE
JULY 1956

143. The cover/title page of the combined War Office Parts List for the "Gun, Sub-Machine, 9mm, L2A2" and "Gun, Sub-Machine, 9mm, L2A1", first produced in 1956.

The L2A1 Parts List appears at the end of Chapter Five. (MoD Army, REME)

Catalogue No	Designation	Qty	Mk4/12A3 Equiv
CR 1014	Plunger, block	1	C 21
CR 870	Plunger, extractor	1	C 20
CR 871	Spring, extractor plunger	1	C 20
CR 1015	Spring, block, plunger	1	C 20
CR 892	Bush, retaining, backsight lever	1	C 6
CR 8 MA	Butt, assembly	1	B 1
CR 876	Bush	1	–
CR 113 SA	Catch, butt	1	B 8
CR 877	Catch	1	B 9
CR 878	Rivet	1	B 11
CR 879	Spring	1	B 10
CR 880	Pin, catch, butt	1	–
CR 881	Pin, tube, butt	1	–
CR 882	Pin, butt plate and tube	1	B 14 – 17

Catalogue No	Designation	Qty	Mk4/12A3 Equiv
CR 1016	Plate, butt, rear	1	B 7
CR 1034	Plate, butt, side	1	–
CR 110 A	Tube, butt, assembly	1	B 2
CR 1017	Catch	1	B 6
CR 887	Pin, catch	1	B 5
CR 889	Spring	1	B 4
CR 126 SA	Tube, butt	1	B 2 – 3
CR 886	Pin, spring, retaining ring	1	–
CR 888	Ring, retaining, spring	1	–
CR 1019	Tube	1	–
CR 891	Washer, butt plate and tube pin	2	–
CR 127 SA	Cap, return spring	1	C 27
CR 1020	Cap	1	C 27
CR 1000	Locator, outer return spring	1	–
CR 1001	Plate, swivel	1	–
CR 875	Swivel, sling	1	–
	OR		
CR 139 SA	Cap, return spring	1	C 27
CR 1119	Cap	1	–
CR 1001	Plate, swivel	1	–
CR 875	Swivel, sling	1	–
CR 1136	Casing	1	C 3 – 4
CR 902	Catch, magazine	1	C 31
CR 903	Cup, inner return spring	1	C 25
CR 904	Ejector	1	C 30
CR 972	Foresight, 0.530	1	C 35
CR 973	Foresight, 0.550	1	C 35
CR 907	Foresight, 0.570	1	C 35
CR 906	Foresight, 0.590	1	C 35
CR 905	Foresight, 0.610	1	C 35
CR 974	Foresight, 0.630	1	C 35
CR 975	Foresight, 0.650	1	C 35
CR 1025	Grip	1	T 32
CR 1026	Handle, cocking	1	C 28
CR 1027	Lever, backsight	1	–
CR 128 SA	Lever, locking, return spring cap	1	C 10
CR 1028	Lever	1	C 11
CR 1029	Pin	1	C 12
CR 879	Spring	1	C 13
CR 1002	Pin, axis, return spring cap lever	1	C 14
CR 1030	Pin, centre	1	C 23
CR 911	Pin, locating, trigger assembly	1	T 33
CR 1032	Pin, locking, butt retaining pin	2	B 19
CR 899	Pin, retaining, butt	2	B 18

Catalogue No	Designation	Qty	Mk4/l2A3 Equiv
CR 1035	Screw, catch, magazine	1	C 32
CR 915	Screw, ejector	1	–
5305-417807	Screw, set, BA, steel, hex socket, cup point,		
	zinc coated No 0 × ¾	3	C 39
CR 1033	Spring, backsight	1	C 7
CR 916	Spring, catch, magazine	1	C 32
CR 901	Spring, locating pin	1	–
CR 917	Spring, return, inner	1	C 24
CR 918	Spring, return, outer	1	C 26
CR 102 A	Trigger assembly	1	–
CR 116 A	Cradle, sear	1	T 15
CR 919	Guide, spring, main	1	T 18
CR 920	Pin, distance, side plates	3	T 17
CR 921	Plate, side	2	T 16
CR 922	Roller	1	T 19
CR 117 A	Guard, trigger	1	T 30
CR 923	Block, spring, main	1	T 14
CR 924	Block, thrust	1	T 4
CR 925	Guard	1	T 11 – 12
CR 1003	Lever, change, part 1	1	T 6
	OR		
CR 926	Lever, change, part 1	1	T 6
CR 927	Lever, change, part 2	1	T 8
CR 928	Pin, axis, spring detent	1	T 5
CR 960	Pin, detent	1	T 9
CR 929	Pin, stop, part 2 change lever	2	T 13
CR 970	Pin, thrust	1	–
CR 930	Plate, side	2	T 3
CR 931	Rivet, plate, side	3	T 5
CR 932	Spring, pin, detent	1	T 10
CR 933	Lever, tripping	1	T 20
CR 934	Pin, sear and trigger	2	T 23
CR 935	Pin, tripping lever	1	T 21
CR 936	Plunger, sear and trigger	1	T 25
CR 937	Sear	1	T 22
CR 939	Spring, sear cradle	1	T 26
CR 938	Spring, sear and trigger	2	T 24
CR 940	Trigger	1	T 27 – 28

Chapter Seven

The Crown Jewel

Sterling Sub-Machine Gun, 9mm, Mk4 (Gun, Sub-Machine, 9mm L2A3) and Sterling 'Police Carbine' 9mm Mk4

Date adopted by UK Military:		September, 1955
Date introduced:		16th July, 1956
Date production ceased:	Fazakerley:	October, 1959
	Sterling:	1988
Date obsoleted in UK Military:		1994
Quantities manufactured:	Sterling 'KR' and 'S':	195,644
	Sterling 'US':	15,250 (total)
	Fazakerley 'UF':	163,475 (total)
Unit price at 31-1-84:		£256.00

A General-Issue Sterling at Last

The commercial Sterling Mk4 was adopted by the UK Military as the L2A3, and so we will generally refer to it as the Mk4/L2A3.

The signing of the British contract for the Mk.4/L2A3 guns in September, 1955 was marked by a cocktail party on 13 October, 1955 at the Savoy Hotel in London, which was attended by 54 members of the Sterling staff and other dignitaries.

However, the Military had to wait until 1956 before the first few hundred Sterling-made Mk4/L2A3s were hastily diverted and issued to paratroopers bound for Suez (more below), and indeed until 1957 before substantial deliveries were made to UK forces.

The introduction of the Mk4 was an important event. Unlike the earlier MkII/L2A1s, hybrid MkII/MkIIIs and MkIII/L2A2s, which had been ordered

144. Right side view of the Mk4/L2A3 Sterling, with sling and bayonet fitted. This is a commercial gun (fig 175) with UK Military-style matt finish. Form certainly follows function in this excellent piece of kit! (Peter Laidler collection)

145. Left side view of a typical UK Military matt-finish L2A3, with butt folded.
First adopted in 1955, the superb Mk4/L2A3 served the British Military well for 40 years, until 1994. (MoD Army, REME)

in limited numbers only, the Mk4 Sterling was to be Britain's new *general-issue* sub-machine gun, destined to completely supplant the Mk2 and Mk5 Sten throughout the British Army and Royal Air Force, and, eventually, to replace the Lanchester in the Royal Navy.

Consequently, it would be needed in large numbers, not only within the UK Military, but overseas as well. A LOT of other nations were still equipped with Stens, which would also soon need replacing.

The Mk4/L2A3 Sterling was issued with the NATO part number of B3 (indicating a sub-machine gun) 1005-99-960-0029 following from the Sterling/Ministry of Supply manufacturers' drawing number B3/CR 53 GA. It was approved for production in May, 1955 but Sterling production did not commence until June, 1956.

By this time, earlier Marks of the Sterling were in worldwide service with the British and other Allied armies, although they were still relatively few in number. The British Armies were at that time operating in every type of terrain known to man, and Archive reports from the period state that the MkII/L2A1 and MkIII/L2A2 guns were behaving admirably. The reports do say that there were doubts about the strength of the butt, but that problem was well in hand with the Mk4.

STERLING

STERLING ENGINEERING COMPANY, LIMITED, have been designing and developing automatic small-arms since 1939, when their first success, the LANCHESTER Sub-Machine Gun, was accepted and used by the Royal Navy.

To meet the need for a lighter weapon for use by the Commandos and the Airborne and Parachute troops, the Company, in 1942, began to develop the present weapon, and a few early models were brought into service just before the end of World War II. Since the war the Company have further developed and improved their Sub-Machine Gun to the requirement of a General Staff specification.

The final model—the STERLING SUB-MACHINE GUN 9-mm.—described overleaf, has been adopted by H.M. Government as a supplementary weapon to the F.N. Rifle, and reflects the achievement of the Company's team of skilled engineers and technicians.

STERLING ENGINEERING COMPANY LIMITED, Sterling Works, Dagenham, Essex, England.

Telephone : Dominion 4545/55.   Telegrams : Sterling Dagenham.

146. The proud announcement by the Sterling Works in Dagenham that their "final model", the "Sterling Sub-Machine Gun 9mm", had been "adopted by HM Government as a supplementary weapon to the FN Rifle". Little did Sterling know at the time that they would only get to make 14% of the total UK Military order! (Courtesy David Howroyd)

New Mk4 Sterlings Help "De-Nationalise" Suez

As noted, production of the Sterling Mk4/L2A3 guns commenced in mid-1956, just as the War Office decided to get these new Mk4/L2A3 guns quickly into the hands of paratroopers who with other forces were about to invade Egypt in order to de-nationalise the Suez Canal, unthoughtfully nationalised by Colonel Nasser.

The Sterling company released several thousand Mk4/L2A3s held in bond (originally bound for Nepal) and some actually did make it to Suez. Ironically, however, most of the paratroopers who flew in from Cyprus went in armed with Mk5 Stens, only to find some of the Egyptian Army using MkIII/L2A2 and early Mk4/L2A3 Sterlings, originally supplied to Iraq-the rascals!

MoD policy was that overseas orders were to be manufactured first, in order to test the quality of the tooling. Iraq had been the first major buyer of the Mk4/L2A3, and was already partially equipped. Iraq purchased a total of 13,241 of this Mark between 1956 and 1963, not to mention the 70 MkIIIs purchased in 1955.

As noted, first substantial deliveries to UK forces were not made until 1957.

Meeting the Worldwide Demand

Given that large orders were coming in thick and fast, an internal memo from Kenton Redgrave dated 31st October, 1956 required that the production of Mk4/L2A3 guns at Sterling had to be 250 guns per week, rising to 300 when possible, with the exception of Christmas week. Magazines had to be produced at a rate of 2,500 per week, rising to 3,000 when possible.

Spare parts, the sale of which formed a substantial portion of the company's income, had to be made in sufficient quantity to ensure they were ready at the same time as completion of the substantial (Iraqi) orders in hand.

Bayonet production was completed mainly in Sheffield, but sufficient castings (supplied by Sterling to Hopkinson, the manufacturer) were to be made available. A figure of 1,000 castings a week was suggested.

A Fazakerley in the Ointment

Introducing the Ministry of Supply "X9E1"

While it had been known for some time that an improved version of the MkIII Sterling would be the next general-issue SMG, it was not so well known that the British Government had no intention of buying all these new sub-machine guns from Sterling. In fact, the Ministry of Supply had already decided that, once a design was finalised and adopted, the lion's share of the manufacturing would be done by the Royal Ordnance Factory at Fazakerley (known to Armourers as ROF 6) in Liverpool.

As evidenced in the *Report of the Director-General of Ordnance Factories for the Year Ended 31 March, 1954*, this decision had obviously been taken some time ago:

> *[ROF] Fazakerley ... carried out preparatory work in aid of the production of the new L2A1 Carbine ...*
>
> *... Hence each factory was engaged simultaneously upon two problems, each of considerable magnitude. The maintenance of a strict schedule of deliveries*

> *of their normal production, and the putting into production new designs and in some cases new services ... during the year extensive preparatory work was undertaken to put ... into production in the near future [the] Machine Carbine ...*

At Fazakerley, the resulting gun was· codenamed the X9E1. It was decided that the X9E1 (later L2A3) and the Sterling Mk4 specifications would be identical, as the interchangeability of components was essential.

By 1955 engineers at the UK Ministry of Supply had formulated a stronger folding butt. This involved a fundamental geometrical redesign of the butt members, and a relocation of the butt trunnions on the casing, which is why Mk4 and later butts are not interchangeable with earlier Marks of Sterlings. However, the rest of the X9E1 was an exact copy of the new 9mm Sterling Mk4.

At first, Sterling were unaware that the MoS intended to manufacture the new L2A3 at its own facility. To keep the project quiet, Fazakerley tool room guns were called, and marked, "Pioneer".

A major departure from the normal commercial nature of business between the Sterling company and the British Government came when it was announced that ROF Fazakerley were to make 90% of the British Government L2A3s, under a 'licence' agreed between the Ministry of Supply and, well; whoever it was, it certainly wasn't Sterling.

The reason given for Fazakerley manufacture, quoted by the UK Ministry of Supply, was that as a small company, Sterling would be unable to supply the substantial UK Military order in the necessary three year rearmament period allotted under the Government's Rearmament Programme. As Ministry officials later explained to the High Court, the TOTAL UK Military production order had to be completed by October, 1959.

Fazakerley Steals a March: the X9E1 "Pioneer" in Pre-Production

The Report of the Director-General of Ordnance Factories for the Year Ended 31 March, 1955 recorded:

> *... A great deal of preparatory work has been done in the group in connection with the production of the X9E1 (Patchett) Carbine ... Production of the new Carbine is due to start at Fazakerley this year ...*
>
> *... Whole sections of Fazakerley were completely replanned for the production of the Patchett Carbine and the purchase of new machine tools, some for the introduction of novel and unusual methods of manufacture, proceeded apace. Most satisfactory progress was made toward the aim of producing large quantities of Carbines in the coming year.*

Ironically, production at Fazakerley actually commenced BEFORE production at Sterling, and although reports dated May, 1955 mention this, they do state that this is PROPOSED X9E1 production. The first pre-production guns made at Fazakerley were marked 'PIONEER' on the magazine housing.

One particular 'PIONEER'-marked gun examined carries no proof or other markings. This gun also has the magazine housing butt-brazed to the casing Sterling-fashion, unlike production Fazakerley guns, which were flange-brazed.

147. Top closeup view of the first Fazakerly "Pioneer". ROF production actually began a month or so ahead of Sterling, and to conceal that fact, the first guns were marked as shown rather than with the military designation "X9EI".
On these initial guns the magazine housings were buttbrazed to the casings, but for series manufacture a concession was granted which allowed Fazakerley to flange-braze the housing. In all other respects (except for markings), Fazakerley- and Sterling-made guns were identical. (MoD Pattern Room collection)

Problems with Fazakerley Production: Hurry Up and Wait

Naturally, the Chief Inspector of Armaments was eager to test the quality of Fazakerley production and in May, 1955, ordered that six guns from the first production run of 200 be supplied for examination and testing. It was to be a long wait.

Due to severe production difficulties, discussed below by David Howroyd, he had to wait until August, 1956 before six production guns were available, and only two of these came from the first 200! Guns tested between 24 August and 18 October, 1956 were UF56A-16, -132, -277, -549, -677 and -832.

The *Report of the Director-General of Ordnance Factories for the Year Ended 31 March, 1956* recorded that "Fazakerley made its first issues of the L2A3 (Patchett) carbine", but admitted,

> *... although success was not achieved in producing the new Patchett Carbine in the numbers originally promised it is pleasing to record that the first issue of weapons to the Services was made during the year.*

Heat Distortion: Fazakerley Ruins 7,000 Casings

Wasted body casings due to heat distortion were a real problem at Fazakerley. As further discussed by David Howroyd later in this chapter, Fazakerley ruined 7,000 L2A3 casings due to warpage alone in three years of their manufacturing programme. These were sent to RSAF Enfield for possible rectification, who turned to Sterling for assistance!

In contrast, Sterling had been dealing with heat distortion in perforated drawn steel tube casings since 1942. In David Howroyd's words, Sterling's Mk4 casing rejects due to heat warpage totalled "just the under 300 in 32 years".

Interchangeability Tests of Sterling and Fazakerley Production

In November, 1956, six Fazakerley and six Sterling Mk4s were taken at random from stock to test the interchangeability of component parts of the guns AND parts produced as spares. These guru:, included UF56-A 5851 and-1645 plus US56-A 12 and-13.

Other guns used were simply referred to by code numbers. These tests proved that parts switched between the Fazakerley and Sterling guns interchanged and functioned correctly.

Also during November 1956, the Chief Inspector of Armaments expressed great concern over production problems with Fazakerley guns, stating that:

> *... to date, there have been 4 (different) major problems with the ovality of Fazakerley guns, each one of which has required a relaxation in the inspection criteria.*

Testing the Sterling Mk4

Sterling were only required to supply three guns for examination and testing. These were supplied on 22nd January, 1957 and were numbered US56-A 2, –A4 and-A5.

Describing the Mk4/L2A3

The Mk4 gun evolved through the Sterling Engineering Company's striving for improvements and the worldwide search for reliability–and sales of course! Many of these latter improvements, some major and some minor, were due to the manufacturers listening to those users who were equipped with the earlier Marks of guns. Apart from some minor machining differences, such as patterns of knurling on the change lever (or safety catch) and the magazine catch button, the interchangeability of components between the Fazakerley and Sterling Mk4/L2A3s held good throughout production.

148. Top view of the magazine housing of the very FIRST Mk4 Sterling, no KR 5001, showing markings.

The Sterling Mk4 had the military designation 'L2A3' added in parentheses, to indicate that the Mk4 Sterling was in fact identical to the UK Military gun. (MoD Pattern Room collection)

Component Parts of the Mk4/L2A3 Casing Assembly

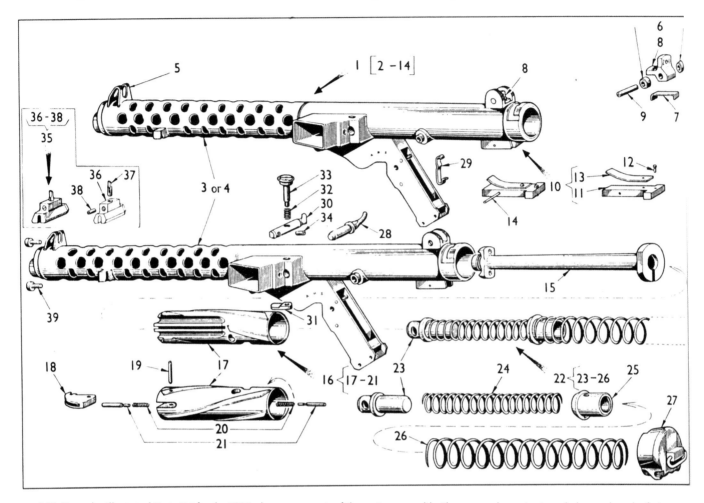

149. From the Illustrated Parts List for the L2A3, the components of the casing assembly. The nomenclature is given, below and on the facing page.

Item	NSN	Item Name and Description	Part No/Dwg No	No Off
1	1005-99-960-0029	Submachine Gun, 9 millimeter, L2A3	CR 53 GA	1
2	1005-99-960-0033	Casing Assembly	CR 113 A	1
3	1005-99-960-2170	Casing, submachine gun	CR 1077	1
		OR		
4	1005-99-960-2258	Casing, submachine gun	CR 1184	1
5	1005-99-960-8557	Guard, foresight	WP 8158	1
6	1005-99-960-2169	Bearing, rear sight	CR 1075	2
7	1005-99-960-2175	Spring, rear sight	CR 1080	1
8	1005-99-960-2168	Sight, rear	CR 1081	1
9	1005-99-960-2257	Pin, axis, backsight	CR 1182	1
10	1005-99-960-0034	Lever, locking, return spring cup	CR 135 SA	1
11	1005-99-960-2171	Lever	CR 1089	1
12	1005-99-960-2172	Pin, locating	CR 1090	1
13	1005-99-960-2252	Spring, locking lever	CR 1177	1

Item	NSN	Item Name and Description	Part No/Dwg No	No Off
14	5315-99-942-3915	Pin, grooved, headless, steel, phosphate coated, 3/32 in nom dia, 3/8 in nom lg	James Mills Ltd, GP 5	1
15	1005-99-960-2485	Barrel, submachine gun	CR 1207	1
16	1005-99-960-0030	Breechblock	CR 136 SA	1
17	1005-99-960-2153	Block	CR 1093	1
18	1005-99-960-2154	Extractor, small arms cartridge	CR 1094	1
19	1005-99-960-2155	Pin, extractor	CR 1p95	1
20	1005-99-960-2240	Spring, helical, compression	CR 1164	2
21	1005-99-960-2239	Plunger, extractor and block	CR 1163	2
22	1005-99-960-0035	Main spring assembly	CR 137 SA	1
23	1005-99-960-2186	Block, handle, cocking	CR 1100	1
24	1005-99-960-2188	Spring, helical, compression	CR 1102	1
25	1005-99-960-2187	Cup, main spring assembly	CR 1101	1n
26	1005-99-960-2189	Spring, helical, compression	CR 1103	1
27	1005-99-960-2116	Cap, main spring assembly	CR 1204	1
28	1005-99-960-2179	Handle, cocking	CR 1073	1
29	1005-99-960-2082	Spring, locking	CR 1202	1
30	1005-99-960-2177	Ejector, small arms cartridge	CR 1105	1
31	1005-99-960-2176	Catch, magazine	CR 1109	1
32	1005-99-960-2184	Spring, helical, compression	CR 1111	1
33	1005-99-960-2183	Screw, catch, magazine	CR 1110	1
34	5305-99-943-3809	Screw, grub, UNF, steel, socket drive, full dog point, $\frac{1}{4} \times \frac{1}{2}$ in lg. Zn coated	BSI BS 2470 table 3	1
35	1005-99-960-0047	Foresight assembly, adjustable	CR 146 SA	1
36	1005-99-960-2254	Body, foresight	CR 1179	1
37	1005-99-960-2255	Foresight	CR 1180	1
38	1005-99-960-2069	Screw, grub, BA, steel, socket drive, cone point, no 4 × 3/16 in, phosphated	CR 1199	1
39	1005-99-960-8938	Screw, socket head, UNF, steel, $\frac{1}{4} \times \frac{5}{8}$ in lg, flat fil hd, knurled	BSI BS 2470–1954	2

Casing Assembly Improvements Over the MkIII/L2A2

Ministry of Supply Demands Simplified Foresight

150. Sterling Foresights, old and new.

Below, right: one of the seven old-style fixed foresight blades of varying heights, a good selection of which was required with each lot of guns.

Centre: the adjustable foresight assembly, fully interchangeable with the fixed foresight fitted to the Patchett, and the Lanchester!

Above, from left: Allen key, locking grub screw, threaded foresight.

The first and most obvious thing will be that where necessary, the Foresight body (36) reverts to the old Lanchester/MkII Patchett style, wherein one of seven different-sized (Lanchester-type) foresight blades was fitted into a dovetailed slot within the body casing and heavy nose-cap, the blade being protected by the dog-legged stamped foresight guard (5). The seven different foresight blades themselves were re-placed by the new-style Foresight (37) with a single, height-adjustable blade.

This change to a single adjustable foresight was instigated by the Ministry of Defence/Ministry of Supply, and caused quite a stir at Sterling. Before this, each batch of guns was sold with a good selection of the numbered foresight blades, in order to zero the guns as and when they needed re-zeroing in the future. The customer paid for this selection of foresight blades, of course! Once the ADJUSTABLE foresight had been approved and adopted, this source of extra revenue dried up.

Backsight Lever Eliminated

The rear sight on the Mk4/L2A3 was simplified, in that the changeover lever on the left side of the backsight protector was eliminated. Now, the aperture was changed from 100 to 200 yards by simply flicking it over with the index finger. And why not? As a result of this slight variation, the A2 backsight axis pin (which originally had the flick-over

151. Two Sterling backsights, both shown with their axis pins and collars in place.
Left: MkIII pattern backsight with external flipover lever. Right: simplified Mk4 pattern, with axis pin now incorporating rightmost collar. (MoD Army, REME)

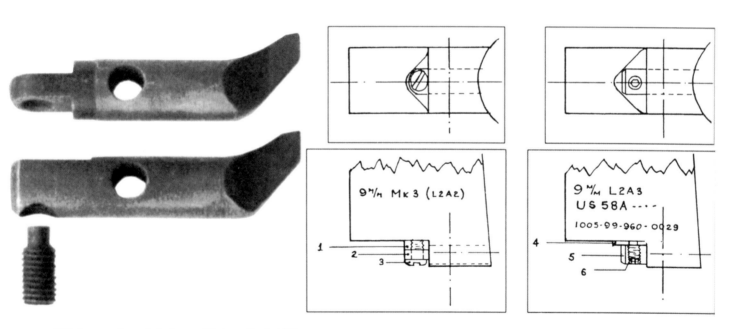

152. A comparison of ejectors and their method of fitting.
Left: stepped pre-Mk4 ejector (above) and Mk4 onwards pattern (below) with stepped retaining screw.
Centre: method of fitting pre-Mk4 ejector. Step of ejector
(2) sits on and is screwed to a thick, threaded anti-rotation plate (1) by a button-headed screw (3). On the MkII/L2A1, this screw could be unscrewed with the cocking handle. Above shows rear view with vertical centre line of magazine catch screw.
Right: method of fitting Mk4 ejector. Threaded ejector (5) is retained by shoulder of stepped grub screw (6) in hole in thin anti-rotation block (4). (MoD Army, REME)

lever attached) was changed to an axis pin pivoted within the backsight protectors on two collars or bearings. In one of the very few modifications that took place during production, this was changed in 1959 to a simplified axis pin that incorporated one of the collars. Both types remain fully interchangeable.

Simplified Ejector and Fitting

The ejector and the way it is fitted have been simplified on the Mk4/L2A3 . Previously, the ejector fitted through the casing and came up against an anti-rotation block. This block was threaded and the ejector was secured to it (and the casing) by a rounded button-headed screw. The threaded portion

153. Sterling return spring caps:
Left: MkIII
Centre: Mks 4, 5, 6 and 8
Right: Mk7 pistol. The spigot on the rear of the Mk7 cap was to allow the fitting of a detachable plastic shoulder stock.

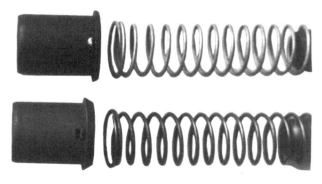

154. Mk4 spare parts were given different Ministry of Supply (MoS) 'CR'-prefixed part numbers from earlier MkII and MkIII spare parts, which indicated that they were not readily interchangeable. However, many differences were minimal and did not affect interchangeability.

Above: a MkII or m inner return spring and cup, made from roll-flanged tubular steel. Note the spring is coiled left-handed.

Below: a machined-from-solid Mk4 inner return spring cup. Note the spring is coiled right-handed!

The Armourer's Engineering Regulations (EMERs) mention this, stating that the springs "... may be encountered either left or right handed. Either type is acceptable." (MoD Army, REME)

within this anti-rotation block was extremely short and tenuous and in the course of disassembling and assembling the gun, the thread would strip. It was extremely difficult to effect a repair to this component, which resulted in the gun having to be scrapped. The Mk4/L2A3 gun has an ejector with a shallow flat that sits against a very thin anti-rotation plate. The hole in the ejector formerly occupied by the button-headed screw is now threaded. Into this hole screws a shouldered grub screw, the shouldered tip of which now sits into a small locating hole.

In reality this could have been simplified further, because the magazine catch screw also holds the ejector in position AND prevents it rotating. Surely somebody must have noticed that this could have saved fitting the anti-rotation plate, drilling and threading the ejector, drilling the magazine housing to accommodate the ejector screw, and machining the flat onto the ejector! That's just what the New Zealand Army Armourers did with their MkIII/L2A2s, until another repair procedure was formulated.

Three Interchangeable Mk4 Barrels

There were three barrels made for the Mk4/L2A3 gun, all of which were interchangeable. The earlier MkIII/L2A2 barrel, numbered CR 1113, is not listed as being interchangeable within a Mk4/L2A3, but a recent range test showed that such a barrel functioned perfectly in a sample Mk4/L2A3 gun PROVIDING it was retained in place by the proper 0–BA screws. The chamber for the early and now obsolescent barrels, numbered on the outside CR 1092 and CR 1165, did not conform to the NATO specification and although these barrels will fire standard NATO 9mm ball ammunition, problems might be encountered with what was described as "locally made, or ammunition of dubious origin".

The NATO standard barrel CR 1165.should have the letter 'L', indicating long chamber (+.012″, or 12 thousandths of an inch) above the small extractor slot on the rear face. The latest barrel will be marked CR 1207, with a chamber depth of .662″. The rifling was still to the well tried and tested Lanchester form. Those barrels made specifically for the Mk4 export guns had a double-entry angle into the breech, whereas those for the NATO L2A3 guns have a single-entry angle into the breech. A gauge of .345″ diameter must run through the bore, and a gauge of .351″ must not enter the muzzle by more than .5″.

Component Parts of the Mk4/L2A3 Trigger Assembly

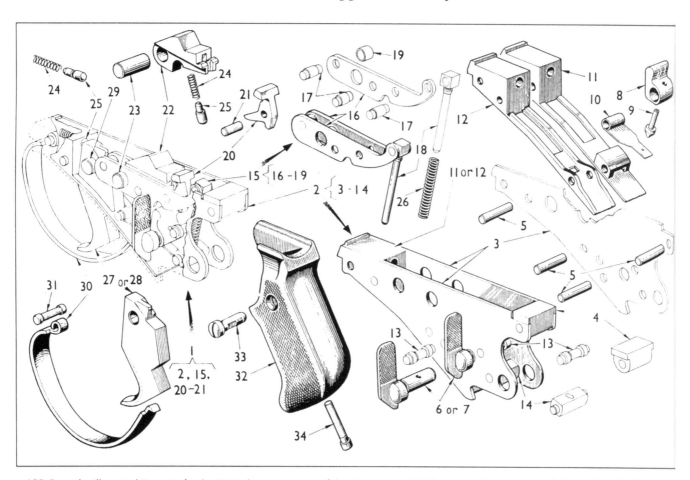

155. From the Illustrated Parts List for the L2A3, the components of the trigger assembly. The nomenclature is given, below and on the facing page.

Item	NSN	Item Name and Description	Part No/Dwg No	No Off
1	NP	Trigger Assembly	CR 112 A	1
2	1005-99-960-0038	Frame, mechanism, trigger	CR 130 SA	1
3	NP	Plate, side	CR 1057	2
4	NP	Block, thrust	CR 1050	1
5	1005-99-960-2201	Pin, rivet	CR 1055	4
6	1005-99-960-2197	Lever, change		
		OR	CR 1052	1
7	1005-99-960-2198	Lever, change	CR 1074	1
8	1005-99-960-2199	Lever, change	CR 1053	1
9	1005-99-960-2200	Pin, detent	CR 1054	1
10	1005-99-960-2256	Spring, detent pin	CR 1181	1
11	1005-99-960-2196	Plate, guard	CR 1071	1
		OR		
12	1005-99-960-2110	Plate, guard	CR 1203	1
13	NP	Pin, stop	CR 1056	2
14	NP	Block, spring, main	CR 1049	1
15	1005-99-960-0037	Cradle, sear	CR 129 SA	1
16	NP	Plate, side	CR 1046	1
17	NP	Pin, distance, side plate	CR 1047	3
18	NP	Guide, spring, sear cradle	CR 1045	1
19	NP	Roller, cradle	CR 1048	1
20	1005-99-960-2206	Lever, tripping	CR 1037	1
21	1005-99-960-2208	Pin, lever, tripping	CR 1040	1
22	1005-99-960-2211	Sear	CR 1041	1
23	1005-99-960-2209	Pin, sear and trigger	CR 1039	1
24	1005-99-960-2213	Spring, helical, compression	CR 1042	2
25	1005-99-960-2210	Plunger, sear and trigger	CR 1039	2
26	1005-99-960-2212	Spring, helical, compression	CR 1042	1
27	1005-99-960-2214	Trigger	CR 1044	1
		OR		
28	1005-99-960-2259	Trigger	CR 1186	1
29	1005-99-960-2209	Pin, sear and trigger	CR 1039	1
30	1005-99-960-2205	Guard, trigger	CR 1051	1
31	1005-99-960-2207	Pin, guard, trigger	CR 1072	1
32	1005-99-960-2178	Grip, handle	CR 1107	1
33	1005-99-960-2180	Pin, locating, trigger assembly	CR 1108	1
34	1005-99-960-3806	Screw, socket head, UNF, steel, flat fil hd, hex, ¼ in × ¼ in Zn coated	BSIBS 2470 Table 1	1

Mk4 Trigger Assembly Improvements Over the MkIII

Semantics about Interchangeable Screws

Literature of the time and the current Electrical and Mechanical Engineering Regulations (EMERs) suggests that the Pistol grip screw was now not inter changeable with the barrel screws. This is only partially correct.

What is correct is that the LENGTHS of the two are different, $5/8''$ for the two barrel screws and $1¼''$ for the pistol grip screw. The reason why the pistol grip screw is now longer is to accommodate the screw-on arctic trigger adaptor. However, both are ¼″ UNF Allen screws, and it would be a poor Armourer who waited for a 1¼″ long screw when the ⁵⁄₈″ long barrel screw was available and had sufficient thread. The fact is that although they are a- different length, they ARE interchangeable.

In fact, the longer pistol grip screw was useful when the barrel was tight in the casing. Armourers would insert the long screw into the barrel thread and tap it with a mallet to free the barrel.

For the Mk4/L2A3 series of guns, the screw thread pattern of the two barrel and single pistol grip was changed–from OBA thread to ¼″ UNIFIED. The unified threads within the barrel muzzle end and in the threaded boss of the pistol grip mounting can be identified with three touching circles, signifying unified threads therein.

A Tale of Two Triggers

The profile of the Mk4/L2A3 Trigger was altered, and made more concave at the front to provide the trigger finger with a more positive feel. This redesign also allowed a small hole to be drilled into the underneath whereby the (short-lived) Sterling arctic trigger adaptor could be used. A small plug on the adaptor went into this hole, and the trigger could then be operated with a gloved hand.

Early triggers with the hole in the base were numbered CR 1044, whereas the later triggers were numbered CR1186. A recent inspection of a quantity of triggers shows that this hole was deleted from production in about 1957, after the appearance of the arctic trigger guard, described below, made the additional hole redundant.

The Arctic Trigger Guard

The arctic trigger mechanism offered by Sterling was of questionable value, and, at the insistence of the Ministry of Defence, the Mk4/L2A3 had a folding trigger guard built into the trigger mechanism, although by then the real need had abated.

Sterling commented that unlike the earlier guns, the Mk4/L2A3 trigger guard was a separate part that

156. Left side closeup of a crackle-finish Mk4/L2A3 Sterling, showing arctic trigger guard in forward position.

Note the selector markings: 'A', then (partially hidden by selector) 'R' overengraved 'FIRE' and 'S' overengraved 'SAFE'. This gun is actually an early Mk4 Police Carbine. (Courtesy Adrian Bull)

could be removed for use in arctic warfare conditions. This was done by releasing the trigger assembly, pushing out the front .10″ trigger guard retaining pin, then swinging the trigger guard down and back

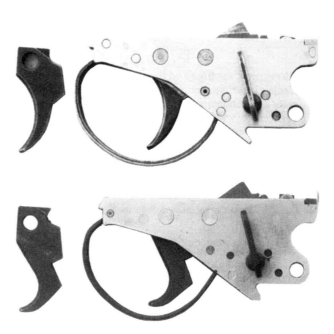

157 (right). The two basic production Sterling selective-fire trigger mechanisms, showing the distinctively shaped triggers of each alongside.

Above: MkI through MkIII/L2A2. Trigger guard is non-detachable.

Below: Mk4/L2A3, Mk5/L34A1 and Mk7A. Trigger guard may be detached, reversed, and remounted forward for use in arctic conditions. (MoD Army, REME)

to unhook the rear. You then rotated it horizontally through 180°, and replaced the retaining pin through the trigger guard as per assembly, but with the guard now back to front, with the rear lip hooked into the corresponding hole in the body casing. The whole assembly was then replaced, and the trigger mechanism retaining pin inserted and turned to the 'LOCK' position.

Read that again, and just imagine doing it in a frozen dug-out in bleakest Korea, with thick padded mittens on! The Military User handbook wisely does not mention this. Like the 7.62mm L1A1 rifle, the removal of the trigger guard WAS possible, and although Peter Laidler never served anywhere colder than Hohne (in northern Germany), he has been reliably informed that colleagues quickly became ex-colleagues if you ever removed your trigger guard. And rightly so.

A Proud Sterling Tradition: the Stainless Steel Trigger Unit

The stainless steel trigger frame side plates and axis pins were retained in the Mk4 Sterling, and on every subsequent Mark thereafter.

This meant that if the Sterling trigger mechanism got full of dust or mud, it was a simple matter to remove the whole unit from the gun, rinse it out in water, oil it, replace it, and you'd be ready to go once again.

Fazakerley Fouls the Trigger Group's Sterling Reputation

As noted, Sterling-made trigger mechanisms (and spare parts) have the trigger and sear/sear cradle axis pins made from stainless steel in order to eliminate trigger mechanism failure due to rusted or seized components. However, some of the trigger and sear/sear cradle axis pins made at Fazakerley were manufactured from phosphated steel.

While the phosphated steel axis pins remained in good condition, they were fine with just a wipe of oil. But once the weather turned to rain and they started to rust … British Army Armourers always replaced steel axis pins with stainless. The same applied to the guide rod for the sear cradle spring (Mk4 parts list, part 18). Sterling, stainless; Fazakerley, phosphated steel.

Redesigned Butt Geometry Requires Altered Pistol Grip

As noted below, the butt axis point on the Mk4/L2A3 body was relocated very close behind the pistol grip. As a result, the rearmost part of the plastic pistol grip

158. Left side view of a stripped L2A3 trigger frame. Being well-made of stainless steel by both contractors, these rarely gave any trouble. After prolonged heavy use the sear cradle axis pin could elongate the sear hole, causing rough action and malfunctioning.

Note the 'F/58', indicating manufacture at ROF Fazakerley in 1958. (MoD Army, REME)

159. Sear cradles, guide rods and axis pins as made by ROF Fazakerley (top) and Sterling (bottom).

As shown, early Fazakerley manufacture used phosphated steel for the guide rod and axis pins, while Sterling used stainless steel. In the field the phosphated items were quickly replaced with stainless parts. (MoD Army, REME)

160. Right side view of two plastic Sterling grips.

Left: pre-Mk4 .

Right: Mk4. Note the reduced and angled section at top rear, necessary to clear the repositioned butt trunnion hinge. (MoD Army, REME)

(the overhang that fits in the fleshy web between the thumb and fore-finger) is noticeably shorter. The plastic pistol grip, manufactured by Helix Plastics incidentally, was also altered at the front in order to accommodate the later-shaped trigger mechanism side frames.

Sterling stressed that although the earlier MkIII/L2A2 grip differed from this Mk4/L2A3 grip, the later grip could be used on the early gun without modification. The reverse is not true, however, as the longer rear overhang of the earlier MkII/L2A1 or MkIII/L2A2 grip fouls against the Mk4 butt trunnion block.

How the Sterling Trigger Mechanism Works

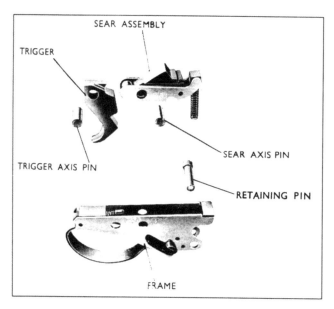

161. The Patchett/Sterling trigger mechanism, showing frame stripped into major components.

Although the Mk4 version is shown, all follow the same patttern, with many individual parts being interchangeable.

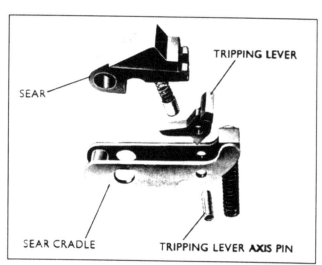

162. Enlarged view of sear assembly from Patchett/Sterling trigger mechanism, stripped to show internal parts.

Only Armourers could strip the trigger mechanism further, to remove the inner/outer change levers and change lever detent spring. They were also the only ones permitted to separate the frame side plates.

Action of the Trigger Mechanism in Automatic Fire

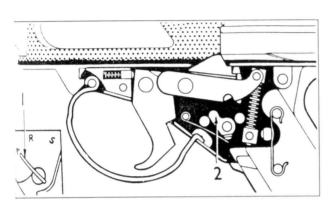

163. Gun cocked and change lever (1) set for 'A' (automatic fire). The inner arm (2) of the change lever is rotated forward clear of the tripping lever (3).

Note the front edge of the bolt, retained by the sear. (Excerpted from the UK Military User Handbook *Gun, Sub-Machine, 9mm L2A3*)

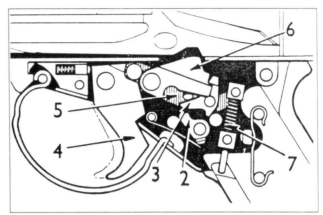

164. When the trigger (4) is pressed, the sear cradle (5) is rotated about its axis pin, the sear (6) is depressed and the breech block moves forward to feed, chamber and fire a round. At the same time the sear cradle spring (7) is compressed.

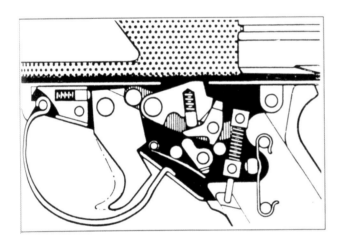

165. Since the inner arm of the change lever does not obstruct the tripping lever, the tripping lever is not rotated clear of the sear, therefore for as long as the trigger is pressed the sear will remain depressed, and the gun will continue to fire while there are rounds in the magazine.

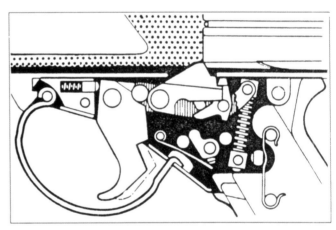

166. As the trigger is released the cradle spring forces the sear cradle to its normal position thus raising the sear into the breech block way, and as the block moves forward the sear engages against the bent on the breech block and holds the breech block in the cocked position.

Action of the Trigger Mechanism in Single Shot Fire

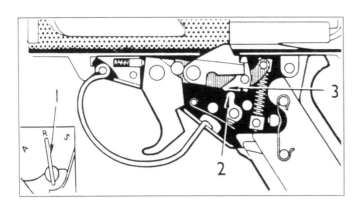

167. Gun cocked and change lever (1) set for 'R' (single shot fire). The inner arm of the change lever (2) is positioned under the toe of the triping lever (3).

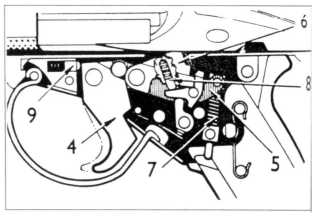

168. Trigger (4) pressed. The sear cradle (5) is rotated about its axis pin, the sear (6) is depressed and the breech block moves forward to feed, chamber and fire a round. At the same time the sear cradle spring (7) is compressed.

During this movement the toe of the tripping lever contacts the inner arm of the change lever causing the tripping lever to rotate until the upper arm disengages from the step on the sear. At the same time the sear plunger and spring (8) are compressed.

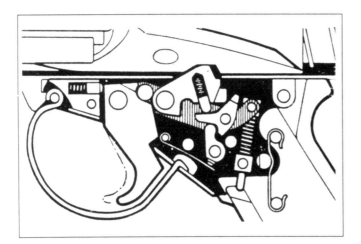

169. When the round is fired, the sear is held down by contact with the sear ramp, but as the block reaches the end of its rearward travel and is clear of the sear, the sear is forced upward by the pressure of the sear plunger and spring. Then as the breech block moves forward the sear engages against the bent on the breech block and holds the block in the cocked.

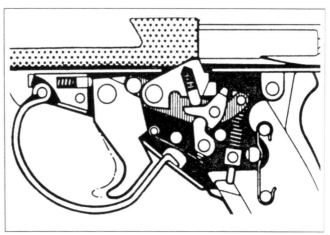

170. As the trigger is released the cradle spring forces the rear end of the cradle upward, which lifts the tripping lever, and this action combined with that of the sear spring causes the tripping lever to rotate about its axis pin until its upper arm re-engages on the sear.

The trigger must be fully released and again pressed for each single shot.

Component Parts of the Mk4/I.2A3 Butt Assembly

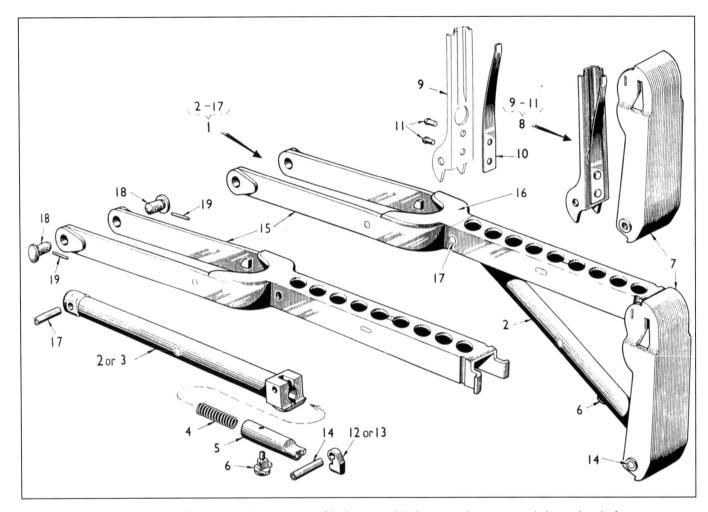

171. From the Illustrated Parts List for the L2A3, the components of the butt assembly. The nomenclature is given, below and on the facing page.

Item	NSN	Item Name and Description	Part No/Dwg No	No Off
1	1005-99-960-0053	Butt Assembly	CR 122A	1
2	1005-99-960-2387	Strut, butt assembly		
		OR	CR 1206	1
3	1005-99-960-2166	Strut, butt assembly	CR 1155	1
4	1005-99-960-2228	Spring, helical, compression	CR 1154	1
5	1005-99-960-2227	Plunger, strut	CR 1153	1
6	1005-99-960-2229	Catch, locking, strut	CR 1152	1
7	1005-99-960-2080	Plate, butt	CR 1201	1
8	1005-99-960-0032	Catch, assembly	CR 140 SA	1
9	NP	Catch, butt plate	CR 1122	1
10	1005-99-960-2162	Spring, catch	CR 1123	1
11	5320-99-943-1547	Rivet, solid, steel, tinners, hd, $^3/_{32}$ in x $^7/_{32}$ in lg	BS 641-1951 Table 4	2

Item	NSN	Item Name and Description	Part No/Dwg No	No Off
12	1005-99-960-2233	Lever, plunger strut	CR 1162	1
		OR		
13	1005-99-960-2260	OR		
		Lever, plunger, strut	CR 1185	1
14	1005-99-960-2163	Pin, axis, butt frame	CR 1124	1
15	1005-99-960-2079	Butt frame	CR 1200	1
16	1005-99-960-2458	Reinforcing plate, butt	WP 17898	1
17	1005-99-960-2164	Pin, axis, strut	CR 1125	1
18	1005-99-960-2182	Pin, retaining, butt	CR 1078	2
19	1005-99-960-2181	Pin, locking, butt retaining pin	CR 1076	2

Butt Assembly Improvements Over the MkIII

Geometrically Redesigned Butt Assembly

The whole Butt Assembly of the Mk4/L2A3 gun had been re-designed, courtesy the Ministry of Supply, from the weak and flimsy MkIII/L2A2 offering.

The butt axis point on the Mk4/L2A3 gun has been moved forward about 1″ to 4.9″ from the rear end of the casing, and now sits a hair's breadth behind the

172. (right). Left side closeup views comparing the butt trunnion points of Sterling SMGs.

Above: Up to and including MkIII/L2A2, the trunnion point was 3.5″ from the rear of the casing and about 1″ from the pistol grip. Note the distinctive early trigger and the MkIII ('L') backsight lever.

Below: On the Mk4/L2A3 and later Marks the butt trunnion point is 4.9″ from the rear of the casing, and closer to the (bobbed) pistol grip. The revised butt geometry, devised by MoD and Sterling engineers, was the principal difference between the Mk4 and earlier Marks. (MoD Army, REME)

173. Plan view of the MkIII butt (above, in crackle-black commercial finish) compared with Mk4, 5, 6 and 8 butt (below). The positions of the hinged trunnion points relative to the butt locking lugs are clearly shown.

The geometry of the buttstock remained the same from the MkI through the MkIII. Various small attempts at strengthening were made, but the weakness of the open-topped early design is clearly apparent. (MoD Army, REME)

bobbed pistol grip. To accommodate this apparent shortening of the overall length of the gun, the forward extended arms have been lengthened by 1″, while the top bracing section has been shortened by 1″.

This repositioning of the butt trunnion point and geometry was also to ensure that the Mk4/L2A3 butt cleared the trigger guard when it was rotated to the arctic position. The top bracing section was also strengthened by making it an inverted open square section down its total length. It was lightened by piercing 6 × $^7/_{16}$″ holes down its spine.

In a change from the original brazed fabrication, the Mk4 main butt frame was stamped out in one piece by William Still and Co, who had the necessary double-action presses required for this operation.

A Small Slip, Soon Rectified

For some reason the small nibs and recesses incorporated on the MkII/L2A1 and MkIII/L2A2 butt plates and frames were not carried forward into the first Mk4/L2A3s. However, quite soon into Mk4/L2A3 production, during late 1956 and early 1957, the literature of the time mentions that the design of the butt plate had been improved "… in order to ensure positive engagement of the butt plate at all times when the butt is extended." This was accomplished by recess-punching an elongated dimple into each side of the butt frame, just where the top of the butt plate folded over and onto it In turn, the butt plate also had a similar dimple punched into place. This simple modification ensured that when the butt was folded, the strut locking catch positively engaged the body and could not shake loose.

The Commercial Sterling Mk4: Markings and Finish

The Mk4/L2A3 Sterling guns crune with two principal methods of finish. The first was a black crackle paint finish, used on the vast majority of guns including those for export.

On these export and commercial guns, the top surface of the magazine housing is marked as shown in fig 175. Underneath, the magazine housing is marked with the Sterling patent numbers (fig 176).

The first Mk4/L2A3 guns produced were numbered from KR 5001 onwards, and thus the 'KR' prefix with a number higher than 5000 indicates a Mk4

174. Closeups of two Mk4 butts.
　Above: 1957 and later pattern butt. Note the small nibs and recesses (highlighted in white). Without these, the folded buttplate was liable to pull away, releasing the butt frame from the casing.
　Below: first (1956/57) pattern. Thousands of these are still giving 'Sterling' service. (MoD Army, REME)

175. Top closeup view of the magazine housing of Peter Ladler's matt-finish Mk4 Sterling, showing typical commercial markings. All markings were roll-stamped into place except the serial number (KR 45082), which was deeply engraved and is virtually impossible to alter or conceal, short of complete removal of the metal on which it sits.
　Note the '4' is Arabic, while earlier guns were marked 'II' or 'III'. (Peter Laidler collection)

176. Bottom closeup view of commercial Sterling Mk4 magazine housing, showing patent numbers that applied to the original Patchett Machine Carbine.

From top, left to right: 559,469 (trigger); 566,875 (folding butt); 579,660 (helically-ribbed breech block); 686,628 (double return springs). The debt to George Patchett looms large! While not applied to UK Military L2A3s, these markings continued to be applied to commercial Mk4s long after the patents themselves had expired. (Peter Laidler collection)

gun. The reason why the gun numbers started at 5001 was to allow a space between the approximately 4,500 MkIs, MkII/L2A1s and MkIII/L2A2s previously produced.

Numbers KR5001 and 5002 formed part of the Sterling historical collection, which was taken over by British Aerospace/Royal Ordnance at the closure of the Sterling factory in 1989. These guns are now housed in the MoD Pattern Room at Nottingham. The next 5,000 guns, starting from number 5003, went to the army of the Kingdom of Iraq.

Identifying Mk4 Year of Manufacture from 'KR' Prefix SN

This list covers commercial Mk4 guns only. A degree of fluidity exists at the extreme ends of these figures:

Serial Number	Date Produced
KR 5001	16 July, 1956
KR 5500	August, 1956
KR 6000	August, 1956
KR 6500	September, 1956
KR 7000	September, 1956

Serial Number	Date Produced
KR 7500	October, 1956
KR 8000	November, 1956
KR 8500	November, 1956
KR 9000	December, 1956
KR 9500	December, 1956
KR 10000	17 December, 1956
KR 10500	January, 1957
KR 11000	February, 1957
KR 11500	February, 1957
KR 12000	March,1957
KR 12500	March,1957
KR 13000	April, 1957
KR 13500	May,1957
KR 14000	May, 1957
KR 14500	May, 1957
KR 15000	May,1957
KR 15500	May, 1957
KR 16000	June, 1957
KR 16500	July, 1957
KR 17000	July, 1957
KR 17500	July, 1957
KR 18000	August, 1957
KR 18500	August, 1957
KR 19000	October, 1957
KR 19500	March, 1958

production of large UK Military order during this time

Serial Number	Date Produced
KR 20000	date unclear
KR 20500	date unclear
KR 21000	August, 1958
KR 21500	date unclear
KR 22000	November, 1958
KR 22500	November, 1958
KR 23000	November, 1958
KR 23500	November, 1958
KR 24000	November,1958
KR 24500	January, 1959
KR 25000	February, 1959
KR 25500	February, 1959
KR 26000	March, 1959
KR 26500	March, 1959
KR 27000	March, 1959

Serial Number	Date Produced	Serial Number	Date Produced
KR 27500	April, 1959	KR 48000	March, 1963
KR 28000	April, 1959	KR 48500	April, 1963
KR 28500	April, 1959	KR 49000	April, 1963
KR 29000	May, 1959	KR 49500	May, 1963
KR 29500	May, 1959	KR 50000	02 June, 1963
KR 30000	04 June, 1959	KR 50500	July, 1963
KR 30500	July, 1959	KR 51000	July, 1963
KR 31000	September, 1959	KR 51500	August, 1963
KR 31500	September, 1959	KR 52000	September,1963
KR 32000	September, 1959	KR 52500	September, 1963
KR 32500	October, 1959	KR 53000	September, 1963
KR 33000	October, 1959	KR 53500	September, 1963
KR 33500	October, 1959	KR 54000	September, 1963
KR 34000	November, 1959	KR 54500	October, 1963
KR 34500	November, 1959	KR 55000	November, 1963
KR 35000	December, 1959	KR 55500	November, 1963
KR 35500	December, 1959	KR 56000	December, 1963
KR 36000	January, 1960	KR 56500	December, 1963
KR 36500	January, 1960	KR 57000	December, 1963
KR 37000	January, 1960	KR 57500	December, 1963
KR 37500	February, 1960	KR 58000	January, 1964
KR 38000	March, 1960	KR 58500	January, 1964
KR 38500	August, 1960	KR 59000	January, 1964
		KR 59500	February, 1964
factory reorganisation during this time		KR 60000	13 February,1964
		KR 60500	February, 1964
KR 39000	June, 1961	KR 61000	March, 1964
KR 39500	July, 1961	KR 61500	March, 1964
KR 40000	08 August, 1961	KR 62000	March, 1964
KR 40500	October, 1961	KR 62500	March, 1964
KR 41000	October, 1961	KR 63000	April, 1964
KR 41500	November, 1961	KR 63500	April, 1964
KR 42000	December, 1961	KR 64000	April, 1964
KR 42500	January, 1962	KR 64500	May, 1964
KR 43000	January, 1962	KR 65000	May, 1964
KR 43500	February, 1962	KR 65550	June, 1964
KR 44000	February, 1962	KR 66000	June, 1964
KR 44500	June, 1962	KR 66500	June, 1964
KR 45000	June, 1962	KR 67000	June, 1964
KR 45500	September, 1962	KR 67500	June, 1964
KR 46000	September, 1962	KR 68000	June, 1964
KR 46500	November, 1962	KR 68500	June, 1964
KR 47000	January, 1963	KR 69000	July, 1964
KR 47500	January, 1963	KR 69500	July, 1964

Serial Number	Date Produced
KR 70000	03 August, 1964
KR 70500	August, 1964
KR 71000	August, 1964
KR 71500	September, 1964
KR 72000	October, 1964
KR 72500	October, 1964
KR 73000	October, 1964
KR 73500	October, 1964
KR 74000	November, 1964
KR 74500	November, 1964
KR 75000	November, 1964
KR 75500	November, 1964
KR 76000	December, 1964
KR 76500	December, 1964
KR 77000	December, 1964
KR 77500	January, 1965
KR 78000	January, 1965
KR 78500	January, 1965
KR 79000	February, 1965
KR 79500	February, 1965
KR 80000	13 February, 1965
KR 80500	February, 1965
KR 81000	November, 1964
KR 81500	March, 1965
KR 82000	March, 1965
KR 82500	March, 1965
KR 83000	April, 1965
KR 83500	April, 1965
KR 84000	April, 1965
KR 84500	May, 1965
KR 85000	May, 1965
KR 85500	May, 1965
KR 86000	May, 1965
KR 86500	June, 1965
KR 87000	July, 1965
KR 87500	July, 1965
KR 88000	July, 1965
KR 88500	July, 1965
KR 89000	July, 1965
KR 89500	August, 1965
KR 90000	09 August, 1965
KR 90500	August, 1965
KR 91000	September, 1965
KR 91500	October, 1965

Serial Number	Date Produced
KR 92000	October, 1965
KR 92500	October, 1965
KR 93000	October, 1965
KR 93500	October, 1965
KR 94000	November, 1965
KR 94500	November, 1965
KR 95000	November, 1965
KR 95500	November, 1965
KR 96000	December, 1965
KR 96500	December, 1965
KR 97000	December, 1965
KR 97500	January, 1966
KR 98000	January, 1966
KR 98500	January, 1966
KR 99000	February, 1966
KR 99500	February, 1966
KR 100000	13 February, 1966

The Sterling records are incomplete after this date, but the following data on serial numbers produced within subsequent years are quite accurate:

Year	From	To
1967	KR 103036	108164
1968	KR 108165	110550
1969	KR 110551	111726
1970	KR 111727	113158
1971	KR 113159	113752
1972	KR 113753	114000

This was the end of the 'KR' prefix. The exact changeover number is not known, but 114000 is mathematically correct.

Commercial Mk4s produced after a further change of ownership of the Sterling Armament Company in 1972 were prefixed by the letter 'S', in honour of owner James Edmiston's wife, Sisi. So, after mid-1972, commercial Sterling Mk4s were marked:

STERLING
SMG
9mm Mk4 (L2A3)
No S —

Identifying Mk4 Year of Manufacture from 'S' Prefix SN

Year	From	To
1972	S 1001	4411
1973	S 4412	8672
1974	S 8673	11067

Serial numbering of guns was strictly adhered to, and apart from a mistake made when two foreign governments each got a wrongly numbered gun, serial numbers were all sequential.

Sterling would add a specific government crest or other identifying logo if requested. Many government organisations marked their guns with their own serial numbers too, New Zealand being an example.

The UK Military L2A3: Markings and Finish

Explaining the Military Coding System

The manufacturer and the year of manufacture of any given UK Military-contract L2A3 can be found within the serial number of the gun. For example, serial number UF57-A 12345 or US57-A 12345 can be broken down thus:

12345 = Consecutive serial number.
Codes of other manufacturers, not manufacturers of Sterling guns, are:

- U = United Kingdom manufacture
- F = Royal Ordnance Factory No6, Fazakerley, Liverpool
- S = Sterling Engineering Co, Rainham Road (South), Dagenham, Essex
- 57 = year of manufacture, 1957
- A = indicates first batch of 99,999 guns
- BL = FN Herstal (Pistol, 9mm, L9A1)
- UA = Accuracy International, Portsmouth
- UB = BSA Guns Ltd, Small Heath, Birmingham
- UE = Royal Small Arms Factory, Enfield
- UN= British Aerospace,Kings Meadow Road, Nottingham
- UP = Parker Hale Ltd, Birmingham.

The Sterling-Made L2A3

The finish specified by the UK Military, and by some commercial buyers, was a hard satin black 'SUNKORITE' 259 paint over a rustproofed phosphated casing. Sterling-made UK Military L2A3s are marked thus:

GUN
SUB MACHINE
9mm L2A3
No US58A —
1005-99-960-0029

(Number 7287 taken as a sample of many thousands examined).

As noted, the first 5,000 Mk4s, starting with number 5003, were commercially marked and sent to the army of the Kingdom of Iraq. The next 5,000 were L2A3s for the UK War Office, supplies from Sterling being augmented by production coming on stream at ROF Fazakerley in 1956.

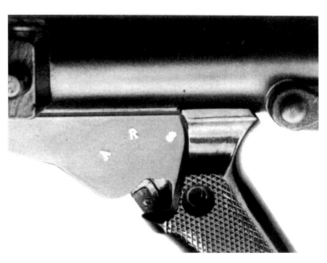

177. Left side closeup of Sterling-made UK Military L2A3 with trigger mechanism removed, showing select fire markings 'A' – 'R' – 'S'. Note the matt black 'Sunkorite' finish.

Several other types of markings were used on commercial guns: some Mk4 and Mks Sterlings were marked '34' – '1' – '0', or '34' – '1' – 'SAFE'. As a rule, where English was not the principal language, the markings were numerical. (MoD Pattern Room collection)

The lowest number we have seen, incidentally, was US56A 81, the 81st Sterling-made UK Military contract gun.

UK Military figures given for those guns supplied by the Sterling company are:

US56A   1–2772
US57A   2773–8592
US58A   8593–14250
US59A   15001–16000

This would indicate that a total of only 15,250 Sterling Mk4/L2A3s were supplied to the UK Military. There is clearly a mistake somewhere, because in a random selection of 24 UK Military 'US5-A —/L2A3' marked guns, five do not equate to these production figures. Indeed, the example given

above of gun number 7287, is marked as having been manufactured in 1958, but the Military production figures say it was manufactured in 1957. Not a point to lose friends about, but it does indicate just how wrong or confusing official figures can be.

Identifying Fazakerley Production

In conformance with the above, the first Fazakerley made L2A3s were marked with a special batch of serial numbers prefixed 'UF 56 A —'.

According to the Royal Ordnance Factories' official annual report of production the *Statement of Output of Major Services*, the following total numbers of L2A3s and magazines were manufactured at Fazakerley (magazines manufactured at Fazakerley and Woolwich):

178. A smiling group from ROF Fazalcerley pose proudly with the 20,000th L2A3 produced at that facility.
According to production figures quoted in the text from the *Statement of Output of Major Services*, this occurred around the beginning of 1957. (Courtesy MoD Pattern Room)

Period	L2A3s	Magazines
1956–1957	24,773	–
1957–1958	69,347	115,000
1958–1959	59,272	581,982
1950–1960	10,227	516,369
	163,619	1,213,351

Fazakerley were also given a free reign as to manufacturing procedures, which allowed them to make the best use of their facilities. The only noticeable thing simplified on Fazakerley guns (or 'UF' guns as Armourers describe them) is the magazine housing, which was made with top and bottom flanges, rounded to the curve of the body. These flanges were brazed to the body, unlike the Sterling procedure where the flangeless magazine housing was butt-brazed directly to the body. We cannot explain why Sterling did the magazine housing their way, because they certainly used this flanged method when fitting and brazing the trigger mechanism housing to the casing. From a purely engineering point of view, the flanged method is stronger, and damage in the magazine housing area in Service was certainly easier to repair on Fazakerley-made guns.

L2A3s manufactured at Fazakerley in 1958 were marked:

GUN
SUB MACHINE
9mm L2A3
UF 58A —
(Number 107148 taken as sample of many
thousands examined)
CR 53 GA

Fazakerley-made L2A3s from 1959 were marked as shown in fig 179.

Identifying Spares Production

Fazakerley-made parts were marked 'F56' (or whatever date), and Sterling's were marked 'S82' (or whatever date).

RSAF Enfield subsequently made certain spare parts for the Sterling Mk4 under licence. During negotiations for the 60,000 "Aid to India" Mk4s (Chapter Ten) it was agreed that some of the work would go to RSAF Enfield. Enfield successfully cast the return spring caps, and also manufactured magazine catches and butt assemblies dated 1965. Enfield marked all their production with the distinctive 'E within D' logo.

By the time the agreement with India had been negotiated, ROF Fazakerley had finished its

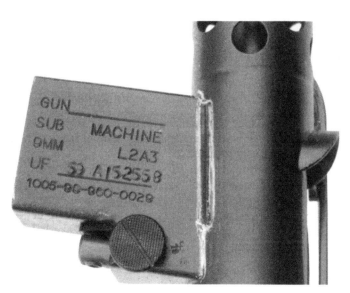

179. Top closeup view of magazine housing of L2A3 made by ROF Fazakerley in 1959, showing markings.
    Note the housing is flange-brazed to the casing. (MoD Army, RLC Donnington)

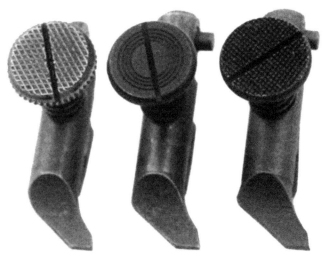

180. Three versions of the magazine catch screw, all of which are interchangeable:
    Left: earliest Patchett (and Lanchester).
    Centre: Sterling Mk4/L2A3 pattern, used from 1956 onwards through all Sterling production.
    Right: finely chequered Fazakerley pattern.

181. Closeup of breech flange area of 9mm Sterling barrel made by RSAF Enfield in 1956.

It has been suggested that Enfield merely rifled a few hundred barrels for Sterling. Not so! This example is distinctly marked as Enfield-made, with RSAF examiners' AND proof marks visible. (MoD Army, REME)

The Mk4/L2A3: the Most Reliable Sub-Machine Gun in the World

In all, the modifications embodied in the Mk4/L2A3 made it one of, if not THE most reliable sub-machine gun in the world. In respect of the privately manufactured Sterling, Major Robert Turp, then the head of the Army Purchasing Board, stated that: "… It fires in all conditions when the trigger IS pulled; and it does not fire UNLESS the trigger is pulled. For safety's sake, the second is more important than the first." This is not to say that the gun had no faults, but a lack of safety precautions was not one of them.

… But Still a Few Degrees Short of Perfection

One flaw was that the hinging butt trunnions soon became worn, allowing an unacceptable degree of end-play. A repair instruction was formulated whereby the holes could be ring-punched to take up this wear. However, this could only be undertaken once before the butt frame had to be scrapped.

New Zealand Army sources reveal that they purchased 6 Mk4 guns in 1956, and a further 2,000 in 1959. British (and New Zealand) REME Armourers soon devised better methods to· repair worn butt trunnions. These are discussed in Chapter Fifteen under "Four Miscellaneous Instructions".

production run of L2A3s and spare parts, and were unable to take part.

Several hundred externally machined barrels were supplied by Sterling to Enfield, to establish whether they could rifle them. It appears that Enfield went further than just rifling Sterling barrels, however. Two such barrels seen recently bear the 'ED' logo and 1956 date, plus RSAF examiners' and proof marks. Another identifying feature is that the part number (CR)1165 is engraved in the extractor slot.

Manufacturing the Mk4 Sterling

A Personal Insight by David Howroyd

1953: The 4,000 Surplus Lanchester Barrels Dry Up

Until midway through MkIII/L2A2 gun production, the Sterling Company were using the approximately 4,000 production Lanchester barrels that remained in stock after Lanchester production had ceased in October, 1943. These were converted for use with the Sterling guns then being produced. These barrels were ex-wartime stock, externally turned by various engineering companies but internally rifled by Lanes, a firm of barrelmakers from Birmingham. By 1953, Lanes, like so many other companies, had disappeared. Sterling were then faced with having to buy-in barrels, or manufacture their own.

Certainly, the trials appeared to confirm that the Sterling gun would be adopted as the next generation of sub-machine gun and barrels would be needed in great quantity. The task ahead certainly concentrated the mind on the enormity of the problems. I was tasked with setting up the complete separate manufacturing

182. In-the-white barrel casings undergoing final inspection by Mr Blackery, Chief Inspector of the Sterling Shop Floor (left) with a female assistant, circa 1957.

At Sterling, casings were moved from one operation to the next in 60-gun lots on the trolley racks shown in the gangway at right. Here the casing assemblies are awaiting inspection and clearance to the next stage of manufacture. (Courtesy Sterling Archives)

unit for the Mk4/L2A3. We had made body casings, breech blocks and individual components, but not the barrel!

In 1953, Sterling purchased two ex-wartime Pollard Twin Head deep gun-drilling machines. These had been used for Sten gun barrel production.

I converted one of these machines into a draw reaming machine and installed a force-feed cutting oil supply. This forced the steel swarf clear of the reamer. At that time the reamers were manufactured from high speed steel (HSS). We encountered problems with the HSS 'D' shaped drill bits and approached the Royal Small Arms Factory (RSAF) at Enfield to see their method of barrel production. Stan Wingrove

and I had considered asking RSAF to manufacture the Sterling L2 barrels for us. In 1954, RSAF did rifle several hundred barrels.

We were shown the rifling machines that cut each rifling groove separately. The machines could rifle two barrels simultaneously. A mandrel was passed through the barrel and a rifling cut was automatically set. An ingenious circular brush cleaned the cutting tool as it passed through the end of the barrel. This rather long-winded process would cut the 6 rifling grooves, indexing each as it proceeded. It took 20 minutes per cycle and maximum production was 6 barrels per hour. At this rate, we would need a LOT of machines!

We were also shown the Spill boring machine with which the skilled operator would pack a sliver of wood beneath the boring tool in order to obtain the exact bore size. We were learning fast.

The machined barrels were lead-lapped. This involved placing a steel insert down into the centre of the bore, then pouring molten lead down the bore to make a lead plug, which when cooled, could be pulled clear. This plug was loaded with graphite paste and passed in and out of the barrel until the desired mirror finish was achieved.

However, while the RSAF top-brass were talking to Stan Wingrove, I got talking to the Spill boring operator about our reaming of the Sterling barrel. Not one to be bettered, he showed me the latest RSAF gun-drilling 'D' bit. It was a gun-drill with Wimet carbide tips brazed to the cutting edge with an insert in the underside which acted as a rubbing plate. This in turn reduced drill friction. He then went on to inform me that with this drill and carbide tips, the deep hole drilling machine could run at 4,750 revolutions per minute (rpm). Against our Pollard drilling machines, this phenomenal 4,750 rpm head speed was like something out of science fiction!

We had found the answer. The Wimet carbide manufacturers were contacted and their representatives came to the factory with samples of the tips, drawings of the cutting angles and the clearances. At the same time the Pollard deep boring machine was modified to give the 4,750 rpm head speed. From then on, we were in business and production barrel drilling commenced.

The next problem was that of rifling the barrel. Matrix of Coventry had adapted a broaching machine for rifling purposes. It had a leader bar fitted to match the twist of the rifling. Thus, in one pull of the broaching machine, the barrel would have the 6 rifling grooves cut to depth, with a 6-8 micro finish. All was not that simple though. During the first trial of this machine, I broached the first 3 barrels and the broach snapped. We established that it was caused by the barrel expanding to the 1.5-ton pressure of the broaching action, then closing down on the broach buttons, causing them to break. Mr Spall from the hardening shop came to my aid by heat treating a barrel forging to 50/51 tons tensile strength. This time the barrels remained firm during the broaching operation. The steel from the rifling cut was brittle and did not interfere with the rifling process.

The only problem for the Sterling Company with these harder barrels was that they cut down on the need for spares! In a Ministry of Defence report, they concluded that "… after 10,000 rounds, the barrel showed no sign of wear and the test was discontinued."

In one celebrated case, a barrel was returned with multiple bulges and rifling absent throughout part of its length. It was ground away to reveal a line of stuck bullets forced into the bulged barrel wall, through which subsequent bullets had punched their way!

No Sterling barrel *ever* failed a proof test. (What an accolade!)

To finish the bore we had two redundant lathes modified with the lead plug in the head and the barrel held in a moveable fixture on the lathe bed. It was a painstakingly slow process but the honing operator, Greg Coogan, always one for bright ideas, suggested that given a honing mandrel and stones long enough not to fall into the rifling grooves, he could hone them. The tool-room made the honing mandrel and Delapena & Co, who supplied us with all our honing material, supplied us with the special stones suggested by Greg. It worked.

All Sterling barrels were hand-polished in the chamber and leed-in angles. The small ledge at the base of the chamber, just before the lead into the rifling, was hand finished to ensure that the ledge was sharp and square. If this ledge was not sharp and square, some soft brass-cased ammunition would partially feed into the barrel lead-in causing hard extraction, or in some cases, no extraction at all!

The inspection department checked all dimensions and afterwards each inspector stamped his or her own inspection stamp mark onto it, once before phosphating and painting and once after phosphating and painting.

The Sterling barrel was very cheap to manufacture. Excluding the machine loading and unloading time, the three independent operating slides of Churchill-Redman copy lathe could turn out a complete Mk4/L2A3 barrel from the raw forging in 90 seconds. The broaching of the rifling passing through a pressurised oil box was completed in 20 seconds and the honing of the bore in another 20 seconds. Since our first tentative steps at barrelmaking in 1953, we were soon regarded as one of the quality manufacturers of broached 9mm and button-rifled barrels up to 20″ in length. We also manufactured by button-rifling .223″

(5.56mm) ArmaLite [AR-18 and AR-180 barrels as part of Sterling's licensed production of ArmaLite rifles; Chapter Fourteen], and .177 and .22″ air rifle barrels. The rifling buttons were all manufactured in the USA from Ramnet 3, and the best lubricant for the button was found to be molybdenum disulphide.

The Barrel Casing

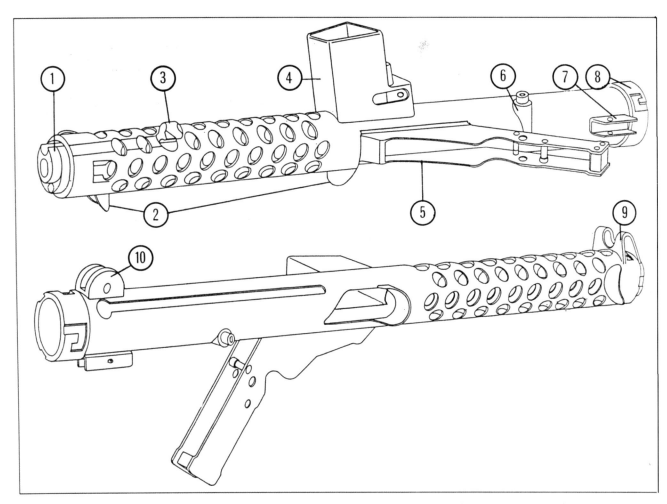

183. Two views of the Mk4 casing assembly, part no CR 53 GA, showing the ten components attached. On some early guns the components were arc welded, but for the Mk4/L2A3 and later guns, the assembly was entirely by brazing.
     The ten components are listed in the text below, clockwise from top left. (Drawing by K E Jenkins)

The barrel casing consists of a 1.5″ diameter tube, manufactured by Accles and Pollock, who supplied them to us cut to length with the air cooling holes pierced. Due to the fact that one set of holes are offset, the holes were punched on two sets of press tools.

The first and the sixth set of holes from the front edge were reamed to an exact size in a reaming fixture.

These holes were subsequently used as datum holes from which all other fixtures, gauging and dimensions were taken.

The next operation was to put the barrel casing into a press tool locating in the first datum hole, the press tool then accurately punching four .125″ holes which in later brazing operations were accurately

184. Sterling officials, interspersed with high-ranking military attaches from around the world, look on as Ron Houghton, who assumed responsibilityfor the entire welding and brazing staff when Percy Byrne retired, demonstrates the process of high-frequency brazing the casing of a Sterling Mk4.

  Second from left: Fred Reed, Chief Inspector of All Products for Sterling Works; fourth from left: David Howroyd. (Photo dated 20 February, 1959, courtesy Sterling Archives)

aligned with corresponding location holes in the pistol grip assembly, the locking ring for the return spring cap, and the locking latch support bracket. The oblong sear aperture hole was also punched in the same operation.

Ten pressed and/or machined components were then attached to the barrel casing by high frequency induction brazing. On some early guns, components were arc welded but for the Mk4/L2A3 gun onward, the assembly was entirely by brazing.

Clockwise from top left (fig 183), these components are:

1. front barrel support/nose cap
2. front and rear finger guards
3. bayonet standard
4. magazine housing assembly
5. pistol grip frame assembly
6. butt pivot
7. return spring cap locking lever housing
8. return spring cap locking ring
9. foresight protector
10. rear sight base

Overcoming Heat Distortion

The problem we faced during early production was that when heat is applied to one side of the tube, expansion takes place unevenly and upon contraction this caused the tube to take a stressed contorted position. In other words, it retains the bend!

Fazakerley encountered this problem to their cost and their first 7,000 Mk4/L2A3 guns destined for the British Government were so misaligned that they could not be zeroed at the factory after assembly. The RSAF at Enfield had the job of troubleshooting and to try to cure the problem before further production at Fazakerley could be contemplated. They turned to us at Sterling.

We had several years' previous experience with this type of production on the MkI, MkII/L2A1, MkIII/L2A2 and we were already successfully producing our first Mk4/L2A3 guns for Iraq. How we overcame the distortion problem will become apparent in the next few paragraphs.

The first component to be brazed to the casing was the pistol grip assembly. To overcome the heat distortion, the body casing was fitted to a front and rear niandrel and bent $^3/_{16}''$ out of true in the OPPOSITE direction to which the heat was to be applied. The grip assembly had a .125" locating peg inserted which fitted into the requisite datum hole on the casing. This ensured that it remained accurately in position while being induction brazed. After the cooling cycle, due to being pre–stressed (bent $^3/_{16}''$) the barrel casing returned to its original straight position. Each casing was checked on the mandrel fixture and if necessary, corrected to a concentricity reading of a maximum of .004" of true.

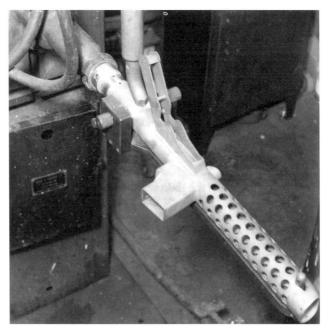

186. The foot-operated Spot Welder, a familiar component at Sterling that was used for many spot welding tasks dating from the 1940s until the company was wound up in 1989.

Here the butt pivot (6, fig 183) is being spot welded to the casing assembly, prior to being high-frequency brazed.

Note the fixture is locating in the first Datum Hole (front) to give the correct position from the known source. (Courtesy MoD Pattern Room, Nottingham)

185. Two Sterling components shown in-the-white in the production sequence as used on the MkIII and onwards:

Left: return spring cap locking ring (8, fig 183).

Right: nose cap (1, fig 183). This was a VERY expensive component, requiring machining of both ends. The Canadian C1 SMG (Chapter Nine) virtually eliminated this component, certainly in this form. (Courtesy David Howroyd)

One other problem encountered was that during the grip brazing operation, the actual tube length shrank! To overcome this, the case assembly was placed into a butt reaming fixture, located by the .125" return spring cap locking ring datum hole. Then, the first datum (cooling) hole was reamed out again ready to accurately position the magazine housing in the brazing fixture.

The brazing of the magazine housing was similar to that of the pistol grip. Once again, the barrel case was placed on a mandrel and the casing bent $^3/_{16}''$ out of true opposite to the area to which the heat was to be applied. Once again, after cooling, the barrel casing was checked for concentricity.

The return spring cap locking ring was a tight fit to the case and was located and locked by the .125" peg during the high frequency induction brazing operation so that during the expansion and contraction the locator held the ring in the correct position.

187. Machining the Mk4/L2A3 Sterling casing.

The unflappable Mrs Tyrell, last seen expertly range-testing a MkIII Sterling (fig 141), here completes the penultimate stage of milling the casing, milling out the cocking handle slot.

The last machining operation was to pantograph-engrave the serial number on top of the magazine housing, after which the gun became a controlled item. (Courtesy David Howroyd)

The Front (and Only) Barrel Support

The next most important component of the assembly was the front barrel support. This must be inserted absolutely square because any minute error would bend the barrel when the barrel screws were tightened. This operation used a drill jig mandrel which accepted the barrel support and was locked into position through the 6th datum (cooling) hole. Then three .093" holes were drilled through the casing and into the front barrel support. Dowel pins were then driven into the holes. This extremely accurate operation held the front barrel support accurately in position during the induction brazing operation.

We have outlined the important components in the high frequency brazing operation. Sterling, like Fazakerley, scrapped some barrel casings but our

quality ensured that during production of the Mk4/L2A3, it was just under 300 (in 32 years) unlike the 7,000 (in 3 years!) from Fazakerley.

Our endeavour was to manufacture a perfect component. The objective being that it would accept its assemblies from the master gauge set. From there on, it would proceed to the range and pass its zero test without alteration at the first shoot, on the 2½" zeroing square.

This accuracy was achieved by the labourious work of Mr Percy Byrne and myself. Percy was the welding shop superintendent. A significant breakthrough came through late one night. I had over 30 Mk4 gun barrel casings in the assembly shop. The barrels had been fitted and tightened up with their 2 × ¼" UNF screws. The 9" long bore gauge which should pass through the barrel under its own weight would not pass. When this occurred we knew that the gun casings had distorted during manufacture and that the casings had slightly bent the barrels during assembly. We also knew that the guns would fail the accuracy test.

Percy said to me words to the effect "… you make me a large, sturdy solid barrel, without the central bore hole, that we can screw into the barrel position. I will make a high-frequency coil to go around the casing in the area behind the bayonet stud. I'll bring it up to brazing heat and this will take all the stress out of the casing. Then whatever is bending the barrel will correct itself, overcoming the last few thousandths of an inch of squareness that has built up between the rear and front barrel support area."

Sure enough, it worked to perfection! What Percy designed was one of the most important additions to the barrel casing manufacture layout. After Percy retired in the early 1980s, his important work was undertaken by Ron Houghton, whom Percy had trained since he was a young man.

High frequency brazing was used on the remainder of the components and the same sound· engineering principles were employed to avoid casing distortion with these components too.

The last operation on the production line was to pantograph engrave the serial number to th magazine housing. Thereafter the casing became an accountable item, and went off to the 90 gauge inspection station.

Manufacturing the Breech Block

The breech block is made from case hardening quality steel, received from British Steel in 1.4" diameter ground stock. It was received at the factory with release notes detailing the composition of the steel batch. This batch number was subsequently stamped on the information line of every breech block. This will enable the steel to be traced back to its material source.

The first operation after an inspection of the material was carried out on the automatic turret lathe. This machined a ½" diameter × .⅝" stub on the front end of the block and centre drilled it. The second operation faced and drilled the rear end to facilitate the grinding of the external diameter. At the front end in the stub a .187" Datum tool hole was machined.

All subsequent milling and drilling operations were carried out from this .187" reamed datum hole and the ground external diameter. Once the breech block was completed in the white metal stage, it was 100% inspected and passed to the hardening shop.

If you look at a breech block, you will immediately notice that it has a very heavy section at the front end

188. A further view of the 60-gun trolley racks that were used to transport guns between production stages.

Here three New Zealand Army Armourers inspect in-the-white L2A3 casing assemblies of guns destined for New Zealand. Staff Sgt David 'Jock' Annandale (centre) was the senior Armourer at the Northern District Ordnance depot in Ngaruawahia, New Zealand while Peter Laidler served there in 1967–1968, when the SMGs in New Zealand stores were still Mk2 Stens!

New Zealand purchased an initial batch of 6 Mk4/L2A3s for trials in 1958 and a further 2,000 in 1959. Their Owen and Sten guns on active service in Malaya were replaced with L2A3s from UK Ordnance stocks in Johore Bahru.

Note longtime Sterling employees Percy Byrne (left background) and (between New Zealanders, in white coat) Mr Setram, who hand-finished the shoulder on the feed horns of each breech block made. (Courtesy David Howroyd)

and at the rear, it is very thin and light. The design of this component was a hardening shop nightmare. They decided that to avoid the bolt bending like a banana, it had to be heat treated by being individually wired heavy side up and lowered into the cyanide furnace. It was then quenched in oil absolutely vertically. Any bending of the bolt would change the centre-line and affect the radial positions. It would

189. British paratroopers practising close-quarter-battle (CQB) techniques at a training base in West Berlin in the 1960s. Here, two paras have stormed a house through a smashed-in window, while their comrade covers the inside door with his L2A3. The Sterling was a favourite of most lightly-armed paratroopers, who were well used to this type of infighting.

The Sterling was a favourite of most, but not all British troops. As James Edmiston recalled bitterly in The Sterling Years,

… Almost as ludicrous is the SAS connection, although one criticises that elite body at one's peril. In the field of small arms, the SAS rejects whatever is standard in the British Army or available from British sources. Certainly, it would appear that SAS soldiers are the only ones who cannot jump through a window with a loaded Sterling. The side-loading magazine, apparently, gets in the way … (Courtesy Central Office of Information)

also affect the long slow angle of the sear flat. Just .002″ error from the centre line would not allow the bolt to slide onto the .187″ master gauge. For this reason all breech blocks had to emerge from the heat treatment process absolutely straight.

After hardening, the inspectors checked the hardness and depth of hardness. The breech block holes were then honed to size and the large internal bore where the return spring cup seats was ground to the required size, concentric to the external diameter. This internal diameter was used to accommodate a special mandrel to facilitate the grinding of the external diameter. This method ensured 100% acceptance in the master receiver gauge for radial and central positions. Finally it was inserted into a master gauge where the sear flat was checked and surface ground to its precise dimension.

After final inspection, the last operations were phosphating, de-embrittlement and oil dipping.

Marking the Breech Block

Coded identification numbers were engraved on all breech blocks. A sample of these, as found on British Military breech blocks, reads:

- 1005-99-960-2153/883-W711-CR1093: full NATO code number (1005-99-960-2153), the presence of which indicates a breech block manufactured for the UK Ministry of Defence; date code (883 = 8/1983); steel batch (W711); Ministry of Supply code number (CR1093).
- S66-9-602-153-M2494 Sterling manufacture in 1966 (S66); abridged NATO code (960-2153); steel batch code (M2494).
- S87-9-602-153-M4746: as above but 1987 manufacture; steel batch code (M4746).

The Materials

Many experiments were carried out by the Company on materials for the manufacture of component parts. These included sintered steel (compressed steel powder), lost wax castings, drawn or extruded section and hot steel forgings.

The problem with sintered components was that due to the porous nature of the material, it was penetrated during the phosphating process. During subsequent painting, residue from the phosphating operation bubbled through the surface.

Lost wax castings have their limitations of accuracy but save many machining hours where aesthetics are of little importance. Components were cast oversize where an accurate dimension was required as this allowed subsequent machining to those tight tolerances.

Drawn sections were extensively used but the accuracy of the dies were of paramount importance. They usually lasted for many years without being remanufactured. This material came in 10- to 12-foot lengths and the milling machines cut the components six at a time through jig fixtures. A good example of this is the sear. You can see the savings in machine time by using the drawn section process.

Hot forged steel forgings were used for the barrel and the return spring cap. These were cast by the steel founders and supplied 'as cast'. The return spring cap was also made by the lost wax method. However, experience and cost dictated that the cast method was re-introduced.

The following list details components and the method used for their manufacture:

Lost Wax

- backsight housing (horizontal knurl pattern only)
- butt catch
- return spring cap

Hot Forged Steel

- barrel
- return spring cap

Drawn Section

- backsight
- backsight housing (diamond knurl pattern only)
- bayonet stud
- blocks on trigger plate
- butt tube block
- butt tube cam

190. A New Zealand sentry, wearing no rank or other insignia except for the cap badge and armed with a Mk4 Sterling, during "the forgotten war" in Borneo, 1964.

The New Zealanders were natural bush fighters and were quite at home operating in the jungle. Note the British-issue Bedford RL and Series 2 Land Rover, far right background. (Courtesy New Zealand Army Archives)

- foresight block
- inner change lever
- magazine catch
- magazine housing
- pistol grip front block
- sear
- trigger
- trigger frame rear locating block
- tripping lever

A Proud Moment Sterling Armament Becomes a CIA-Approved Supplier

Until 4 February, 1958, Sterling submachine gun inspection was under the control of examiners from the Chief Inspector of Small Arms (CISA). At Sterling, Ivy Henry and other female examiners were responsible to CISA for the examination of components and guns. Sterling in-house inspection was overseen by Fred Reid.

Due to the continued high quality and standards of the production, in-house inspection and finish of the guns, the Chief Inspector of Armaments (CIA) decided that Sterling would become CIA-approved suppliers, and be their own inspectors and examiners. Thereafter the only parts that would be examined by an outside body would be the breech blocks and barrels submitted for proofing. UK Military contract barrels and breech blocks were all proofed at RSAF Enfield, while commercial production was proofed at the London Proof House.

Stressing Good Customer Relations

Sterling did not normally offer foresight protectors or small rounded handguards (found on the right side of the casing at the muzzle and ejection port) as spares or replacement parts. However, as these parts suffered like any others from normal wear and tear in UK Military service, the Ministry of Defence insisted that Sterling make them available to UK Ordnance stores for replacement by Armourers when necessary. Although these components were never officially offered as commercial spare parts, a formal letter to Sterling usually resulted in a jiffy-bag full, free of charge. British Armourers in Malaya regularly 'exchanged' these parts with their Malayan, Fijian and New Zealand Army Armourer colleagues.

Good customer relations were stressed by Sterling, especially when those customers might be coming back for more guns!

It was common knowledge amongst users that the Sterling Company would reply to a technical letter within the space of a few days, as Peter Laidler confirmed when a Mk4 User Handbook arrived at a remote Malayan REME workshop within a week of his request.

On the home front, a colleague with a superb collection of bayonets wrote and asked if he could have the front 8″ of a Mk4/L2A3 on which to display one of his No5 bayonets. Along it came, (presumably from a scrap or damaged casing), within a week – and he has it to this day. The Sterling company certainly excelled at Public Relations!

191. In action in Malaya in the late 1960s. Here. a New Zealand dog-handler armed with a Mk4/L2A3 Sterling, and his faithful black Labrador tracker dog, are being helicptered into operations. Helicopters and Twin-Pioneer aircraft were the backbone of jungle transport in Malaya.

This man is a Lance-Corporal, but note the total lack of rank or insignia on his shirt. (Courtesy New Zealand Army Archives)

The 1960 Reorganisation

In 1960, the Sterling Engineering Company was sold out to Land and General, under the chairmanship of Mr Bligh. It was during the late 1960s that the company moved to a rented factory in Selenas Lane, Chadwell Heath, Dagenham, about two miles away from its traditional site on Rainham Road (South). This was to provide vacant possession for re-development, in order to allow the old site to be sold. However, as it turned out, this was not to be.

Taking It to Court

As noted, when the Mk4 Sterling had been adopted as the general-issue L2A3, the Ministry of Supply had decreed that ROF Fazakerley, with their huge arms manufacturing capacity (and equally large labour relations problems) were to make 90% of the UK Government order of 190,087 Mk4/L2A3s, with Sterling only allowed to make the remaining 10 percent. This caused a certain amount of anger at Sterling, and rightly so.

The main thrust of this 'licence' was the fact that the Ministry of Defence/War Office/Ministry of Supply/ Crown were a far bigger organisation than

192. George Patchett resigned from Sterling the very day the £228,000 judgement was announced in favour of Sterling and himself in 1966, in response to their suit against the Government for patent infringements arising from the ROF Fazakerley L2A3 production programme. In this still from a videotape made at his home in the south of France, George was obviously enjoying his retirement! (Courtesy Bert List)

Sterling, and so it became a "sue us if you dare" standoff. Sterling decided to sue; and while they did not prevent production of the L2A3 by the Government, they did win a cash settlement for violation of patent rights (unlike Webley, who had been bullied into submission over a similar incident in the early 1930s).

The case went to the High Court, where in 1966 the Crown settled out of court and paid. Sterling and Patchett £228,000 for breech of patent rights, the judge ordering that the money was to be divided equally between Sterling and George Patchett.

The £228,000 was considerably less than the £500,000 that had been requested for breeching the patent rights, but nevertheless George Patchett resigned the day the judgement was announced, and retired to live in the South of France, where he died in April, 1978.

The court also reduced the number of guns to be made at Fazakerley to 86% of the total required, with 14% to be made by Sterling. (Fazakerley's allowable

193. The Sterling in South Vietnam, with New Zealand Infantry operating from Nui Oat.

The L2A3 is being carried by the second man, probably the patrol leader. The third man is carrying an L4A4 7.62mm Bren, favoured by the New Zealanders over the Australian L2A1 heavy barrelled automatic rifle.

The long grass, similar to pineapple leaves, was sharp with barbed edges and would quickly rip long OG trousers and legs to shreds. The webbing is a mixture of British Pattern '44 and US, and each soldier is heavily loaded around the waist and back. Only the Bren is fitted with a sling: other weapons were always carried 'at the ready'. (Courtesy New Zealand Army Archives)

total of 163,474 guns matches very well with the official stated production total of 163,619.)

The full story of this bullying by the Ministry of Supply is told in detail by James Edmiston in *The Sterling Years*.

Under the terms of the settlement, the Government was prohibited from selling Fazakerley-made L2A3s commercially in competition with the Mk4 Sterling.

Peter Laidler has never seen a Fazakerley gun outside UK Military service, except with New Zealand and Fijian Infantry. The reason this occurred was that on active service, Ordnance stores were generally pooled.

Insofar as rest-of-the-world sales were concerned, despite the vast quantities required, Sterling coped magnificently.

Mk4 Variations

The Sterling company, being in the private commercial sector, regularly made feasibility studies of customer requirements. For example, post-1972 Mk4 guns could be ordered with the Mk6 type optical sight rail mounting points, discussed in Chapter Eleven. One such Mk4 gun, S 34430, is resident in the MoD Pattern Room. Another Mk4 gun, S33487, has been fitted with a .22″ sub-calibre adapter of US origin. The sub-calibre kit takes the usual form of a barrel insert, magazine insert which accepts a .22″ magazine, and a modified breech block assembly. Two such studies were undertaken with .22″ inserts, and both were cancelled due to technical difficulties that do not concern this study.

Gilding the Lily

The Mk4/L2A3 was exported to so many countries that it is easier to simply say that almost every Commonwealth nation eventually adopted it, as did many other countries with military allegiances to Great Britain, such as certain Middle Eastern and African states.

In addition to the normal black finish to the guns, the customer could in reality specify ANY finish. As a result some were supplied hard chrome plated, and some were completely 24-kt gold-plated. Whether these were actually used, perhaps by ceremonial bodyguards or simply as presentation pieces, is not known. It does emphasise the degree to which Sterling would go to keep their customers satisfied.

194. A Sterling data sheet, in English and Arabic, depicts the two 'luxury' finishes offered: 24-kt gold (above), or high-gloss chrome (below). Even the bayonets, scabbards and magazines are plated. (Courtesy James Alley)

195. David Howroyd in the Pistol and SMG Room at the MoD Pattern Room, displaying one of the gold-plated 'presentation' Mk4 Sterlings. Gold plated or not, these guns were fully operational. (MoD Pattern Room, Nottingham)

At least 25 chromed models were manufactured, together with at least 21 gold-plated, all bearing then-current serial numbers. Several were displayed at the London premises of Cogswell and Harrison. These gold-plated guns, with gold-plated magazines, bayonets, and scabbards, went to Qatar and Kuwait to name but two nations. The chromed guns, magazines, bayonets and scabbards also went to Qatar, Kuwait and Tunisia.

The Later 'Solid-Butt' Mk4

A later variation of the Mk4 gun was produced in 1984, when it was suggested that guns fitted with solid Mk7 butts (Chapter Twelve) might be more acceptable to certain buyers. This was a simple modification, as both the Mk4 and Mk7 guns were then in simultaneous production. The Mk4 hinging butt trunnion block was omitted and the Mk7 type return spring cap and locking catch added. It was then a simple matter to fit the plastic Mk7 butt.

One advantage to the plastic butt was that it was adjustable for length. However, this was not a great success and only eleven such guns were produced with fixed stocks.

Interchangeability Throughout Mk4 Production

Throughout this work we often discuss the interchangeability of components. This is of vital importance to the user and Armourers in the field, who are attempting to keep their equipment in running order. The Sterling engineers at the Research and Development offices made much of the claim in their literature, that whereas their production techniques were amended as necessary to remain up-to-date, *every part* of the Mk4/L2A3 gun was interchangeable from the start to the end of production.

A Minor Change in Designation

During the 1970s, the UK Military changed the designation of the Mk4 Sterling from 'Gun, Sub-Machine, 9mm L2A3' to 'Submachine Gun, 9mm L2A3'. Although the official designation changed, nothing else did and the gun was known to soldiers worldwide as 'the Sterling' and to Armourers as simply 'the L2'.

Notes on Zeroing All Sterlings

Zeroing the Mk4 gun was identical to zeroing the other marks in the Sterling series, and the method is worth repeating here. With the gun zeroed at 25 yards and the backsight set at '100'(yards), 5 shots should be fired from the prone position with the left forearm

196. British paras in Northern Ireland, one armed with an L2A3 Sterling, leap from their Land Rover as they rush to the aid of their colleagues following a city-centre bomb blast one terrible day. The leftmost man (with the L1A1) is Graham Jones, a friend of Peter Laidler's.
The Series 2 Land Rover and cotton dennison smocks date this photo to the very early 1970s. (MoD Army, Parachute Regiment)

rested. The mean point of impact (MPI) should fall within a square 1.5″ above and .5″ below and between .5″ left and 2.5″ right of the point of aim. It will be found that with a gun zeroed to this specification, it will be correct for elevation at all ranges when fired in the open and from the shoulder.

As discussed in the Accessories Chapter, there was a zeroing tool named 'Tool, foresight cramp No5 Mk1' with a part number B3 CR 116A available for this gun. Peter Laidler confesses that, in all his time on the ranges as Armourer or Range Officer, he has never seen one of these tools used, although he admits to having had one in his tool box! A brass drift and judicious use of the small hammer was just as effective.

The Mk4/L2A3: a Selected Bibliography

Readers interested in other publications covering the Sterling Mk4/L2A3 should consider acquiring and reading the following:

Later Sterling Handbooks and Parts Lists

The Mk4 Sterling SMG was manufactured commercially for nearly 40 years. During that time, Sterling produced various editions of their own illustrated Parts Lists and brief User Handbooks for the Mk4/L2A3 and its silenced follow-on, the Mk5/L34A1 (Chapter Eight). Over the years these booklets (and other miscellaneous fact-sheets on the Mk4 and Mk5) were produced in English, French, Italian, Spanish, Portuguese, and Arabic.

One copy of the Sterling Mk4 User Handbook was issued with each weapon. The Sterling Spares Catalogue, only issued with the Mk4 and Mk5, was supplied one per ten weapons to overseas buyers.

The Sterling User Handbook is clearly a revamped issue of the previous MkIII/L2A2 handbook, as some obsolete parts are still shown within it. As an example, the first Mk4/L2A3 User Handbooks and Parts Lists issued by Sterling do not mention the new adjustable foresight (assembly no 35, fig 149).

Sterling User Handbooks issued after James Edmiston sold Sterling Armament in 1983 featured a rampant lion logo on the front cover.

UK Military User Handbook

There was only one UK Military User Handbook, WO Code 12042, 26/Mans/3911, HB (handbook) 15, dated 1956. User Handbook, 26/Mans/3911 was later replaced by a combined User Handbook with Army Code 12042 (revised 1977) 2G/Mans/4347, which also contained a section covering the silenced L34A1.

The L2A3 UK Military User Handbook does mention the adjustable foresight, stating that each revolution of the blade would increase or decrease the mean point of impact by 1.3″ at 25 yards, or 5.5″ approx at 100 yards. Hardly a point in favour of pin-point accuracy, but the gun was never meant for such accuracy anyway.

Other Mk4 Instructions

INFANTRY TRAINING, Volume 1. Infantry Platoon Weapons, Pamphlet number 4, THE SUB-MACHINE GUN. Army Code 8948 dated 21st November, 1955, or as above, but reprinted 1968.

INFANTRY TRAINING, Volume 2. Skill at Arms (Personal weapons), Pamphlet number 9. THE SUB-MACHINE GUN. Army Code 71028, dated 1975.

197. Cover/title pages of two Sterling Mk4/L2A3 Manuals.
Above: Spares Catalogue, in English.
Below: User Handbook, in Arabic. (Courtesy Michael Gruber)

And for the REAL masochists, the Provisional Drill Book·, WO Code 9707, dated 1961, or as above but superseded in 1965 with book WO code 70166.

Hand in glove with these UK Military publications, were the Electrical and Mechanical Engineering Regulations. These are the Armourers' equivalent of the Workshop Manual for your car. Relevant sections have been reproduced herein.

... and a Small One for the Wife, Please, Mr Patchett!

The Single-Shot Sterling 9mm Police Carbine

During the 1950s, 60s and 70s, as Sterling sub-machine guns became available to armies worldwide, there were sometimes violent political disorder problems in parts of the Commonwealth. The politics do not concern us here, but sections of the civilian population within these countries, such as the rubber planters in Malaya, the tea and sisal planters in Kenya and the arable and tobacco farmers in Southern Africa, asked Sterling whether such a gun could be made available to them. Being light, flexible and reliable, the Sterling could be used by all but the smallest members of the family, and when used in anger, it would leave any assailant in no doubt as to how deadly it could be.

Both Britain and Sterling were anxious to promote overseas trade, but the governments of these other countries were not keen on the civilian population, or even some of their paramilitary Police, possessing modem, fully-automatic firearms.

Sterling came up with a solution to the problem by introducing a version of the then current Mk4 gun with a single shot or self-loading facility only.

First 17 PCs Based on the MkIII Sterling

The first Police Carbine, serial no P 0001, was manufactured on 10 June, 1955, and was based on the commercial MkIII gun. These guns were numbered consecutively, and this numbering continued when guns numbered from P 0018 were built using Mk4 casings.

A Sterling sales brochure of the period confirmed that the single shot Police Carbine "... is no longer a prohibited weapon (a machine gun) as defined by the UK Firearms Act of 1937, part 2, section 17 ...", a

POLICE MODEL — STERLING CARBINE
(9 mm.)

STERLING

The well-known STERLING SUB-MACHINE GUN recently adopted by H.M. Government for the Armed Forces of the Crown, has now been modified for use by Police and Civilians in troubled parts of the world.

STERLING ENGINEERING COMPANY LIMITED
STERLING WORKS. DAGENHAM. ESSEX. ENGLAND

198 (right). The front page of an early Sterling pamphlet on the semi-automatic-only Police Carbine, developed "for use by Police and Civilians in troubled parts of the world."

The gun depicted is the MkIII: the first 17 Police Carbines were based on the commercial MkIII SMG. (Courtesy David Howroyd)

DESCRIPTION

The new Police Model, which is no longer a prohibited weapon as defined by the Firearms Act of 1937, Part II, Section 17, while remaining largely inter-changeable as to major parts with the Military Model, is now a single shot, self-loading weapon. It can now serve both as a short range pistol or as a light carbine which is extremely accurate up to 200 yards.

It weighs only 6 pounds, fires the standard 9 mm international ammunition from a 34-round magazine and is extremely simple to handle and maintain with perfect safety to the user. During a recent demonstration the weapon was handled with safety and accuracy by a twelve-year-old boy and two untrained young women.

Although its potential rate of fire is even higher, an average user can, in an emergency, fire up to 60 well aimed shots per minute and group within an 18-inch rectangle at 200 yards range. The safety mechanism is such that, even cocked, the carbine will not go off if dropped.

Its short overall length of 19 inches with butt folded makes the weapon easy to carry and handle either slung or in a vehicle and it can be brought into action with extreme rapidity.

The Police Model Sterling Carbine therefore provides the perfect weapon of self-defence for those who are obliged to take such precautions.

199. The single-page description provided in Sterling's original Police Carbine brochure ends rather ominously by recommending the Sterling Police Carbine as "the perfect weapon of self-defence for those who are obliged to take such precautions." (Courtesy David Howroyd)

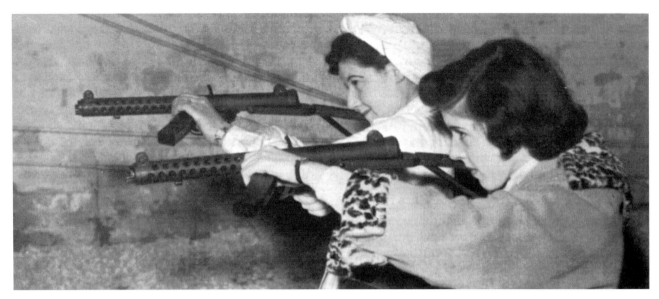

200. The Sterling Police Carbine brochure featured another photograph of Mrs Tyrell, rear, and Miss Butts, right foreground, both illustrating the correct stance for firing the (MkIII) Police Carbine from the shoulder with butt extended. Compare with fig 141: the two photos were taken at the same range test. (Courtesy David Howroyd)

phrase that would come back to haunt the Sterling company some years later! However, judging from the commercial sales of these single-shot guns overseas, it appears that this assurance was perfectly acceptable to foreign governments!

The Police Carbine brochure also shows the gun being fired, by Major Turp, both as a pistol from the waist with stock folded, and as a sub-machine gun from the shoulder with the stock extended.

Interestingly, the guns shown in the brochure are from the first batch of 17 Police Carbines which were based on the commercial MkIII design.

These guns were not adopted by the Military, but until recently could be seen in the hands of several Police forces. They were marked on the magazine housing:

POLICE CARBINE

9mm Mk4

No. P —

(Number 0807 examined.)

The 'P' serial number prefix was to indicate its single shot Police Carbine status.

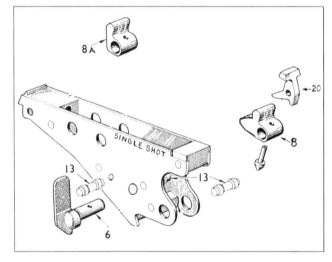

201. The Single-Shot trigger mechanism used in the Sterling Police Carbine, marked 'SINGLE SHOT'.

With the change lever (6) set to 'FIRE' or 'R' (repetition), the solid block at the front of the special inner change lever (8) bears on the front left-hand stop or spacer pin (13). In this position the top of the inner change lever is under the toe of the boot-shaped tripping lever (20), allowing single shot fire only.

If the block on the inner change lever were removed OR a new L2A3 change lever (8A) were fitted, the top of the inner change lever would be able to rotate forward, clear of the toe of the tripping lever. Rock and Roll is still alive …

In the 'SAFE' or 'S' position, the inner change lever is positioned under the heel of the tripping lever boot.

Dipping into the Mk4 Production Pool

A total of 507 SMGs (17 MkIIIs and 490 Mk4s) were converted to single-shot Police Carbines between 1956 and 1975, with further batches made up as and when required. We have examined many of these guns, all in the typical civilian black crackle finish.

It is blatantly clear that these Police Carbines were merely commercial automatic guns converted to semi-automatic. The wording 'POLICE CARBINE' on the top of the magazine housing has been engraved extremely deeply with a wide-pointed engraving cutter, but the former lettering 'SMG' is still slightly visible. Likewise, while the change lever markings of 'R' 'S' (for 'Repetition' and 'Safe') on the left side of the pistol grip have been over-engraved with 'FIRE' and 'SAFE', the former 'A' 'R' and 'S' letters are still clearly visible, indicating their origin as automatics.

The conversion of the trigger mechanism to single shot was completed by simply changing the automatic inner change lever (Sterling part number S4-12-9, NATO part number 1005-99-960-2199) to a modified one (Sterling part number P4-12-9) which could not rotate forward to the 'A' Automatic position. These semi-automatic trigger mechanisms were also marked 'SINGLE SHOT'. That was the extent of the modification: the inner change lever is the only part that differs between the Automatic Mk4/L2A3 and the semi automatic Mk4 carbine.

Overcoming the Modifications

Quite quickly some of these single-shot 9mm carbines found their way into the hands of legitimate target shooters in the United Kingdom (only 36 units) and the USA, plus of course, those other Commonwealth countries where semi-automatic or self-loading guns were permitted but NOT full automatics.

Peter Laidler had personal experience of some Malayan rubber planters who simply ground off the blocking projection from the inner change lever so as to have what they really wanted: a gun that fired as though it meant business. One planter from Batu Pahat in Malaya told him that when he heard noises outside at night, he went out with his 'carbine' and cocked it. Animal noises remained but human noises immediately abated. "Sten gun speak", he said as he patted his trusty Sterling Mk4. Nor would his Sterling ever fail him.

The Police Attempt Prosecution for Selling Prohibited Weapons

Sterling Police Carbines were initially offered for sale within the United Kingdom, until, after the mentioned 36 units had been sold, one Police Force decided, unwisely as it transpired, to prosecute the Sterling company for supplying prohibited weapons, in this case, sub-machine guns.

According to press reports of the time, this prosecution was NOT based on the fact that an owner of a Police Carbine might grind off the inner change lever to attempt to make it an automatic, but much more loosely on the fact that if an owner of such a weapon left the trigger mechanism out, he would be able to put a full magazine onto the gun, pull the cocking handle to the rear, let it go and immediately have an (uncontrollable) sub-machine gun with automatic fire.

"We agree", said Sterling: after all, isn't that exactly what George Patchett did in his own office one evening when he accidentally fired off a magazine of bullets into his desk, filing cabinets and floor from a triggerless gun? But what was more, the prosecutor argued, once this gun WAS fired in such a manner, because it was being held one-handed (the other hand having just released the cocking handle), it was uncontrollable and unstoppable. The consequences of such foolhardy action could only be imagined, the prosecutor went on, especially in the wrong hands.

"We agree with that too", said Sterling, whose lawyer quickly countered by asking whether any of the 36 Police Carbines sold in Britain had ever been traced to 'wrong hands'?

"Not that we are aware", the prosecutor sheepishly replied. "We'll take that as 'NO' then," said the Sterling lawyer, who asked, "then have you any evidence that ANYBODY has tried this 'no trigger mechanism' stunt?"

Once again, when the legal jargon had ceased, it became clear that no, there was no evidence that a member of the PUBLIC had tried it. But what DID emerge was that the POLICE had tried it; "in order to prove the point to the satisfaction of the court"! Uncontrollable and unstoppable indeed …

But ex-Royal Marines Major Keen, Sterling's unflappable Sales Manager, was a representative of the company AND by definition an expert witness. He told the court that, as MAKERS of sub-machine guns, Sterling were at liberty to test and fire their products in any way they liked (and regularly did), but that did not express or imply that others might follow their example. He also stated that the Police Carbines were MADE and SUPPLIED as semi-automatic carbines, and NOT automatic sub-machine guns. He was also able to supply evidence that, true to the Sterling brochure, the office of the Secretary of State for Home Affairs had earlier clearly determined that the single-shot Sterling carbine "… is no longer a prohibited weapon (a machine gun) as defined in the UK Firearms Act of 1937, part 2, section 17".

What was more, Major Keen told the court that if a BUYER or other user chose to convert his carbine to fire automatically BY WHATEVER MEANS, then HE must answer to the court, not the Sterling company. After all, he successfully argued, what is the difference between one user taking out the trigger mechanism to get auto fire, and another taking the more difficult (but quite possible) route of modifying the inner change lever?

He also put forward other comparisons. For example, he pointed out that while most Ford cars (also locally produced in Dagenham) would readily exceed the speed limit, nobody was prosecuting Ford, although plenty of Ford drivers were getting speeding tickets!

The Police lost their case, due to total and complete incompetence. It was said that the prosecution did not have even the most basic understanding of the operation of the gun. The Police left the court licking their wounds after having considerable financial costs awarded against them. They did not come back for more.

By that time, of course, the damage had been done, as every gun-buff in Britain had been furnished with step-by-step instructions on how to convert the semi-automatic Police Carbine into a sub-machine gun, courtesy of the Police! Surely a lesson in how NOT to wield a big stick!

Following this case, there was an unwritten "gentleman's agreement" between the Sterling Company and the United Kingdom Police forces that after the sale of the initial 36 guns, further Police Carbines would not be sold on the UK market. However, it did not take long for enterprising dealers to simply purchase the guns back from countries whence they had been legally exported. The rascals!

As discussed in later chapters, the BATF-approved closed-bolt Mk6 and Mk8 guns that eventually replaced the Mk4 Police Carbine were a different kettle of fish entirely. Even so, it did not take long before an enterprising US entrepreneur produced a small booklet detailing how to make the closed-bolt Mk6 and Mk8 fire fully automatically. Where there's a will, there's a way; says the old proverb!

There it is. Due to the fact that the Mk4 Sterling was so tough and reliable, it never 'hit the headlines', but just got on quietly with the job. So reliable was it, that it formed the basis of the next gun in the series. This surreptitious little gun got on with the job in an even quieter way. Enter, stage right, the magnificent Silenced Mk5 or Gun, Sub-Machine, 9mm, L34A1. All be very quiet, or you'll miss it!

Chapter Eight

The Silent Sterling

Sterling-Patchett Silenced Gun Mk5 (Gun, Sub Machine, 9mm L34A1)

Date introduced:		20 June,1966
Date adopted by UK Military:		January, 1967
Date production ceased:		September, 1988
Date obsoleted in UK Military:		still in service
Quantity manufactured:	Sterling commercial	3,500
	UK Military 'US67A': restricted (+/− 500)	

The De Lisle: the *First* Silenced Sterling

The full history of the mystical De Lisle Carbine has been written elsewhere, and for those interested in further reading we suggest *The Lee Enfield Story* and the booklet *Small Arms Series, Number 1, The De lisle Carbine*, both published in Australia by Ian Skennerton and in the USA by IDSA Books of Piqua, Ohio.

Like the Lanchester, the De Lisle was not a true Sterling design, but it was another gun made by Sterling under the direction of the Ministry of Supply and thus must be regarded as "from the Sterling stable".

The information that follows is taken from those records that existed at Sterling Armament Co Ltd at its closure in 1989, the memory of George Patchett's assistant Bert List, and the remaining archives of Holland and Holland. It follows therefore that this information might differ somewhat to details found elsewhere and documented at the Public Records Office. Certainly some information held at the Sterling works differs from the facts shown on the guns examined. This can only be put down to wartime pressures and hasty bookkeeping.

Like the Lanchester, De Lisle guns were built by several firms, including Sterling, under contract to the Ministry of Supply, who controlled the production.

Several Sterling factory personnel, including Bert List, were involved in both silenced projects, the De Lisle and the Patchett. In fact, while examining a De Lisle gun for this research, we established that the design and application of both silencers was too similar to be coincidental. It has been said that there is nothing new in small-arms design, and this is a case in point. It is quite obvious that the Sterling Patchett Mk5 silencer owes its origins to the De Lisle, and the De Lisle silencer owes its origins to previously patented ideas.

Origins of the De Lisle Silenced Carbine

William Godfray De Lisle lived at Letcombe on the Berkshire Downs, and worked as an engineer for the Ministry of Aircraft Production at many of the aircraft factories nearby. He had a .22″ Browning self-loading rifle and in 1942, he built himself a silencer in order that he could quietly kill game for his family. Meat was in short supply, but game on the Downs was plentiful. He also fitted the rifle with a WWI Periscopic Prism Company telescope in ring mounts.

Major Sir Malcolm Campbell, who also lived nearby, got to hear about this silenced rifle, if you'll excuse the pun, and invited De Lisle to London to show it to fellow Officers from the Combined Operations Executive S6 Department. They fired the gun many times from the top of the Adelphi building, down into the Thames. They considered that it was worthy of further development, but not in .22″ calibre. Major Campbell asked William De Lisle to build him a prototype, based on "a larger calibre rifle action", but in 9mm calibre.

This .22″ gun has gone into history as being the first prototype, although whether scholars should consider this gun to be the first "prototype" or just De Lisle's original is a matter of conjecture.

The "larger rifle action" is now well documented as being the action body of the No1 rifle, into which De Lisle fitted a modified 9mm Lanchester barrel.

Problems with Early De Lisle Silencers

The silencer built around that Lanchester barrel introduced many problems, the first being that the 9mm bullet was supersonic. This was overcome by venting the barrel, a feature that was later copied in the silenced Sten and Sterling Mk5/L34A1.

The second problem was that the ragged edges of the vent holes within the barrel shaved slivers of copper/cupro nickel from the jackets of the 9mm bullets, making them unstable in flight and the gun totally inaccurate.(During Sten Mk2S and Mk6 production, this problem was overcome by filling the barrels with molten lead, allowing it to cool, then drilling the holes.)

In order to eliminate these two problems in the De Lisle, it was decided that the gun should be in .45ACP calibre, as standard-issue .45″ ammunition was sub-sonic, which made venting the barrel unnecessary.

Although it was not necessary to vent the adapted .45 calibre Thompson barrel next used, a series of small holes was drilled close to the muzzle end "… to allow some of the escaping gases to build up the back pressure within the expansion chamber and to reduce the volume of gas flowing at high velocity behind the bullet. The short length of barrel left intact [at the muzzle end] serves to steady the bullet if it should become upset due to the gases escaping behind it."

A One-Off Production De Lisle from Bapty & Co

De Lisle himself did not have the time, facilities nor official authority to continue his work on the silenced carbine, so Major Campbell took it to Bapty & Co, who were, and still are, Armourers to the British film industry. Their Armourers completed the task to De Lisle's specifications and sketches. The Bapty gun, number 001, was returned to Major Campbell for evaluation. Right from the start, it was found to be successful. There was no flash at night, it was inaudible at 50 yards, and even closer it was totally unrecognisable as a firearm discharging.

De Lisle Patents "His" Ideas

In the meantime, De Lisle, aware of the possibility that large quantities of this gun might be manufactured (not a wise assumption there I'm afraid, Bill), set about patenting "his" ideas. On 7 June, 1944, Roult, Wade and Tennant, chartered patent agents of 111-2 Hatton Garden, London, [just up the road from the long-defunct Maxim Gun Co, at no 57D] registered the design, giving William Godfray De Lisle a security address of 43 Belgrave Road, London SW1. Provisional patents had previously been granted.

The Bapty & Co De Lisle Prototype Proves Popular

The .45ACP Bapty & Co gun no 001 certainly caused quite a stir, and in February, 1944, Warren Lothrop, who was head of technical aid to Division 19 of the United States OSS (the UK equivalent of the SOE) asked Wing Commander "Dickey" Bird, a UK Military attache based in New York, if he knew anything about the De Lisle carbine apart from descriptive reports.

Major Campbell wanted a small number produced immediately for use by Commandos operating along the French coast. He wanted them made by Holland and Holland, but they were fully committed with other important war work. But more about the Holland and Holland connection later.

First Series Production at Ford Motor Company

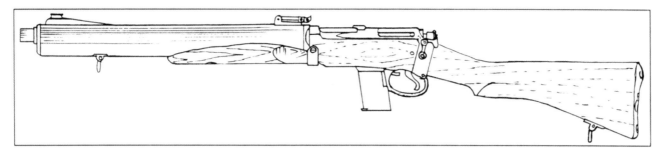

202. Left side view of a Ford-made De Lisle Carbine.

The first twelve Ford-made De Lisles were fitted with simple folded steel sporting rifle backsights. Six of these guns were subsequently retrofitted at Holland and Holland with luminised No1 Mk3 rifle backsights, and a further three guns, fitted with No1 rifle tangent backsights during manufacture, were luminised as well.

After the war the Ford De Lisles were withdrawn and scrapped, and thus very few of the (very few) Ford-made De Lisle guns remain in existence. (Drawing by Peter Laidler)

For reasons best known to himself, Major Campbell suggested that the British Ford Motor Company at Dagenham undertake the manufacture of the first production batch of De Lisle guns.

Ford too were fully occupied with war-work, but nonetheless, were "invited" by the Ministry of Supply (in wartime language, this equated to being "ordered") to undertake the initial production run.

The First Connection with Sterling

The Sterling Engineering Company, just down the road from Ford in Dagenham, were by this time involved in production of the Lanchester, and were developing the Patchett. Two factory foremen experienced in small-arms production were seconded to the Ford toolroom.

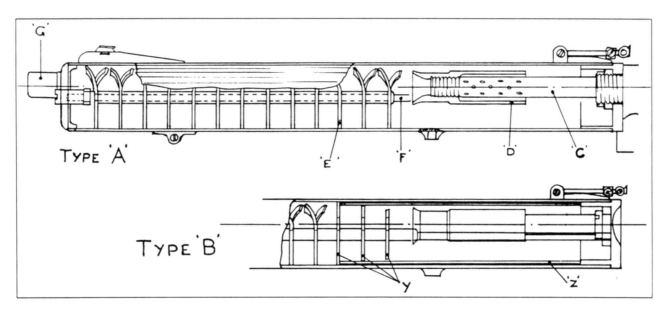

203. Skeletonised views of two patterns of De Lisle silencer. Above: type 'A', the most common silencer. Note the vented barrel (C), the barrel sleeve (D), the eccentric baffles (E), locating rod (F) and nozzle (G), the latter a feature of the Ford-made De Lisle .

Below: the type 'B' silencer. Note the first three baffles (Y) are eccentrically bored flat plates. Surrounding the barrel is a sandwich (Z) consisting of "… a sound-absorbing, yieldable material, which may be felt, rubber or rubberised fabric, asbestos or lead-wool, protected on the inside and outside by a thin metallic sheath". (Drawing by Peter Laidler)

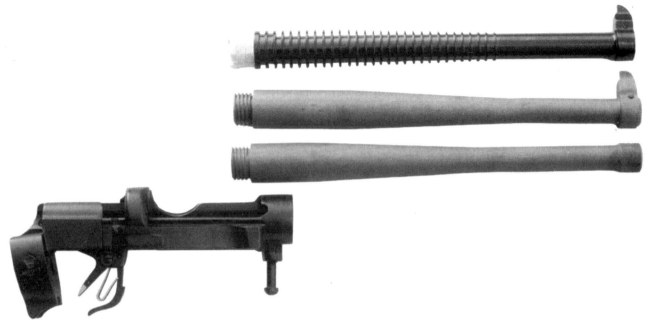

204. De Lisle carbines were assembled using surplus, well used No1 Mk3 rifle receivers, left, mated to .45" Thompson SMG barrels (right, in three versions as described below).

Above: original M1928 finned TSMG barrel (with protective grease paper wrapped around breech threads). It was soon found that there was not enough material left at the breech end of the finned barrels to accept the No1 rifle body thread, so this type of barrel was not used.

Centre: non-finned M1928Al or MI/MIAl Thompson barrel, as used exclusively in De Lisle conversions.

Below: non-finned MI 928 barrel, front sight stripped prior to modifications. (MoD Army, REME)

There the No1 rifle bodies, supplied from Enfield, were mated with the Thompson sub–machine gun barrels, which were supplied machined to size by Greener.

Ford got the first 17 production De Lisle guns into operation, then immediately into service. These guns were reportedly numbered 1002 to 1018, the Bapty gun being number 001.

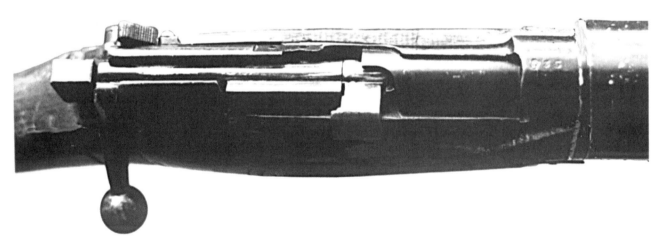

205. Right side closeup of the receiver of a typical De Lisle. Note the modified No1 rifle receiver, shortened No1 rifle bolt, and modified Thompson barrel.

Serial numbering was a relatively haphazard affair which included numbers stamped in one of two sizes, $^3/_{32}$" or $^3/_{16}$" in a number of locations. Clockwise from 9 o'clock: rear of bolt handle; left side of receiver close to ejector screw; left and right sides of breeching-up ring (where they are easily confused with old No1 rifle serial numbers); right side of receiver; forestock above magazine.

These Ford guns have the silencer jackets made from drawn steel tube. They can be further identified by having a short length of (what appears to be barrel) tube protruding from the end of the silencer jacket.

There has been some speculation as to the exact date these first seventeen Ford guns were made. Indeed, even an approximate date has been disputed. We do know that on 12 August, 1943 an order (dated 28 April, incidentally) was placed with Holland and Holland to supply and fit six sets of luminised night sights to De Lisle carbines. Later this was increased to nine sets, priced at £3:10s:6d (£3:52p) each.

This order was placed by the shadowy War Department Experimental Station (6) operating from Whitehall, London SW1. They also arranged to have night sights fitted to over 700 Sten guns, 500 Thompson SMGs and a similar number of .45″ Colt pistols. Holland and Holland also fitted silencers to a quantity of Thompson guns, and the first silencers to

Mk5 Sten guns, leading to the adoption of the Mk6 Sten. They also assembled the Welrod silenced pistol for this secret ES(6) department.

The De Lisles, Stens, Thompsons and Colts were sent directly to 41, 46, 47 Commando and 45 Scottish Brigade. We therefore know that the De Lisle was operating with Commandos after August, 1943.

The First Sterling-Made De Lisle Carbines

Following the success of the Ford-made De Lisle guns, the Combined Operations Executive ordered a production run of 500 De Lisle carbines, this time from the Sterling Engineering Co Ltd.

Once again Enfield supplied the stripped, secondhand bodies from disassembled .303″ No1 rifles, and the .45 calibre Thompson barrels were supplied machined to size from Greener, who,

206. Right side view of a Sterling-made De Lisle carbine, with magazine removed. This gun was part of the Sterling collection, where it was fitted with a magazine marked '.455 Eley'. (MoD Pattern Room collection)

207. Left side closeup of the markings on a Sterling-made De Lisle carbine.

Note the lightly engraved second line, reading 'COSD 2111 SECo'. COSD was the Special Operations Executive's Stores Division; 2111 was the contract number; and SECo stood for Sterling Engineering Co Ltd.

Guns so marked are quite rare, as are all De Lisle guns today. (MoD Army, RMCS Shrivenham)

along with Holland and Holland, were involved in rebuilding war-weary British Army Thompsons.

Initially it was thought that there would be a considerable build-up of pressure within the silencing chamber, and drawn-steel tubing was used for the silencer jackets. The Sterling engineers discovered that this was not the case: Sterling-made De Lisles would have duralium alloy silencer tubes and baffles.

The V-Bomb Fire at Sterling: De Lisle Records Destroyed

If there is a lesson to be learned for all future researchers of small-arms, it must be that you should never accept previous research at face value, regardless of its pedigree.

The 500 Sterling De Lisle carbines were supposed to be numbered 1019 onwards, but one Sterling-made gun examined is distinctly numbered 1015, with a bolt to match.

We have mentioned the V-bomb fire at the Sterling factory on 21 March, 1945, and the handwritten factory record (fig 73) dated 26 March which recorded that 101 Patchett Carbines and 4 De Lisle Carbines had been manufactured and dispatched to the War Department, with none remaining in stock.

The Sterling Company records show that they only made a total of 106 De Lisle carbines before the order was cancelled on 20 December, 1945.

In theory, this should mean that the last Sterling-made De Lisle would be number 124 (1024). However, it appears that the last serial number was actually 2089 or 2090.

The most realistic explanation of why later Sterling-made De Lisle guns have numbers out of sequence is that, while the "Troop Trials 101" Patchetts were already numbered and ready to go, the serial numbers of De Lisle carbines already delivered were lost in the V-bomb fire.

Additionally, two extra guns were ordered for the Ordnance Board. Whether these guns were made as supernumerariesor taken from known production is not clear. But this could have a bearing on the final production figures given later. In any case, this Ordnance Board order was cancelled on 16 November, 1944.

The Sterling "De Lisle Commando Carbine, MkII"

Plans were soon well advanced for the production and assembly of these guns at Sterling, largely because the small parts had been swiftly subcontracted out to manufacturers who specialised in like components. For example Webb and Co, who made Mk1 Lanchester tangent backsights, were contracted to supply 500 sets of sights for the De Lisle. According to factory records, Webb had supplied a total of 428 "recalibrated Lanchester backsights and 476 foresights" before the De Lisle procurement order was cancelled on 20 December, 1945. Similar quantities of other De Lisle components were also stockpiled at Sterling when the production order was cancelled.

The manufacture of De Lisle guns at Dagenham was highly labour-intensive. As a result, they were relatively expensive, and the small number involved meant that it was not viable to produce them by

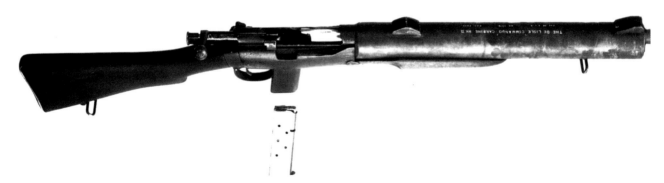

208. Right side view of the Sterling-made "De Lisle Commando Carbine MkII", serial no 1015, with .45 pistol magazine removed and bolt open. Note the simplified Lanchester Mk1* flipover rear sight, and the protruding 'nozzle', supposedly a feature of Fordmade De Lisles. (MoD Pattern Room collection)

production-line methods, as was the case with the Lanchester and the later Patchett.

The serial number on Sterling-made De Lisles was supposed to be stamped on the right side of the body, between the two rivet holes vacated by the absent bridge charger guide. The serial number may also be found stamped into the wooden fore stock adjacent to this. Once again, fact differs from record, because some guns are certainly not numbered between the rivet holes.

Traces of the former No1 rifle markings are usually obvious too, including the former serial number. Additionally, rifle serial numbers may be found on the left and right of the breeching-up ring, the rear of the bolt handle, the left side of the body above the ejector screw, and the right side of the body.

One particular hiccup concerned the No1 rifle receiver. To accept the large-diameter breech of the Thompson barrel (you can only turn so much steel from it), it was necessary to line-bore the left side of the boltway in the receiver, to give the barrel clearance. Any engineer will confirm that line-boring 20% of a full diameter is not easy. This inherent difficulty was compounded by the fact that, given the age and degree of wear inherent in most of the receivers, which were all secondhand, none was the same. Each receiver had to be set up and machined on an individual basis.

The Thompson barrels were partially machined at the rear where the chamber portion intrudes into the boltway. The remainder of the rear section of the barrel, being 1" in diameter, was threaded with the 1" × 14 TPI thread that enabled it to be screwed into the No1 rifle body. The muzzle was threaded to accept the sleeve. That was easy.

Consummating a Difficult Union

As manufactured, neither the British-made No1 rifle bodies and bolts nor the American-made Thompson SMG barrels had been intended to interface with one another. This made what was ordinarily a relatively simple task, that of setting cartridge headspace (CHS), into something far more difficult.

The No1 rifle barrel is breeched *inside* the receiver ring, and not by abutting outside, as on the No4 rifle. Furthermore, due to the differences in the start point of the re-cut bolt head threads within the shortened bolt, the length of each bolt could differ by up to .050" (fifty thousandths of an inch). This was the norm throughout the whole of the manufacturing process. CHS in the De Lisle was set during the conversion by adjusting the barrel to the bolt and bolthead with breeching washers.

In fact, every De Lisle was virtually a "one-off", with components manufactured individually for each gun. Close examination of individual parts will show the serial number scribed or stamped in.

Staff Sergeant Harry Weeks, an Armourer of that era with knowledge of Sterling De Lisles nos 26, 28, 31 and 39, described them as "an absolute nightmare".

Sights on the Sterling-Made De Lisles

Early Sterling-made De Lisles have the re-graduated Mk1 Lanchester rear sight rivetted to the silencer casing. These are marked up to 200 yards in 50-yard intervals, allowing for the difference in velocity and trajectory between the Lanchester 9mm and De Lisle .45" ball ammunition. Later 'MkII' De Lisles use the two-position, flipover rear sight from the Lanchester Mk1*.

The foresight blade was not adjustable for height after assembly. Initial zeroing was completed by Sterling and the backsight bed marked accordingly. Deflection adjustment was made by swinging the articulating blade left or right.

However, some early Sterling De Lisles have a simple spring steel Winchester rifle tangent sight, and one is known to exist with a modified No1 Mk3 rifle rear sight fixed to the casing.

From Maker to User–in 24 Hours

Sterling Archive records show that some of their De Lisle guns were in the hands of European resistance fighters within 24 hours of production.

It is recorded fact that these guns were used in France, Burma and later, in the Malayan counter-terrorist campaign.

Night Sights from Holland and Holland

From Webb and Co, the De Lisle sights were sent to Holland and Holland to be converted into night sights. Under Sterling order 30011, dated 6 March, 1945, Holland and Holland were required to drill the rear of the foresight blade, slot the backsight, bronofix (blacken) the assemblies and luminise, all for 6/9d (34p) per set.

The luminising consisted of filling the slotted and drilled recesses with zinc sulphide mixed with an active radium compound. Little did they then realise just how long this old-fashioned luminising compound would remain active!

The One-Off, Folding-Stock "Airborne" De Lisle Carbine

The original 500-gun order from Sterling was later amended to read 450 'MkII' guns plus 50 "airborne" models, the latter to be fitted with the folding butt taken straight from George Patchett's MkI SMG.

The 50 airborne models were to be numbered from 451 to 500, although the only one actually manufactured, now housed at The School of Infantry, has no serial numb er. The bolt is numbered 1017 which, if the official records are to be believed, was taken from a Ford-made De Lisle.

Postwar Refurbishing of De Lisles at RSAF Enfield, with Sterling Assistance

About 80 needy De Lisle guns were refurbished during the post-war Factory Thorough Repair (FTR) programme at RSAF Enfield. Due to the fact that Enfield had not been involved in the original project, they had to turn to Sterling for the necessary expertise and, where necessary, spare parts. Luckily, Sterling had stocks of many components (especially sights and silencer components) left over from the cancelled 500-gun order.

There was never a published parts list for the De Lisle. Parts that had a No1 rifle equivalent (such as a butt or locking bolt) were readily available, but there could be problems with special parts such as magazines and bolts.

Those guns overhauled at Enfield have the 'FTR-48' mark lightly engraved below the knob of the bolt handle.

Scrapping the Ford-Made De Lisles

As a result of the availability of Sterling spares, and the fact that the Ford De Lisles differed in many (albeit minor) ways, the Ford guns were sifted out, withdrawn and scrapped. It is for this reason that very few of the (very few) Ford-made De Lisle guns remain in existence.

The Demise of the De Lisle – Quietness, Yes; but Accuracy, No

Stories abound as to the accuracy of the De Lisle, at ranges out to 400 yards, no less. However, after a recent spell on the range at the School of Infantry with a De Lisle under controlled conditions and using modern factory ammunition, Peter Laidler

209. Right side view of the one-off Sterling "Airborne" De Lisle, fitted with George Patchett's patented folding SMG butt.
Fifty such guns were ordered, but only one was ever completed. (MoD Pattern Room collection)

has to report that grouping, and therefore accuracy, were not among the gun's finest attributes, certainly beyond 50 yards. Quietness, yes; but accuracy, no.

During a recent test firing, with a noise meter situated 30 feet away, the De Lisle recorded 46 decibels. Of course, this was a field test and not a scientific one.

Tests at the British National Physics Laboratory showed the silenced Sten to be as quiet as the De Lisle and, if used in the single shot mode only, just as reliable.

Moreover, Mk2S and Mk6 Sten were in plentiful supply, and were more easily understood by users. Spare parts were readily available, and in Peter Laidler's experience until at least 1971 and as recently as 1992, canvas silencer gaiters were still in a small box of odd Sten parts. Finally, while the Stens were not regarded to be as "accurate" as the De Lisle, they did use the far more readily available 9mm ammunition.

These facts caused the demise of the De Lisle, and by 1954 it had been completely withdrawn from service.

De Lisle Production Totals

9mm Prototype (De Lisle):	1
.45″ Prototype (Bapty and Co)	1
Production (Ford)	17
Production (Sterling)	106
Prototype airborne	1
Total	125

Serial Numbers

Ford:	1002 to 1018
Sterling:*	19 to 289 or 290
Prototype "airborne"	1

Requiem for the Mystical De Lisle

The De Lisle has slipped into history surrounded by an almost mystical air. It was certainly no match for the equally mystical Welrod pistol or the Mk2S or Mk6 Sten. Nor, dare we say it, the Mk5 Sterling. For all its mysterious background, we hope that uncovering its faults hasn't diminished its worthy reputation and its deserved place in the annals of small arms history.

Cost per De Lisle: no definite figure is available but the total conversion cost to Sterling, less parts supplied by Enfield and Greener, was £27.15. Given that an entire Bren gun cost only £34, the De Lisle was very expensive. By definition the De Lisle could only be used in the offensive role, but as the saying goes, "offence is no expense".

The Silent Stens

210. Right side view of the famous Mk2S Sten, the silenced successor to the De Lisle.

Quite as quiet as the De Lisle if used correctly (i.e., single-shot ONLY). Said to be less accurate than the De Lisle, but modern shooting trials prove this to be a myth. The Mk2S and Mk6 silenced Stens served for many years, and were the predecessors to the superb Sterling-Patchett Mk5/L34A1. (MoD Army, REME)

---

* But not sequentially. These serial numbers should be treated with a degree of suspicion in the light of recent findings.

During the 1960s, the silenced sub-machine gun in front line service with those armies that had a requirement for such a weapon, was the Mk2S and/or the Mk6 Sten gun, whose origins dated back to the mid-1940s.

Certainly in Malaya during the mid to fate 1960s, Peter Laidler encountered both Mk2S and Mk6 Stens in Military service.

Full-Auto Fire Destroys Sten Silencer Baffles

The major drawback with the Mk2S and Mk6 Sten was that, although they should not be, they could be used in the automatic role. When this was done, the silencer overheated and very quickly burned or blasted out the baffling medium.

Soldiers being soldiers, no matter what was told them, they would insist on trying the automatic role. A two-second burst (20 rounds) would effectively seal the silencer's fate.

Although spare Sten silencer parts were kept in the Armourers' shop, they were not replaced as a matter of course, and the guns were left with burned out baffling or none at all.

They still tried it. Peter Laidler recalls one trooper coming into the Armourer's shop, commenting "… I

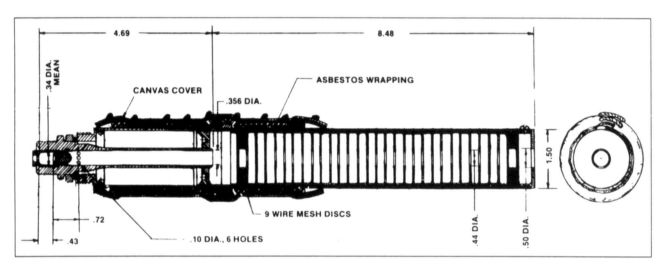

211. 9mm Sten SMG Silencer Assembly, Type I.
   Note the six .10-dia holes bored into the barrel around the breech end.

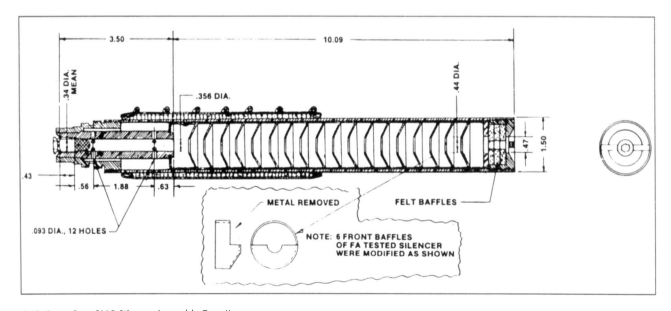

212. 9mm Sten SMG Silencer Assembly, Type II.
   The number of .093-diaholes bored into the barrel has been doubled to 12, in two rings of six holes each.

fired it single shot, then automatic, and it sounds just as loud as an 12 [Mk4 Sterling]!" Of course it did; we didn't replace the baffling, and without it, it sounded like a normal gun. But we didn't tell them.

Another favourite trooper's trick was to quickly swing the gun from side to side while firing it. Getting it just right wasn't difficult, and the bullet would leave the muzzle of the very short (some were 4.7″ and others were only 3.5″ long) barrel set back inside the silencer casing, and hit the last stepped baffles and then the solid silencer casing end plate, sending it whining off downrange.

There was no excuse for this, and a degree of backside kicking was the order of the day for miscreants. All protested their innocence, the rascals.

While this is not about the Mk2S and Mk6 Sten, Peter Laidler recalls that there was no illustrated parts list for the silenced Stens either (or if there was, he never saw one). Parts had to be identified from the Vocabulary of Army Ordnance Stores (VAOS or just Vocab) lists, which were placed almost at random within the B3 section.

Relying on Sub-Sonic Ammunition

The First Silenced Patchetts

OB Proc Q4,532, dated 16 August, 1946, introduced a proposal from George Patchett for a silencer that simply attached to a relatively standard Patchett machine carbine. The Proc reported that the clip-on silencer had already undergone sound tests at the National Physics Laboratory in May, 1946, using the necessary "reduced charge ammunition".

A Clip-On Silencer for the First Six "MkII" Patchetts

As noted in Chapter Four, an initial series of six "MkII" Patchetts with 82° magazine housings was first supplied in the early postwar years, although the gun (and hence the designation) was not officially adopted until July, 1953.

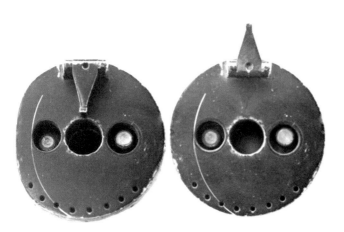

213. Three end-on views of Patchett's clip-on silencer.
  Left: front view, front sight folded down.
  Centre: front view, front sight raised. Note the vent-holes around the lower periphery, another feature copied from the De Lisle, used to drain moisture from the silencer, produced by the continual compression of air.
  Right: rear view of Patchett's clip-on silencer. Note the two side clamps, which mate with the slots in the sides of the gun casing (fig 89), and the recessed locating pin (under the rear sight) which mates with the hole in the top of the muzzle cap (fig 90) of the first six "MkII" Patchetts, serial nos 01–06. (MoD Pattern Room collection)

214. Two views of the Patchett clip-on silencer, attached to "MkII" Patchett No 06.

Above: left side view, showing front sight raised. The silencer tube is marked "PATCHETT. MKII."

Right: top three-quarter view, showing clamps rotated into the slots in the gun casing. (MoD Pattern Room collection)

These guns (figs 89 through 92) were factory modified with square slots in the front sides of the casings and a round hole in the top front of the muzzle cap, to take Patchett's clip-on silencer.

OB Proc Q 5,127 dated 3 June, 1947 mentions this "New Model" Patchett and the "Silencing attachment using a special cartridge", but indicates that development was to proceed on a "low priority" basis only, as "we have decided that there is no general requirement for a silent machine carbine".

The principal drawback of the Patchett clip-on silencer was that it was by definition useable on a (relatively) standard gun fitted with a regular barrel, and thus depended on specially produced, reduced charge (sub-sonic) ammunition. The project was shelved.

Early Silent SMG Research at RSAF Enfield

The Design Department of RSAF Enfield had been quietly working on a replacement for the Sten Mk2S and Mk6 since the mid–1950s, although the Chairman of the Sub-Machine Gun Steering Committee appeared not to have been aware of this when he later told his Canadian counterparts that he hoped they (the Canadians) would collaborate on a joint silenced gun project in the future.

The RSAF Enfield silencer design, which did not require any modifications at all to the standard sub-machine gun, was intended to function with special, sub-sonic 9mm rounds, loaded with heavy 150- or 170-grain bullets. For this purpose a short, curved

10-round magazine was proposed, which could be kept full of the special rounds in the soldier's pocket until required, the gun otherwise functioning normally with standard ammunition and magazines.

215. Unnumbered ex-Fazakerley L2A3 (with butt-welded magazine housing), showing identification marking 'DD3' on top line of nomenclature group.

A small number of unnumbered L2A3s were so marked by the the Design Department at RSAF Enfield when taken in for in-house testing. (MoD Pattern Room collection)

216. Left side view of a standard L2A3 fitted with the silencer unit developed by the RSAF Enfield Design Department.
   To attach the unit, the sprung rear half-cylinder is clipped around the bayonet standard as shown. (Courtesy MoD Pattern Room, Nottingham)

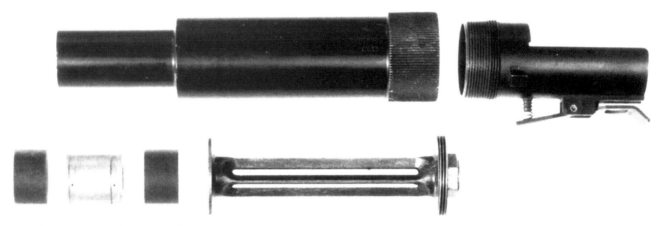

217. The components of the RSAF Enfield Design Department silencer.
   Top row, from left: silencer body; clip-on half-cylinder. Note the spring-loaded clip, which attaches to the bayonet standard of the gun.
   Bottom row, from left: 1st rubber plug; spacer; 2nd rubber plug; diffuser unit.
   This silencer was to be used with special LV (low velocity) heavy bullets in 150- and 170-grain weights. (Courtesy MoD Pattern Room, Nottingham)

218. Front closeup view of the RSAF Enfield silencer, showing the 1st solid rubber muzzle plug. These plugs were disposable, and designed to be pierced by each shot. (MoD Pattern Room collection)

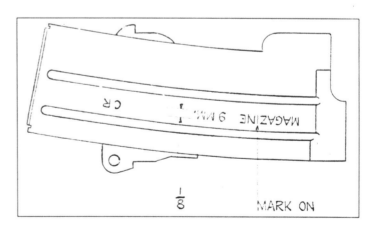

219. Enfield drawing dated 28 June, 1956 showing proposed curved 10-round magazine. Intended to be kept separate and filled with special LV heavy-bullet sub-sonic loads, to be used with the Enfield-designed clip-on silencer. Not adopted. (Courtesy MoD Pattern Room, Nottingham)

As shown, Enfield Design Department engineers utilised ex-Fazakerley L2A3 casings; after all, they had about 7,000 defective casings to experiment with.

The heavy-bullet option was at length discarded in favour of the permanently silenced Sterling-Patchett, which used regular 9mm ammunition.

A Third Contender-the Saben & Harts "Shutter" Silencer

220. Left side view of an L2A3, mounting the Saben & Harts "shutter" silencer.
    Note the absence of cooling holes in the special casing. (MoD Pattern Room collection)

A third design in hand during 1958 was the Saben & Harts silencer, which incorporated a flap or shutter mechanism, controlled by the bolt working a pushrod, that opened and closed the gas venting ports between the silencer and atmosphere. This was not a new idea, having been previously incorporated on certain diesel engines.

As fitted to the Patchett, the flaps/shutters would only operate during the last 5mm of forward and first 5mm of rearward movement of the bolt.

Unfortunately, this resulted in a massive buildup of carbon within the silencer unit. As every shooter knows, carbon buildup becomes VERY hard, and will jam up any moving parts within a short time. This problem could not be overcome, and caused the demise of the Saben & Harts shutter silencer, although in May, 1963 George Patchett patented a similar device within his SV (Silenced Version) gun.

Developing the Truly Silenced Sterling

New Requirements and Standard Ammunition

The Ministry of Defence Procurement Executive made it known that they were looking for a new silenced gun to replace the venerable Sten. They stated that this newgun, for logistical reasons, should be based upon the existing Sterling L2A3/Mk4 submachine gun. They also stated; "… the silencer must reduce the sound of the shot so that it is unrecognisable (as a gunshot) at a distance of 50 metres and that mechanical noise from the gun not be detectable at 30 metres."

Like the silenced Stens, the new design was to function with regular ball ammunition. Unlike the Stens, it would be capable of silenced, full-automatic fire. This effectively ruled out any form of rubber or neoprene buffers or baffles, which would be destroyed within several seconds of fire.

George Patchett's Debt to the De Lisle

In addition to fitting the "airborne" De Lisle carbine with a folding butt, George Patchett, ably assisted by Bert List, had cut his teeth with the design of the silencer unit on the De Lisle. The later silenced Mk5 gun owes many of its features to the De Lisle, and one of Patchett's first attempts at silencing the Sterling utilised a De Lisle silencer.

George Patchett got busy with his old pal, Bert List. Between them they incorporated the remains of an old De Lisle silencer casing onto an old hybrid' MkII/MkIII casing. The results were promising. This silencer contained no moving parts, nothing that would be affected by carbon (beyond that usual with firearms), and no parts that would deteriorate in intense heat.

In fact, the Sterling factory had a large quantity of De Lisle alloy silencer casing tubes in stock fot many years, and many of the remaining De Lisle silencer components were utilised by George Patchett and

Bert List in their development of the silenced Mk5 gun during the early 1960s.

Sterling and Enfield Pool Resources

George Patchett was well aware that the Enfield design and development engineers were working on a silenced Sterling gun, and what is more, HE knew that THEY knew his designs were at an important phase. But this time, in the face of a degree of mistrust stemming from the then-ongoing Patchett-Sterling/Crown litigation (that soon after found in favour of Patchett and Sterling), there was a meeting of minds.

Enfield gave George Patchett and Bert List some reject Fazakerley casings with which to further their experiments. These tests were conducted completely independently of the Sterling company.

The Experimental SV (Silenced Version) Patchett

The Patchett Push Rod-Activated Silencer

221. Three views of the SV (Silent Version) Patchett, built on a very late ex-Fazakerley casing no UF59A 162823, overstamped "SV 01 EXP".
   Above: right side view with butt folded.
   Below, left: closeup of markings on silencer tube.
Below, right: closeup view through ejection port, showing bolt-operated push rod which operates the "trap door" in the silencer.
   Only gun no SV1 retains this feature: on other SV models the push rod has been removed and the hole sealed up. (MoD Pattern Room collection)

Two guns that did feature in these Patchett/List experiments were very late Fazakerley casings nos UF59A 162119 and UF59A 162823, overstamped with the experimental SNs SV (silenced version)–01 EXP and SV-2 respectively. These guns must be regarded as the final Mk5 prototypes.

Turnabout Sterling Works for Patchett

Right from the start, the design of the new silenced gun was George Patchett's, and the Sterling designers and development engineers, with Bert List, worked on the project under his supervision. This time, the patents were George Patchett's alone.

The authors have chosen not to include details of George Patchett's silencer patents, no 757,640 covering the push rod–activated SV silencer, and no 966,934 dated 6 May, 1963, which relates to "Silencers and Flash Eliminators for Firearms".

The reason for this is that, unfortunately for the Sterling Company, there is no patent obtainable on the laws of physics. Many of the methods and principles for which Patchett claimed patent protection were copied from the earlier silenced Stens, and were to be copied by others later.

To be fair, patent 966,934 as detailed, does contain two "new" ideas that were incorporated into the eventual Mk5/L34A1 silenced SMG of 1967, and these are discussed below.

The Sterling company were reluctant to undertake the silenced SMG project on their own, because the MoD order was very small, so in this project, Sterling were to be George Patchett's sub-contractors. George knew that although the UK Military order might be small, many other governments were actively looking for a new silenced gun.

Building On the Standard Mk4 Casing

It was decided that in the interests of commonality, an EXTREMELY powerful sales point, the standard Sterling casing was to be used as the basis for George Patchett's new silenced SMG. Thus, rearward of the magazine housing, this silenced gun casing is identical to the Mk4/L2A3.

This casing is fitted with front and rear spacers, over which the silencer casing, a metal tube enclosing the component parts of the silencer, locates. A special locating sleeve for the barrel is fitted inside the casing, forward of the magazine housing.

Foresight protectors are fitted to the top of the silencer casing, and the foresight block slides into an inner locating sleeve. A small Allen bolt prevents the outer casing from rotating.

Taming the Supersonic 9mm Bullet

222. Top three-quarter right side view of the 'heart' of the Mks-the internal locating sleeve which was brazed into the casings of all Mks and Mk7 Sterlings to seal the breech cavity and act as the rear barrel support. The barrel is inserted from the rear and the flat on the bottom of the rear barrel flange is positioned on the protruding lip, which ensures that the barrel's extractor slot is perfectly aligned with the extractor.

Each example of the Mks Sterling-Patchett silenced gun was produced to tool room standards and virtually as an individual order: their price did not truly reflect the amount of handwork involved in their production. (MoD Army, REME)

Before attempting to silence the supersonic 9mm bullet, the engineers had noted that, "To silence a firearm effectively it is necessary not only to silence the noise of the discharge, but also to ensure that the bullet leaves the weapon below the speed of sound

(1,140 ft/sec or about 330m/sec in still air). This is achieved by reducing the energy of the propellant by diverting some gases from behind the bullet into the silencer unit. After the bullet leaves the weapon, the gases are quickly dissipated."

Thus the first problem encountered by the designers of both the silenced Stens and Sterling was the 9 × 19mm cartridge, as used by most of the major armies of the world, which gives a muzzle velocity from a 7.8″ long Mk4/L2A3 barrel of 1,280 ft/sec (390m/sec). It was also established that the velocity of the 9mm bullet fired from such a barrel did not fall below the speed of sound (1,140 ft/sec) until it had travelled 184 yards.

Clearly the use of these cartridges would cause a problem, but even more so was the alternative, the logistical one of having to use a special sub-sonic cartridge. The only way around the problem was to make sure that the bullet never reached the speed of 1,140 ft/sec while it made its way up the bore. To do this, the engineers enlisted the aid of the laws of physics and calculated mathematically that by drilling six rows of 12 small holes accurately in the rifling

grooves, each spaced equally up the 7.8″ length of the barrel, then a standard 9mm Mk2Z ball round would only reach between 960–1,020 ft/sec. Which was JUST what they wanted.

One of George Patchett's new ideas as detailed in patent 966,934 eventually incorporated into the Mk5 was drilling the barrel vent holes *along the path of the barrel rifling*. The exact pitch of the holes was an easy tolerance but the first line of holes from the breech face was tightly controlled by gauging this dimension 100%. During a test carried out with an old Mk4 on a chronograph-equipped test range, it was established that the exact position of the vent holes was of no consequence in reducing the speed of the bullet, although problems of imbalance might arise if the holes were drilled unequally around the barrel.

But the holes allowed a lot of hot gas to escape into the atmosphere, which had to be controlled, so the barrel was surrounded by a substantial steel diffuser tube, which did exactly as it says. It diffused.

The diffuser tube was also perforated BUT, it was drill-punched where each hole was partially drilled, then punched through. The end result was that the

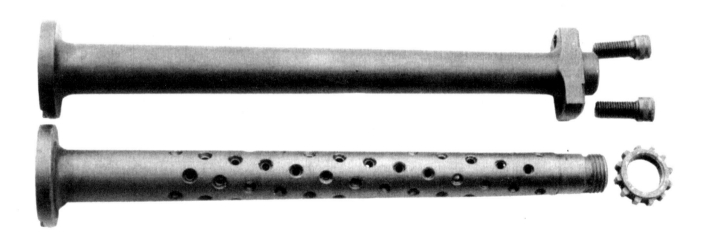

223. Right side views of two Sterling barrels.
   Above. Mk4/L2A3 barrel, with its two socket-headed securing screws.
   Below: Mk5/L34A1 barrel, with its castellated barrel nut.
   There are 12 vent holes in each of six spiral rows, a total of 72 holes. These follow the path of the rifling, as described in George Patchett's patent no 966,934. (MoD Army, REME)

inside was full of sharp, jagged punched metal edges. These sharp, jagged edges broke up the jets of flame and unburned propellant that exited through the 72 holes in the barrel in a most effective way. Peter Laidler can say from experience that firing one round from one of these guns WITHOUT the benefit of the diffuser tube or foil wrap to control the escaping gas is an awe-inspiring sight.

Once the vented gases passed out of the diffuser tube they were further controlled by a wrapped cylinder of expanded metal mesh, fitted between the diffuser tube and the original gun casing. From the gun casing, these gases were now vented via the muzzle opening in the outer silencer casing.

Adding the Muzzle Diffuser

The next problem faced by George Patchett and his team was what to do about the report. This is the loud bang or distinctive Sterling 'crackkkkk' caused by the high-pressure gases escaping into the atmosphere. Here, the problems were different but once again the laws of physics came to their aid. They put another diffuser, this time a SPIRAL diffuser, immediately in front of the front face of the barrel. All the escaping gases must pass through this spiral diffuser, which increases the distance they must travel to an incredible 5 ft (60″ approx), and slows them down before they are dissipated into the atmosphere from the front of the gun. The spiral diffuser slides on three tie rods.

In front of this spiral diffuser there is a forward expansion chamber. The other of George's patented silencer ideas incorporated into the Mk5 was the cupped design of the silencer end cap. The front plate of the expansion chamber features a design whereby some gas is swept back into the plenum chamber and further broken up before it escapes into the atmosphere.

This arrangement effectively slows the bullet down and eliminates the 'crack' as it passes through the air. The Sterling-Patchett was a truly silenced firearm, not merely a supressed or moderated one. There is just a 'whizzzzzzz' as the sub-sonic bullet passes close by, followed by a dull thud as it hits home, preferably into somebody else!

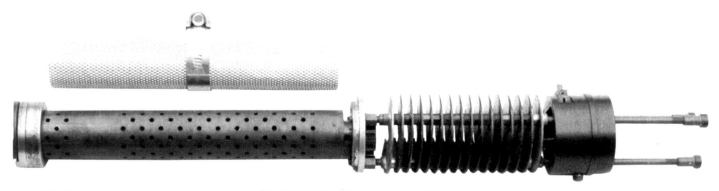

224. Right side view of the internal components of the Mk5/L34A1 silencer, shown partially assembled.
Above: the roll of expanded metal mesh, held in the wrapped position by the jubilee clip supplied in the special Armourer's tool kit (fig 363).
Below: the rear barrel flange (left) is shown positioned on the lip of the internal locating sleeve (fig 222; normally part of the Mk5/L34A1 casing assembly). The rest of the barrel extends through the diffuser tube, and the threaded muzzle end is clamped to the barrel support plate by the castellated barrel nut (centre).
Ahead of the diffuser tube is the spiral diffuser and extension tube (with front sight), showing how these are held in position by the tie rods. (MoD Army, REME)

The Commercial Foregrip vs an Old Woollen Sock

225. Left side view of the wooden foregrip, fitted to the commercial Mk5 silenced Sterling-Patchett. The centre of the foregrip was slightly recessed, and the forward end of the folded butt clipped to a steel button within this recess. The UK Military L34A1 dispensed with such fripperies. (Courtesy Adrian Bull)

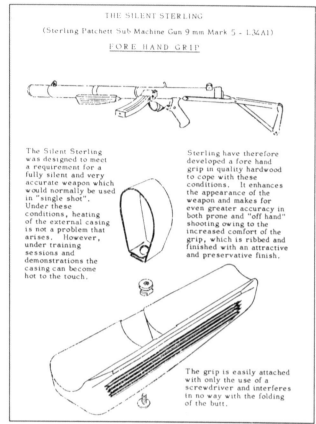

226. The one-page Sterling leaflet on the Mk5 "Fore Hand Grip", showing its method of installation. (Courtesy Sterling Archives)

The fact that the extremely hot propellant gases vent initially into the silencer casing meant that in a short space of time the casing gets, well, jolly hot. This isn't quite how an agitated soldier would describe his scorched hand, but nonetheless, the heat just HAS to go somewhere.

As a result, commercial Mk5s were equipped with a bulky wooden foregrip, suspended under the silencer casing by a steel band. The centre of the foregrip was slightly recessed, and the forward end of the folded butt clipped to a steel button within this recess.

The military-specification guns did not warrant such fripperies, so where a canvas sleeve, Sten-gun fashion, could not be improvised (in Peter Laidler's experience, from a webbing gaiter), then an old woollen sock pulled over from the muzzle did the job just as well.

Modifying the Breech Block to Improve Elevation and Depression Fire

One problem that did manifest itself with the prototype SV silenced Patchetts was that, whereas they operated perfectly in the horizontal plane, they did not operate satisfactorily in the depression mode. The depression and elevation modes allow firing at an anti-aircraft angle and, at the other extreme, down into a slit trench (or into the turret of a tank). These were important tests, which the early silenced SV Patchetts failed.

The reason was that, due to the lower muzzle velocity, the weight of the breech block would not allow it to recoil far enough to engage the sear. This condition produces one of three results: automatic fire only (a runaway gun); a jam because the breech block feed horns do not pick up the next round in the magazine; or a misfire caused by a diminished force of striker blow.

David Howroyd modified a standard breech block by concentrically lightening the inside surfaces. This cured the problem, but the modification was re-designed by George Patchett, who offset these lightening cuts .075″ to the right (when viewed from the rear). Quite why he did this remains somewhat of a mystery. It has been said that it was to prevent the borings breaking out into the rear of the feedhorns, but this is not correct. Perhaps it had to do with hardening, or maybe just, to quote David Howroyd, "… Patchett had some funny ideas"!

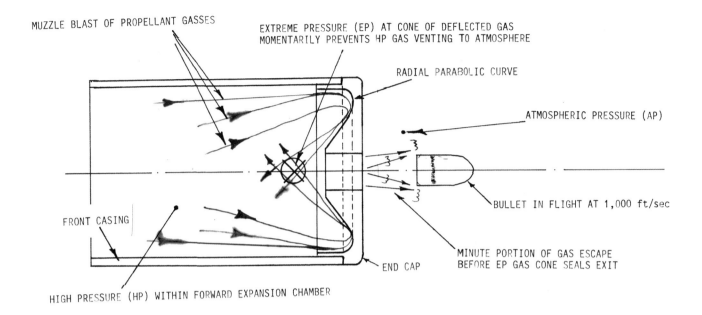

MUZZLE BLAST OF PROPELLANT GASSES

EXTREME PRESSURE (EP) AT CONE OF DEFLECTED GAS
MOMENTARILY PREVENTS HP GAS VENTING TO ATMOSPHERE

RADIAL PARABOLIC CURVE

ATMOSPHERIC PRESSURE (AP)

BULLET IN FLIGHT AT 1,000 ft/sec

FRONT CASING

END CAP

MINUTE PORTION OF GAS ESCAPE
BEFORE EP GAS CONE SEALS EXIT

HIGH PRESSURE (HP) WITHIN FORWARD EXPANSION CHAMBER

DIAGRAM SHOWING THE ACTION OF THE RADIAL PARABOLIC CURVE WITHIN THE END CAP
ON THE RELEASE OF PROPELLANT GASSES INTO THE ATMOSPHERE

Diagram showing the action of the radial parabolic curve within the end cap on the release of propellant gasses into the atmosphere.

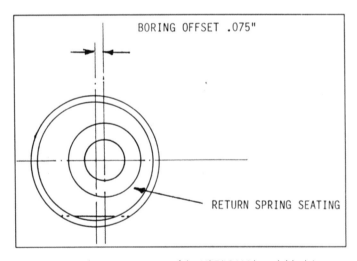

BORING OFFSET .075"

RETURN SPRING SEATING

227. Rear diagrammatic view of the Mk5/L34A1 breech block (part no CR 179 SA). For reasons of his own, George Patchett modified David Howroyd's initial concentric lightening cuts forward of the return spring seating to the .075" offset borings shown here. (Drawing by Peter Laidler)

Tailoring for Heavy 9mm Loads

No sooner had the lightened bolt cured short recoils in the elevation and depression fire modes, when another early problem manifested itself. Firing ammunition with heavy loads caused the locking lugs on the return spring cap to burr up the corresponding lugs of the cap locking ring on the rear of the casing, making stripping extremely difficult.

This problem was solved by Frank Waters, who incorporated a hard neoprene buffer ring into the return spring cap for export and commercial guns where users might encounter "… ammunition of doubtful origin or dubious manufacture". Or should that read "dubious origin or doubtful manufacture"! Peter Laidler encountered a similar problem with a UK Military L34A1 while firing stocks of captured Iraqi 9mm ball of supposedly French manufacture. Doubtful origin indeed! This problem was not encountered while using standard UK military very hot '2Z'.

Adopting the Sterling-Patchett Mk5 as the L34A1

228. Right side view of the UK Military-issue silenced L34A1, with stock extended .
Note the matt finish, and absence of the commercial wooden foregrip. (MoD School of Infan try, Warminster)

The Mk5 was perfected in May, 1966 and was manufactured exclusively by Sterling Engineering at Dagenham, under licence from George Patchett. In fact, the civilian version was known as the "Sterling-Patchett 9mm Sub Machine Gun Mk5".

The Mk5 was put into production by David Howroyd, who was required to amend certain drawings in the interests of standardisation.

After being subjected to user trials, the Mk5 silenced Sterling was adopted by the Ministry of Defence for UK Military service in 1967 as the "Gun, Sub-machine, 9mm L34Al", which immediately paved the way for worldwide sales. The gun was described as "… able to provide a short range, silenced weapon for use at ranges up to 100 metres where an element of surprise is essential".

L34A1 Finish and Markings

Like the L2 series, two types of finish were offered with the Mk5/L34Al: either hard-baked black matt finish Sunkorite paint over a phosphated casing, or crackle-finish black paint.

The UK MoD also purchased some crackle-finish commercial pattern Mk5 guns to augment their

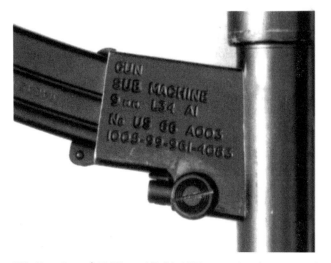

229. Top view of L34Al no US 66 A003 magazine housing and magazine, showing markings. This was the third L34Al gun produced to UK Military specifications by Sterling.
'1005-99-961-4083' was the NATO Vocabulary of Army Ordnance Stores number, which would usually be prefixed by the code 'B3', indicating that this was in fact a sub-machine gun. (Courtesy MoD Pattern Room, Nottingham)

stocks. These guns were the remainder of a Rhodesia/Zimbabwe order, cancelled part way.

As discussed below, the Mk5 silenced Sterling Patchett was also offered for sale to foreign buyers in single-shot form if required.

Describing the Mk5/L34A1

The Mk5/L34Al is 34″ long with the butt fully extended, and only 26″ folded. Fully loaded it weighs 9lbs 8ozs. The sight radius is 20½″. It delivers a cyclic rate of fire of between 515 and 565 ronnds per minute.

The whole of the silencing unit is held together by the rear of the barrel being pulled against the special internal rear barrel seating (fig 222). As illustrated in fig 230, the diffuser tube (27) and roll of expanded metal mesh (30) slide over the barrel, inside the original perforated casing, and the barrel is secured to the front barrel support (5) by the barrel nut (37). The three tie rods (3) anchor at the rear in the front barrel support (5), and go forward through holes in the spiral diffuser (1) within the extension tube (31), and are secured by the tie rod nuts (9) to the end cap

(28). This simplicity makes both the Ann ourer's and the user's life easier.

The L34A1 was described as follows in official documents:

… an adaptation of the Sub-machine gun, 9mm L2A3, designed to operate as a silenced weapon. It is capable of both repetition and automatic fire. It will normally be used for single aimed shots at ranges between 50 and 75 metres.

Component Parts of the Mk5/L34A1 Silencer Assembly

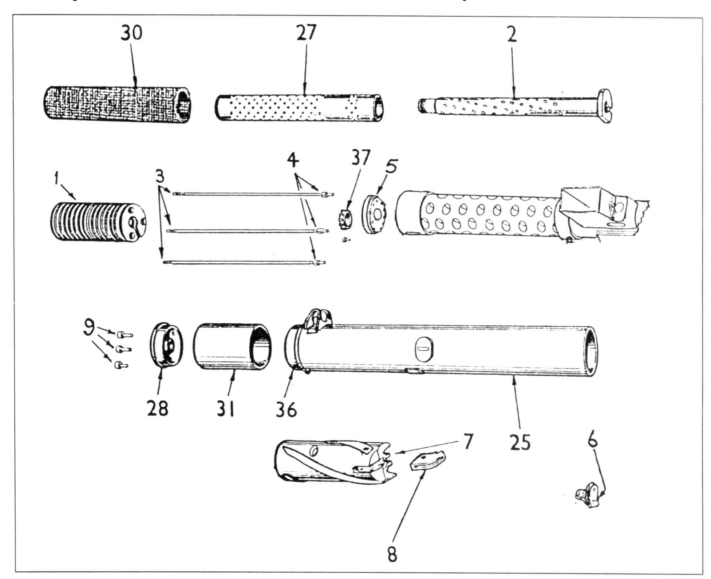

230. From the illustrated Parts List, the internal components special to the Mk5. The nomenclature is given, opposite.

Item	NSN	Item Name and Desaiption	Part No/Dwg No	No Off
1	1005-99-961-4089	Spiral diffuser assembly	CR 180 SA	1
2	1005-99-961-4084	Barrel, sub-machine gun	CR 1382	1
3	1005-99-961-4087	Tie rods	CR 1395	3
4	1005-99-961-4088	Nut, plain, hexagon	CR 1391	3
5	1005-99-961-4091	Plate assembly, barrel support	CR 1392	1
6	1005-99-961-4093	Sight, rear	CR 1394	1
7	1005-99-961-4096	Block, breech	CR 179 SA	1
8	1005-99-960-2154	Extractor, small arms	CR 1094	1
9	1005-99-961-4097	Nut, tie rod	CR 1396	3
25	1005-99-961-4240	Casing, silencer	S5 29 G	1
27	1005-99-961-4090	Diffuser tube	CR 1385	1
28	1005-99-961-4094	End cap	CR 1386	1
30	1005-99-961-4086	Expanded metal wrap	CR 1387	1
31	1005-99-961-4095	Extension tube	CR 1388	1
36	1005-99-961-4092	Mount, foresight	CR 1389	1
37	1005-99-961-4085	Nut, barrel	CR 1390	1

The absence of parts that would be affected by the hot gases means that the Mk5/L34Al can be fired in the automatic role. The noise is reduced to below 90 decibels, which is about the noise of an electric typewriter key. In Peter Laidler's experience, a shot, at night from a trooper close by, sounded like a muffled cough.

The effect on morale during the dawn changeover, at finding all the occupants of the next slit trench shot dead overnight, simply cannot be described. It would certainly concentrate the mind on the advantages of staying alert and awake in the future!

The One-Off Single Shot, Closed-Bolt Mk5 with Shortened Silencer

231. Left side view of the one-off single shot, closed-bolt-firing Mk5/L34A1, serial no S 3818.
    Note the shortened silencer with forward chamber deleted, and change lever markings 'SAFE' and 'FIRE'.
    The short gun proved slightly noisier than the standard silenced gun, and the project was shelved. (MoD Pattern Room collection)

232. Cover/title page of the final edition of the official UK Military User Handbook for the L2A3.

As noted, this was a 1977 revision of the original L2A3 User Handbook, WO Code 12042 of 1956, to include a section on the silenced L34A1.

When a customer expressed interest in a shorter silenced single shot gun, the forward expansion chamber of the standard Mk5 silencer was experimentally deleted. The gun so fitted was slightly noisier than the standard silenced gun and the project was shelved, but it proved that a shorter silenced gun was feasible.

The magazine housing of this experimental silenced single shot gun was marked:

STERLING [boxed logo]

EXPERIMENTAL

SINGLE SHOT

9m/m Mk5 S L34Al

No S 3818

Notes on Interchangeability with Other Sterling Marks

Because of the different ballistic qualities of the Mk5/L34A1 compared with its earlier brother the Mk4/L2A3, certain parts were changed. These are listed below with the reasons.

The BODY CASING, fully described above.

There is no facility to fix a bayonet.

The BARREL, also described fully above.

A new, lighter BREECH BLOCK was fitted to this gun, lightened by increasing the depth and diameter of the internal borings which are eccentric.

The EXTRACTOR on the Mk5 does not have the lightening slot. Although given as non-interchangeable, Mk4/L2A3 and Mk5/L34A1 extractors are for all purposes, interchangeable. This heavier extractor was developed from the slotted version by Stan Wingrove as a result of earlier problems.

The RETURN SPRING CAP. On export and commercial guns, a hard round neoprene breech block buffer was available to fit into the internal recess.

Mk4/L2A3 Parts Omitted on Mk5/L34A1

Additionally, the following Mk4/L2A3 parts were omitted from the Mk5/L34A1:

The INNER RETURN SPRING. Due to the lighter recoil and sub-sonic muzzle velocity, the inner spring was not required. As a result of this, the following parts were also made redundant and omitted: the INNER RETURN SPRING CUP, the COCKING HANDLE BLOCK, and the cocking handle block SPRING and PLUNGER.

With the exception of the parts listed above, every other component of the Mk4/L2A3 is fully interchangeable with the Mk5/L34A1.

The Multi-Holed Sniping Backsight

Due to the fact that the muzzle velocity is less than with theMk4/L2A3, the trajectory is different and the sight radius is longer, the apertures are higher up, and thus the backsight leaves are taller.

233. Top closeup view of the Mk5/L34A1 backsight with multi-holed 100-yd backsight leaf folded forward.

This ingenious idea gives a cross-hair effect resulting in improved sight definition and a greater field of view than the standard 100-yd aperture on the forward leaf. (Courtesy MoD Pattern Room, Nottingham)

On the Mk5, BOTH leaves are calibrated to 100 yards, the more FORWARD of the two leaves incorporating an ingenious multi-holed sniping sight.

It is said that George Patchett was sitting on the beach one day, when one of his trouser buttons fell off. He picked it up, blew the cotton out, and looked through it. He noticed the greater field of view, and the fact that the eye naturally fell into the centre.

He immediately incorporated this pattern of holes into a sniping sight, which gives a cross-hair effect resulting in improved sight definition and a greater field of view.

Contrary to popular belief among some soldiers AND Armourers, whereas this multi-holed backsight will fit on a standard gun, there is insufficient thread on the foresight to re-zero the standard gun once it is so fitted.

Production Dates for the Commercial Mk5

Serial Number	Date Produced
S 001	20 June, 1966

break in commercial production to concentrate on UK Military order

S 050	November, 1968
S 100	June, 1969
S 150	January, 1970
S 200	January, 1970
S 250	January, 1970
S 300	December, 1970
S 350	December, 1970
S 400	December, 1970
S 450	May, 1971
S 500	May, 1971
S 550	May, 1971
S 600	May, 1971
S 650	May, 1971
S 700	November, 1971
S 750	November, 1971
S 800	November, 1971
S 850	November, 1971
S 900	November, 1971
S 950	December, 1971
S 1000	26 December, 1970
S 1050	December, 1971
S 1100	January,1972
S 1150	February, 1972

production temporarily ceased to clear backlog

S 1200	April, 1973
S 1250	May, 1973
S 1300	May, 1973
S 1350	May, 1973
S 1400	June, 1973
S 1450	November, 1973

production temporarily ceased to clear backlog

S 1500	October, 1974
S 1550	October, 1974
S 1600	May, 1975
S 1650	October, 1976
S 1686	following records incomplete

234. Three versions of the Sterling User Handbook for the silenced Mlc5/L2A3.

    Above: English, pre-1972

    Centre: Arabic

    Below: English, post-1983. The rampant lions were added by the new owners after James Edmiston sold Sterling Armament in 1983.

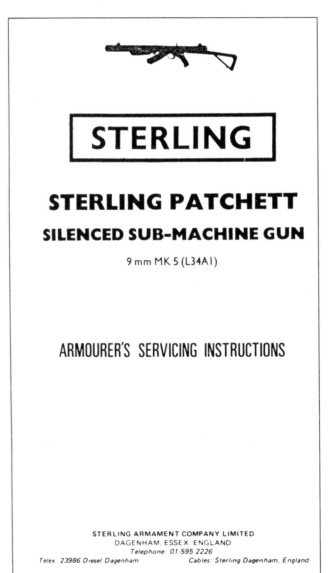

235. Cover/title page of the commercial Armourer's Servicing Instructions for the Mk5 Sterling-Patchett, produced by Sterling to support the silenced Mk5 in other armies.

    This manual was part of the magnificent Armourer's kit supplied with the Mk5/L34A1 (Chapter Sixteen).

A military night sight bracket was available, that fitted around the front of the outer silencer casing and locked at the rear over the backsight ears. This enabled NATO users using first- and second-generation night sights with NATO-standard (STANAG) mountings to fit their night sights to Mk5/L34 guns.

The 'see-through' design of the brackets also allowed the use of the standard iron sights. Sterling also offered an oversize diameter (to cater for the

236. Left side view of the Sterling IWS (night sight) mount, specifically designed to adapt the Mk5/L34Al for night sights fitted with standard NATO (STANAG) mounts.

The large ring (left) is dimensioned for the 1¾″ diameter of the silencer casing. Note the extended backsight axis pin and collars (cen tre), with which the rear of the bracket is anchored around the rear sight housing. (MoD School of Infantry, Warminster)

237. Left side view of a UK Military-issue silenced L34Al, fitted with the Sterling IWS mount and Dutch STANAG night sight. This sight was used on the L34Al because it was shorter than the British-made Pilkington and Rank night sights (used on the GPMG, Carl Gustav and L1A1 rifle).

This is the most feared weapon in the clandestine armoury. Except for equal cunning and guile, there is no defence against it. At between 30 and 80 metres, even on the darkest night, a sentry stands two chances, slim and none!

In the UK Military, such specialised combinations are reserved for "… those specialist troops whose operational needs require weapons of such a clandestine nature". What troops are these? No names, no pack drill! (MoD School of Infantry, Warminster)

oversized casing) foresight adjusting tool to fit the Mk5/L34A1. Like the Mk4/L2A3 sight adjusting tool, it did nothing a sensible Armourer couldn't do with a small hammer and a brass drift!

In the chapters on the Mk6 and later guns, we learn more of specially studded casings and the optional Sterling sight rail, which mounted on the studs to accommodate a series of telescopic sights.

Non-UK military Mk5 guns could also be ordered with these sight rail locating studs installed, thus enabling the buyer to fit a variety of commercial telescopic sights or night sights. The night sight makes even the PC version of the Mk5 an EXTREMELY potent weapon. Additionally, as noted, the commercial guns were offered with the optional no-cost wooden foregrip.

Third and subsequent generation ('coke-tin' or CWS) night sights were usually manufactured with integral mounting studs/threads, and can be fitted to almost any commercial rail that will fit the Sterling locating studs. Thus virtually any current CWS can be adapted to fit the Mk5/L34Al.

Marking the Commercial Silenced Mk5

Commercial Mk5 silenced Sterling/Patchetts were marked on the magazine housing:

STERLING
SMG
9mm Mk5 (L34A1)
No. S — (number 1929 examined)

The serial number of the civilian guns was always prefixed by the letter 'S' to indicate a silenced gun.

On full-auto Mk5s we have seen two styles of lettering on the top left side of the pistol grip. The first is the standard 'A', 'R' and 'S' for Automatic, Repetition and Safe. The second and more recent style is '34', '1' and 'O', indicating 34 shots (Automatic), 1 shot (Single shot), and O shots (Safe). The last 70 guns were marked '34', '1' and 'SAFE'. The Police Carbine-type guns sold with no automatic facility were simply marked 'FIRE' and 'SAFE'.

Mk5/L34A1 Variables

The variables likely to be found in the Mk5/L34Al series include the following:

- black crackle or satin Sunkorite paint finish
- safe, single and automatic fire trigger mechanism marked 'A-R-S' or '34-1-0' or '34-1-SAFE' (Mk5/L34Al)
- safe and single-shot-only trigger mechanism marked 'FIRE' – 'SAFE' (Mk5PC)
- casings with or without sight rail studs
- casings with or without wooden foregrip
- MoD 'Gun Sub-Machine, L34 Al' marking on magazine housing
- commercial guns with 'Sterling SMG Mk5' markings on magazine housing.

The Late-Issue Mk5 with Solid Butt

238 (above). Left side view of commercial Mk5/L34A1 Sterling, fitted with the Sterling night-sight mount and the late-issue Mk7- type nylon butt. Note the selector markings: '34', '1', and 'SAFE'.

INSET, right: the plastic Sterling buttstock 'kit'.

Above left: special return spring cap with butt retention spigot.

Centre: buttstock; two plastic spacers, the use of one or both of which increases the length of the stock; buttplate; buttplate screws.

Below: spring pin, which fits through hole in small of stock and hole in return spring cap locking lever housing. (Courtesy MoD Pattern Room)

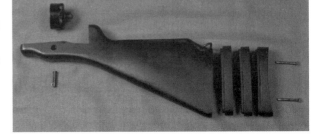

Another version of the Mk5 gun was produced in 1984, when it was suggested that guns fitted with the solid Mk7 type butt would be more acceptable to certain buyers. This was a simple modification as both the Mk5 and Mk7 guns were in simultaneous production. The hinging butt trunnion block was omitted, and the Mk7 type return spring cap and locking catch added. It was then a simple matter to fit the plastic Mk7 butt.

One advantage to this plastic butt was that it was adjustable for length. Whatever the advantages, however, this was not a great success and only eight Mk5 guns were produced with fixed stocks.

The Commercial 'Mk5PC'

The silenced Sterling-Patchett Mk5 was also offered commercially in a single-shot-only version called the Nfic5PC. It must be assumed that, as with the singleshot 'Police Carbine' version of the Mk4, Police forces were not anticipating the need for automatic fire!

The Mk5PC was identical to the commercial Mk5, except it was fitted with the Mk4 Police Carbine SINGLE SHOT trigger mechanism (marked SAFE and FIRE only).

239. The silenced L34A1 in action with the Australian SAS at Dui Nat, South Vietnam. L34A1s with magazines fitted but butts removed are seen here in the hands of the 4th trooper from left (top row) and first from right (bottom row).

The Australian and New Zealand Governments purchased a total of 94 L34Als, all of which were used in South Vietnam. Peter Laidler's first experiences with the L34 were with these Australian guns in 1968.

Note the webbing, a motley collection of British '44 and '58 pattern plus some US issue thrown in for good measure. (MoD Australian Army, Perth, Western Australia)

Notes on Zeroing the Silenced Mk5 Sterling-Patchett

Whether selective-fire or not, the silenced gun must be zeroed at 25 metres with the left forearm rested, using five single shots. All five shots must be in or touching a 4″ diameter circle. The mean point of impact of the five shots must fall within a rectangle measured from a point 2″ up and 2″ to the left of the point of aim. This somewhat haphazard method of zeroing is to ensure that the bullets fall on the point of aim when the gun is fired from the prone unsupported position at 75 metres.

Readers and researchers desiring associated material relating to the Mk5/L34Al might wish to obtain the UK Military User Handbook titled "User Handbook, Gun, Sub-machine 9mm L2A3 and L34A1. Army code 12042-26-Mans/4347" (fig 232). The UK Military Engineering Regulations relating to the L34A1 can be found in section SA&MG, E740.

Sterling printed their own User Handbooks (fig 234), Spares Catalogues, Armourer's Servicing Instructions (fig 237) and numerous brochures (fig 240) for the Mk5, in several different languages.

A Change of Ownership and George Patchett's Name Enshrined

Soon after he had purchased Sterling Armament Company in 1972, James Edmiston acquired the rights to manufacture the Mk5/L34A1 from George Patchett, who was living in retirement in the South of France.

In his fine book *The Sterling Years*, Edmiston recalls,

> ... *The fact that the company had called his design by their name had long rankled with Patchett. Not surprisingly, therefore, when I finally settled with him and bought the silenced gun for Sterling, but agreed that it should always carry his name, he was delighted.*

The Last Service Sterling

At the time of this writing, the L34A1 remains the only Sterling still in service with UK Military forces.

240. Sterling produced one- or two-page brochures on the Mk5/L34A1 in several languages.

From top: English, French, Spanish, Portuguese. (Courtesy Mike Gruber)

Part II

The Commonwealth Sterlings

Guns large and small at the British Army Equipment Exhibition at Aldershot 1974.

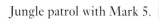

Jungle patrol with Mark 5.

Northern Ireland; protecting democracy.

Malaysian Rangers suitably equipped.

James Edmiston and Lawrence Kormornick - joint authors of "The Sterling Redemption ", enjoying a lunch break during a ski trip to Les Portes du Soleil.

James Edmiston paying respects at the grave of Frederick Courtney Selous, the big game hunter, killed at the age of 63 fighting the enemy in German East Africa (now Tanzania) on 4th. January 1917. Selous and Edmiston both attended Rugby School.

Shooting was not the only leisure pursuit of James Edmiston.

Pride of product.

Discussing developments with H.R.H. The Duke of Kent.

Sterling SMG's mounted in an armoured fighting vehicle.

Our partner in USA.

Roma Skinner partner in Lanchester
USA Inc and wife Elaine.

Skeletonised Lanchester.

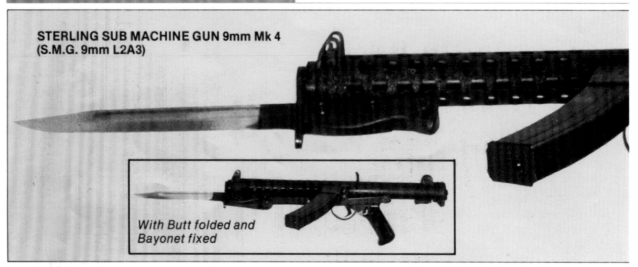

STERLING SUB MACHINE GUN 9mm Mk 4
(S.M.G. 9mm L2A3)

With Butt folded and Bayonet fixed

The standard sub-machine gun with the British Armed forces and in service in over 90 countries throughout the world.

A light and easily handled weapon which can fire full automatic and single shot, using standard 9mm Parabellum ammunition being operated by case projection or "blow back". With exceptional accuracy and with renowned reliability it continues to function in the most adverse conditions of mud, sand, snow and ice. It is a short to medium range weapon used for engagement at ranges up to 200 metres.

Folding butt for ease of carrying and stowage. Illustrated with optional bayonet, 15 and 34 round magazines.

With Butt folded

Developed to meet a British General Staff requirement for a fully automatic silent weapon and in service with the British Armed Forces. The bullet is slowed to subsonic speeds by the silencing arrangements giving a truly silent weapon. There is nothing to wear out in the built in silencer and thousands of rounds can be fired without attention except normal cleaning. Using **standard** 9mm Parabellum ammunition a maximum size group at 30 metres (100 feet) of 63.5mm x 63.5mm (2½" x 2½") is achieved on every gun prior to its leaving the factory. The Mark 5 retains all the other features of the Mark 4, for example, the folding butt for ease of carriage, the helical ribs on the bolt for efficient functioning under adverse operational conditions. A close bolt semi automatic version is also available for Police use. Many of the spare parts are fully interchangeable between the Marks 4 and 5 giving continuity of manufacture and availability.

STERLING SILENCED GUN 9mm Mk 5 (L34A1)

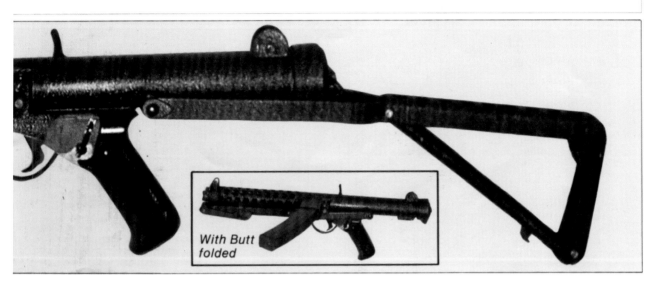

With Butt folded

SPECIFICATIONS:

Calibre		9mm	9mm
Length – butt folded		48.2cms	19 inches
– butt extended		69cms	27 inches
Weight – machine gun only		2.7kg (approx)	6 lbs (approx)
– with full magazine		3.5kg (approx)	7lb 10oz (approx)
– with full magazine and bayonet		3.73kg (approx)	8lb 4oz (approx)

Barrel	– length	19.8cms	7.8inches
	– number of grooves	6	
	– pitch of rifling	25cms	1 turn in 9.84 inches
	– twist of rifling	Right hand	
Sights	– radius	41cms	16.1 inches
	– type	Rear-aperture Fore blade	
	– range settings	100 and 200 metres	100 and 200 yards
Cyclic rate of fire		550 r.p.m. approx	
Magazines		10, 15 and 34 round capacity or permanent twin stacked 20, 30 and 68 round capacity	

STERLING SILENCED GUN 9mm Mk5 (L34A1)

Night sight

SPECIFICATIONS:

Calibre		9mm	9mm
Length – butt folded		64.4cms	25¾ inches
– butt extended		85.6cms	33¾ inches
Weight – machine gun only		3.54kg	7 lbs 13 oz
– with full magazine		4.25kg	9lb 6oz
Barrel – length		19.8cms	7.8inches
– number of grooves		6	
– pitch of rifling		25cms	1 turn in 9.84 inches

	– twist of rifling	Right hand	
Sights	– radius	50.2cms	20.5 inches
	– type	Rear-aperture Fore blade	
	– range settings	100m only	100 yards only
Magazines		The Sterling Mk 5 silent gun accepts all Sterling magazines	
Decibel Reading		81 dcb	

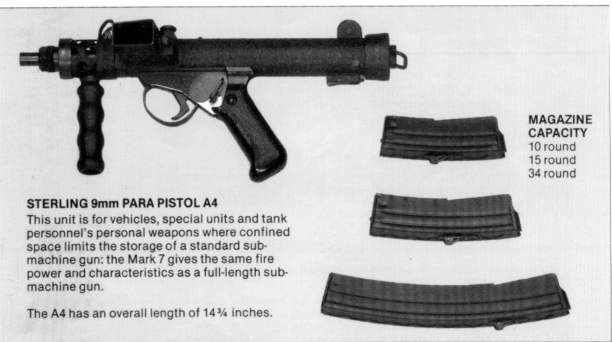

STERLING 9mm PARA PISTOL A4

This unit is for vehicles, special units and tank personnel's personal weapons where confined space limits the storage of a standard sub-machine gun: the Mark 7 gives the same fire power and characteristics as a full-length sub-machine gun.

The A4 has an overall length of 14¾ inches.

MAGAZINE CAPACITY
10 round
15 round
34 round

STERLING 9mm PARA PISTOL A8

All A series weapons fire from the open bolt and have the capability of firing single shot or automatic rapid fire at 560 rounds per minute. The A4 and A8 have a forward pistol grip fitted as standard which enables the user to have a rugged hold to have complete control of the gun in continuous rapid fire.

A8 Denotes open bolt firing 7.8 inch barrel length.

The A8 has an overall length of 18½ inches.

Twin stacked (Permanent) Magazine 2 x 10, 2 x 15 or any other combination.

ACCESSORIES AVAILABLE:—

1. 10, 15 or 34-round Magazines
2. Forward Holding Strap
3. Long Sling
4. Wall Stowage Bracket
5. Sterling suppressor/silencer (4¼" Barrel only)
6. Twin stacked (Permanent) Magazines 2 x 10, 2 x 15 or any other combination

	METRIC		IMPERIAL	
	A4	A8	A4	A8
Approx. Weight:	2.2 Kgs	2.3 Kgs	5 lbs	5 lbs 4 oz
Overall Length:	38cms	47cms	14.75"	18.5"
Barrel Length:	108mm	198mm	4.25"	7.8"

STERLING 9mm PARA PISTOL C4

C4 Denotes closed bolt firing 4¼ inch barrel length.

The C4 has an overall length of 14¾ inches.

The "C" series fires from a closed bolt and has a floating firing pin. All closed bolt units fire in the single-shot mode only. As the bolt is forward and stationary when the firing pin strikes the round it gives the firer maximum accuracy.

STERLING 9mm PARA PISTOL C8

C8 Denotes closed bolt firing 7.8 inch barrel length.

The C8 has an overall length of 18½" inches.

All "C" series guns have 2 locating buttons on the upper side of the gun casing to enable a dovetailed 'scope rail to be fitted. The buttons are ready-drilled and tapped, and the Sterling 'scope rail fits on them direct.

The 'scopes recommended on this unit, after testing, are:—

A. 3/9 x 32 rubber armour "Sterling Bisley De-Luxe"
B. 4 x 40 rubber armour
C. Hakko Electro-point
D. Aimpoint

CCESSORIES AVAILABLE:—

10, 15 or 34-round Magazines
Forward Holding Strap
Long Sling
Wall Stowage Bracket
Sterling suppressor/silencer
(4¼" Barrel only)
Twin stacked (Permanent)
Magazines 2 x 10, 2 x 15 or
any other combination

	METRIC		IMPERIAL	
	C4	C8	C4	C8
Approx. Weight:	2.2 Kgs	2.3 Kgs	5 lbs	5 lbs 4 oz
Overall Length:	38cms	47cms	14.75"	18.5"
Barrel Length:	108mm	198mm	4.25"	7.8"

STERLING

STERLING POLICE CARBINE Mk 7
9mm C8

Sterling 9mm Para Pistol C4 and C8 fitted with a light plastic fixed butt with 3 add on sections to adjust to the user's own arm length.

This unit was designed at the request of police marksmen and also shooting clubs requiring maximum stability in placing shots when the telescopic sight is used.

The butt is removed by pushing out a simple spring retaining locking pin.

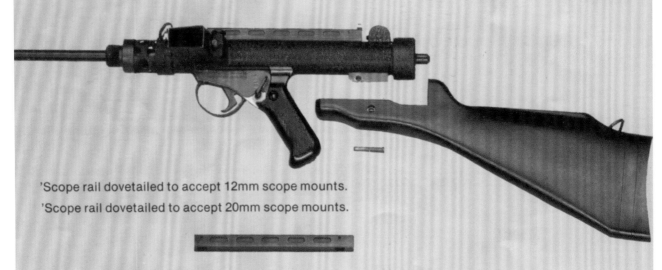

'Scope rail dovetailed to accept 12mm scope mounts.

'Scope rail dovetailed to accept 20mm scope mounts.

The 'scopes recommended on this unit, after testing, are:—
A. 3/9 x 32 rubber armour "Sterling Bisley De-Luxe"   **B.** 4 x 40 rubber armour
C. Hakko Electro-point   **D.** Aimpoint

ACCESSORIES AVAILABLE:—

. 10, 15 or 34-round Magazines
. Forward Holding Strap
. Long Sling
. Wall Stowage Bracket
. Sterling suppressor/silencer
  (4¼" Barrel only)
. Twin stacked (Permanent)
  Magazines 2 x 10, 2 x 15 or
  any other combination

Dims. with butt:	METRIC		IMPERIAL	
	C4	C8	C4	C8
Approx. Weight:	2.9 Kgs	3 Kgs	6¼ lbs	6½ lbs
Overall Length:	64cms	73cms	25"	28¾"
Barrel Length:	108mm	198mm	4.25"	7.8"

STERLING

With Butt folded

STERLING Mk 6 9mm SEMI-AUTOMATIC CARBINE

Sterling, the most widely sold Submachine Gun in the world (100 nations) is now available in the U.S.A. as the Mark 6 semi-auto carbine. The Mark 6 is identical in appearance to the Sterling Submachine Gun except that the barrel has been lengthened to conform with U.S. regulations.

Sterling Mark 6 is manufactured to the same high standards as the Submachine Gun. Each weapon is 100% tested and proofed by the British government before shipment. Sterling's battle proven design is acknowledged by arms experts as the ultimate in reliability, accuracy and smoothness of operation. Each Mark 6 is supplied with a 34 round magazine, carrying sling, owner's manual and 8" display barrel.

SPECIFICATIONS:

Type:	Semi Auto Carbine
Calibre:	9mm Parabellum
Operation:	Blowback W/Floating Firing Pin
Type of Fire:	Semi Auto only
Weight unloaded:	7.5 lbs (3.4 kg)
Length (stock folded):	27 in (685mm)
Length (stock extended):	35 in (889mm)
Barrel Length:	16.1" (410mm)
Max Range:	200 yds (200 metres) at 30° angle
Magazines:	All Sterling magazines

With Butt extended & 34 round magazine

With Butt folded

STERLING Mk 8 9mm CLOSED BOLT SINGLE SHOT

The single shot closed bolt Sterling 9mm Mark 8 was developed for greater accuracy in the 100-200 metre range for security forces using standard 9mm parabellum ammunition. Hand guns used by security forces are unreliable in accuracy at these ranges when innocent members of the public are present during terrorist incidents.

SPECIFICATIONS:

Calibre	9mm	9mm
Length – butt folded	48.2cms	19 inches
– but extended	69cms	27 inches
Weight – gun only	2.7kg (approx)	6 lbs (approx)
– with full magazine	3.5kg (approx)	7lb 10oz (approx)
– with full magazine and bayonet	3.73kg (approx)	8lb 4oz (approx)

Barrel	– length	19.8cms	7.8inches
	– number of grooves	6	
	– pitch of rifling	25cms	1 turn in 9.84 inches
	– twist of rifling	Right hand	
Sights	– radius	41cms	16.1 inches
	– type	Rear-aperture Fore blade	
	– range settings	100 and 200 metres	100 and 200 yards
	– Semi-automatic	single shot	
Magazines		All Sterling magazines	

STERLING

STERLING 9mm ACCESSORIES AND TRAINING EQUIPMENT

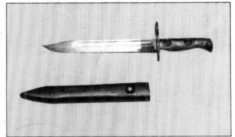
BAYONET AND SCABBARD FOR SMG

SLING

FORESIGHT ZEROING TOOL   CLEANING KIT

ARMOURERS KIT FOR SILENT GUN

MAGAZINES 10, 15 & 34 ROUNDS OR PERMANENT TWIN STACKED 20, 30 & 68 ROUNDS

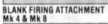
BLANK FIRING ATTACHMENT
Mk 4 & Mk 8

BLANK FIRING ATTACHMENT
Mk 7, A4 and C4

AMMUNITION — BALL, TRACER, ARMOUR PIERCING, BLANK, DRILL

**STERLING SILENCED GUN 9mm Mk 5
(L34A1) AND 34 ROUND MAGAZINE**

Sectionalised weapons are available for training purposes.

STERLING

STERLING ARMAMENT COMPANY

DAGENHAM · ESSEX · ENGLAND

Telephone: 01-595 2226   Telex: 896895 STERLN G   Cables: STERLING DAGENHAM, ENGLAND.

CONTRACTORS TO MINISTRY OF DEFENCE HER MAJESTY'S GOVERNMENT, CROWN AGENTS, AND OVERSEAS GOVERNMENTS

Photographed, Designed, Reproduced & Printed in England by Fidelity Colour Printers, Basildon, Essex · Basildon (0268) 44066   FSM8416a/1

STERLING HR 81

A high powered British air rifle of all-new design

STERLING HR 81

New design with greater accuracy
Maximum permitted muzzle energy
All-metal to last a lifetime

Here is the brilliant new HR 81 – an all-round advance in the development of high powered air rifles and the culmination of years of research and gunmaking experience* at Sterling.

The HR 81 has a lightweight 1" diameter piston coupled with a 3¾" stroke, resulting in a very high pressure build-up with minimum spring strength which reduces recoil.

A constant air seal is created by the bolt shaft swelling the skirt of the pellet to size when it is chambered. The pellet leaves the barrel only when the piston has completed its stroke thereby ensuring a more constant and higher pressure, resulting in greater accuracy.

As the weapon is cocked with an underlever, the barrel is not strained. Furthermore, when a telescopic sight is used, the sight line is constant as the mounting tracks and the barrel are a permanent assembly.

The stock is well balanced and ensures ease of handling whilst the firm recoil pad gives added confidence.

The single stage match trigger is manufactured from hardened steel and is adjustable for sear engagement and pressures down to 2lbs.

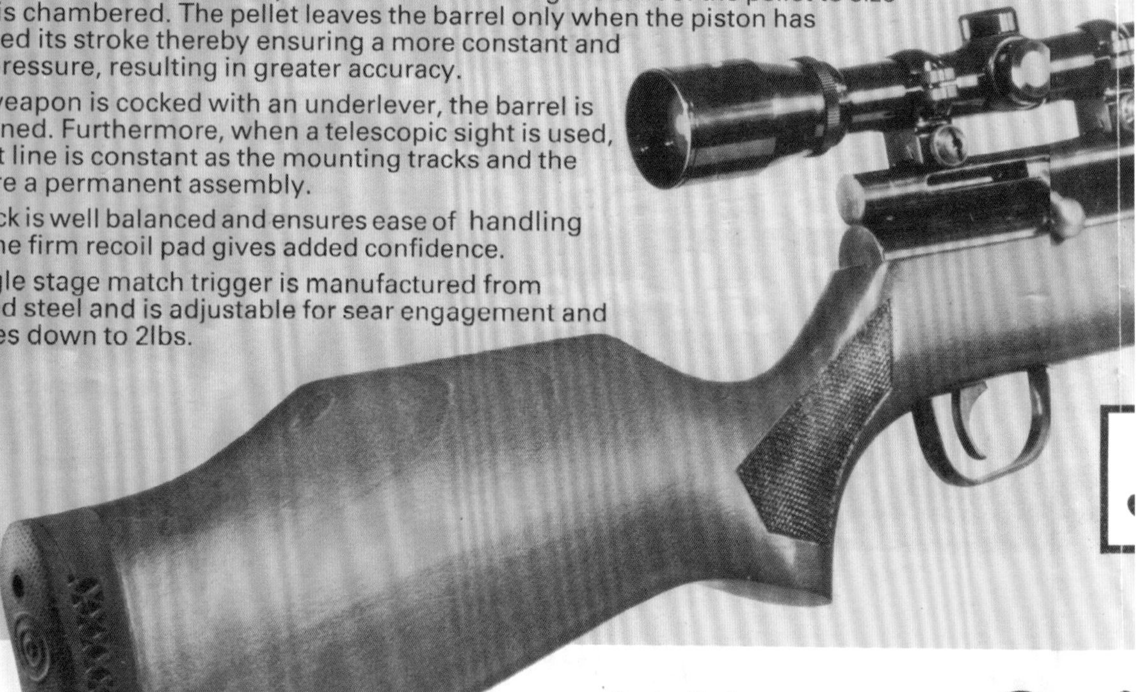

Each rifle is tested to give the maximum permitted muzzle energy that the Law allows and will amply meet the demands of the sporting airgunner.

Only high grade steels are used in the manufacture of this outstanding British weapon—no diecastings or plastics are employed in its construction. The Sterling HR 81 is built to last and will give a lifetime of high performance shooting. It has been designed to meet the requirements of today's serious air rifle shooters.

Opti
Ext
SPECIALLY
FOR USE W
STERLIN

Sterling
4-plex ret
All the quality fea
nitrogen filling,
centred reticul
adjustment for

*Our design team have a wealth of gunmaking experience behind them and their expertise is backed by the success of the Sterling Sub Machine Gun, manufactured for the British Army and exported to over 100 countries throughout the world, and by the Sterling AR-180 Rifle used word-wide by police forces and sportsmen alike.

OLT ACTION

ovides a fast, positive feed
oothly and faultlessly, aiding
eater accuracy.

UNIQUE LOADING

Adopted to give a fixed
alignment of barrel and sight
system yet allows the pellet to
be loaded in a straight line to the
breech.

PRECISION SIGHTS

The V-type adjustable rearsight
and tunnel type, 3-element
interchangeable frontsight are
precision engineered to provide
perfect sighting control.

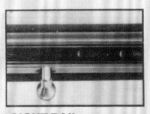

SIGHT RAIL

The sight rail permits instant
scope mounting and is
compatible with different sight
systems. It is drilled to accept
arrester studs.

Specification

Calibres	.177" 4.5mm, .20" 5.0mm, .22" 5.5mm
Length	42½" 1080mm
Weight	8½lbs 3.95 kg
Barrel	
Length	19½" 500mm
No. of Grooves	6
Pitch of Rifling	1 turn in 11,34"
Twist of Rifling	right hand
Sights	
Rear	V-type adjustable
Front	Tunnel-type 4 element interchangeable
Stock	Hardwood with cheekpiece, fitted rubber recoil pad
Accuracy	Better than 2" at 45 yards.

STERLING

onal
ras
DESIGNED
VITH YOUR
G HR 81

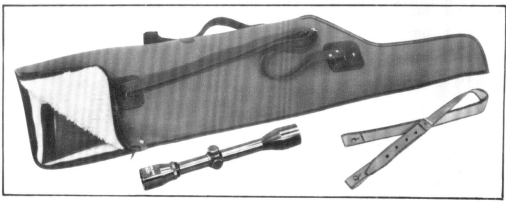

4 x 40 Wide Angle Scope with
ticule. Complete with mounts

atures—coated lenses, click adjustment,
correction for parallax and accurately
le. Image moving with ¼ minute click
both elevation and lateral movements.

Protect your HR 81 with this ideal cover and
sturdy sling

The well-made Sterling ST7 cover is fully lined in a deep,
soft fleece to provide maximum protection for your
HR 81 with scope. The Sterling LSP leather sling is strong
and of good quality. In light tan.

STERLING HR 81
Spare Parts List

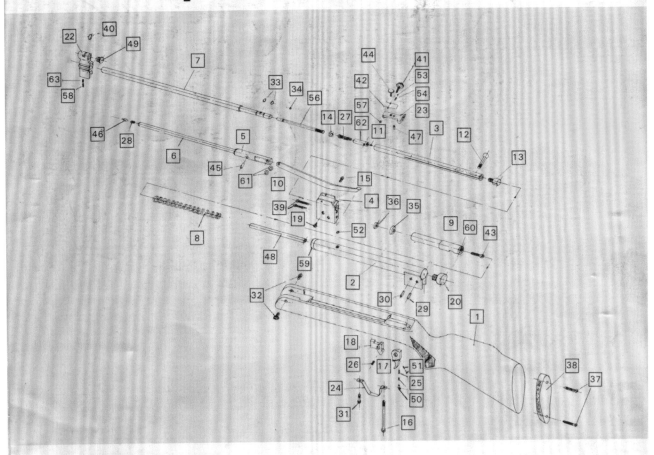

1	Stock	22	Front Sight
2	Cylinder	23	Rear Sight
3	Bolt Tube	24	Trigger Guard
4	Main Block	25	Trigger Spring
5	Lever Hinge	26	Sear Spring
6	Lever Cocking	27	Bolt Spring
7	Barrel	28	Plunger Spring
8	Main Spring	29	Trigger Hinge
9	Piston	30	Sear Hinge
10	Link Cocking	31	Trigger Guard Screw
11	Screw	32	Butt Screw
12	Charging Handle	33	O - Rings
13	Bolt Tube Plug	34	O - Ring A . 220 B . 200 C . 177
14	Locking Nut A - 220 B - 200 C - 177	35	Leather Washer
15	Pivot Screw	36	Washer Retainer
16	Main Trigger Guard Screw	37	Recoil Pad Screw
17	Trigger	38	Recoil Pad
18	Sear	39	Locking Screw
19	Pivot Lock Screw	40	Front Sight Element x 3
20	Cylinder Plug	41	Windage Screw
21	Spring Housing	42	Rear Sight Spring

43	Screw
44	Rear Sight Elevation Screw
45	Cocking Lever Hinge Pin
46	Lever Handle Plunger
47	Ball Plunger
48	Spring Guide
49	Front Sight Screw
50	Screw
51	Screw
52	O - Ring
53	Steel Ball
54	Spring
55	Trigger Plate (LH - RH)
56	Pellet Pusher A - 220 B - 200 C - 177
57	Clip
58	Screw
59	Cylinder Plug
60	Piston Bung
61	Shim
62	Screw
63	Shuttle A - 220 B - 200 C - 177

STERLING

STERLING ARMAMENT CO. LTD.,
Rainham Road South, Dagenham,
Essex RM10 8ST

Chapter Nine

The Canadian Connection

Gun, Sub Machine, 9mm L2A4 and SMG, 9mm C1

by Armourer WO Gary Crocker, Canadian Forces EME, with Capt Peter Laidler REME(V)

Date adopted by Canadian Forces:		1957
Series Production	from:	April, 1959
	to:	January, 1969
Date obsoleted in Canadian Forces:		1987
Number produced:		30,000

It is a well established fact that since the birth and formation of the Canadian Military machine, as members of the Commonwealth and NATO, the Canadians have followed the remainder of the Commonwealth in their choice of Military small-arms within their Order of Battle. There was one notable exception, that of the ill-fated Ross rifle, although this was born of necessity and not through any desire to go it alone.

After being first in the world to adopt the FN FAL rifle in 1954, the Canadians became prime movers within the Rifle Steering Committee, which oversaw the development of the "inch-measurement" FAL. Canadian Arsenals Limited was designated the design authority in the conversion, which ensured that when Britain, Canada and Australia eventually adopted the anglicised FN as the Commonwealth standard 'Rifle, 7.62mm L1A1' (the C1, in Canada's case), every component, or at least every assembly, would be interchangeable, regardless of whether it was made at Long Branch by Canadian Arsenals Ltd, the Government Small Arms Factory at Lithgow in Australia, or in Britain by BSA Guns Ltd or the Royal Small Arms Factory at Enfield.

The Canadians Look to Replace their Worn Mk2 Stens

For some years after World War II, the Canadian Forces seemed quite happy with their Long Branch Mk2 Sten guns. But like Britain's Mks Stens, these guns were getting old and tired, and a replacement was considered and sought.

The Canadians took note of the exhaustive British sub-machine gun trials which had taken place in the late 1940s and early 1950s, which had confirmed the Patchett as the only real contender. The improved production version, then called the Patchett MkII, adopted by British forces as the L2A1 in September, 1953, was quietly studied and tested by the Canadians.

It has emerged quite recently that Canada acquired a small quantity of hybrid MkII/III Patchett/Sterlin in the early 1950s. Quite where or how these guns were obtained is not clear, but obtain them the Canadians did, as they feature prominently in a 1955 Canadian-issue EMER which largely copies the UK "EX" User Handbook (fig 107).

Establishing the Sterling Foundation

It was on the improved Mk4/L2A3 Sterling that the Canadians wanted to base their replacement for the Mk2 Sten. One drawback with the Sterling was that it was not cheap. It was seven times as expensive as the Mk2 Sten (at £21:10s [£21.50] against £3 for the Sten), although only half the price of the previous offering, the .45 calibre M1928 Thompson.

The reason for this expense was IMAGE. Sterling were attempting to break away from the cheap and cheerful image that the Sten gun portrayed.

For the Sterling, gone were the rough edges, the loose fit, fabricated this, that and the other, and general unfinished appearance. The Sterling product offered a high standard of workmanship and finish. Everything fitted well, the sharp pressed edges were linished or tumbled, and the components precision brazed into place on the casing. The gun was also rustproofed in a phosphate dip, and finished with a choice of crackle black hard-baked paint or matt black Trimite oven-baked paint, the finish chosen by the UK Military.

Now there were several thin that the Canadians were not short of, and one of these was spare gunmaking capacity. Another was the expertise with which to undertake the task of manufacturing a new sub-machine gun for the Canadian Forces. In short, the Canadians liked the Sterling Mk4 and expressed a wish to adopt it, on condition that they could build it, under licence, at Canadian Arsenals Limited, the Government arms factory at Long Branch near Toronto, Ontario.

The UK – Canada Sub-Machine Gun Steering Committee

A Sub-Machine Gun Steering Committee was set up between Britain and Canada, with observers from Australia (who were armed with the aging Owen gun). The Committee's first meeting was held on 15th November, 1956.

The Canadians were impressed with the Mk4 Sterling, which they had only recently first seen,

and the first impression might have been that the production gun was there, and anything else was academic; a case of take it or leave it.

However, during this first meeting the Canadian members of the Board insisted that they did not wish to be tied to a particular method of manufacture on any given component. The meeting was to establish just how the Canadian gun would differ from the UK-made Mk4.

One item that was discussed was the return spring cap. The Canadians stated, quite rightly, that so long as it was interchangeable with the UK version, the method of manufacture was not important. There was to be more to this than first met the eye, though.

Canada also stated that the arctic trigger guard must be easier to adapt. They also stated that, for logistical reasons, the Canadian-made gun must be fitted with the then-current C1 rifle bayonet (interchangeable with the UK L1A1 rifle bayonet). On the face of it, these were simple modifications which the Enfield engineers promised to look into, keeping interchangeability in mind.

As it turned out, things were not quite that simple. Because the muzzle/bayonet configuration differed for the Canadian gun, the horizontally adjustable foresight could not be used. Any horizontal adjustment would have to be made with the backsight Vertical adjustment" would have to be made with the foresight.

All participants agreed at the outset that the interface of magazine and "mouthpiece" would be totally that of the Mk4 Sterling. As th transpired, even when the Australians later adopted the Lithgow-made F1 gun, it too came with a Sterling magazine interface.

The trigger mechanism frame was altered to allow a simplified method of releasing the arctic trigger guard. Hand in hand with this, the Canadians were invited to try an interchangeable but totally different trigger mechanism assembly, designed by Sterling designer Les Ruffell. They liked Les Ruffell's design!

Six Fazakerley L2A3s Converted to Canadian Specifications: the "L2A4"

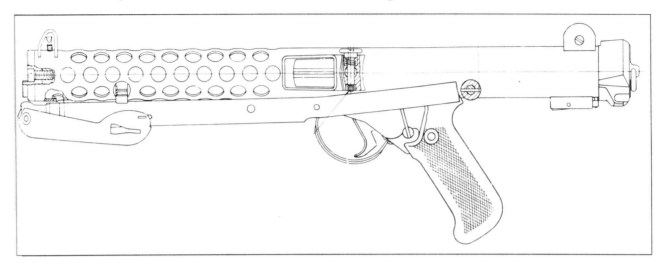

241. British ARDE (Armament Design Research Establishment) drawing dated 1 October, 1956, entitled "Gun, SMG L2A4".

Six ex-Fazakerley L2A3s were converted and re-marked as shown in fig 242 as pilots for the Canadian C1 SMG programme. (Courtesy MoD Pattern Room, Nottingham)

These ideas were all incorporated into six specimen guns were all marked with the usual Fazakerley ex-Fazakerley guns by engineers at Enfield. The markings but the marking 'L2A3' was changed by "Gun, Sub-Machine 9mm L2A4" was born. These barring out the '3' and inserting a '4'.

Differences in the L2A4

242. Top view of magazine housing of Enfield L2A4 No 6, showing markings. Converted from an ex-Fazakerley 'UF' casing, the '3' of 'L2A3' has been barred through and a '4' added to read 'L2A4'. (MoD Pattern Room collection)

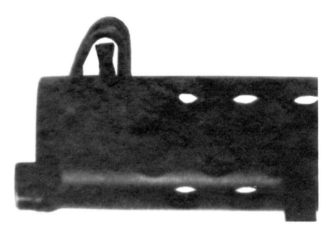

243. Left side closeup of L2A4 muzzle configuration. Note the L1A1 rifle foresight blade.

The L1A1 (or C1) rifle bayonet idea was much admired: during this time the L2A4 was mooted as the next conversion/replacement for the L2A2 in UK Military Service. (MoD Pattern Room collection)

These guns were examined at the next Steering Committee meeting, held in February, 1957. The L2A4 differed from the commercial/UK Military Mk4/L2A3 as follows:

1. flat muzzle configuration, without No5 bayonet boss
2. small bayonet boss for L1A1 (C1) rifle bayonet

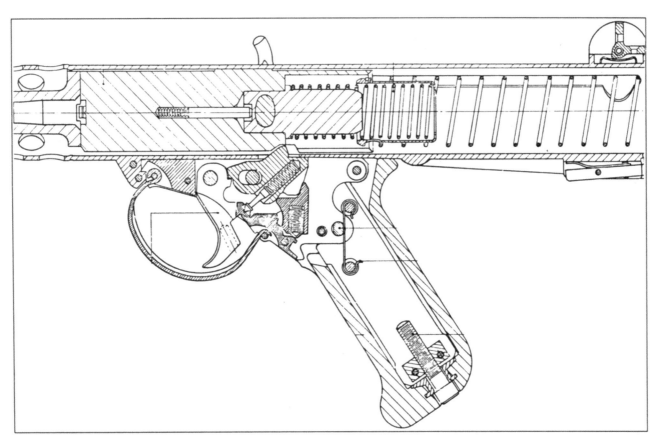

244. From the ARDE drawing "Gun SMG L2A4" dated 1 October, 1956, an enlarged view of the breech area of the L2A4, showing Sterling breech block, cocking handle block and spring-loaded plunger, (components eschewed by the Canadians in the final Ct design), and the admirably simple Ruffell trigger mechanism, which the Canadians did choose, thereby avoiding royalty payments on Patchett's patented helical-ribbed breech block and trigger mechanism.

This simplified trigger was the brainchild of Les Ruffell, a brilliant designer and head of the Sterling drawing shop. (Courtesy MoD Pattern Room, Nottingham)

3. extended and redesigned rear casing bayonet standard

4. adjustable-for-height, screw-in, L1A1 (C1) rifle foresight blade

5. foresight blade locked in position by grub screw from front

6. rearsight adjustable for horizontal deflection

7. wider rearsight protector ears to allow for 6

8. hole for removal of cocking handle adjusted to allow for 7

9. different trigger mechanism and frame.

Signing the Pennywise Licensing Agreement

A licensing agreement was reached while the engineers at Canadian Arsenals Ltd were examining the Mk4 and L2A4 guns sent over from Enfield for

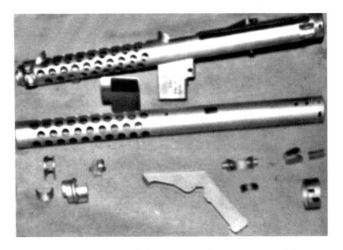

245. An historic photo of the two sample casing assemblies-one complete, in-the-white brazed (above) and another left in component form (below)-*before* they were sent by Sterling to Canadian Arsenals Ltd, for use in formulating the production techniques to be used in manufacturing the C1 SMG. (Courtesy David Howroyd)

this purpose, as well as two complete Mk4 gun casing assemblies, one in un-brazed component form, which were sent over from Sterling.

After a thorough examination of these, the Canadians proposed that their fabrication and production facilities, which had improved a great deal since the Sten gun era, would allow them to produce a good, well-finished and presentable SMG locally, using predominantly stamped and spot-welded components. In turn this meant faster and cheaper production, the use of local materials and a higher proportion of cheaper unskilled labour.

How much cheaper the Long Branch engineers were able to make the C1 gun is not clear. Certainly, as we shall see, they went to great pains to avoid royalty payments on Patchett's patented trigger, ribbed bolt, double return springs, and magazine feed rollers. However, the cost of tooling, gauges, setting up plant facilities, redrawing components for manufacture, stamping dies, fixtures and specialised machinery was probably three or four times the cost of buying the necessary number of standard Mk4/L2A3s direct from Sterling.

Canadian Arsenals Ltd (CAL) Toolroom Production Begins

246. Left side view of Canadian TRM (toolroom) trial gun no TRM02, sent to RSAF Enfield for evaluation and inspection by the Sub-Machine Gun Committee, shown with trigger guard reversed in the arctic position.

Enfield were impressed with the "Ruffell" trigger (which was interchangeable with George Patchett's patented trigger, but different enough that it was not liable for royalty payment), the fabricated L1A1 (C1) bayonet standard-and-boss, and the foresight configuration, which used the standard rifle foresight blade. Also, the fabricated return spring cap was found to perform better than the original Sterling cap in dusty climates. (MoD Pattern Room collection)

Serial numbers for toolroom C1 and C2 (automatic) rifle prototypes had already been set aside in 100-number blocks, the C1s beginning with TRM001 and the C2s beginning with TRM101. In the records, at any rate, Canadian Arsenals Ltd toolroom C1 SMGs were begun at TRM201, although the guns themselves were simply numbered with the last two digits.

The CAL toolroom order for the production of the first four C1 prototypes, guns nos TRM (2)01 – TRM (2)04, was issued on September 4, 1957 and closed on February 21, 1958. CAL Data Sheets from

the period make brief mention of two later guns, nos TRM (2)05 and TRM (2)06.

Keeping the Product Local

While the Sterling Company licensing agreement allowed the Canadian Government to produce the gun locally, it did not allow the commercial sale of the Canadian-made C1 SMG to other nations, who still had to go through Sterling direct. The exact wording of the licensing agreement was "… guns are for use by our own Armed and Security Forces and will not

247. Top closeup view of (flange-brazed) magazine housing of Canadian trial gun no TRM 02, showing markings. (MoD Pattern Room collection)

It was agreed that the magazine housings and magazine interfaces should be fully interchangeable. This of course allowed Canadian soldiers to use British made and -filled magazines, and vice-versa.

But next, the vexing question of the component parts. If the magazines and housings were to be interchangeable between the British and Canadian guns, then by definition the magazine catches would also have to be, and so on, and on. The end result was that, whereas the guns might LOOK different, the vast majority of the internal component parts

be resold". For this reason, it is extremely unusual to see a C1 SMG outside the Canadian Military.

In keeping with the Canadian spirit of truthfulness and fair-play, when C1 SMG production ceased, the Canadian Government turned to Sterling for spare parts.

Manufacturing the C1 SMG

were designed to be, and were, fully interchangeable. Just to emphasise this point, in the C1 SMG Parts Lists printed in this chapter, every part (such as the butt assembly, trigger mechanism assembly, magazine assembly and return spring cap) with a NATO Stock Number (NSN) beginning '1005-21-960-' was made in Canada, and as an assembly, is directly interchangeable with the Mk4/L2A3 Sterling then current with British, New Zealand, Indian, and a hundred other nations' forces.

Similarly, NSNs beginning '1005-99-960-' indicate an original British stock number, signifying, for troops stationed in such places as Germany, that if Canadian parts were unavailable they might draw on British stores for an interchangeable component.

From this, and in the experience of Canadian and British Armourers, if a damaged gun could not be repaired locally using the British or Canadian parts available, then the gun was probably damaged beyond repair. This was a remarkable achievement by the Canadians.

248. Right side view of production Canadian 9mm C1 SMG, with buttstock extended and breech block closed. (Courtesy Diemaco Inc, Kitchener, Ontario)

Interfaces Established; the C1 Still Unique

Once this major degree of interchangeability had been designed into the gun, the designers got on with the features that would be applicable only to the Canadian model.

In place of full induction brazing and a heavy reliance on machining, as favoured by Sterling, CAL elected to stamp, fold and fabricate as many components as practicable, and spot-weld these to the C1 "casing tube" assembly. The rear and fore sight guards, the front and rear hand guards, grip plate assembly, bayonet stud and boss assembly, and the magazine "mouthpiece" were all such.

The two exceptions were the "barrel support" at the front of the casing and the return spring cap ring at the rear, which were silver-alloy induction brazed. During this process a solid copper cylinder was pushed inside the casing, to draw away the heat and alleviate warping.

Mounting the C1 (L1A1) rifle bayonet to the gun required that the strong fabricated bayonet standard and boss assembly be spot-welded to the casing 45° from vertical on the left-hand side, so as to clear the folding butt. When mounted, the ring on the bayonet crossguard had to clear the bullet path from the muzzle, so the bayonet was mounted slightly away from the body casing. This idea was so successful that a similar idea was tried with a view to modifying the L2 guns in British Military service: in fact for a time, the L2A4 gun was mooted as the next UK Sterling!

The fact that the barrel support of the L2A4 and C1 versions of the gun did not have to provide the boss for the bayonet mounting ting significantly reduced the cost of producing what was for Sterling an intricate and VERY expensive machining.

Component Parts of the a SMG Casing Assembly

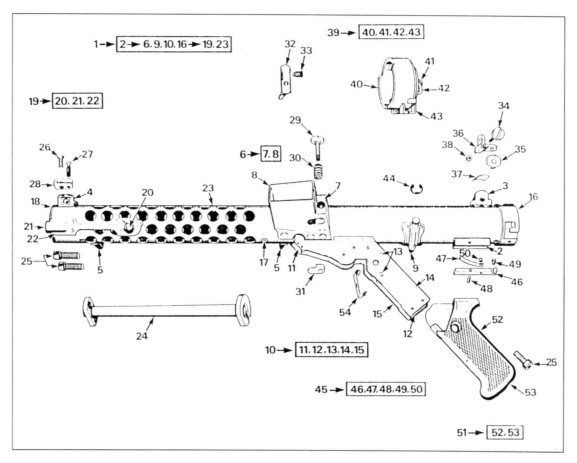

249. From the Illustrated Parts List for the Canadian C1 SMG, the components of the casing assembly. The nomenclature is given, below and on the following page.

The two-digit number in the NSN is the country code, indicating the origin of the part number: 21 = Canada; 00 and 01 = USA; 99 = Britain.

Item	NSN	Item Name and Description	Mfr No	No Off
1	1005-21-842-3374	Casing assembly, gun	301257	1
2	1005-21-842-3836	Bracket, casing	301258	1
3	1005-21-842-3837	Guard, rearsight	301259	1
4	1005-21-114-6039	Guard, frontsight	301260	1
5	1005-21-842-3375	Guard, hand	301261	2
6		Mouthpiece, magazine	F 301262	1
7		Block, ejector	B 301263	1
8		Mouthpiece	D 301264	1
9		Pivot, butt	C 301265	1
10		Plate assembly, grip	F 301266	1
11		Block, front	C 301267	1
12		Block, rear	B 301268	1
13		Pin, distance	B 301269	2
14		Plate, left	F 301270	1
15		Plate, right	F 301271	1
16		Ring	D301272	1
17		Stud, barrel positioning	B 301273	1
18		Support, barrel	B 301274	1
19		Support assembly, bayonet	B 301275	1
20		Boss, bayonet	B 301276	1
21		Stud, bayonet	B 301277	1
22		Support, bayonet	C 301278	1
23		Tube, casing	F 301279	1
24	1005-99-960-2485	Barrel, gun	301222	1
25	5305-00-057-1273	Screw, cap, socket head, fil hd, 1/4-28 UNF-3A, 0.750 in fas lg	MS 35460-23	3
26	5305-21-107-7097	Screw, machine 60° countersunk oval hd, st dr, 8-36 UNF-2A, 0.500 in fas lg	436217	1
27	1005-21-102-3797	Sight, front	103136	1
28	1005-21-107-2769	Block, foresight	301229	1
29	1005-99-960-2183	Screw, magazine catch, special O/S pan hd, sl dr, 10-32 UNF-2A	301292	1
30	1005-99-960-2184	Spring, magazine catch, 0.380 in OD, 2.212 in free lg	301294	1
31	1005-99-960-2176	Catch, magazine	301280	1
32	1005-99-960-2177	Ejector, cartridge	301281	1
33	5305-21-107-7087	Set screw, headless, socket drive. full dog point, 1/4-28 UNF-3A, 0.500 in O/A	BCTX2-11	1
34	1005-21-107-2778	Pin, axis, rearsight	301290	1
35	1005-21-107-3048	Washer, positioning, rearsight	301318	1
36	1005-21-107-2768	Sight, rear	301293	1
37	1005-21-107-2784	Spring, rearsight	301293	1
38	1005-21-107-2777	Nut, rearsight axis pin 0.195-32 UNC-2B	301289	1

39	1005-21-107-2772	Cap, return spring	301251	1
40		Cap	D 304701	1
41		Cleat	B 301253	1
42		Loop	B 301254	1
43		Plate, cap	D 301255	1
44	5365-00-944-4911	Ring, retaining extension 'C' or 'E' type external 0.207 in ID, 0.027 in thk	MS16633-3025	2
45	1005-99-960-0034	Lever assembly, locking, return spring cap	301285	1
46		Lever	C 301286	1
47	1005-99-960-2252	Spring, locking lever	301288	1
48	5315-00-797-8039	Pin, grooved, headless 0.094 in dia both ends, 0.101 in dia centre, 0.375 in O/A lg	GP5-094X375-12	1
49		Pin	B 301287	1
50	5320-00-068-6922	Rivet, solid, universal head, 0.065 in shk dia, 0.323 in shk lg	MS20613-2P5	1
51	1005-99-960-2178	Grip, pistol	301282	1
52		Grip	33188CS1790E	1
53		Insert	B 301283	1
54	1005-99-960-2082	Spring, locking, locating pin	301295	1

Features of the Canadian C1 Casing Assembly

250. Left hand view of the Canadian 9mm C1 SMG, with buttstock folded and 10-round alternate magazine in place.
While the C1 *looks* like a Mk4/L2A3 Sterling and all components are interchangeable as assemblies, innovative stampings have largely replaced expensive machinings. (Courtesy Centre of Forensic Sciences, Toronto)

The grip plate assembly and the magazine housing, or "mouthpiece", were spot-welded to the body side by their flanges, an idea copied from the production method used by ROF Fazakerley during their Government-ordered production of the L2A3 (although the Fazakerley components were brazed).

The threaded (C1 rifle) foresight blade followed the modified Sterling pattern of being adjustable for elevation. The backsight differed in that the axis pin, which allows the sight to be flipped over to either 100 or 200 yards, was screw-threaded. This allowed the backsight to be moved either left or right, to zero the gun.

251 (Left). Two return spring caps.
  Left: Canadian Cl, fabricated
  Right: Sterling Mk4, machined .
  The Canadian version was much cheaper to produce than the cast-and-machined Sterling product, and fared better than the Fazalcerley-made L2A3 cap during comparison trials. (MoD Army REME)

The stamped return spring cap followed the Sterling pattern but the locating recesses that hold the butt in the extended position were fabricated and welded onto the cap. This fabrication and welding saved a LOT of the expensive machining usually required on these small but important parts (which at Sterling were later precision cast but still finish machined).

Component Parts of the C1 SMG Butt Assembly

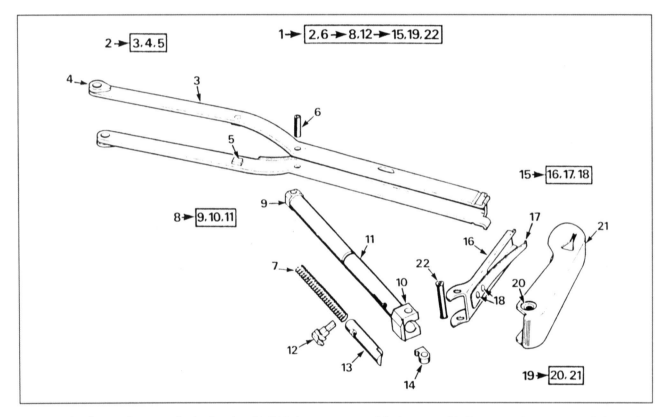

252. From the Illustrated Parts List for the Canadian C1 SMG, the components of the butt assembly. The nomenclature is given, below and on the facing page.

Item	NSN	Item Name and Description	Mfr No	No Off
1	1005-21-107-2771	Stock, extension, gun	301230	1
2	1005-99-960-2386	Stock, extension, gun	301231	1
3		Frame	D 301232	1
4		Pad	B 301233	2
5		Stud	B 301234	2
6	1005-99-960-2164	Pin, axis, strut	301241	1

Item	NSN	Item Name and Description	Mfr No	No Off
7	5360-99-960-2228	Spring, plunger, strut 0.360 in OD, 2.212 in free lg, A/A coils	301246	1
8	1005-21-107-2787	Strut, butt	301247	1
9		Block, pivot, front	B 301248	1
10		Block, pivot, rear	B 301249	1
11		Tube	C 301250	1
12	1005-99-960-2229	Catch, locking	301238	1
13	1005-21-107-2780	Plunger, strut	301245	1
14	1005-21-846-5208	Lever, strut plunger	371686	1
15	1005-99-960-0032	Catch assembly, butt	301235	1
16		Catch	C 301236	1
17	1005-99-960-2162	Spring, butt catch	301237	1
18	5320-00-721-8972	Rivet, solid, universal head 0.097 in shk dia, 0.260 in shk lg	134773	2
19	1005-99-960-2080	Plate, butt, shoulder gun stock	301242	1
20		Bush	B 301243	1
21		Plate	F 301244	1
22	1005-99-960-2163	Pin, axis, butt plate	301240	1

Improving the Sterling Butt

The butt assembly of the Canadian gun was fabricated to a local design, but remained fully interchangeable as a unit, including most of the internal components.

One absurd piece of illogical engineering was designed out of the Sterling butt by the canny Canadians. On the Sterling, the butt is hinged on two trunnions, one at each side, positioned just behind the pistol grip, each butt frame member being retained by a button-headed retaining pin, itself retained by a small pin. The simple Canadian method of using a spring-steel circlip to retain the butt frame to the trunnion is just as effective, simpler, easier to repair, less likely to go wrong, and far easier to produce by fabricating. Any British Armourer will tell you that repairing this part of the L2A3 has caused a great deal of head-scratching over the years!

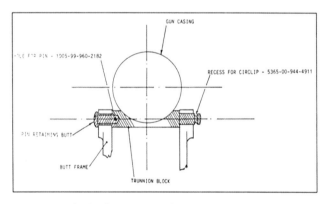

253. Two methods of securing the folding butt assembly to the butt trunnions, described in the text.
Left: Sterling (trunnion block machined and brazed).
Right: Canadian Arsenals Ltd (trunnion block stamped and spot-welded). (Drawing by Peter Laidler)

Component Parts of the a SMG Breech Assembly (fig 254)

Item	NSN	Item Name and Description	Mfr No	No Off
1	1005-21-107-2774	Guard, trigger	301298	1
2	1005-21-107-2775	Housing, trigger mechansim	301299	1
3		Bracket, support, trigger guard	C 301300	1
4		Pin, axis, shield	B 301301	1
5		Pin	B 301302	1
6		Plate, housing, left	B 301303	1
7		Plate, housing, right	B 301304	1
8		Plate, stop	B 301305	1
9		Stiffener, housing	B 301307	1
10	1005-21-107-2776	Lever, assembly, change	301307	1
11		Ann	B 301308	1
12		Stem	C 301309	1
13	5315-21-107-2779	Pin, sear and trigger, 0.025 in dia, 0.460 in lg	301310	2

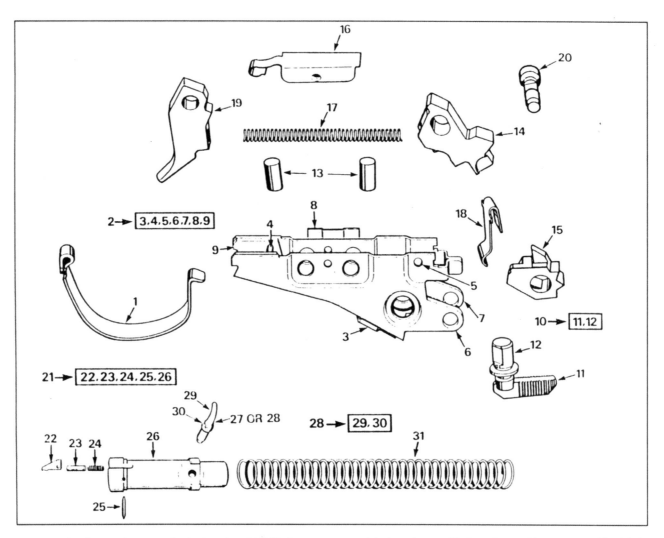

254. From the Illustrated Parts List for the Canadian C1 SMG, the components of the breech assembly. Interchangeable as an assembly with the Sterling Mk4/L2A3. The nomenclature is given, beginning on the facing page.

14	1005-21-107-2781	Sear	301311	1
15	1005-21-860-3956	Selector, change lever	301312REVD	1
16	1005-21-107-2783	Shield, trigger mechanism	301313	1
17	5360-21-107-2785	Spring, trigger and sear 0.192 in OD, 2.250 in free lg, 41 coils	301315	1
18	1005-21-860-3780	Spring, change lever selector red	388489	1
19	1005-21-107-2788	Trigger	301316	1
20	1005-99-960-2180	Pin, locating, trigger assembly	301291	1
21	1005-21-107-2770	Bolt assembly, breech	301233	1
22	1005-21-107-2773	Extractor, cartridge	304702	1
23	1005-21-107-	Plunger, extractor, straight headless 0.188 in dia, 1.078 in lg	301227	1
24	5360-21-107-3045	Spring, extractor, 0.181 in OD, 0.750 in free lg, 13 coils	301228	1
25	5315-21-107-3044	Pin, extractor, straight, headless, 0.125 in shk dia, 1.109 in 0/A lg, end style 03	301226	1
		Bolt	F 301224	1
27		Handle, cocking, obsolete – replaced by item 28	301284	1
28	1005-21-864-5707	Handle assembly, cocking, w/detent	390138	1
29		Handle, cocking	C 389294	1
30	5330-00-542-1420	O Ring, synthetic rubber, 0.234 to 0.244 in ID, 0.067 to 0.073 in 0/A h	MS29561-010	1
31	5360-21-107-3047	Spring, return 1.332 in OD, 13.00 in free lg, 18 coils	301296	1

Declining the Helically Ribbed Bolt

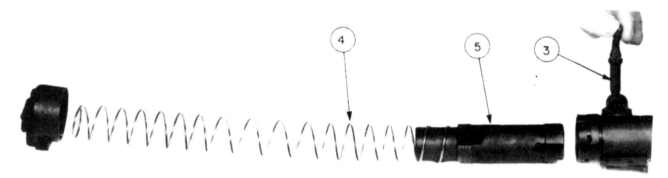

255. From Issue 2 of the Canadian Army EME Manual, dated 12 December, 1960: Breechblock and return spring. Removal of the return spring cap is followed by removal of the cocking handle (3), after which the breech block (5) may be withdrawn. Note the single return spring and 'ribless' Sten-style bolt. (Courtesy Capt Wm Etter)

While designing OUT the nightmare Sterling butt trunnion pins, the Canadian designers at Long Branch ignored the superb design of the Sterling breech block (Patchett patent number 579660 dated 25th October, 1943). The external raised helical lands of the Sterling block reduce friction to an acceptable minimum while allowing sand, mud, water, ice and most other terrestrial rubbish to be swept forward under the flat on the rear barrel flange, and thence out of the gun via the cooling holes in the casing. This feature made the Mk4/A3 gun so effective and trouble-free in service with the British Armies in the Middle East, and recently in Kuwait. It seems as though mud and sand just will not stop the gun functioning.

In the Cl, however, the Canadians opted for an improved Sten breech block. However, during trials of early toolroom guns fitted with these breech blocks, several problems appeared, notably a series of 'double-taps' where with the change lever set to 'SINGLE SHOT', two or more shots fired automatically.

Other breech blocks were fabricated to drawing number XP 199-81, using the Sterling double return spring, return spring block, and cup. The problem was eventually solved by repositioning the sear bent in the original breech blocks. Ironically, during the tests set up to iron out this problem, one of the UK-made L2A4s also suffered a 'double-tap' problem, although this was traced to a defective trigger mechanism detent spring. Guns used during these breech block interchangeability and 'double-tap' trials were UF57A 15525, Canadian tool room guns nos TRM 203 and TRM 204.

The reason the Canadians wished to retain the old pattern un-ribbed breech block is not stated in the committee papers, but one school of thought, put forward by senior Canadian Armourers, was that the Achilles' heel of the Sten had always been the quality of the magazines and the magazine housing. By designing out the magazine and housing faults, the Canadian Forces were happy to keep the Sten-style breech block. Another reason might have been that this avoided royalty payments on Patchett's patented ribbed bolt.

The Canadians also eliminated the complex . Sterling cocking handle plunger and spring without detriment. Additionally, they avoided the patented inner and outer return spring idea of the British gun. The Canadian C1 uses one return spring only.

Adopting the Admirably Simple "Ruffell" Trigger Mechanism

The production C1 trigger mechanism was not the original Patchett pattern. The simplified trigger mechanism the Canadians adopted came from the fertile mind of Les Ruffell, a brilliant designer and head of the Sterling drawing office. This "Ruffell" trigger mechanism is shown in exploded form in fig 264. So radical was the design change that no royalties were payable on Patchett's patent number 559469 dated 17th August, 1942.

The cold arctic weather associated with the Canadian winters spurred development of an arctic trigger guard easier to deploy than the Sterling version. As complete assemblies, the Sterling and Canadian trigger mechanisms remain interchangeable.

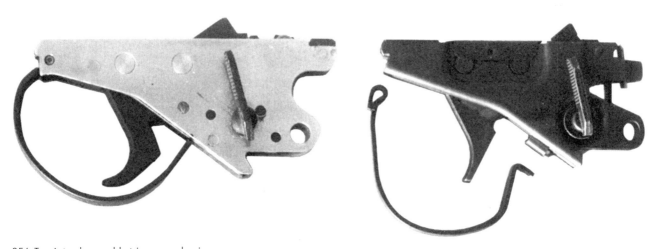

256. Two interchangeable trigger mechanisms.
Left: George Patchett's patented trigger mechanism, as featured in the Sterling Mk4/L2A3. (MoD Army REME)
Right: the fabricated trigger housing and simplified mechanism designed by Sterling draughtsman Les Ruffell, as used in the Canadian C1 SMG. The Ruffell trigger was cheaper and used fewer parts, and actually fared better during Canadian acceptance trials. It was tested in England but was found to offer "no significant improvement" over the Sterling mechanism. (Canadian Forces EME)

The UK Chief Inspector of Armament Design was slightly taken aback by the Canadian decision to use the Ruffell trigger mechanism, and ordered that Enfield take a good look at it as a suitable (and cheaper) alternative to the Sterling pattern. The Ordnance Board concluded that the Ruffell trigger "… offered no significant improvement over the existing mechanism."

The Steering Committee were also concerned as to how the Canadian-made guns would fare during the mud, sand and salt water corrosion tests, the procedures of which standard tests are explained in detail in Chapter Fifteen. As it turned out, the UK made Sterlings fared better in the mud tests, and the Canadian C1s fared better in the sand tests. Both compared equally well during the salt water corrosion test. The Canadian (Les Ruffell) trigger mechanism fared better throughout the tests, as did the Canadian fabricated return spring cap, which proved to be easier to remove throughout the whole series of trials. All. of the UK versions had to be tapped off with a hammer during the blown sand test!

How the C1 Trigger Mechanism Works

As noted, although interchangeable as assemblies with the Sterling Mk4, the simplified trigger mechanism used in the Canadian C1 contained fewer parts and featured a different searing action, although the C1 could still be put on Safe with the bolt either closed or cocked, as with the Sterling.

The Ruffell trigger mechanism is described in Issue 1 of the Canadian Forces EME Manual, dated 28 January, 1960, as follows:

Automatic Fire

On pressing the trigger, the nose of the sear is forced upward thereby rotating the sear and disengaging the bent of the sear from the bent on the breechblock. The gun will now continue to fire until the magazine is empty or pressure on the trigger is relaxed.

When the trigger is released, the sear is free to return to its former position under the influence of the sear spring. The nose of the sear rubs against the flat surface on the bottom of the breechblock until the

breechblock has passed over it to the rear. The sear now completes its upward movement and stops the breechblock on its forward travel.

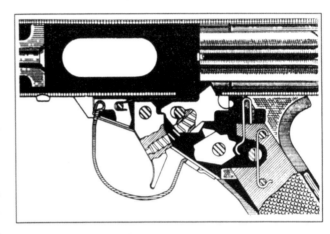

257. C1 SMG, Automatic fire: Breech block cocked. (Courtesy Capt Wm Etter)

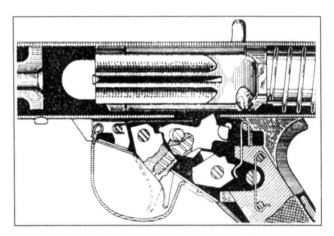

258. C1 SMG, Automatic fire: Trigger pressed, beech block in motion. (Courtesy Capt Wm Etter)

Repetition fire

When the change lever is placed at 'R' (Repetition), the selector is rotated clear of the sear. When, with the gun cocked, the trigger is pressed, the step on the trigger engaging the underside of the nose of the sear rotates the sear about its axis pin, and sear is lowered.

As the sear disengages from the breechblock, it is forced rearward and upward under the influence of the compressed sear spring. The nose of the sear is now positioned behind the step on the trigger and the sear rubs against the flat undersurface of the breechblock.

During recoil, the sear is held down by the flat undersurface of the breechblock, but as the breechblock approaches the end of its rearward travel and is clear of the sear, the sear is forced further upward by pressure of the sear spring. As the breechblock commences to move forward, the bent on the sear engages with the bent on the breechblock and the front face of the nose of the sear is forced upward against the rear face of the step on the trigger,holding the action to the rear.

When the trigger is released, the trigger is rotated on its axis pin, lowering the rear face of the step of trigger out of engagement with the nose of the sear. The breechblock and sear are forced forward until the nose of the sear is over the step of the trigger and the breechblock is cocked on the sear. The trigger must be fully released and pressed again for each single shot.

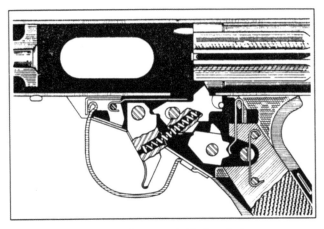

259. C1 SMG, Repetition fire: Breech block cocked. (Courtesy Capt Wm Etter)

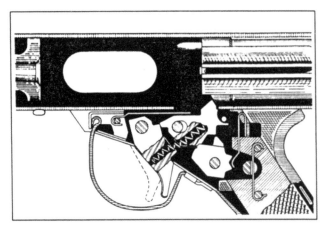

260. C1 SMG, Repetition fire: trigger pressed, breech block in motion. (Courtesy Capt Wm Etter)

Applied safety

When the change lever is placed at 'S' (Safe), the inner shoulder of the selector is rotated directly under the lower rear shoulder of the sear. Pressure on the trigger when the gun is cocked, results in direct metal to metal contact between the sear and selector preventing the sear from rotating.

When the change lever is placed at 'S ' (Safe) with the bolt in the forward position, the sear engages the rear bent on the bottom of the breechblock. The sear cannot be depressed as it is locked, as described above, thereby preventing the breechblock from being withdrawn rearward.

First C1 Production: Numbering and Markings

The first pre-production guns were shown to RCEME Armourers at the Training School at Kingston, Ontario in 1959. The last Sub-Machine Gun Steering Committee meeting was held on 28th October, 1959, where it was reported that the first Canadian guns were now ready for distribution, the first production gun having been completed in April, 1959. Production was to be initially 1,000 per month and the gun was issued with the Canadian NSN (B3) 1005-21-102-8202.

Serial numbers for the first ten thousand C1 SMGs were assigned the prefix OS followed by a four-digit number (fig 261), the second thousand were 1S plus four digits, and so on. The Canadian C1s examined for this study were marked on the top of the magazine housing:

SMG 9mm C1
2S XXXX
(numbers 2S 5182, 2S 5217 and 2S 5222 examined)
(Maple leaf)

and on the underside of the housing:

CAL 1968
(indicating the year of manufacture by Canadian Arsenals Ltd)

The Canadian Forces have expressed total satisfaction with their Sterling-designed, locally-produced C1 SMGs, which featured in the Canadian Order of Battle until superseded by the C7 rifle and CB carbine (Canada's updated versions of the 5.56mm NATO calibre M16 rifle and carbine) in 1987.

Early Interchangeability Trials

Featured in early interchangeability trials were L2A4s converted from Fazakerley L2A3s SNs UF59A 152082 and 152083, alongside early Canadian production guns nos OS 0582 and OS 0585.

The Canadian Magazine Story

At the start, the Canadian engineers decided that the C1 magazine should hold 34 rounds in a staggered formation, with a double feed position. Having had experience with the 50-round Lanchester and later Sten magazines, they did not seriously contemplate using these earlier, single-feed magazines in their new SMG, although like the British Sterling, the Canadian guns will operate with Sten magazines.

George Patchett designed and patented the superb curved design we all now associate with the Sterling. The full description and technical aspects of these curved, friction-reducing, roller-platform magazines are detailed in chapters Four and Sixteen. The Canadians found they could do without the patented roller platform by designing out of their magazines the friction problems that had dogged the Sten and Lanchester magazines. The top and bottom surfaces of the Canadian magazine follow the Sterling pattern, by having two shallow recesses rolled down the curved length. This presents a much-reduced friction-bearing area to the platform. The top and bottom surfaces are then folded over to form the front and rear. However, these folded edges are not just welded together as in Bren and (some) Sten magazines. Strips of seam-free spring steel are spotwelded to the internal front and back walls, making an extremely smooth internal section that allows the successful use of a platform instead of the Sterling rollers. A point worthy of praise, considering that the Israeli UZI

magazines follow the same principle. Be that as it may, the Canadian magazines are not as friction-free as the Sterling ones.

Because of the increased friction encountered with the early Canadian 34-round prototypes, the production C1 magazine only holds 30 rounds against the Sterling's 34, and as a result, the Canadian magazine is 1.4″ shorter. The Sterling magazines also incorporate a positioning/anti-rattle spring, which the Canadian ones do not. Canadian magazines will operate perfectly in UK-made guns, and vice versa.

The Alternate 10-Round Magazine, and the Sling

Also supplied with the Canadian C1 SMG was a 10-round magazine, the design of which follows exactly the design of the 30-round magazine, except the casing is straight. The concept of reduced-capacity magazines was later copied by Sterling. Although intended for their commercial Sterling Mk7 'Pistols', ten and fifteen round magazines were readily available for the sub-machine gun series, too.

The sling issued with the Canadian C1 is identical to the Sterling sling issued by UK Military Ordnance, except that the attachment hook is larger and appears to be more robust.

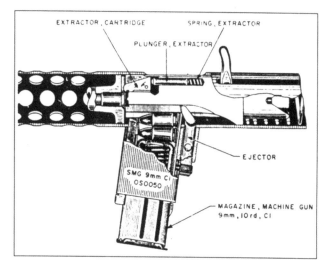

261 (right). Top, partially-sectioned view of C1 SMG no OS 0050, showing 10-round alternate magazine in place. (Courtesy Diemaco Inc, Kitchener, Ontario)

Component Parts of the C1 SMG Magazines and Sling

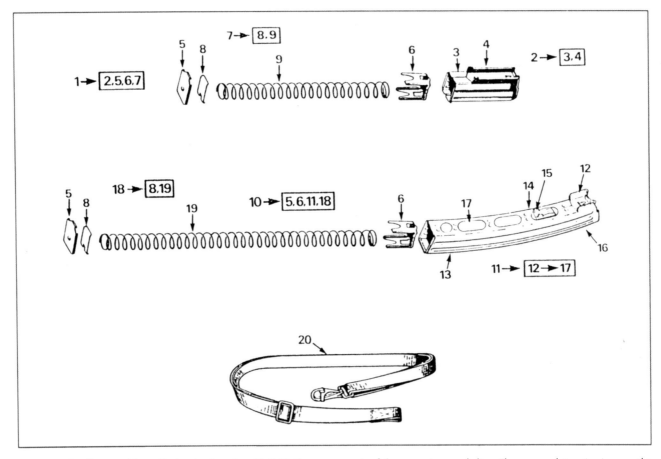

262. From the Illustrated Parts List for the Canadian C1 SMG, the components of the magazines and sling. The nomenclature is given on the next page.

Item	NSN	Item Name and Description	Mfr No	No Off
1	1005–21–103–7354	Magazine, cartridge, 10 rounds	301201	1
2		Case, magazine, 10 round, welded	C 301202	1
3		Case, magazine	F 301203	1
4		Guide, bullet	D 301204	1
5	1005–21–107–2790	Plate, bottom	301209	1
6	1005–21–107–2792	Platform, magazine	301208	1
7		Spring assembly, 10 round magazine	B 301205	1
8	1005–21–107–2791	Plate, distance	301207	1
9	1005–21–107–2793	Spring, platform., 0.7707 in OD, 6.200 in free lg, 18 coils	301206	1
10	1005–21–103–7355	Magazine, cartridge, 30 rounds	301210	1
11		Case, magazine, 30 round, welded	F 301211	1
12		Guide, bullet	F 301214	1
13		Plate, magazine, left	E 301213	1
14		Plate, magazine, right	E 301212	1
15		Stop,magazine,lower	B 301215	1
16		Stop, magazine, upper	B 301216	1

17		Strap, backing	B 301217	1
5	1005–21–107–2790	Plate, bottom	301209	1
6	1005–21–107–2792	Platform, magazine	301208	1
18		Spring assembly, 30 round magazine	B 301218	1
8	1005–21–107–2791	Plate, distance	301207	1
19	1005–21–107–2794	Spring, platform, 0.717 in OD, 12,600 in free lg, 35 coils	301219	1
20	1005–21–103–5406	Sling, small arms	301319	1

The Silent C1

Long Branch engineers manufactured two silenced versions of the C1 SMG, as a proposal to replace the Mk2S and Mk6 Sten guns within the Canadian Military. These guns were not adopted and the silenced gun in service to date with the Canadian Military Forces is the Mk5/L34A1, manufactured by Sterling.

Accessories for the C1 SMG

Different Muzzle Configuration Mandates Different BFA

As the muzzle configuration of the Canadian guns differed from the UK Sterling pattern, so did the blank firing adaptor.

The bowed left leg is to clear the bayonet standard, while the straight leg fits to the right hand side of the casing. The locating studs fit into two of the cooling holes in the gun casing.

The articulating spigot/choke extends into the muzzle of the gun, while the curved spring plate beneath the choke pulls forward, ensuring that the shouldered attachment lugs remained locked within the holes in the casing.

Like all military blank firing adaptors, the Canadian pattern is painted with a high-temperature yellow paint.

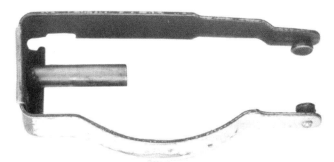

263. The yellow-painted blank firing attachment (BFA) for the Canadian C1 SMG. The bowed leg was necessary to clear the bayonet standard on the left side of the casing.

The Superb C1 Cleaning Kit

The Canadian climate and topography ensure that reliability associated with weapon cleanliness is paramount.

The cleaning kit for the C1 SMG consists of a sturdy khaki plastic hinged box, about the same size as a two-ounce tobacco tin. This contains a moulded

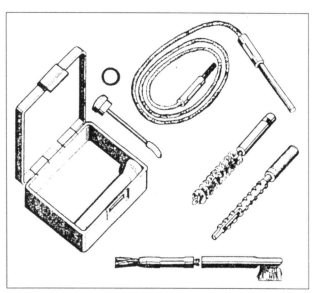

264. The Canadian C1 SMG cleaning kit, perhaps the most comprehensive ever issued with a sub-machine gun.

A sturdy, hinged khaki plastic box with built-in oil bottle contains, clockwise from 11 o'clock: oil spoon and 'O'-ring; double-ended pull through; wire bore brush; brass jag; 2-pc plastic screw-together nook-and-cranny brush.

in oil bottle with an applicator spoon sealed at its top by a synthetic rubber 'O'-ring.

Inside there is a double-ended nylon pull through, one end threaded and the other weighted. A brass jag, onto which a piece of 4″ × 3″ flannelette wraps, and a bronze wire barrel brush both may be screwed onto the threaded pull through end.

There is also a short, two-piece screw-together plastic rod, bearing a toothbrush-type brush at one end and a rounded stiff bristle brush at the other.

This must be the most comprehensive but compact cleaning kit ever devised for a sub-machine gun. It is interesting that it took Great Britain another 25 or so years before it copied the double-ended pull through and brush idea from the canny Canadians for its 185/86 weapon system. Even then the soldier had to use an old toothbrush to supplement the absence of a sensible nook-and-cranny brush!

The (Short-Lived) Carrying Chest

265. The sturdy wooden carrying chest, looking remarkably similar to a shortened No4(T) sniper rifle chest, as originally issued with the Canadian C1 SMG.

Each chest had spacers and keepers to securely hold one SMG, 1 magazine, a bayonet, and a cleaning kit.

Each new C1 was originally issued from CAL in a returnable stout wooden chest. These chests have dovetailed ends and sides with a hinged top, fastened with a hasp and staple, looking remarkably similar to shortened No4(T) sniper rifle chests. Each is marked 'C.A.L. 9MM: CARBINE LONG BRANCH'.

Needless to say, once the guns were taken out, these heavy chests were phased out, never to be seen again.

Notes on a Diemaco-Developed Recovery Process

With the demise of Canadian Arsenals Limited on June 30, 1976, responsibility for further thorough repair and overhaul procedures to all Canadian Forces small arms was transferred to the private firm of Diemaco Inc, of Kitchener, Ontario.

266. Right side view of three C1 SMG casings, showing recovery of trigger mechanism locating pin hole.

Above: conversion complete, after grinding, redrilling, and line-reaming.

Centre: after TIG welding.

Below: elongated hole in need of repair.

Note the CAL-developed method of flange-spot-welding mostly fabricated sub-assemblies to the casing. (Courtesy Diemaco Inc, Kitchener, Ontario)

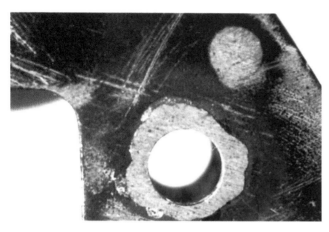

267. Left side closeup of finished repair. Trigger mechanism locating pin hole has been restored to original size and location. (Courtesy Diemaco Inc, Kitchener, Ontario)

There a procedure was developed to recover C1 SMG casings and trigger housings which had become worn.

It was found that, after prolonged use, the continued shock of the breech block stopping on the sear, which caused the trigger mechanism to attempt to rotate forward about its locating pin with each cessation of shots, would elongate the holes in the stamped grip plates, and also deform the material at the front end of the stamped trigger housing.

This two-part repair procedure consisted of welding up the grip plate holes and then re-establishing them, along with recovery of the material and geometry at the front end of the trigger mechanism housing. This returned the trigger mechanism location and function to original specifications.

When the C1 was finally withdrawn from service, the 30,000 or so that were retired, were destroyed in a furnace.

However, the Long Branch Arsenal very kindly sent James Edmiston a complete set of their production drawings.

The whole of the Canadian inventory for this gun was completely accurately accounted for.

268. Right front closeups of two C1 SMG trigger housings.
　Left: deformed material has been built up with weld in first stage of recovery process.
　Right: after machining to shape. (Courtesy Diemaco Inc, Kitchener, Ontario)

Chapter Ten

The Indians Curry Favour

The "Indian" Mk4 and the SAF Machine Carbine 1A

Number produced:	Sterling commercial Mk4s:	51,000
	SAF Cawnpore 1A Machine Carbines:	
	restricted; probably over	1,000,000
Date discontinued:	still in production	

First Enquiries

It was in 1956 that Mr Sinnah, the head of Indian Arms Production came to the Sterling factory. Stan Wingrove and Major Turp asked David Howroyd to entertain Mr Sinnah for the period. Mr Sinnah was made most welcome and given the run of the factory.

The Sterling board were under the impression that the Indian Government did not want the Sterling Mk4 gun, but, like the good businessmen they were, they and David Howroyd duly entertained the small party. David Howroyd recalls taking Mr Sinnah home to enjoy a real English cream tea with his wife and daughter, both of whom still remember him to this day. Mr Sinnah did take two Mk4 guns home with him to India, where the guns were subjected to extensive trials.

The Indian Mk4 – A Deal Gone Wrong

This all paid off in 1961, when the Indian Government signed a contract worth £16,000 with Sterling for the drawings, tools, gauging and expertise to manufacture the Mk4 version of the Sterling SMG at the Indian Small Arms Factory at Kanpur (anglicised as Cawnpore).

A proviso was that Sterling would furnish the first 60,000 finished Mk4 guns under contract to the UK Ministry of Supply, who would pass them on under an Aid for India agreement. There were to be no restrictions on further Indian production, and furthermore, no royalties. What a bargain!

During negotiations for these 60,000 "Aid to India" Mk4s it was agreed that some of the production work would go to RSAF Enfield. They successfully cast the return spring caps, and marked all their production with the logo highlighted here. (By the time this agreement had been negotiated, ROF Fazakerley had finished its production run of L2A3s and spare parts,

269. Inside view of Mk4 return spring cap from one of the planned 60,000 "Aid to India" Mk4s, showing 'E within D' marking indicating manufacture at RSAF Enfield. (Courtesy Indian Army, MoD)

and thus they did not take part in producing L2A3s for the Indian order.)

The outcome was that by 1963 the British Government had placed orders with Sterling for 20,000, then a further 16,000, and then a final 15,000 guns, making a total of 51,000 of the 60,000 Sterling Mk4 guns they had agreed to supply to India.

Unfortunately, India went to war with Pakistan in 1965, and the British Government revoked the export licence part way through shipping the Indian Mk4 order, and abandoned plans to procure the last 9,000 guns.

At first it seemed fortunate for Sterling that their contract was with the UK Ministry of Supply, who had to pay the final bill regardless of whether the guns went to India or not. The full order of 20,000 bayonets and 296,000 magazines reached India unscathed, but in 1965, 18,466 remaining undelivered Sterling Mk4s, numbered from approximately KR 81000, went into bonded secure storage with the UK Ministry of Defence at its huge Ordnance Depot at Donnington in Shropshire.

Ironically, in 1964 and again in 1966, Sterling were able to obtain licences to sell 75 guns and 150 magazines to the other belligerent nation, Pakistan!

Sauve Qui Peut

The 18,466 Mk4s from the aborted Indian order now belonged to the British Government of the day, and they set about selling them to other friendly (and subsequently NOT so friendly) nations. As an ironic blow to Sterling, the Government sold them at the 1961 contract price. After all, the Government didn't have to operate at a profit, whereas Sterling did!

Rubbing it In: Stripping Ex-Indian Guns for UK Army Spares

In the late 1960s the remaining 6,000 Mk4s still left over from the aborted Indian order were stripped for spares by Armourers at the REME workshops attached to the Donnington Ordnance Depot, and for many years, these ex-Indian contract guns formed the bulk of the spare parts stock for the British Army. There was a catch for the British, though. The barrel chambers of these ex-Indian guns did not conform to the NATO 0.662″ depth specification. Only by a relaxation of this specification were these barrels approved as replacement spare parts for UK Military guns.

Like the barrels, for many years and until quite recently, spares from these ex-Indian contract guns have turned up to repair L2A3 Sterlings in the UK Military, especially the distinctive black crackle painted butts and return spring caps.

In 1973 Sterling were able to re-purchase the remaining 6,000 stripped gun casings, which were hastily made back into complete guns, including 2,000 which were immediately assembled and shipped to the Kuwaiti Army who were experiencing problems with a neighbour along her Northern border; a problem that would haunt little Kuwait for a long time thereafter until things reached a head in 1990.

Once these ex-Indian contract Sterlings had been disposed of, Sterling again became the masters of their own product, in so far as setting prices and supplying spare parts were concerned.

The Licence Kicks In – The Machine Carbine 1A

Once the Indian Government had their own production lines up and running at their Cawnpore factory, they could and certainly did cock-a-snook at the UK Government and their remaining Sterling guns. In fact, they implied where they could stick their guns. After all, incomplete guns in Ordnance stores are simply an expensive way of storing fresh air.

A Close Look at the Indian 1A

At first glance, the Indian 1A gun looks identical to the commercial Sterling Mk4s manufactured for the UK Military, with the crackle black paint finish over a phosphated casing. Under the skin however, things are quite different.

270. Left side closeup of the breech area of the crackle-finish Indian 1A Carbine, serial no JJ 9417.

Note the distinctively large markings, and the unusual rounded Indian-pattern change lever. Variations in roughening (prick-punching or chequering) have been noted, but the distinctive identifying feature is the shape. (MoD Pattern Room collection)

In spite of having all the production drawings, the Cawnpore guns are generally not interchangeable with those produced by Sterling or Fazakerley. Most, if not all of the sub-assemblies, such as butts, trigger mechanisms, casings and barrels (not made to the .012″ deeper NATO spec) will interchange, but many component parts certainly will NOT.

As an example, it would be a waste of time trying a Sterling extractor or return spring cup in a Cawnpore gun, and vice-versa. The shape of the change lever on the 1A differs from the UK-made version, being half-round in section, and the small screw used to retain the adjustable foresight is operated with a small screwdriver instead of an Allen key.

"Snotty Joints", but Complete Satisfaction

The overall finish of the Indian-made guns was more akin to the Sterling Mk4 than the Canadian C1. Whereas the Canadian C1 was designed to be and looked fabricated, the Cawnpore guns were not, but somehow did. We think the expression of a fellow

271. Top closeup view of the magazine housing of the Indian SAF Carbine, showing markings.

The serial number is usually prefixed with double letters: 'DD', 'KK' and 'LL' have neen noted, as well as the 'JJ' shown here. (MoD Pattern Room collection)

Armourer who assisted in Peter Laidler's examination of several samples just about sums the finish up. From the purely cosmetic point of view, the problem appeared to be that the Cawnpore factory lacked the induction brazing facilities used on the casing by the Sterling company. This resulted in what a plumber might call "snotty joints". Other distinctive identifying features include unexpected sharp edges on some of the punch-pressed parts.

Whereas the external fit and finish might leave something to be desired, the SAF Carbines functioned as faultlessly as their Sterling counterparts. The well-trained and disciplined Indian Army have seen extensive active service with their SAF Carbines in the north, west and east of their massive country, through Indian winters and summers and in the most appalling conditions ranging from monsoons to arid desert, and have expressed full satisfaction with their reliability.

The SAF Carbine will remain in the Indian Army Order of Battle for many years to come. As a sub-machine gun, it excels.

Sales Out the Back Door

Shady Dealings with Non-Interchangeable Components

Armourers know from skill and experience that hand (or selective) fitting of individual components can usually rectify any given problem. Perhaps this is what motivated certain UK arms suppliers, who purchased Indian-made "Sterling" spares in order to supply other nations with spares for UK-made Sterlings. This was an unfair contravention of the original purchaser's guarantee statement, which India had signed, which stated:

> … *components and guns are for the sole purposes of the Forces of this [buyer's] Country and will not be resold or exported.*

It is no secret that world tension and gun sales increase (or decrease) at the same rate. This was good for Sterling when the buyers were on our side, but things changed when those nations who already had Sterling guns moved to the 'other side of the fence'. Many of these Middle Eastern nations had large quantities of Sterling guns, and were more than happy with them. And they wanted to keep them serviceable, which

272. The front of a double-sided brochure describing the SAF Carbine, produced as an aid to export sales by the Indian Ordnance Factory Board's Marketing and Export Section.

Note the calibre, erroniously listed as "9 × 29" (!)mm. (Courtesy MoD Pattern Room, Nottingham)

meant they needed access to more guns, and to spare parts. The dilemma faced by Sterling was that, while buyers were eager to buy, try as they might, getting the necessary export licence could prove frustratingly difficult, and was often impossible.

This problem could be solved by having the buyer "referred" to the non-aligned and reasonably neutral Indian Government, who happily sold vast numbers of SAF Carbines and spare parts. In one sense it was fortunate for Sterling that there was no licensing agreement to cover where the SAF guns could or could not be sold, but Unfortunately, no royalties were payable under the licensing agreement, which meant that Sterling got nothing and the Indian Government got the sale price IN FULL. Indeed, Sterling often had to compete against SAF Cawnpore for overseas sales of Mk4 Sterlings.

Attempting to Licence an Indian Silenced Gun

After its introduction in 1967 Sterling were forced to turn down sales of the Mk5 Sterling-Patchett silenced gun to several nations, because the UK Board of Trade refused to grant export licences for these "warlike stores". Sterling approached the Indian Government, who were producing the SAF Carbine, to see whether they might be interested in manufacturing the Mk5 under license, reasoning that potential buyers would at least be assured a more congenial reception at Cawnpore. This time, however, the licensing agreement included a royalties clause, so

that by referring a potential customer to the Indians, Sterling would be entitled to a portion of the sale price for each silenced gun sold.

Talks got under way, but because the referral orders were (comparatively) small, and the Mk5 was precision-manufactured to toolroom standards, the Indian Government declined the offer as uneconomical.

Accessories for the 1A Carbine

The Indian guns were equipped with the standard UK-issue slings and bayonets, but they could also mount a locally-made, 12"-bladed "No5" bayonet.

Whether these were made for the Indian-issued No5 rifles or their SAF Carbines is unclear, but both bayonets can be interchangeably mounted on the 1A.

273. Rear view of the Indian-made magazine for the SAF 1A Carbine, showing markings. (MoD Pattern Room collection)

274. The ingenious adaptor, of recent Indian manufacture, to enable a front pistol grip to be fitted to the SAF Carbine.

The adaptor is threaded at the proper angle to accept the long bolt, which is tightened to hold the front plastic pistol grip in place. (The ejector and barrel must first be removed before the adaptor can be inserted into the casing.)

Note the small anti-rotation stud, rivetted to the rear of the adaptor, which seats in one of the cooling holes in the casing of the matt-finish L2A3 shown here. (Courtesy MoD Indian Army)

Photographs of Indian soldiers on duty in the disputed mountains to the north of their large country shows SAF guns fitted with what appears to be SAF-manufactured arctic trigger adaptors.

Recent Front Pistol Grip Adaptation

Recent pictures of Indian soldiers on peace-keeping duty in Sri Lanka show some SAF 9mm Carbines equipped with a front pistol grip. The front grip, which appears identical to the regular pistol grip, is held to the gun by a vertical bolt which screws into a suitably shaped and threaded plate held in place inside the inner casing. The major drawback to this adaptation would be that the butt could not be folded with the front grip fitted, defeating the object somewhat!

Part III

The Late Commercial Sterlings

Chapter Eleven

Closing the Bolt

The Sterling Semi-Automatic 9mm Carbine, Mk6 and the Mysterious Mk9

Date introduced: 1972
Date deleted: 1988
Numbers produced: 1,600
Unit price as at 31-1-1984:   £256.00

This chapter is dedicated to the late Frank Waters, who passed away in January, 1992.

Introduction

The Sterling "Empire" Before 1970

Sterling Electric Holdings Limited, the overall holding company (fig 1), consisted of several diverse businesses in addition to the Sterling Armament Company, some of which were: Russell Newbery Co Ltd, Diesel engines; Sterling Heating Systems; and J Caslake and Co, Oil Drilling Equipment.

Following is a list of some of the items manufactured by the Sterling companies, many of which will still be in use today. Certainly, there are thousands of Russell Newbery engines still giving excellent service:

1. Russell Newbery Co Ltd, Diesel engines
2. Caslake oil drilling equipment
3. Hobbs of Barbican cycles
4. 1 to 4kw central heating units with fan blowers
5. 63 variations of hot water central heating units with fan blowers producing from 10,000 to 20,000 BTUs
6. cylinder-type vacuum cleaners which were distributed under store or customers' trade names
7. spraying units
8. floor polishers
9. drying cabinets
10. incubating cabinets for bacteriological chemists
11. blood centrifuge units
12. Blue Flame oil heaters and a 3kw single bar oil heater
13. mechanical car parking equipment
14. the first do-it-yourself electric drill-polisher
15. Shorrocks superchargers, including the unit for Goldie Gardiner's land speed record
16. EK Cole (ECKO) 2 and 3Kw electric bar element fires (including some in 22 carat gold plate!)
17. 250,000 Hoover flat irons. Tooling then sent for in-house production at Hoover factory in Cambuslang, Scotland
18. Morphy Richards rotary ironers
19. Hotpoint table pressers
20. last, but not least, Sterling sub-machine guns.

The Circle is Broken: Sterling Armament is Cut Loose

In 1970, Mr Clive Raphael took over the overall Sterling company, only to be killed while flying a Beagle twin-engine aircraft that he had purchased with the profits of a large sale of guns to the Malayan

Government. Unfortunately however, he still owed £105,000 of the purchase price. This, unexpectedly, was an intolerable financial burden, and as a result, the company was split up and the separate divisions were sold off separately.

The Edmiston Years: Sterling Goes Commercial

The newly-separated Sterling Armament Company was purchased by James Edmiston on 30 March, 1972. Fate was to turn its hand because shortly after James purchased the Sterling Armament Company, it moved back to its ancestral home at Rainham Road (South) in Dagenham.

Organisation of Sterling Armament Co

At the time of the Edmiston takeover the company was organised into the following departments:

1. Tool Room
2. General Machine Shop, with the following machines: capstan, automatic, Swiss and turret lathes. Drilling machines, tapping machines, welding bays, cylindrical, surface and centreless grinding machines, horizontal and vertical milling machines, gear cutting and hobbing machines.
3. Press Shop with all types of presses, from hand to automatic feed press machines.
4. 3 Spray Shops
5. Assembly Shops
6. Electro-plating Shop
7. Metal Finishing Shop which would degrease, phosphate, aluminium etch, boil and shot-bead/blast.
8. Hardening Shop
9. Drawing and Design Office
10. Packing and Dispatch Department
11. Stores

The company continued in the armaments field but was financially restricted because research and development and new machinery had to be funded from profits generated by sales of products in hand, in this case the Mk4/L2A3 and Mk5/L34A1 submachine guns.

275. The affable James Edmiston, who purchased the Sterling Armament Co Ltd in 1972 and guided the company through changing and interesting times until forced to sell out in 1984. Well-liked and respected by the staff, his story is told in *The Sterling Years*. (Courtesy James Edmiston)

It was during James Edmiston's aggressive time as owner that the product line of the Sterling Armament Company began to diversify as never before.

276. A present-day view of a later brick building, which had been added to the Sterling complex in the late 1930s.

At one time the press and metal shops were located on the ground floor, which was connected via an underground passageway to the gun production shop, shown in fig 135.

"Hobbs of Barbican" cycles were hand-made to individual customer order on the first floor. The second floor housed the drawing and technical offices, plus a light assembly shop.

Sports and social matters were a major component of the Sterling "family compact". The top floor thus housed a wellequipped sports and social club, complete with its own magnificent sprung dance floor. (Courtesy David Howroyd)

David Howroyd's jibe about investment is not accurate. Apart from the purchase price paid by James Edmiston and the parent company Paul Escare' Engineering which was subcontract engineering to the automotive industry and hence very well-equipped with new production plant, money was channeled into the development of the SAR-80, the Mark 6, the AR-18 and its derivatives, the HR-81/3, and into Yaffle Importers & Exporters Ltd. Much of this involved extensive purchase of new items of plant.

There were forays into the prospect of acquiring complimentary manufacturing businesses including Mecar in Belgium, famous for its Energa rifle grenades, its 90m gun, and ammunition. It was felt that administration and difficult labour relations in the area were too much of a risk.

Another firm that was of interest was Manufrance in Saint-Etienne, the home of the French firearms industry. Supported by Banque Stern, Sterling had the intention of importing the Manufacture range of shotguns suitably altered cosmetically for the British market, while using Manufacture to front sales of the Mark 4 and Mark 5 sub-machine guns to the French Ministry of Defence and Francophone Africa.

James Edmiston attended a most cordial meeting with the French Defence Minister at the Rue Fauborg St. Honore' – the smartest area of Paris. He was told that there could be no military armaments in private hands in France. Edmiston pointed out that much of the aircraft industry was owned by M. Marcel Dassault, to which the reply came, "Yes, but he's French." In the context of Brexit, one can see the funny side.

Two Meanings of the Word "Commercial"

Up to now we have used the word "commercial" to denote sales by the Sterling company of their military-pattern automatic weapons, spares and accessories to foreign governments (or their agents), as approved by the British Government. Here in Part ill we discuss a whole new and growing "commercial" market for Sterling, wherein carbines (and later 'pistols'), intentionally restricted to single shot fire capability only, were produced expressly for sale to civilian gun collectors and shooters.

The Police Carbine version of the Sterling Mk4/L2A3 submachine gun had been the first such semi-automatic, and it satisfied the needs of shooters and farmers for many years. That is, until the firearms control authorities in several countries learned that, although it was marketed as semi-automatic, it could soon become fully automatic in the right (or wrong) hands, depending at which end one was standing!

The BATF Gets Wise

In the United States, where Sterling guns were enjoying healthy annual sales, the Federal Bureau of Alcohol, Tobacco and Firearms (BATF) soon realised that the Sterling Police Carbine was in reality just a single shot version of the fully-automatic Mk4 S MG, and that it was simplicity itself to restore the full-automatic fire capability.

The BATF slapped a ban on the Sterling Police Carbine, and decreed that thereafter, ANY former fully-automatic gun, no matter how extensively 'redesigned' it was, had to be submitted for extensive testing by the Bureau before it could be approved for sale within the United States. In effect, these rules and testing meant that the gun had to be "impossible of conversion" to the automatic fire role.

Hands Across the Waters: Origins of the Mk6

Sterling guns were sold on the US commercial market in direct competition with the UZI, which was available in a superb, but heavy, single shot version of their sub-machine gun.

The Mk6 project was instigated by an American gun dealer named Roma Skinner who, with another dealer named Kenny Yee, owned a company called Parker Arms. A deal was struck with Sterling for the design and manufacture of a single shot, folding stock SMG lookalike, that would meet the approval of the ATF, for marketing in America by Parker Arms.

277. Left: Bert List, George Patchett's old pal who helped design the De Lisle and the silenced Sterling, and subsequently formed his own company to manufacture sound suppressors. Centre: L James Sullivan, a brilliant American designer who had worked at ArmaLite on the AR-10 project, and was part of the two-man team who redimensioned the 7.62mm NATO AR-10 into the .223 calibre AR-15. At the time of the photograph Sullivan was 'testing the waters' in the UK with an invention drawn and made in the UK, to escape a US Federal law which stated that all automatic weapons designed in the USA were subject to US export restrictions, regardless of where they were manufactured. Among many other designs, Sullivan later produced the excellent Ultimax 5.56mm light machine gun for CIS (Chartered Industries of Singapore).

Right: Frank Waters, an expert draughtsman, who trained under Les Ruffell. He designed the single-shot Mk6 Sterling carbine, and his own 5.56mmrifle, later produced in Singapore (Chapter Fourteen). (Courtesy David Howroyd)

The Uzi was being sold in the USA in a closed bolt single shot form with a 16″ barrel. It was being imported by a company called Action Arms which was being run by a personable American called Mitch Kalter. James Edmiston approached Kalter at a Shot Show and suggested that if Sterling produced an equivalent version, Action Arms might be interested in handling it as an importer and distributor. This was on the basis that if someone bought an Uzi the chances were high that they would want a Sterling equivalent for their collection as well. Kalter thought it was definitely a good idea but said that he would have to check back with his principals. Directors apart, the main principal was Israeli Military Industries and they lodged an objection, and so the whole subject was dropped.

The Mark 6 project was really instigated by two American gun dealers; Kenny Yee and Roma Skinner of Parker Arms of Texas. The two had a falling out, and Edmiston had to choose which way forward to go. Roma Skinner had the expertise, and Kenny Yee had the money. On the basis of expertise and excellence, Edmiston formed a joint company with Roma Skinner called Lanchester USA Inc.

The reason for using the Lanchester name was because there was already a Sterling company making pistols in New York State. Edmiston at a later time met Eugene Sauls the proprietor, and asked the question, "Why Sterling?"

Sauls was straightforward and replied that it was the only name he could find of a known European manufacturer that had not been registered in the USA.

A deal was struck with Sterling for the design and manufacture of a single shot, folding stock SMG lookalike, that would meet the approval of the BATF, as it was then, for marketing in America by Lanchester USA Inc.

The design was accomplished in Dagenham, by Frank Waters. As Sterling's later Company Profile described it, the Mk6 was developed "… essentially for the American Police and enthusiast market." What emerged as the semi-automatic Mk6 was as close as one could get to a gun that could not(?) be retro-modified to its brother's automatic form. Now, nothing is impossible, but importantly, Frank Waters' design passed the strict BATF testing. In fact, a cutaway gun used as a demonstration model was subsequently presented to officers of the Bureau.

However, despite the terse paragraph on page 1 of the Mk6 manual (headed: *WARNING – THIS GUN CAN KILL YOU!*) that modifications were unsafe, illegal, and would void all warranties, quite soon after the Mk6 was introduced onto the US market, a US entrepreneur with a bent for home gunsmithing produced a small but widely distributed booklet detailing exactly how to convert a Mk6 SEMI-automatic gun into a Mk6 AUTOMATIC fire gun. The rascal!

Three experts in modern gun design.

Jim Sullivans's successes in design work are worth mentioning. As already mentioned he was part of the AR-10, AR-15, and AR-18 design team at Armalite. He had come to their notice as he was originally employed by the "Duke", none other than John Wayne, a "gun nut" for whom Jim designed and produced all sorts of exotic firearms.

Much of this working life was spent in working for Bill Ruger, the founder of Sturm Ruger, where his best known creation was the 5.56mm. Mini 14 rifle that is like a small Garand, and the Ruger M-77. He also designed and developed the 100 round Beta-C magazine which is a clever drum magazine for the M-16/M-4 and most other military small-arms.

Jim also spent three years working at Chartered Industries in Singapore where he developed the quite amazing Ultimax light machine gun which can be fired in fully automatic mode whilst held in one hand without it climbing.

He was invited to the 70th birthday celebration of the famous Mikhail Kalashnikov where they compared notes. Probably the AK-47 outnumbered everything else in terms of numbers sold or given, but Jim has made a lot more money.

The company (Sterling) is still in touch with Jim as it intends to take up a licence for a clever personal defence weapon that Jim has designed.

Features of the Mk6 Semi-Automatic Carbine

New Multiple-Length Barrels

At first view, from the outside, the Mk6 carbine looks IDENTICAL to the Mk4/L2A3 SMG, with the familiar hinged butt, 34-round magazine and perforated casing,except that the Mk6 has no offset bayonet mounting point on the nose cap. The reason for this is two fold: the Mk6 will not accept the No5 bayonet, and Mk6 barrel is not interchangeable with the Mk4/L2A3 sub-machine gun barrel.

The Mk6 barrel is secured into the front of the gun casing by a uni-directional knurled nut designed by Frank Waters. This uni-directional nut was developed after an original nut continually unscrewed during prolonged firing trials. The Frank Waters design would not loosen due to the vibration of shooting, and could only be unscrewed to release the barrel by first pressing in a spring-loaded plunger.

The Mk6 barrel was heavier and longer than the Mk4/L2A3 barrel, which made these particular guns extremely accurate. The large-diameter rear barrel flange was absent. Instead, a smaller machined diameter of about .75″ sat inside a sleeve within the

278. Right side closeup of the front of the Mk6 Sterling Carbine, showing the nose cap configuration.

This example is fitted with the shorter UK 9.5″ barrel. Note the uni-directional barrel nut, designed by the late Frank Waters. Can only be unscrewed by first pressing in the spring-loaded plunger. (Courtesy Adrian Bull)

rear of the casing. The .75″-diameter barrel extended through the perforated gun casing to within about 2″ of the muzzle. It was then stepped, threaded and pulled firmly forward by the uni-directional barrel nut against the muzzle seating.

The versatility of the uni-directional barrel nut allowed an even longer barrel to be fitted to the US-bound Mk6 guns. This was necessary to satisfy US BATF regulations, which specified that barrel length must be a minimum of 16″. The UK-specification guns were sold with a 9.5″ long barrel, although the 16″ barrel could also be fitted. (Whether any US buyer shortened his 16″barrel to the 9.5″ UK length is quite another matter.)

This was not the first time that Sterling had toyed with the idea of making a 9mm gun with a longer barrel: the first experiments had been done with the MkII Patchett.

The rifling of the 16″ barrels was done by the simplified and cheaper "button rifling" method, a process subsequently used in all Sterling-made barrels.

The Closed-Bolt Firing System

The Mk6 closed-bolt firing mechanism was the first such commercial attempt by Sterling. The earlier open-bolt single-shot Police Carbine functioned like most sub-machine guns, in that the bolt was held to the rear. Squeezing the trigger released it, to undertake the small arms cycle of FEED, LOAD, FIRE; EXTRACT, EJECT, COCK. With the closed-boltMk6, the cycle on squeezing the trigger was: FIRE, EXTRACT, EJECT; COCK, FEED, LOAD.

The breech block was an entirely new part, machined to Sterling pattern S8-8-A in such a way that it could not be held to the rear in the open-bolt firing position. The centre was drilled through, and slotted longitudinally through its lower surface, to allow the inclusion of the separate firing pin and spring. The tang at the rear of the stepped firing pin rides in this slot. With the arm assembled, the narrow

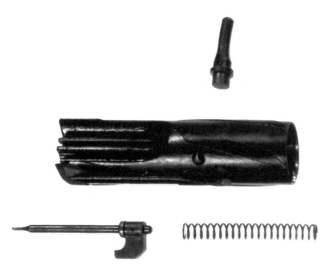

279. Components of the closed-bolt firing system used in the Mk6 and subsequent 'civilian' Marks.

From top: shortened cocking handle; breech block (Sterling part no S8-8-A); firing pin and spring. (Courtesy MoD Pattern Room, Nottingham)

nose of the sear (item 22, fig 283) also rides inside this slot.

As the breech block goes forward to the load position at the end of each firing cycle, the sear catches and holds the firing pin in the cocked position. On pressing the trigger, the sear is depressed, allowing the firing pin to go forward under pressure from the compressed firing pin spring, to fire the chambered cartridge.

In addition to the separate firing pin and spring, what would be the cocking handle block in the Mk4/L2A3 was used as the firing pin spring retainer/inner return spring block in the Mk6.

The Mk6 breech block cannot be used in earlier Sterling guns, nor can the Mk4/L2A3 breech block be used in the Mk6.

The top of the sear cradle return spring guide incorporates an extension whereby, however weak the rearward energy imparted to the breech block, once it has moved rearwards a fraction, the tripping lever will trip the sear cradle to release the sear and prevent the curse of all Armourers, a 'runaway gun'. Well thought-out, David Howroyd and Frank Waters!

Because the centre of the breech block was hollow and the underside slotted, the cocking handle was cut short, and only about .5″ went into the breech block. Any earlier cocking handle could be modified to fit, and the Mk6 cocking handle would operate an earlier gun.

280. Another view of the components of the Mk6, Mk7C and Mk8 breech block.

From left to right: outer return spring; return spring cup; inner return spring; firing pin block; firing pin spring; firing pin; breech block (Sterling part no SS-8-A).

The breech block has been positioned bottom up to show firing pin tang slot in underside. (Courtesy Dunmore Shooting Centre)

The Short-Lived Mechanical Safety Plate

On the earliest Mk6 (and Mk7) guns, the underside of the breech block contained a small hinged springloaded plate, called the mechanical safety plate. This was designed to prevent the gun from firing unless the breech block was fully forward and touching the barrel face, as the plate will not allow the sear to release the firing pin until the breech block is fully forward and touching the rear of the barrel.

It was soon established that the mechanical safety plate was redundant, and it was quietly deleted from production. If the gun WERE fired when the breech

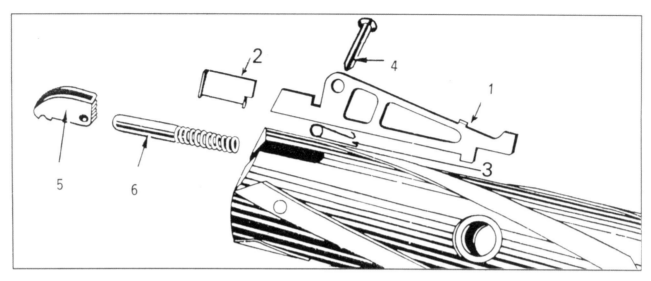

281. The Mechanical Safety Plate (7C-3), as fitted to early Mk6 and Mk7 C guns. Described in the text. The numbered components are as follows:
1. mechanical safety plate
2. abutment shoe
3. spring
4. special split extractor axis pin.
The mechanical safety plate was soon found to be redundant, and was quietly deleted from production.

block was not fully forward, the firing pin spring would not be fully compressed and the firing pin not fully cocked, resulting in a diminished force of blow by the firing pin on the cartridge primer. Moreover, the mechanical safety plate was manufactured from thin steel which, once damaged or distorted, could become a safety HAZARD.

Owners of guns with these components fitted can remove them by pushing out the extractor axis pin (4, fig 281), taking care to control the extractor (5), spring and plunger (6). The plate (1), shoe (2) and spring (3) can be removed and discarded, and the extractor reassembled.

As an Armourer used to firing and using the Mk4 and Mk5 guns, Peter Laidler found the initial cocking of a Mk6 (and the subsequent Mk7C and Mk8) somewhat 'mechanically harsh'. But once the gun was up and running, it operated as faultlessly as its older brothers.

The Single-Shot Trigger

The Mk6 trigger mechanism incorporated the Mk4 Police Carbine inner change lever (8, fig 283), which

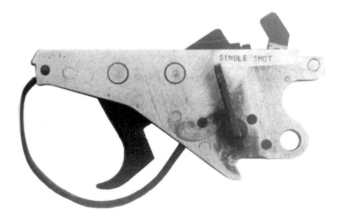

282. The Single Shot trigger mechanism as fitted to the Mk6, Mk7C (Chapter Twelve) and Mk8 (Chapter Thirteen).

Compare with fig 157: note the distinctive dog-leg upper extension on the sear cradle return spring guide, which ensures that the sear spring cradle is positively depressed after each shot, so that only single shot fire is possible.

Also note the stepped cutout at the upper rear of the assembly. This cutout clears a projecting lug welded to the casing just to the rear of the pistol grip side plates, thus effectively preventing the insertion of an automatic Mk4/L2A3 trigger mechanism into the Mk6. (Courtesy Adrian Bull)

only allows rotation of the outer change lever to SAFE or single shot. The pistol grip shows just the markings 'FIRE' (in red) and 'SAFE' (in white).

Unlike the Mk4 Police Carbine, however, modifications to ensure single shot fire only went much deeper in the Mk6 and subsequent 'civilian' models.

To begin with, the Mk6 fires from the closed bolt position. The Mk6 is cocked by pulling the cocking handle sharply to the rear and letting it go FULLY FORWARD on a loaded magazine. A live round will be chambered, with the breech block closed behind it, and with the spring-loaded firing pin held to the rear by the sear.

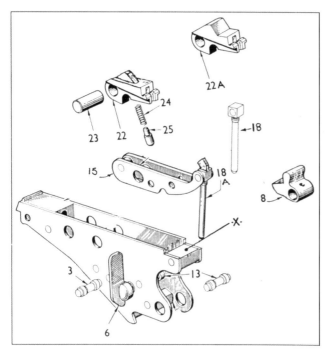

283. The different components of the Single Shot, closed-bolt trigger mechanism.

The closed-bolt sear (22; open-bolt Mk4 part shown as no 22A) holds the firing pin to the rear while allowing the breech block forward to the GUN LOADED position.

The dog-leg extension atop the sear cradle spring guide (18A; Mk4 part no 18) ensures that the sear cradle is positively depressed, so releasing the sear, with each cycle of the breech block.

The inner change lever (8) is identical to that used in the Mk4 Police Carbine. It will not allow the outer change lever (6) to move to the 'A' position.

The small step (X) ensured that a fully automatic trigger mechanism would not fit into the casings of Mk6, Mk7C and Mk8 guns.

To accomplish this, the sear nose is narrower, and travels in a slot in the underside of the modified breech block. The sear thus allows the breech block to travel forward unimpeded to load a live round into the breech, but at the same time it holds the separate firing pin and spring to the rear in the COCKED position.

To further ensure single-shot fire ONLY, a dog-leg upper extension was added to the sear cradle spring guide. This ensures that the sear cradle is positively depressed to release the sear at every cycle of the breech block.

Additionally, the trigger mechanism frame was altered at the rear, with a cut-out to clear a projecting lug welded to the casing just to the rear of the pistol grip side plates. This lug effectively prevents the insertion of an automatic Mk4/L2A3 trigger mechanism into the Mk6 gun.

Even the Casing is Different

The casing on the Mk6 gun, only offered in the black crackle finish, looked similar to the Mk4/L2A3 casing, but was totally non-interchangeable, and could not be modified to Mk4 standards without access to complicated machinery.

284. The cover of an original Sterling User Handbook for the Mk6 Carbine. Most illustrations were lifted directly from the manual for the Mk4/L2A3 SMG, and thus do not exactly depict the components unique to the closed-bolt guns, such as the single shot trigger mechanism. (Courtesy Mike Gruber)

The barrel seating in front of the magazine housing was also a new idea. It was based loosely on the rear barrel seating used in the silenced Mk5/L34A1, but it was positioned further to the rear. This effectively ruled out replacing the Mk6 barrel with either the Mk4/L2A3 or Mk5/L34A1 barrel.

Further, this seating or sleeve incorporated a length of steel, 2.1″ long x .3″ wide, that intruded into the path of the reciprocating breech block. There was a corresponding slot in the Mk6 block to accommodate this length of steel, but no other type of breech block could be inserted.

Markings on the Mk6 Semi-Automatic Carbine

Mk6 carbines were marked on the top of the magazine housing: STERLING [boxed logo]/ SEMI-AUTOMATIC/9mm CARBINE Mk6/No 6AA (Number 0072 examined).

The serial number prefix '6' indicates that the gun is a Mk6 semi-automatic carbine, while the 'AA' stands for Armscorp of America.

A variation of the magazine housing markings reads: STERLING [boxed logo]/SEMI-AUTOMATIC/ 9mm CARBINE Mk6/No SA (numbers 0193 and 0496 examined).

It is a little-known fact that when ordering replacement parts for a particular gun, the only parts that would be supplied would be those applicable to the model to which the serial number prefix referred. In this case, a spare part order against a gun with a 6M or SA serial number prefix would only elicit Mk6 Semi-Automatic Carbine spares, and not Mk4 spares that COULD(?) be used to make a Mk6 gun capable of automatic fire.

BATF Require Extra Markings on US Mk6s

In keeping with BATF firearm importation rules, the name of the importer was roll-stamped on the left side of the trigger housing (above the trigger) on guns offered for sale within the United States. Depending upon the period and who was then the importer, Mk6 guns were marked:

> STERLING, DAGENHAM, U.K. (compulsory)
> (originally) PARKER ARMS
> (later) ARMSCORP OF AMERICA
> (still later) LANCHESTER USA, DALLAS, TEXAS

The tradename STERLING was already registered in the USA, and as the UK Sterling company still owned the long-defunct LANCHESTER name, which was NOT registered in the US, this name was chosen.

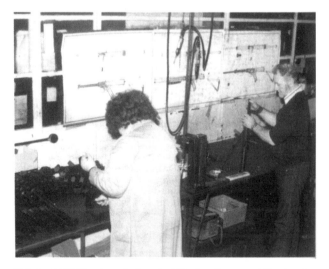

285. A mid-1980s view of a bench at Sterling Armament Co, showing workers assembling Mk6 carbines.
 Note the (coloured) wall charts, showing phantom assembly views of (from left) the Mk4, Mk5 and Mk6 Sterlings. (Courtesy Mike Gruber)

286. A later User Handbook for the Mk6 Carbine.
 Compare with fig 284: note the addition of the name and address of Armscorp of America, the second of three US importers of Sterlings "for the Police and enthusiast market".

Mk6 Accessories

Display Features for US Collectors

The US-market Mk6 guns were sold with a short, UK-spec SOLID barrel for display purposes. Some Mk6 guns imported into the United States were also fitted with the side-mounted bayonet standard and a steel nose cap, retained by a slim barrel retaining screw. Once the US owner had fitted his optional 9.5″ SOLID barrel AND his bayonet, he had a perfectly presentable Mk6 gun that LOOKED like the Mk4 which he probably wanted in the first place.

Telescopic Sight Rail Studs

Because of the gun's extremely good accuracy, thanks to its closed bolt firing system and long, heavy barrel, a telescopic or Singlepoint sight could be fitted (although whether any 9mm gun, even a single-shot carbine, deserves such sighting is another matter altogether!). In any case, as discussed in the next two chapters, commercial Mk6, Mk7 and Mk8 guns were offered with a facility to accept a telescopic sight rail, by means of two .3″-diameter threaded studs, 6″ apart, incorporated in the top of the casing.

Sterling suggested that the following telescopic sights could be fitted to the Sterling telescope rail which bolted to the gun with two Allen screws:

- Sterling DeLuxe, rubber-armoured, 3 – 9 × 32
- Sterling DeLuxe, rubber-armoured, 4 × 40
- Hakko electro-point
- Aimpoint
- Singlepoint.

It was important to use the specially-made Sterling sight rail, which positively lined up with the two mounting studs on the gun casing. It was equally important to use the Allen screws provided by Sterling to lock the sight rail to the gun, because if the &crews were slightly too long, they could distort the casing and impede the smooth path of the breech block. To clear the telescopic sight (if fitted), a special cocking handle, bent downwards, was also provided.

Some literature shows Mk6 guns without the two sight rail buttons. These were usually from the last of the Mk6 importers, LANCHESTER USA, DALLAS TEXAS with serial numbers commencing SA —

287. A snapshot taken at Sterling Armament by an American visitor in 1986, showing a Sterling Mk6 Carbine with sight rail mounting studs and 16″ barrel, ready for shipment from the factory.

Note the compartmented styrofoam case: lid of case and printed cardboard sleeve have been removed to show the gun with stock folded, plus (from left) the Sterling cleaning kit (copied from the Canadian C1 issue); tools (drift and screwdriver); sling; manual; one 20- and one 34-round magazine, separately wrapped in plastic. (Courtesy Mike Gruber)

Mk6 Variables

That virtually sums up this little gun, a 9mm singleshot carbine that fitted into a niche in the market. With the additional nose cap, it also went some way to satisfying those collectors who wished to possess aMk4.

As it was a market-oriented product, the Mk6 came with several variables. As discus ed, these included:

- casings with or without bayonet standard
- casings with or without sight rail mounting studs
- long (US spec) or short (elsewhere) barrels
- one of 3 different US importer names (on left side of trigger housing, above trigger)
- early breech blocks with mechanical safety plate (fig 281)
- later breech block without mechanical safety
- straight or bent-down cocking handle

The Mk9: the Mysterious Canadian Two-Off

There is one other variable of the Mk6 of which you ought to be aware. The mysterious Mk9!During1984 there was a firm order from a Canadian buyer who, for reasons best known to himself, wished to buy two single-shot, closed-bolt guns to the Mk6 specification, but built to look like the Mk5 silenced gun.

This was a relatively simple operation for Sterling, as both guns were in simultaneous production. Although the finished guns looked like Mk5s, with the long, large front casing, it had a correspondingly longer barrel fixed in place with the uni-directional nut. These two guns were marked as .Mk9s.

Mk6 Interchangeability with the Mk4/L2A3

- butt assembly
- long cocking handle can be shortened and bent downwards to fit
- ejector and screw
- extractor, axis pin, spring and plunger
- foresight, rearsight plus axis pin and spring
- magazine catch, spring and operating button
- outer return spring
- pistol grip and screw
- return spring cap and locking lever
- some parts of trigger mechanism; retaining pin and spring.

Chapter Twelve

The Sterling Mk7 'Pistols'

Introduction: Two Types of Mk7 Pistols

In October, 1983 the Sterling Armament Company was acquired by Mr Giles Whittome, and the Sterling Mk7 Pistols (and the Mark 8, discussed in Chapter Thirteen) went into production.

There were two different models of the Mk7 pistol: the automatic, open-bolt Mk7A, and the closed-bolt, single-shot Mk7C.

Both models were offered in two versions, the Mk7A4 or A8, and the Mk7C4 or Ca. The only difference between the two was barrel length, the NC4 barrel being 4″ long, and the NCB barrel, 8″.

The Open-Bolt Sterling Para Pistol 9mm Mk7A

Date introduced: September 1983
Date deleted: 1988
Quantity produced: 300
Unit price as at 31-3-84:   £180.00

Development by David Howroyd

288. Left side view of the 'business' end of a Mk7A4 Para Pistol, with 15-round magazine and fibre foregrip.

Note selector markings, '34', '1', 'SAFE'. (Courtesy MoD Pattern Room, Nottingham)

The Mk7 series was developed by Sterling Works Director, David Howroyd, and was intended to be used by tank and armoured vehicle crews, and those involved in covert operations. The 14.75″ length of the A4 (and 18.5″ length of the A8) made them ideal for these purposes.

As a result of having developed this pistol, David Howroyd (known as DTEH in company correspondence) would be paid 1.5% of the turnover price per gun produced.

The notion that the removal of the butt from a sub-machine gun and reducing the length of the casing makes it a pistol is mere word-play. For that is what this gun was. But such a play on words has its place in the tough commercial world where 'pistol' appears more acceptable than 'sub-machine gun' or 'carbine'. In addition, Sterling were facing stiff competition from Uzi and particularly Heckler & Koch, who were an increasingly hard act to follow.

As far as the British Military was concerned, the Mk7A was not a great success, although it was tried by the UK Ministry of Defence.

289. Left side view of the open-bolt firing, selective-fire Mk7AB Para Pistol, fitted with tough fibre foregrip (made for Sterling by Black & Decker) and Sterling 15-round magazine.
    Note selector markings, '34', 'I', 'SAFE'. (Courtesy MoD Pattern Room, Nottingham)

The Mk7A Adapted for the List Sound Suppressor

After an interest was expressed by the Syrian Government for 5,000 guns, a number of Mk7 pistols were adapted to take the "High Tech Sound Suppressor" offered by Bert List's new firm, List Precision Engineering.

Technical problems with the small 10-round magazines within the housing were corrected quite quickly, but the project was abandoned after it was discovered that an Export licence would not be granted in any case.

The List suppressor was marketed for the Mk7A and C guns with 4″ barrels only, and threaded onto the gun in place of the barrel nut. It was intended for use only with sub-sonic ammunition.

Features of the Sterling Mk7A

Let us look at the Sterling Mk7A The first thing that should be apparent is that the 'A' indicates AUTOMATIC. This gun was equipped with a fully automatic fire facility as well as a singleshot mode. This will indicate that it also fires from the OPEN bolt position as per the Mk4/L2A3.

The Mk7As were only supplied finished in the crackle paint finish.

LIST Precision Engineering

THE HIGH TECH SOUND SUPPRESSOR

This Suppressor has been designed to use Sub Sonic ammunition and really comes into its own where it is imperative to attack targets without drawing return fire or in a Hostage or Terrorist situation where it is necessary to eliminate the cause without panic or distress to the general public.

Using Sub Sonic ammunition all that can be heard is the mechanical noise of the weapon and the bullet flight. Fitting is by screwing onto existing barrel thread, by replacing the Barrel Nut, by Collet Arrangements, or as on the HK MP5 by a Bayonet Fitting.
The Suppressor is of an all Aluminium construction and being so light it affects the weapon balance to a minimum.
A Steel bush fixing is optional, and a Barrel threading service is available in our own workshops.

SUPPRESSOR DATA:
    Length: 322mm
    Diameter: 44mm
    Weight: .738 KG
    Construction is of machined aluminium HE30 TF.
    Fitted with Neoprene Wipes that can be replaced very simply.
    Replace Wipes after 500 rounds.
    Standard finish Matt Black.
    Cleaning interval 1500 rounds.
    To clean is a simple operation of rinsing in Paraffin.
    A recent comparison test between the Sterling MK7 fitted with this Suppressor and the Sterling L34 A1 with integral Silencer showed a difference of only 1 to 2 decibels.

    Unit 1, Ingley Works, 13 River Road, Barking, Essex IG11 0HE.   Tel: 01-594 1686

290. A single-page data sheet produced by Bert List's company, List Precision Engineering, to support the List "High Tech Sound Suppressor" that could be fitted to the 4″ barrel version of the Mk7 pistol in place of the barrel nut. (Courtesy David Howroyd)

Modifying the Mk4 Casing

The casing of the Mk7A is of the Mk4/L2A3 pattern that allows the fully automatic fire facility, cut short about 1.5″ forward of the magazine housing. The foresight block and protectors have been moved back and mounted on a ring that circles the casing, about ½″ forward of the magazine housing. The foresight is a stubby version of the usual thin blade. The backsight also differs in that the 100-yard leaf has been cut off horizontally across the centre line, leaving a primitive 'U'-shaped battle sight. The 200-yard rear leaf is left standard but is unmarked. All this leaves no doubt about the Mk7A's Mk4 origins.

The selective-fire trigger mechanism is identical to that of the Mk4/L2A3 SMG. The change lever positions are marked 'AUTO'-'FIRE'-'SAFE', or '34'-'1'-'0', or '34'-'1'- 'SAFE', to indicate the fire sequence. This Mk4/L2A3 trigger mechanism only allows for OPEN bolt fire.

291. The cover of the original Sterling User Handbook for the selective-fire Mk7A "Para Pistol".

A Pistol; so Buttless

There is no provision to fit a hinged folding butt to the Mk7 pistol, as there is no butt trunnion fitted. The Mk7 return spring cap has been machined so as to remove the butt locating recesses.

The removal of the butt has made this 'pistol' extremely difficult to hold, even with two-handed. In this regard the Sterling engineers thoughtfully provided a tough front hand grip (made by Black & Decker, incidentally) which is fitted below the repositioned foresight.

While this might make the gun controllable when fired from the waist, it does nothing when firing the gun pistol-fashion.

Also offered with the guns were a wall stowage bracket and, for the 4″ barrel, the extremely efficient List sound suppressor for use with subsonic ammunition. The plastic stock offered for the Mk7C guns cannot be fitted to the Mk7A, due to the different method of retaining the return spring cap locking lever.

Why Not Use the Mk6 Uni-Directional Barrel Nut?

The barrel, either 4″ or 8″ long, is inserted from the rear of the gun in the usual manner. It is then pulled tight against an internal collar (Mk5/L34A1 fashion) and secured within the front of the casing flange by a large knurled nut, and tightened with a spanner across two flats. This large locking nut is additionally locked in place by a small grub screw that is screwed through the nut from front to rear, into a locking recess.

There MUST be a logical reason why the Mk6 uni-directional barrel nut was not used, but 'the Armourer's point of view is not always the same as the user's, nor indeed the manufacturer's!

The 8″ barrel guns use the Mk4/L2A3 return spring assembly. Due to the shorter barrel of the 4″ guns and the lesser amount of gas available to operate the reciprocating parts, the 4″ gun does not use the heavy centre pin (nor by definition, its spring and plunger).

Mk7 A Accessories

Ten- or fifteen-round capacity magazines were also offered with the Mk7 pistols. These were fully interchangeable with the 34-round magazines, and although fitting the latter to the Mk7 pistol might look the part, in reality it was too cumbersome. The Sterling engineers also cleverly offered any combination of two magazines permanently "Double Stacked", tip-to-toe.

292. A view of the interior of a Vickers Challenger Tank, showing the Sterling stowage brackets for the Mk4/L2A3 and Mk7A4 Para Pistol, the personal weapons of the crew. Note the Black & Decker foregrip on the Mk7.
The tank is an export version, destined for "a Middle Eastern customer …" (Courtesy Ravenswood Studios)

For training purposes a blank firing adaptor could be screwed onto the 4″ barrel, replacing the barrel nut. Like all blank firing adaptors, the Mk7 unit came finished in a hard, high-temperature bright yellow paint.

A Minor Variable

Externally, the Mk7A and Mk7C look identical, except for the selective fire markings on the Mk7A Peter Laidler has only encountered one very minor variable on any of the Mk7 guns examined, that being that some of the hexagonal barrel locking nuts were locked with the additional grub screw, whereas others were not.

Mk7A Components Interchangeable with Mk4/I.2A3

- backsight axis pin and spring with (modified) leaf
- breech block and cocking handle assembly
- ejector and screw
- foresight block with (modified) blade
- magazine catch, spring and operating button
- pistol grip and screw
- return spring assembly
- return spring cap (can be modified to fit)
- return spring cap locking lever
- trigger mechanism, retaining pin and spring.

The Sterling Pistol Mk7C (Closed Bolt, Single Shot)

Date introduced:	September 1983
Date deleted:	1988
Quantity produced:	900
Unit price as at 31-3-84:	£180.00

293. Left side view of an early Sterling Mk7C8 with 8″ barrel, bearing no US importer's legend, and fitted with 10-shot magazine.

Note the selector markings, 'FIRE' and 'SAFE', and the return spring cap, made from a Mk4 cap casting with the butt and cap locking notches left unmachined and the sling swivel unfinished. (Courtesy MoD Pattern Room, Nottingham)

This gun was the commercial version of the Mk7A automatic pistol. It was known as the Mk7C, the 'C' indicating 'Closed Bolt'. The Mk7C was introduced by the Sterling Company to gain a foothold in the "close protection" bodyguard market. It retailed in the UK for about £320.

The Mk7C looks identical to the Mk7A from the outside, except that the trigger group is marked FIRE and SAFE only.

294. Left side view of a Mk7C4 with 4″ barrel.

Note the US Importer's legend (Armscorp of America) on the trigger housing, above the trigger. (Courtesy MoD Pattern Room, Nottingham)

As with the Mk7A series, David Howroyd was paid 1.5% of the turnover on all Mk7 guns in recognition of his having developed it.

Like the Mk7A, the Mk7C Pistol was offered with two alternative barrel lengths and these are incorporated within the designation Mk7C4, or Mk7C8; indicating either a 4″ or 8″ barrel length.

Mk7C Markings

The Mk7C was only available in the standard black crackle finish. They are marked on the magazine housing:

STERLING [boxed logo]
PISTOL
9mm Mk7
No SA — (Numbers 0024 and 0054 examined).

Although some early UK-spec guns did not include the 'A' within the serial number prefix, the serial numbers were all sequential.

295. A Sterling worker in 1986, hand-painting the white letters 'SAFE' on a Mk7C Sterling (he has already done the red 'FIRE'). (Courtesy Mike Gruber)

Additional Markings for US Sale

As these guns were offered for sale within the United States, in accordance with US Firearms import laws they were additionally marked on the left side of the trigger housing, above the trigger: STERLING, DAGENHAM, UK/ARMSCORP OF M-1ERICA SILVER SPRING MD USA/READ MANUAL BEFORE OPERATING FIREARM or, later, STERLING, DAGENHAM, UK/LANCHESTER USA, DALLAS, TEXAS.

Differences Between Closed- and Open-Bolt Models

Internally there are several differences between this gun and the Mk7A. These restrict the Mk7C to firing single shot only from the closed bolt position, making it immediately acceptable to most commercial markets.

The trigger mechanism is taken from the Mk6 (and Mk8) guns. These mechanisms use the Mk4 Police Carbine inner change lever (P4-12-9) with the special Mk6/8 sear, which only permits closed bolt firing. Like the Mk6 (and Mk8), a projecting block of steel in the Mk7C casing makes it impossible(?) to fit the automatic trigger mechanism.

The casing used in the Mk7C has been adapted from that of the Mk6. The internal bar of steel intrudes into the path of the breech block, only permitting the use of the special single-shot, closed-bolt breech block (S8-8-A). This special single-shot breech block, fully described in Chapter Eleven, incorporates the separate firing pin, spring and firing pin block (fig 280).

296. The cover of the original Sterling User Handbook for the closed-bolt, single-shot Mk7C Pistol.

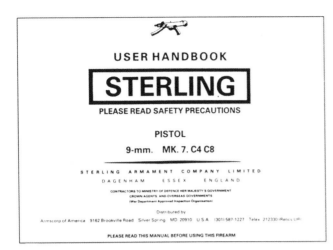

297. The cover of the later Sterling User Handbook for the closed-bolt, single-shot Mk7 C Pistol.

Note the addition of the name and address of Armscorp of America, the US importer of the day.

Everything else within this gun is identical to the earlier Mk7A.

As noted in Chapter Eleven, early Mk6 and Mk7C guns (and this might include several very early Mk8s too) incorporated a mechanical safety plate assembly (fig 281), which was soon found to be redundant and deleted from production. Later Mk7C guns DO NOT have this mechanical safety plate within the underside of the breech block.

Scoping the Mk7C Pistol

The foresight on the Mk7C gun is identical to the short stubby blade fitted to the Mk7A, but for the Mk7C gun, the Sterling engineers used the higher Mk5/L34 backsight leaf, which features the Patchett designed multi-hole sniping leaf with a standard hole on the other leaf, both calibrated for 100 yards.

Like the Mk6, the commercial Mk7C gun could be ordered with two .3‴-diameter threaded telescope rail studs fitted 6″ apart on the top of the casing, to which a telescope mounting rail could be attached to accept either a 12mm or 20mm diameter telescope tube. Sterling suggested that the following telescopes were suitable for fitting to these guns:

• Sterling De-Luxe rubber-armoured 3 – 9 × 32
• Sterling De-Luxe rubber-armoured 4 × 40
• Hakko electro-point
• Aimpoint
• Singlepoint

298. Top left-hand view of a Sterling Mk7C8 Pistol, showing optional telescope rail mounting studs factory-fitted on top of the casing. (Courtesy MoD Pattern Room, Nottingham)

299. Left side view of the Mk7C8 Pistol fitted with Sterling telescope rail, mounted on locating studs, and fitted with optional Nikko-Sterling telescopic sight.
   Note the spigot on the special return spring cap, used to locate the optional plastic buttstock. (Courtesy MoD Pattern Room, Nottingham)

300. Right side view of a Sterling Mk7C8 Pistol, fitted with the 4 × 20 Hakko Electro-Point Mark VIII telescope, and the optional Sterling nylon butt.
   The butt is shown with one of the available two (fig 238) plastic spacers inserted between the stock and buttplate.
   The stock is located over the spigot on the special return spring cap and affixed by a spring pin passed through the stock and the hole in the return spring cap locking lever housing. (MoD Pattern Room, Nottingham)

A Shooter's Frank Critique of the Mk7 C 'Pistol'

As an Armourer and keen practical pistol shooter, Peter Laidler cannot understand quite what on earth possessed the Sterling engineers to market this gun as a pistol. The US market certainly insisted that it

be termed a PISTOL for legal purposes, and in the tough commercial world, you supply what the buyer wants or is allowed.

Having said that, and never having fired the Mk7 series with the plastic butt, it must be added that the Mk7C is purgatory to fire from either the single- or two-handed pistol shooting position, the front pistol grip doing nothing to really aid shooting.

As for the *official* word on its performance, however, the later Sterling Company Profile commented, "British police forces using the Mark7C8 version with butt and bipod regularly obtain 2″ groups at 100 metres."

Mk7C Accessories

The fixed nylon butt, adjustable for length by means of plastic spacers added between the stock and the buttplate, was marketed for use with the Mk7C 4/8. It attaches to a spigot on a special return spring cap, and was retained by a spring pin through an enlarged hole in what on the Mk4 was called the return spring cap locking lever housing.

There was also a short webbing strap that could be used as a foregrip (standard where the fixed fibre foregrip would have classified the Mk6 as a 'carbine'), and the mentioned List suppressor (fig 292) that could be fitted to the 4″ barrel version.

There was also a wall bracket, like that for the Mk7A.

Mk7 C Variations

There have been several variations of the Mk7C guns. Some sales literature shows Mk7C guns WITHOUT the two telescope rail mounting studs, although all the guns sold commercially were fitted with them, and those without should be regarded as early trial/experimental guns.

The complicated rules covering the sale of guns into certain countries also affected the engineers' plans. Some Mk7C guns were sold with the front hand strap, as the fitting of the front pistolgrip would have meant that the gun was a CARBINE and not a pistol. Of course, the buyer could add an aftermarket pistol grip if he so wished, and the butt, as well!

Some early Mk7C bolts were fitted with the spring-loaded "mechanical safety plate", whereas later guns were not.

Like the Mk7A, this gun came fitted with 10- or 15-round magazines, but the 34-round SMG magazines are fully interchangeable.

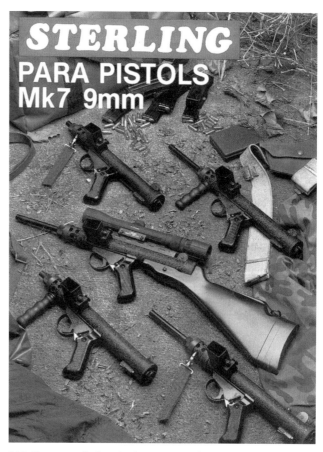

301. The cover of a late Sterling 4-page colour brochure on the Mk7 Para Pistols, showing some of the options available.

10-, 15- and 34-round magazines (top) were available singly or permanently "Twin Stacked", in any combination of sizes desired.

These guns bear 'LANCHESTER, USA, DALLAS, TEXAS' importer's markings.

Mk7 C Components Interchangeable with Mk4/L2A3

- backsight axis pin, spring and (modified) leaf
- cocking handle (can be modified)
- ejector and screw
- extractor, axis pin, spring and plunger
- foresight block with (modified) blade
- magazine catch, spring and release button
- pistol grip and screw
- rear return spring
- return spring cap (can be modified)
- return spring cap locking lever (can, be modified)
- some parts of the trigger mechanism.

Chapter Thirteen

The End of the Line

A Last Hybrid

Closed Bolt, Single Shot (CBS) 9mm Gun Mark 8

Date introduced:	October 1983
Date deleted:	1988
Quantity produced:	70
UK Unit price as at 31-1-84:	£256.00
UK Unit price as at factory closing in 1988	£380.00

302. Right side view of the "CBS Mark 8", a latter-day entry that looked exactly like a Mk4, but functioned like a Mk6. The Mk8 was the last production Sterling. (Courtesy MoD Pattern Room, Nottingham)

The closed-bolt, single-shot, 9mm Mk8 gun (referred to in the Sterling literature as the "CBS Mark 80) was the last in the line of Sterling guns based on the tried and trusted designs of George Patchett and incorporating Frank Waters' closed-bolt-firing, single-shot design.

The Sterling Mk8 went into production alongside the Mk7 Pistols after the Sterling Armament Company was acquired by Mr Giles Whittome in October, 1983.

When Is a Carbine Not a Carbine?

The Sterling commercial managers deemed the Mk4 Police Carbine and the Mk6 to be designated 'Carbines', but not the Mk8 in its official sales brochure title. Importantly, however, it WAS stamped on the gun, to mark a clear distinction between the Mk8 and its Mk4 sub-machine gun brother.

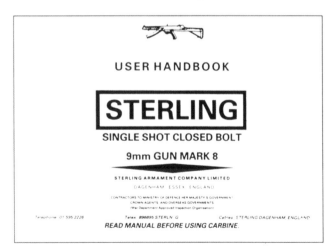

303. Cover of the Sterling User Handbook for the "Single Shot Closed Bolt 9mm Gun Mark 8", dated August, 1983.

The CBS Mark 8 guns were marked:

STERLING [boxed logo]
SEMI-AUTOMATIC
9mm CARBINE Mk8

No. CBS – (Number 0006 examined).

The 'CBS' prefix indicates that the gun is a Closed Bolt, Single-Shot Carbine.

The reasoning behind the 'carbine' designation concerned the American regulatory authorities, the BATF, who most emphatically did NOT favour any potentially legal, semi-auto gun being called a 'sub-machine gun'. Ironically, however, as offered with its 7.8″ barrel, the Mk8 contravened US law and was not importable into the USA for general commercial sale.

Describing the Closed Bolt, Single Shot (CBS) 9mm Mk8 Gun

The Mk8 was a hybrid of the Mk4/L2A3 SMG and the Mk6 Carbine. Externally, the Mk8 looks *identical* to the Mk4/L2A3 and the Mk4 Police Carbine. It uses the Mk4 casing, complete with the folding butt, bayonet boss within the nose-cap and bayonet standard on the casing, to which the No5 rifle bayonet could be secured.

Additionally, the casing on the production model incorporated the two .3″-diameter threaded studs, 6″

apart on the top of the casing, into which an optical or Singlepoint sight rail could be fitted. The universal Sterling telescopic sight rail and recommended sights are described in Chapter Eleven.

The locating studs are not present on the early Mk8s examined for this study, nor are they featured in the Mk8 User Handbook, where the illustrations are mainly of the Mk4 SMG.

Accuracy at Over Pistol Ranges

In the Sterling marketing literature, the closed-bolt Mk8 was described as being

> … *developed for greater accuracy in the 100–200 metre range for security forces using standard 9mm parabellum ammunition. Single action handguns used by security forces have been found to be unreliable in accuracy at this range [we'll say they are!] where members of the public are present during a terrorist attack.*

It is a matter of fact that a closed bolt gun will be more accurate than one with a reciprocating bolt, due to the different lock times between the two types.

Where the Mk8 does differ, compared with the Mk4/L2A3, is internally. The Mk8 casing includes the same internal semi-auto-only safeguards as fitted to the Mk6, and the gun fires in the single-shot mode only, from the closed bolt position.

304. Front three-quarter left side view of the Sterling "CBS Mark 8", with bayonet and 15-round magazine fitted. (Note the bayonet is the later 'hybrid' style, discussed in Chapter Sixteen.)

As can clearly be seen, the Mk8 looked EXACTLY like the Mk4 SMG, but it fired single shot only from the closed bolt. (Courtesy MoD Pattern Room, Nottingham)

Inside the Hybrid: Similarities with the Mk4 *and* the Mk6

More On the Closed Bolt, Single Shot (CBS) Conversion

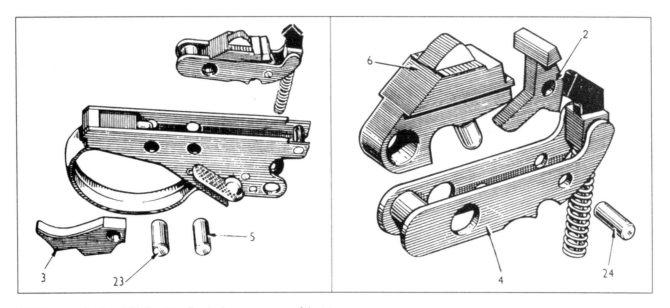

305. From the Sterling Mk8 User Handbook, the components of the trigger group.
Compare with fig 283: note the narrow sear (6) and the dog-leg extension (blacked in) atop the sear cradle spring guide. The Mk8 uses the same Single Shot trigger mechanism and Closed Bolt breech block/firing pin assembly as the Mk6 Carbine and the Mk7C Pistol.

The casing is a conversion of the Mk4/L2A3 casing, and contains all the common parts that one instantly recognises. Internally, however, the casing resembles the Mk6: the lead-up into the rear barrel seating has been modified by the insertion of a steel rib, which prevents the use of the Mk4/L2A3 breech block and barrel, and just to the rear of the pistolgrip side plates, a steel lug has been welded into place, which prevents(?) the insertion of the automatic Mk4/L2A3 trigger mechanism.

The left pistol grip side plate is engraved 'FIRE' (painted red) and 'SAFE' (painted white).

The trigger mechanism housing has a recess machined away at the rear to clear the projecting lug at the rear of the grip side plates. It has the Mk4 Police Carbine inner change lever (P4-12-9), which will not allow the change lever to roll forward to the fully automatic position. Additionally, it incorporates the Mk6 single-shot sear and sear cradle return spring guide, with the raised projection that eliminates the 'runaway gun' problem associated with blowback guns using low-power ammunition.

The Mk8 gun also used the Mk6 breech block (S8-8-A) together with the associated internal components such as the firing pin, firing pin spring, and block. A full description of this breech block and trigger mechanism can be found in Chapter Eleven.

The standard Mk4/L2A3 nose cap has been used on the Mk8 gun, meaning the No5 bayonet can be fitted. A (slightly modified) standard-length (7.8″) Mk4-type barrel is fitted, attached to the standard Mk4 front cap by the usual two Allen screws. The longer Mk6 barrel cannot be used within the Mk8 gun.

The Mk8 was offered only in the black crackle finish paint.

Summing Up: Why the Mk8?

From this description you will see that the only practical differences between the "CBS Gun Mark 8" and the earlier Mk6 Carbine are the different methods of attaching the barrel, and the fact that the Mk8 can mount a bayonet.

As with the Mk7 'Pistols', Peter Laidler has often asked himself just why the Mk8 gun was marketed. It is certainly a Mk4 'lookalike', but at what cost? The fact that the barrel length was shorter than the minimum allowed on a carbine within the United States meant that sales of the Mk8 were prohibited in the US. Perhaps this had something to do with the fact that only 70 Mk8s were ever made!

Component Interchangeability: the Mk8 with the Mk4/L2A3

All components are interchangeable EXCEPT:

- barrel (but Mk4/L2A3 can be slotted at rear flange to fit Mk8 casing)
- breech block assembly (Mk6)
- cocking handle (Mk6) (but Mk4/L2A3 can be cut short to fit)
- inner return spring
- trigger mechanism *assembly* (some *components* interchange).

The Final Windup – Bad News & Good

On January 1, 1985 Barncourts (Tietel) purchased the Sterling Armament Company. Mr Patrick Giles was retained as the Managing Director. It was sold to British Aerospace in 1989.

Archive records show that over 5,000 Mk4/L2A3 guns, 322 Mk5/L34A1s, 229 Mk6s, 351 Mk7Cs, and 15 Mk8s were transferred to British Aerospace on closure of the Sterling factory in 1989. For some time, British Aerospace sold off existing stocks of replacement magazines, only to find out that future potential buyers of the guns were put off somewhat, by the lack of magazines! As James Edmiston recalled bitterly in *The Sterling Years*,

> … the Royal Ordnance 'experts' … invited outside contractors to quote for making the 34-round Sterling magazine; the lowest quotation was for £65. Sterling had last made the magazine for £3 and sold it for £11. Whether or not Sterling had been bought just to be closed down, that in fact transpired as the only available option. The way it was run, it never could have survived.

The Lost Late Registers of Sterling Guns

Both authors have searched high and low to locate the latter-day Sterling arms-registers. Upon closure of the Sterling factory, these valuable documents were removed to the British Aerospace works at Nottingham.

The end user of certain Sterling guns featured in a long court case in the early 1980s. As a result of another not related case, the Sterling case went to the appeal court in 1994. The appeal was allowed. The mysterious 'loss' of these valuable records, whether by accident or design, should have been foreseen.

Sadly therefore, we are unable to give any date of-manufacture details against a given serial number, nor do we have accurate production figures, for Mk4/L2A3, Mk5/L34A1, Mk6, Mk7, and Mk8 Sterling guns produced after 1 January, 1975.

The Good News is that for many years the Sterling firearms registers were the sole responsibility of Mr Mowett, the Stores Superintendent and head of the Despatch Department.

Mr Mowett took great pride in his record keeping, often taking the register home at night in order to complete each day's entries. Luckily, these records still exist, and have been made available for examination by the authors.

They are all handwritten in VERY small copperplate, each letter and number perfectly legible in spite of its miniscule size. As an example, for the Mk4 SMG order for Portugal in June, 1962, Mr Mowett records 2,032 serial numbers (all within the KR 325- to KR 464- range) in 25 tiny lines, in a space only $5\frac{1}{2}''$ by $2\frac{1}{8}''$!

Military Purchasers of the Sterling SMG

Guns, Bayonets and Magazines (*ca*) 1950 to Dec 31, 1974

Thus, thanks to Mr Mowett, we *do* have figures for the most important years of worldwide sales of Sterling sub-machine guns and accessories.

As noted, most wartime records were destroyed in the V-bomb fire at Sterling in April, 1945, and no records have been discovered of commercial sales of the MkI Patchett. The following list therefore begins with the earliest small purchases of MkII

Patchetts, and covers all (non-UK) military sales up to December 31, 1974.

All commercial guns bear SN prefixes 'No.' (early MkIIs only), 'KR' (pre-1972), and 'S' (1972–1988). (All Sterling-made UK-Military contract guns bear SNs prefixed 'US [2-digit year] A'.)

The Mk4 column includes earlier sales where relevant. 'Arab State' indicates an unidentified Arab State; 'unk' indicates sales were made, but quantities remain unknown.

Country	Mk4	Mk5	Mk4PC	Mk5PC	Bayonets	Magazines
Abu Dhabi	1,209					3,100
Aden	98				20	501
Arab State	10 (incl 1 MkIII)	10				10
Antigua	5				3	19
Arab State	111					770
Argentina	1	14				50
Australia	1	88			1	6
Austria	1 (MkIII)		1			10
Bahamas	30					180
Bahrein	50 (all MkIIIs)	50				625
Barbados	11				1	35
Belgium	4				2	
Bermuda	9 (incl 8 MkII, 1 MkIII)					
Bolivia	1				1	8
Botswana	55 (incl 4 MkII, 6 MkIII)					570
Brazil	1 (MkIII)					5
Brit Honduras	10				10	50
Brunei	337	20			110	1,742
Burma	22 (incl 20 MkIII)	1			20	211
Canada	11	5	22		6	138
Ceylon	2,260				160	16,806
Chad	75					150
Chile	1	101				404
Colombia	3				3	15
Cyprus	250 (incl 200 MkIII)					1,205
Cuba	23					120
Crown Agents (MoD)		100				200
Costa Rica		12				24
Dubai	200	250			200	1,800
Dominica	5				5	27
Ethiopia	9	3				3

Country	Mk4	Mk5	Mk4PC	Mk5PC	Bayonets	Magazines
El Salvador		1				3
Egypt	1 (MkIII)					10
Equador	2	1			3	14
France	7 (incl 1 MkIII)				1	13
Guyana	241				281	1,077
Gilbert & Ellis Is	2					4
Ghana	5,990				2,978	46,438
West Germany	2		2		3	103
Gambia	28				2	93
Gabon		5				20
Haiti	1	1			1	6
Hong Kong	703 (incl 150 MkII and 233 MkIII)				15	2,515
India	32,536 (delivered – see text)				20,000	29,600
Indonesia	7	3				
Iran		1			6	53
Iraq	13,311	35			11,900	36,430
Israel	5 (MkIII)					50
Jamaica	353				317	1,877
Jordan	34	100			31	557
Kenya	2,297 (incl 550 MkII and 60 MkIII)	15			1,471	10,262
Korea (South)		1				6
Kuwait	4,437 (incl 100 MkIII, 9 gold &16 chrome Mk4)	2			5,014	42,224
Lebanon	511 (incl 5 MkIII)					5,055
Lesotho	23 (incl 22 MkIII)	2				256
Libya	3,095	300			1,625	13,850
Macau	20				20	72
Malawi	980	55			1,057	2,744
Malaya	18,463 (incl 22 MkIII)	51			6	103,763
Maldive Is	10				10	50
Malta	1				1	2
Mauritius	46				46	301
Morocco		15				45
Muscat		unk				
Nepal	1,103					5,515
New Hebrides	2				2	20
New Zealand	2,006	5			776	16,030
Nicaragua	1 (MkIII)					2
Nigeria	5,844				3,854	24,400
N Ireland Office	2,543					20,341
Norway	9 (8 on loan only)				9 (loan)	27
Oman	1,450	18				8,138
Pakistan	75	30			14	150

Paraguay		2				4
Peru	2	1			2	10
Phillipines	2	94	215	5		861
Portugal	2,032				3	8,139
Port W Africa	1,000					4,000
Qatar	1,487	21			1,048	7,603
Rhodesia	1,180 (incl 84 MkIII)		3		821	6,646
Sabah	80				80	580
Sarawak	266				250	1,423
Seychelles	6					34
Sharjah	(magazines only)					125
Sierra Leone	1		26			65
Singapore	375	102				3,265
	(incl 80 MkII and 115MkIII)					
South Africa	4 (incl 3 MkIII)				4	30
Solomon ls	3					12
South Arabia	681				60	3,707
South Yemen (only slings purchased; quantity unknown)						
Spain	2					6
St Kitts	12					60
St Lucia	2					10
St Vincents	8					40
Sudan	1,176		160		1,236	11,572
Swaziland	30	1				300
Sweden	9				5	24
	(incl 7 MkIII)					
Switzerland			6			12
Syria	1 (Mk2)				1	5
Tanzania	110		38			918
	(incl 60MkIII)					
Thailand		1			1	6
Trinidad	178				178	1,060
Tripolitania	143					1,310
	(Libya: incl 28 MkII and 100MkIII)					
Tunis	4,660				2,770	27,150
	(incl 1 chrome Mk4)					
Uganda	1,108				924	5,520
	(incl 12 MkIII)					
Un Arab Emirates	75	unk				428
UK	26,612					
USA	27	9	3		37	144
Venezuela	1 (MkII)				1	5
Virgin ls	2					10
West Cameroon (spares for refurbished second-hand guns only)						
Yugoslavia	1 (MkIII)				1	5

Sterling guns were available internationally from 1953 to 1988 (with limited ex-Sterling stock available to 1994), with prices fluctuating constantly. We have therefore deliberately omitted the cost of these guns, although in the individual chapters we have mentioned some advertised retail prices to give a ballpark figure.

A Word About Surplus Sterlings

The financial facts of life faced by a buyer shopping around for guns are many. The state of the international money market, the quantity he requires, what spares are required at the time; magazines, bayonets, ammunition? Is he coming back for more? Is there a middle-man to be taken care of? James Edmiston quotes an instance where a good and regular but hard-up military customer was unknowingly subsidised by a wealthy state.

While researching this book we learned that buying guns on the international market is the same as buying anything else. Ask the price and the stock answer is "How many do you want?" Give a reply and the next question will be "What currency are you paying in?" See what we mean about variables?

With the influx of cheap and cheerful Soviet bloc assault rifles flooding Britain's former Middle East, far Eastern, Asian and African allies, many of the latter are releasing their MkIII/L2A2 and Mk4/L2A3 Sterling (and Indian 1A) guns onto the international arms markets. A quantity of circa-1959 guns from New Zealand (serial numbers in the KR 23- range) and a large quantity of circa-1962/3 guns (serial numbers in the KR 45- range) seen recently are still in good serviceable condition, most just requiring a re-painting of the hard-wearing, oven baked matt-black Sunkorite 259. And the price for these good serviceable guns? "How many do you want?" On the other hand, another quantity of late MkIII/L2A2 guns (serial numbers in the KR 32- range) showed signs of neglect and were priced accordingly.

Housing the Priceless Sterling Collection

The well-preserved Sterling historic collection of prototypes and other guns was left in limbo for some months after the factory was closed. It is now housed in its rightful place with the Ministry of Defence Pattern Room at Nottingham, the ancestral home of George Patchett, whence numerous valuable photographs, drawings and documents have been made available to enrich our telling of this story. It is the intention of both authors to correctly catalogue all these Sterling guns in the near future.

Lest We Forget the Ultimate Accolade

Even though the Sterling Armament Company has closed, Sterling sub-machine guns will be with us for many years to come. Tough, reliable and gutsy; the L2 is truly the Land Rover of the small-arms world, the butterfly that stings like a bee.

We may recall some words from the Introduction, to the effect that Sterling's success was a very controversial subject. The actual quote is from David Howroyd, and his exact words are as follows:

> ... *It was a very controversial subject in the Government Royal Ordnance Factories and the well known Gunmakers like BSA of Birmingham that the ex-Wireless and Vacuum Cleaner Company beat 30 other entries [and] designs into becoming the Supplier of the British Forces Sub-machine Gun after WW2* ...

Nevertheless, in what was surely the ultimate accolade to George Patchett and the Sterling workforce, at the School of Infantry Barracks at Brecon, Wales, three of the main buildings are named "Enfield", "Vickers" and "Sterling", three names that kept the punch in Britain's fist.

Chapter Fourteen

Other Sterling Arms

The Frank Waters 5.56mm Assault Rifle

Under James Edmiston's aggressive ownership, the fact that the US Government had prohibited the export of even sample quantities of the 5.56mm M16 rifle had led to a mandate for Frank Waters, Sterling's chief designer, to proceed with his own design of 5.56mm rifle.

Two firing prototypes were produced, but the Sterling 5.56mm rifle project lapsed in 1974 in the face of an enticing licensing agreement with Arma-Lite Corporation of Costa Mesa, California.

What is little known is that the Company had already spotted the opportunity of making a 5.56mm rifle in the mid-1960s. Major Robert Turp, the then Sales Director dashed over to the mighty Colt Company in Connecticut and signed up a patent agreement for the complete in-house British manufacture of the M-161A1 rifle which had been licensed to Colt by Armalite. In fact it was mooted that Sterling should

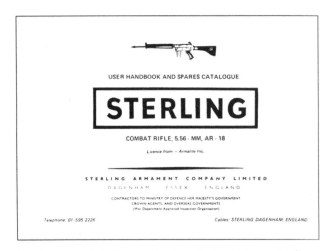

306. The cover of the Sterling User Handbook and Spares Catalogue for the "Sterling Combat Rifle, 5.56mm, AR-18", an exact copy of the ArmaLite AR-18 "solely manufactured by Sterling in the UK for the worldwide market".

be another supplier to the US Government which was heavily involved in the Vietnam War. The large and competent American domestic small-arms producers would have loved that!

It should be noted that Britain had been kept out of that war owing to the astuteness of the then Prime Minister Harold Wilson. The appreciation for this has never really been accorded to Wilson. However, it obviously rankled with those that expected support from "the special relationship", and the export licence from the U.S. Government for the two sample guns was never granted on the grounds that ALL war material was to be sent as top priority to Vietnam. The license could never be "consummated" and had to be dropped.

However, what is also not common knowledge is that the British troops serving in Borneo in the Undeclared War against Soekarno's Indonesia were issued with 5,000 AR-15 5.56mm semi-automatic rifles before the official adoption of the M-16 by the US authorities.

The Sterling/ArmaLite Connection

A license agreement was confirmed in 1974 between the Sterling Armament Company and ArmaLite Corporation of Costa Mesa, California, under which Sterling were to be sole world producers of the ArmaLite AR-18 and AR-180 5.56mm rifles, for sale predominantly in the USA through ArmaLite, and in other parts of the world by Sterling.

Production of Sterling-made AR-180 rifles began in 1976 and ended in 1983. A total of 12,368 were made, 10,946 of which were imported into the United States. The remainder were sold elsewhere by Sterling, with royalty payment to ArmaLite.

Sterling produced several models and variations of the AR-18 and AR-180 rifles, as follows:

ستيرلينغ

بندقية الكاربين إى آر-١٨ إس عيار ٥,٥٦ ملم

(بتصريح من شركة أرمالايت انكوربوريتد)

إى آر - ١٨ إس عيار ٥,٥٦ ملم بعقب ثابت

إى آر - ١٨ إس عيار ٥,٥٦ ملم بعقب قابل للطيّ

307. A Sterling brochure, in Arabic, describing the selective fire 5.56mm Sterling Combat Carbine AR-18AS .
   Above: left side view with stock open.
   Below: right side view, with stock folded (on left side).
   Sterling made magazines in 20, 30 and 40-round sizes for its AR-18s.

The Sterling AR-180 5.56mm Police Rifle

Start: S 15001

End: S 27368

The AR-180 "5.56mm Police Rifle" is described in a late Sterling brochure as:

A modern light weight rifle, simple to handle and easy to maintain. Designed to meet the many varied roles of modern para-military and police forces. Normally supplied with a fixed butt, however, for special roles, e.g. special patrol groups, a folding butt

model can be supplied. A general purpose weapon which fires single shots [with] an operation range of up to 600 metres …

The Sterling AR-18 Combat Rifle

Start: A 1001

End: A 10887

The Sterling AR-180S 5.56mm Police Carbine

Start: SS 225

End: SS 334

The AR-180S 5.56mm Police Carbine is described in a late Sterling brochure as:

... a compact version of the AR-180 using the same cartridge ... all parts are interchangeable with the standard AR-180 except those forward of the receiver. It has an operational range of 450 metres ...

The Sterling AR-18AS Combat Carbine

Start: AS 001
End: AS 327

Sterling AR-180SCS in Wood Stock

Start: PH 00001
End: PH 00385

It was Peter Hart who developed and put into production the wood-stocked version of the AR-180, described as the "AR-180SCS". It was as a result of his development work in this field that, in true Sterling fashion, the serial numbers of all 385 AR-180SCS rifles commenced with his initials, 'PH'.

308. Peter Hart, Works Manager for the Sterling/ArmaLite production programme, who developed the wood-stocked, single shot AR-180CS, all 385 of which bear his initials as a serial number prefix. Peter Hart was highly critical of some of the engineering methods that Armalite had employed, and let Armalite have the "Damn Yanks" bit with both brarrels. He was later to become very friendly with John McGerty his opposite number at Armalite. (Courtesy Mike Gruber)

The Sterling AR-180SCS Hand-Loading (Single Shot) in Wood Stock

This one-off rifle, numbered SW 23178, was manufactured without a gas port in the barrel. It was thus a true single-shot rifle, which had to be loaded and unloaded by hand.

Whoever now owns rifle SW 23178 can be guaranteed that it has already become a valuable collector's piece!

The "Sterling Assault Rifle 1980"

Five years after Frank Waters' 5.56mm assault rifle had first been abandoned, he produced a second design, dubbed the "Sterling Assault Rifle 1980". Despite its name, the Sterling Assault Rifle 1980 was first presented for British Army NATO trials in 1979. A total of ten such rifles were built, and two were extensively tested by Frank Waters and David Howroyd.

However, nothing more became of the "Sterling Assault Rifle 1980". The prototype samples now reside in the Pattern Room at Nottingham.

309. David Howroyd test firing Frank Waters' second design of 5.56mm rifle, in 1986 or 1987, long after it had been passed over by the British Government.

This rifle featured a swinging latch on the side of the bolt which guided the locking bolt into position. (Courtesy David Howroyd)

The First Frank Waters Assault Rifle Becomes the SAR-80

The Sterling Company Profile [circa 1985] commented on the aftermath of the military trials featuring the "Sterling Assault Rifle 1980" as follows:

... These trials were abandoned following a change of Government and the new Government decided; for political reasons, to develop a new weapon

310. Singaporean soldier with the SAR 80 5.56mm Assault Rifle and 30-round magazine, in a photo from a Chartered Industries of Singapore (CIS) brochure. Note the Sterling 'crackle' finish.

CIS modified the original Frank Waters design slightly, to achieve commonality of trigger group components with the M16, a rifle they were also manufacturing, under licence from Colt's.

through the Royal Ordnance Factories. Faced with this change of policy, Sterling sold the design and development of the SAR 80 to the Government of Singapore who now produce the highly successful SAR 80 and its lightweight gun derivative, the Ultimax [designed by L James Sullivan].

The gun bought by the Singaporeans was Frank Waters' original design. As noted, the contract called for the entire gun to be tooled up in England for production by Chartered Industries of Singapore (CIS). The Singaporeans later redesigned the trigger mechanism to take parts common to the M16, which they were also manufacturing, under licence from Colt's.

Curiouser and Curiouser – the Sterling AR-18 Becomes the MoD "Bullpup" (SASO)

The attempted free use of the Sterling Mk4 SMG by the British Government in the Fazakerley 'Pioneer' (L2A3) programme, discussed in Chapter Seven, took place in the 1960s. In the 1980s the Sterling made AR-18 had its turn, and this time, they got away with it.

The AR-18 served as the thankless physical basis for the weapon mentioned above which, developed "through the Royal Ordnance factories", ironically beat out Frank Waters' "Sterling Assault Rifle 1980".

311. Two views of an original prototype of the Enfield 'bullpup' rifle.

Above: left hand view. Note the central wooden pistol grip, reminiscent of the EM-2. The modified AR-18 upper receiver still features a now-useless scope mounting block.

Below: right side view. Compare with fig 307. (MoD Pattern Room collection, photo by Thomas B Dugelby)

This highly controversial bullpup design, originally in 4.85 × 49mm calibre, was later adopted in 5.56mmNATO calibre as the SABO (L85A1).

Among the effects of this adoption was the phaseout and eventual obsolescence of the Sterling L2A3 SMG in British Service.

At this writing the L85A1 remains the standard UK Military rifle.

The One-Off SU "Stamped Sterling"

Introduction: Increased Competition from Heckler & Koch

Until the 1960s, Sterling and UZI had coexisted quite happily, selling their SMGs within well-defined territories, some nations even purchasing quantities of both Sterlings *and* UZIs. The UZI featured the Czech developed 'wraparound bolt' technology within a relatively modem stamped and fabricated square casing. The Sterling used older (but silenceable!) abutting bolt technology, within a longer and more expensive-looking casing.

During the 1960s Sterling began to face competition from a third source, a newcomer on the scene. The competition came in the form of the MP series of SMGs, produced in Germany by Heckler & Koch. These guns featured a revolutionary new roller locked, closed-bolt technology, housed within a sheet-metal casing that raised the art of metal starnping and fabricating to a new high. Interestingly, however, neither the UZI nor the H&K ever successfully completed the course of trials that the Patchett had, in the course of its being adopted as the next British SMG.

Nevertheless, Sterling became concerned over the inroads H&K was ruthlessly forging among Sterling's own well-known trading grounds in the Middle and Far East. They set about to design a new SMG that would retain the good features of the Mk4 Sterling, such as reliable feed from the left side and the Mk4's proven ability to keep firing under all sorts of atrocious conditions, and combine these advantages within a square, pressed housing.

Describing the S11

In 1965 David Howroyd and Harry Goodall fabricated and tested one example of Frank Waters' experimental gun, called the S11. The gun was neat and compact, with a folding butt based upon the strong, double-hinged design used on the third "Lightweight Lanchester" (discussed in Chapter One). The magazine used was the tried-and-true Sterling doublefeed, roller-platform design, feeding from the left side as usual. The trigger mechanism could be either the standard Patchett patented trigger, or the interchangeable Ruffell design chosen by the Canadians for their C1 SMG (Chapter Nine).

The S11 embodied the unique facility of being capable of selectively mounting two completely different bayonets: the No5 rifle/SMG bayonet along the left side, or the L1A3 (L1A1/C1 rifle) bayonet, underneath. It also featured a quick-removable barrel.

Apart from the magazine and trigger mechanism, nothing else was interchangeable with the Mk4.

Field stripping was similar to the UZI with a removable top cover, although a hinged cover was also tried. The square-section breech block was grooved in a similar manner to the helical ribs on the Mk4/L2A3.

This gun reached the preliminary firing trial stage, where the side-mounted magazine was described as a drawback, although the Sterling engineers considered that it would be quite possible to construct a similar gun with the magazine mounted underneath. If height was to be a problem, Sterling already had 10- and 15-round magazines, permanently "Double Stacked" if desired, in production.

Problems with the S11

Problems were numerous, although none actually appeared insurmountable. The top cover kept opening, causing feed problems, and there were trigger failures. Unfortunately these problems were interlinked, creating a 'chicken-or-egg' situation wherein no one was sure just what caused what.

312. Two views of the unorthodox(!) Sterling S11 no EXP 001, with butt extended.

Above: left side view with side-mounted No5 rifle bayonet, standard 34-round Sterling magazine. Compare with fig 16: the double-hingedbutt design was taken from the experimental wartime Third Light Lanchester.

Below: right side view. Note the grip safety, the standard Sterling trigger, and the vertically mounted (!) L1A3 (L1A1 rifle) bayonet. (MoD Pattern Room collection)

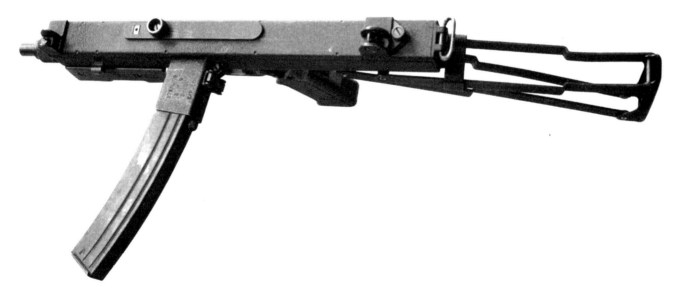

313. Top view of the Sterling S11 no EXP 001, showing the unusual offset of the sights, barrel, and cocking handle. (MoD Pattern Room collection)

314. Top closeup view of the magazine housing of Sterling SMG 9mm S11 no EXP 001, showing pantographed markings.

 Note the altered magazine catch/extractor assembly. (MoD Pattern Room collection)

The initial firing trials were dismissed as a disaster, and a meeting was called of the sales, design and production staffs, with senior management present. During the meeting the S11 was described as "… a donkey in a thoroughbred race". Well let's not mince words here, lads!

The Demise of the S11

It was estimated that tooling up for a major change such as the S11 represented would cost perhaps a million pounds, or even more. Additionally, the gauging, retraining, marketing, etc would add to these costs. However, the biggest problem of all was greater than any engendered by the S11 itself: the worldwide SMG market was shrinking. With diminishing sales apparent for all to see, such a changeover would ensure a case of dwindling returns in which there would probably never be a break-even point.

On the other hand, the existing Mk4 Sterling was proven and reliable. It was still being sold in large numbers to over 100 customer nations worldwide, and it was argued that only a few of these old customers would opt for the cheaper S11, which would necessitate a complete changeover of guns AND

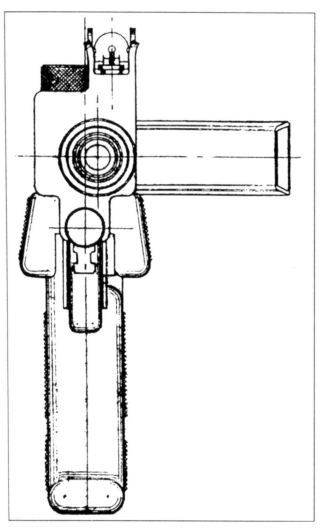

315. From an undated Sterling factory drawing: the Sterling S11, viewed front-end-on.

 Compare with fig 313: note that the barrel, cocking handle and sights are all in different vertical planes, none of which is in the physical vertical centre of the receiver and grip. (Courtesy MoD Pattern Room, Nottingham)

spares stockholding. In any case, most customers would continue to require Mk4 guns and spares, in the interest of standardisation.

With its well-made and carefully brazed components, the Mk4 casing appeared to be expensive, but in fact it was very cheap to produce due to all the production being carried out in-house on well-tried (and long since paid-for) machinery.

All in all, the "stamped Sterling" presented too many variables and drawbacks. The S11 was shelved in 1967, and the drawings were carefully put away.

316. Left side view of the S11, illustrating its ingenious ability to mount two completely different types of bayonets.

Above: the side-mounted Nos rifle-type bayonet is fitted, with its large ring around the muzzle . The squared bayonet standard and small front stud for the L1A3 (L1A1 or C1 rifle) bayonet are shown on the bottom, between the grooved handguards.

INSET, right: with bayonet removed, showing side (Nos) and bottom (L1A1) bayonet standards. (MoD Pattern Room collection)

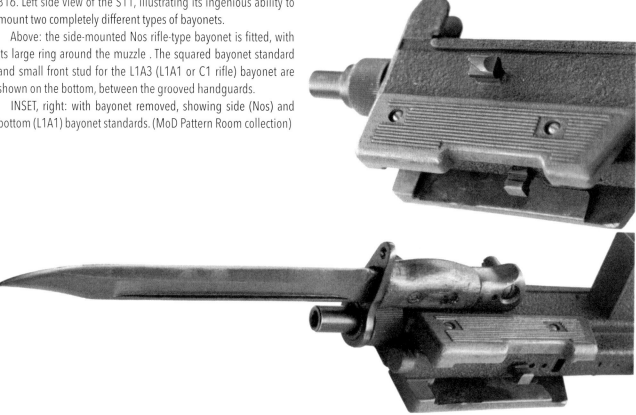

Only one S11 had been produced, and this was consigned to the Sterling vault and forgotten until the company was closed for good in 1989. Then, along with the other historic guns and documents in the Sterling collection, S11 protoype no EXP 001 was transferred to the Ministry of Defence Pattern Room, where it remains to this day.

The Sterling HR 81 Air Rifle

The Sterling HR 81 air rifle was designed by Roy Hutchinson, improved by Peter Hart (who developed the wood-stocked AR-180SCS) and Peter Moon, and put into production in both .177″ or .22″ calibres.

The Sterling .357 Magnum Revolver, and Other Ventures

Additionally, a sample batch of 20 .357″ Magnum calibre Sterling Revolvers was manufactured, with 80% of the tooling completed by the Sterling Armament Company.

On the revolver programme, the circa-1985 Sterling Company Profile commented,

Series production is now commencing on the Sterling .38 Special/.357 Magnum Revolver for the law enforcement and security/civilian market The weapon has been designed to incorporate the highest quality and performance and has many exceptional features including a unique system to ensure constant trigger pressure whilst firing.

Sterling Armament also sub-contracted their press shop capacity to manufacture assemblies for Roneo Vickers printing machines, postal franking machines and Jaguar XJ6 cooling systems.

Patented trigger mechanism giving exceptionally
smooth double action operation.
Short hammer throw for easier cocking and accurate
single action performance.
Fully adjustable target style hammer and trigger.
Full length ejection of empty cases on all models.
Action designed to prevent malfunctions from fouling
build up.
Shrouded ejector rod.
All components manufactured from highest grade
molybdenum steels.

STERLING

SPECIFICATION

Calibre .38 Special/ .357 Magnum
Capacity 6 shot
Barrel 2¾" (70mm), 4" (102mm) 6" (152mm)
Length 9½" (240mm) (4" barrel)
Sights Front fixed ⅛" Serrated Ramp
Rear: Adjustable with Square Notch or Fixed
Finish: Polished, Matt or Stainless
Grips: Checkered wood

317. A Sterling brochure on the short-lived Sterling .357 Magnum calibre revolver.

The basic externals appear to owe much to the Smith & Wesson 'N' series frame design, but internally the Sterling featured a unique, patented "constant trigger pressure" system, said to give exceptionally smooth double action operation. The extended shroud was effected before that of Smith & Hesson. (Courtesy Sterling Archive)

318. With large UK Military contracts a thing of the past, Sterling's success during the Edmiston years (1972–1983) depended largely upon an aggressive stance in foreign sales.

This photo was taken at a demonstration and shoot for the Royal Malaysian Police, held at the National Police Training Centre in Malaysia in May, 1981.

From left, Sterling 'Product' on the line includes a Mk4/L2A3 (bottom left); a Mk5/L34A1 (behind kneeling instructor); a .357 Magnum Revolver with 4" barrel; a 5.56mm Combat Rifle AR-18 (on bipod); a Combat Carbine AR-18SC; a Sterling 7.62NATO calibre Sniper's Rifle. Note also the plastic-stocked Mk4 (or Mk8?) on the table (foreground). (Courtesy Sterling Archive)

319. Sterling proudly 'Show the Flag' with their full product line at British Arms Fair, Aldershot, in 1985.
    From left:"Revolvers from Sterling"; a .50 calibre M2 BMG (Browning Machine Gun, foreground, on M3 tripod; made in England by Manroy, for whom Sterling occasionally did some work); a Mk5/L34A1 wall exhibit (behind the Browning); some coloured wall charts of the Mk6 Sterling and the WWII Lanchester behind David Howroyd (in brown suit); a goldplated Mk4/L2A3 with (gold) bayonet mounted, plus what appears to be a gold-plated Mk5 in a fitted leather carrying case on the glass counter, under which are displayed Sterling cleaning kits (top shelf); a Mk7 Pistol and a wooden-foregripped L34A1 (bottom shelf). Far right: a display of Mk7 Pistol variations. (Courtesy Sterling Archive)

Sterling Sectionalised Training Aids and Presentation Models

Sterling would also supply sectioned or skeletonised versions of its standard guns for training purposes. The full range could be supplied, although we have only ever seen the Mk4/L2A3 and a Mk5/L34A1. At least one Mk6 was sectioned to show the US Bureau of Alcohol, Tobacco and Firearms the modifications done to make it strictly a semi-automatic carbine. These skeletonised guns are works of art which are now extremely valuable and highly prized by collectors.

Sterling regularly presented neutered/deactivated guns, suitably mounted on wooden plinths, to high-ranking dignitaries and buyers. Likewise, an official letter from a recognised body, such as a museum or military establishment would usually see a suitable example arrive quite soon. These mounted de-activated presentation pieces and Sterling skeletonised guns were works of art, and as a result they are extremely sought-after today by collectors.

320. Left side views of two cutaway Sterling SMGs, "Sectionalised for Instruction and Training".

Above: sectionalised Mk4/L2A3 with butt open and magazine inserted. A sectionalised magazine is shown above.

Below: sectionalised Mk5 with butt folded.

Note the left side plates of the trigger mechanisms have been replaced with ones made of clear acrylic, to show the action of the sears and sear cradles within.

As described in a Sterling brochure, "All the parts can be clearly seen by students, providing the Instructor with a professional and useful training aid." (Courtesy MoD Pattern Room, Nottingham)

Part IV

Armourers Talk Shop

Chapter Fifteen

Mods and Sods

A Trials Retrospective: a Paean to the Patchett

It was the success of the Patchett Machine Carbine in the long series of trials held between 1946 and 1953, in climates as diverse as the dry dust of Sudan, through the most bitter freezing winters of Korea to the wettest stinking mangrove swamps in the Malayan jungle that finally proclaimed the Patchett the successor to the venerable Sten.

A study of just what was involved in these trials helps us realise just how tough those early Patchett guns really were!

In the next few pages we describe the details of several such trials. Some were carried out under controlled, almost clinical conditions, while some were not; some were carried out in England, others with British forces serving abroad. We accept that clinical trials are not combat trials, but when carried out in conjunction with combat use, they have an uncanny knack of separating the wheat from the chaff. They certainly weeded out all the opposition to the Patchett!

The Official Salt Mist Test

This test is mainly for the testing of new phosphating and anti-rust proofing processes. Once (if) the phosphating process has broken down, these tests serve a secondary purpose to ensure that the steel used is the best possible bearing the economics of production in mind. It is essentially a comparative test and must therefore be conducted under controlled conditions. The guns for test must be clearly marked for identification purposes in such a way that the markings can be identified during every stage of the test. They must be fully degreased and after degreasing, thoroughly oiled with oil OX52 (or similar) then wiped over with clean flannelette

(4″ × 2″ cleaning swabs). From this point on, the articles are not to be touched by hand until the tests are complete.

Actual sea-water will be used, OR a standard sea-water chemical mix, made up in the following proportions (shown in grams per litre of water):

Calcium Sulphate	*1.5*
Magnesium Chloride	*3.0*
Magnesium Sulphate	*2.0*
Sodium Chloride	*25.0*

The guns will be hung in the salt mist cabinet by a non-metallic medium. The test should start at 07.30 hrs on a Monday morning, when the mist will be turned on for 30 minutes. The mist will be turned off for 4 hours. The mist will then be turned ON for a further 30 minutes. This test will continue during the day.

The guns will be left in the cabinet for 14.5 hours overnight to dry.

This cycle will be repeated every day until the end of the week ensuring that the guns are rotated through 180% to ensure that each side is subject to the same exposure conditions. At the weekends, the guns will be left in the cabinet to dry.

The guns will be examined after each drying period when they may be wiped or fully dried for this examination. Except for this wiping dry, the guns will not be touched with bare hands or oil.

This series of tests will continue until large patches of rust are visible to the naked eye on all (or all but one) of the guns. Rust at the point of suspension or on surfaces not being subject to the test will be ignored. Likewise, in order to obtain good comparative results, guns which obviously fail early in the test will remain in the cabinet until the testis completed with the other guns. All guns will be removed together.

Corrosion will be assessed in accordance with the following standard tables:

Code Letter	Condition
A	*good*
B	*microscopic pitting*
C	*visual pin-point pitting*
D	*enlarged pin-point pitting*
E	*patches of rust up to 0.01 sq" in area*
F	*patches of rust up to 0.1 sq" in area*
G	*patches of rust up to 0.5 sq" in area*
H	*patches of rust up to 1.0 sq" in area*
I	*patches of rust over 1.0 sq" in area*
J	*complete breakdown*

Intensity No	Number of pits or patches of rust
1	*1 to 5*
2	*5 to 10*
3	*10 to 20*
4	*20 plus*

Descriptions of corrosion to guns will therefore comprise of a series of numbers and letters, for example: F1, E3, D4 meaning 1 to 5 patches of rust up to 0.1 square inches in area, plus 10 to 20 patches up to 0.1 square inches and plus more than 20 enlarged pin-point pitted areas. To ensure correct comparisons, guns will be labelled with the amount of wet days and dry weekends that occurred during the tests.

The Practical Rust Test

Of course, all of the above was theory, and as every engineer quickly realises, theory is not quite the same as practice.

For a further practical trial under warlike conditions, the guns were taken onto operations in the tidal mangrove swamps of Johore Bahru by men of the Somerset Light Infantry, fighting in Malaya. This time, the salt water was for real, but now it was saturated with abrasive and clogging salt-water silt. These were real conditions, where the enemy was liable to emerge and fight back with a split second's warning.

Fortunately, in this combined salt water test *and* mud test, the MkII Patchett performed admirably. The gun won many friends in the Far East.

The Official Mud Test

Weapons will be cleaned and prepared for firing. They will be fired to ensure that the weapon is functioning correctly. An Armourer's dummy or drill round will be placed in the chamber and the muzzle will be plugged. The breech block cocked in the ready-to-fire position. If the weapon fails the following test, it may be subject to a repeat test with the breech block forward in the fired position. It must be understood AND STATED ON SUBSEQUENT REPORTS that this is a second-best com promise. A loaded magazine will be placed on the gun.

A mud bath will be prepared using a 25% mixture of garden soil and 75% water by volume. The mixture will be passed through a ¼" sieve before use.

The mixture will be stirred to a uniform consistency. The guns, together with a second full

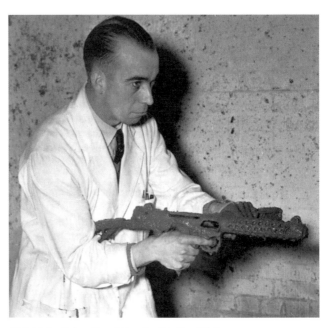

321. Major Robert Turp firing the Sterling MkIII.

This photograph featured in the Sterling broadsheet headed "Replacing the Sten: the British Army's New Sterling Sub-Machine Gun", where it was captioned as follows: "After the Mud Test: the Sterling was lifted from complete immersion in glutinous mud and can be fired immediately without any cleaning." (Sterling Archival photograph dated 8 February, 1955)

magazine, will be hung horizontally into the mixture. The weapons will be moved slowly in the mud for one minute and then removed . It will then be rotated horizontally through 180" and moved through the mixture for a further minute.

Shake off and wipe away by hand all the surplus mud. Remove the plug from the muzzle and the cartridge from the breech. Load the weapon and fire. The first half of the magazine will be fired single shot and the second half will be fired in short bursts. If the weapon will not function correctly, operate the working parts three times and try again.

If the weapon fires successfully with the original magazine, fire the spare magazine which has been in the mud. If the weapon fails to fire the original magazine and the second magazine, fire again with a clean magazine. It is important that the weapon is kept horizontal from the time it is first put into the mud until the end of the test.

Most foreign buyers accepted these tests at face value, but Ecuador carried out a similar series of tests to their own standards. During their mud test, they filled the barrel with mud!

Once again, under real active service conditions, the gun was described as unstoppable.

The Blown Sand Test

The gun will be prepared for firing and testing as detailed in the mud test. The gun will be placed in the sand cabinet together with one spare magazine. A mixture of 75% Pendine like sand and 25% Pendine like quarry dust (by weight) will be prepared. The mixture will be passed through a 144 hole per square inch mesh sieve before use and will be thoroughly dried by heating. A fresh mixture will be used for each series of tests.

The guns will be placed in the sand cabinet and the sand blower turned on. After five minutes or any other specified time in the sand/dust mix, the blower will be turned off and the weapons with the spare magazines will be removed from the cabinet The sand will be shaken off and the breech and muzzle

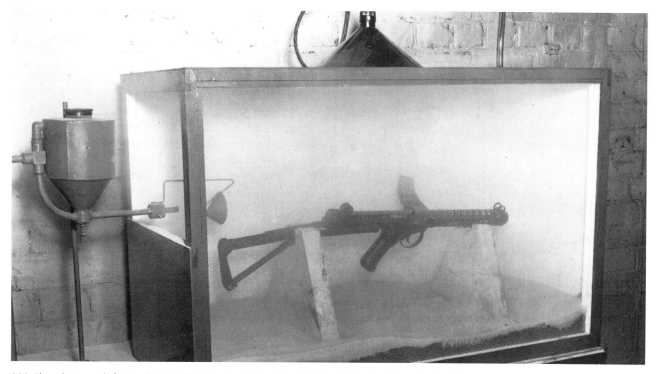

322. This photograph featured in the Sterling broadsheet headed "Replacing the Sten: the British Army's New Sterling Sub-Machine Gun", where it was captioned as follows:

"The Sterling Mounted in a Sand Chamber for the test which simulates sandstorm conditions. It can be fired immediately after removal."
(Sterling Archival photograph dated 8 February, 1955)

plugs will be removed. Load and fire the gun. The first half of the magazine will be single shot fire and the second half fired in short bursts. If the gun will not function correctly, operate the working parts three times and try again.

If the weapon fires successfully with the original magazine, fire the second magazine which has been in the sand cabinet. If the weapon fails to fire the original magazine and the second magazine, fire again with a clean magazine.

Like the salt water and mud tests described above, the sand cabinet test was only a substitute for the real thing, so the guns were taken to the Sudan, the dustbowl of Africa. Dustproofing was a feature not properly

taken into account while the current 185–86/SAB0 rifle was being developed, the gun that was to replace the Sterling! And as UN soldiers discovered recently, fighting in desert conditions is similar to fighting in a giant sandblasting cabinet where, without oil and constant oil changes, everything soon wears out.

It was soon established that the Patchett was quite at home in the arid and dusty atmosphere of the desert, and it was quite happy to work while bone dry, too. Guns and ammunition, heated to 79°C (175°F) for 12 hours, functioned correctly.

It was the success of these exhaustive tests that subsequently saw many thousands of these super little guns being sold to our Arab friends.

Winter Trials in Korea

323. This photograph featured in the Sterling broadsheet headed "Replacing the Sten: the British Army's New Sterling Sub-Machine Gun ", where it was captioned as follows:

"After the 'Alaska Test', in which [the MkIII Sterling] is frozen for several hours. Immediately after being withdrawn from the refrigerator, it can be fired."

Note the large shards of ice, broken from the casing. (Sterling Archival photograph dated 8 February, 1955)

The tests were not only confined to the heat. It is recorded that some guns were taken to Korea with the King's Shropshire Light Infantry. Those who fought in Korea will remind you that the winters are probably the bleakest on earth. The cold is so intense that uncovered hands stick to bare metal. One senior Training Warrant Officer while reading this added, "… conditions for the rest of the year weren't much better either!"

Guns and ammunition were subject to freezing down to –32°C (–25°F) for 12 hours and functioned correctly. The Sterling company test was similar, but their guns were frozen for two days.

The Functioning Test

After each of the above tests but before cleaning, the guns will fire three magazines non-stop and without mechanical fault [after all, you cannot cater for an ammunition fault] three magazines with the gun at 85° depression. This simulates firing into a trench or into the turret of an armoured vehicle. Similarly, the gun will fire three magazines at an angle of 85° elevation. This simulates firing up into a window or at an opponent firing into your trench or armoured vehicle.

The Patchett did not perform faultlessly here, but suffered from light detonator strikes. This was rectified by machining the firing pin integrally into the breech face.

Endurance Deemed "Beyond Reproach"

During a series of trials at Pendine Experimental Establishment and on active service elsewhere, the Patchett was subject to all of the above tests and more, after which it had been passed as "suitable for service". After a further lengthy endurance test with six production weapons, selected from the factory at random, trials reports stated that endurance was "beyond reproach". Such praise is seldom given, and rarely appears in official reports.

In these trials, two of the six guns fired over 10,000 rounds each without a single stoppage, and the remaining four fired 5,000 rounds each. Indeed, only two stoppages of a minor nature were recorded from a total of 42,163 rounds fired. The failure in weapon '4' related to a failure to eject a spent case, and this was reported to be an ammunition fault. The stoppage in weapon '6' was found to be caused by a stuck sear due to dirt from an earlier test, and was easily rectified.

Before-and-After Accuracy Tests

Accuracy tests were conducted both before and after the endurance firing described above.

The results deserve mentioning in full:

Weapon		Rounds fired prior to accuracy test (a) Rounds fired prior to accuracy test (b)	Accuracy in feet Hor × Vert = Sq Ft		
1	a	335	0.5	0.7	.35
1	b	10,696	0.3	0.8	.24
2	a	335	0.5	0.4	.20
2	b	10,685	0.4	0.6	.24
3	a	335	0.8	0.4	.32
3	b	5,921	0.3	0.6	.19
4	a	90	0.4	0.4	.16
4	b	4,940	0.4	0.6	.24
5	a	20	1.0	0.4	.40
5	b	4,961	0.7	0.9	.63
6	a	20	0.6	0.9	.54
6	b	4,960	0.8	0.4	.32

All these figures were obtained at 100 yards and represented 10 single shots with each shot being recorded. It is important to note that even after 10, 000 rounds the accuracy was not affected.

Continuing the Armourer's Tale

After finishing his apprenticeship in 1965, Peter Laidler encountered thousands upon thousands of L2s in service, but even then it was quite common to see Mk5 Sten guns with the rear echelon units of the Territorial Army. He recalls going out with Bob France, the circuit Armourer, and seeing quantities of these Mk5 Stens. During the mid 1960s when supplies of then-current L2s were plentiful, Bob France and the other circuit Armourers would ZF (the Army term for "reduce to scrap") the Mk5 Stens by gently twisting the gun casing, making it impossible for the gun to function properly. Mk5s were still in limited service with the UK Military overseas and· in Malaya, 27 Squadron, Royal Corps of Transport still had a dozen or so.

As for the L2A2 and L2A3 Sterlings encountered, it would be interesting to tell tales of daring-do with these guns. They were tough, hardy and well liked little guns, and apart from having flimsy and therefore weak butts, there was nothing that really caused concern.

In fact, a Sterling gun was simplicity itself. Just a .345″ barrel bore gauge and a set of feeler gauges, plus the normal Armourers tool kit, was all that was needed. Then the gun either worked or it didn't If it didn't, then the problem was investigated and easily put right. The quality of the replacement parts was such that they inevitably went straight in, with perhaps the slightest of fitting. Armourers always polished the breech block face and usually the

324. A contemporary photo of British Armourers and Armourer-Apprentices loading magazines and belts in order to range-test an interesting selection of weapons, including many discussed in this book.

From left (after the double-barreled shotgun!): M1928 Thompson; Mks Sten; Lanchester Mk1*; unidentified large-bore pistol; AK47 with solid butt (Valmet?); H&K MPS; an early MkI Trials Patchett; and last but certainly not least, a German MG42, hence the discussion between REME Armourer WO Ray Davies (rear, with cap on) and Armourer Sgt Kevin Edwards (holding up the non-disintegrating belt). (MoD Army, RMCS Shrivenham, photo by Peter Laidler)

sear face and corresponding slot in the breech block, too.

Whatever the weather, come sleet, snow, driving rain, mud or dust, nothing would stop a Sterling for long. Most soldiers will have seen them operating in the most atrocious weather while in the worst of mechanical conditions. Armourers have cringed to see bridging engineers hosing down their mud-caked Sterlings, along with vehicles and webbing equipment, with a high-power vehicle hose! However, the Sterling could take it-it was the Land Rover of the small-arms world.

However, as the crews of Ferret armoured reconnaissance vehicles quickly found out, when they stowed their L2s in the upright position, the rotating turret that housed the .30" Browning machine-gun would chew them in half when traversed in anger. The crews soon learned to lay their sub-machine guns down behind the radio.

This book is not intended to replace the Electrical and Mechanical Engineering Regulations (EMERs), the Armourers' bible, nor is it intended to replace the Technical Information or User Handbooks supplied with the guns by Sterling. However, there were only one or two modifications and miscellaneous instructions issued for the Sterling during its entire lifetime, and these are discussed below.

Where parts have to be named, we have used the Army designation. To this end, what a civilian would call the "safety catch" we refer to as the "change lever". Likewise the "end cap" is called the "return spring cap", and so on. The Military designates its parts by asking firstly "What is it?" If it is a pin, they follow up, first by asking "What sort of pin?" If it is an axis pin, they ask "An axis pin for what?" The full designation then becomes clear. It is a 'Pin, axis, backsight', or commonly, the backsight axis pin. The same applies to the 'Spring, catch, magazine', or magazine catch spring.

Interchangeability Throughout the Sterling Stable

As we have seen, the official factory designations for some Sterling Marks have a NATO specification too, and these are cross-referenced throughout the book as follows:

Factory Name	British (NATO) Name
Prototypes	
Patchett Machine Carbine 9mm	(Carbine, Machine, Patchett, 9mm)
MkI Patchett Machine Carbine 9mm MkII	Carbine, Machine, Patchett, 9mm, EX
	Gun Sub-Machine 9mm L2A1
Sterling SMG 9mm MkIII	Gun Sub-Machine 9mm L2A2
Sterling SMG 9mm Mk4	Gun Sub-Machine 9mm L2A3
Sterling Police Carbine 9mm Mk4	no NATO designation
Sterling-Patchett SMG 9mm Mk5	Gun Sub-Machine 9mm L34A1
Sterling Carbine 9mm Mk6	no NATO designation
Sterling Para Pistol 9mm Mk7A4/8	no NATO designation
Sterling Pistol 9mm Mk7C4/C8	no NATO designation
Sterling Single Shot Closed Bolt 9mm Gun Mk8	no NATO designation

Throughout this book we have used the Mk4/L2A3 gun as the control, as this was the gun produced over the longest time span and which saw the most extensive worldwide service. It thus follows that these parts will be the most common for the longest time to come, and that the gun itself will also be the most commonly available for students to research.

Of course, some owners will prefer to keep their guns original, and might take heart from the fact that even parts that are not interchangeable certainly bear some semblance to those from the Mk4/L2A3, which are close enough to modify to suit. The exception to this is the closed-bolt firing breech block from the Mk6, Mk7C and Mk8 Sterlings.

There are instances where a PART is not interchangeable, but the WHOLE ASSEMBLY is. Examples of this include the Mk4/L2A3 adjustable foresight blade, which by itself cannot be used on the MkII/L2A1 or MkIII/L2A2. However, the Mk4/L2A3 adjustable foresight BODY can certainly be used on the MkI, MkII and MkIII guns(and on the Lanchester, too!)

Another example is the Mk4 centre pin (cocking handle block). This is not used on the MkII or MkIII, but if the Mk4 BREECH BLOCK is used, then the centre pin certainly can be, as well.

The Casing Assembly

Part No	Proto-type	MkI	MkII L2A1	MkIII L2A2	Mk4 L2A3	Mk4 PC	Mk5 L34A1	Mk6 Carbine	Mk7A Pistol	Mk7C Pistol	Mk8 Gun
3	#	#	#	#	*	*	#	#	#	#	#
5	#	A	A	*	*	*	*	*	*	*	*
6	#	#	#	#	*	*	*	*	*	*	*
7	#	A	*	*	*	*	*	*	*	*	*
8	#	#	#	#	*	*	#	*	#	#	*
9	#	#	#	#	*	*	*	*	*	*	*
10	#	A	A	*	*	*	*	*	*	*	*
14	#	A	*	*	*	*	*	*	*	*	*
15	#	#	A	A	*	*	#	#	#	#	*
17	#	#	*	*	*	*	#	#	*	#	#
18	#	#	*	*	*	*	*	*	*	*	*
19	#	#	*	*	*	*	*	*	*	*	*
20	#	#	*	*	*	*	*	*	*	*	*
21	#	#	*	*	*	*	*	*	*	*	*
23	#	#	#	#	*	*	#	#	*	#	*
24	#	#	#	*	*	*	#	#	*	#	#
25	#	#	#	*	*	*	#	#	*	#	#
26	A	A	A	*	*	*	*	*	*	*	*
27	#	A	*	*	*	*	*	*	*	*	*
28	#	#	*	*	*	*	*	A	*	A	A
29	#	#	*	*	*	*	*	*	*	*	*
30	#	#	#	#	*	*	*	*	*	*	*
31	*	*	*	*	*	*	*	*	*	*	*
32	*	*	*	*	*	*	*	*	*	*	*
33	#	#	*	*	*	*	*	*	*	*	*
34	#	#	#	#	*	*	*	*	*	*	*
35	#	*	*	*	*	*	*	*	*	*	*
36	#	*	*	*	*	*	*	*	*	*	*
37	#	*	*	*	*	*	*	*	#	#	*
38	#	*	*	*	*	*	*	*	*	*	*
39	#	#	#	#	*	*	#	#	#	#	*

325. Components of the Mk4/L2A3 Casing Assembly, numbered as in fig 149, showing interchangeability with all other Patchett and Sterling Marks.

= Mk4/L2A3 part not interchangeable

A = Mk4/L2A3 part could easily be modified to fit

* = Mk4/L2A3 part fully interchangeable.

We have included at the end of each chapter information on component interchangeability among the various Sterling Marks. Indeed, an Armourer or collector with access to a selection of Mk4/L2A3 spares should be able to keep both early *and* late guns in good running order indefinitely.

You might also notice that whereas most of the plentiful Mk4/L2A3 parts will interchange with the MkII/L2A1, MkIII/L2A2 and subsequent Marks of gun, the part numbers in the parts lists, shown at the end of the relevant chapters, certainly don't agree.

Although most of the Mk4/L2A3 part numbers differ from the earlier and later parts, the truth is that the differences are usually slight pattern variations that have no bearing on functioning. One example is the inner return spring, which in the (late) MkII and the MkIII is wound in the opposite direction to the Mk4 (fig 154)! Quite why is anyone's guess, but in all other respects they are identical. Only those interested in ORIGINALITY, or a collector who might desire a CONCOURSE example of a certain Mark of gun would notice.

A group of British Armourers recently spent an enjoyable day on the range with (virtually) unlimited ammunition, testing a MkII/L2A1, a couple of MkIII/L2A2s, and several Mk4/L2A3s, and interchanged many parts as assemblies. All the guns functioned perfectly – didn't they, Ray and Roy?

The Trigger Assembly

Part No	Proto-type	MkI	MkII L2A1	MkIII L2A2	Mk4 L2A3	Mk4 PC	Mk5 L34A1	Mk6 Carbine	Mk7A Pistol	Mk7C Pistol	Mk8 Gun
			Mk4 parts nos 1,3, 4, 5, 7, 13, 14, 16, 17, 18, 19, 27: N/A								
2	#	A	*	*	*	*	*	A	*	A	A
6	A	*	*	*	*	*	*	*	*	*	*
8	#	*	*	*	*	#	*	#	*	#	#
9	*	*	*	*	*	*	*	*	*	*	*
10	*	*	*	*	*	*	*	*	*	*	*
11	#	#	#	#	*	*	*	*	*	*	*
12	#	#	#	#	*	*	*	*	*	*	*
15	#	A	*	*	*	*	*	A	*	A	A
20	A	A	*	*	*	*	*	*	*	*	*
21	*	*	*	*	*	*	*	*	*	*	*
22	#	A	*	*	*	*	*	#	*	#	#
23	*	*	*	*	*	*	*	*	*	*	*
24	#	#	*	*	*	*	*	*	*	*	*
25	#	#	*	*	*	*	*	*	*	*	*
26	#	*	*	*	*	*	*	*	*	*	*
28	#	#	*	*	*	*	*	*	*	*	*
29	*	*	*	*	*	*	*	*	*	*	*
30	#	#	#	#	*	*	*	*	*	*	*
31	#	#	#	#	*	*	*	*	*	*	*
32	#	#	#	*	*	*	*	*	*	*	*
33	#	A	*	*	*	*	*	*	*	*	*
34	#	#	#	#	*	*	*	*	*	*	*

326. Components of the Mk4/L2A3 Trigger Assembly, numbered as in fig 155, showing interchangeability with all other Patchett and Sterling Marks.

= Mk4/L2A3 part not interchangeable

A = Mk4/L2A3 part could easily be modified to fit

* = Mk4/L2A3 part fully interchangeable.

The Butt Assembly

Part No	Proto-type	MkI	MkII L2A1	MkIII L2A2	Mk4 L2A3	Mk4 PC	Mk5 L34A1	Mk6 Carbine	Mk7A Pistol	Mk7C Pistol	Mk8 Gun
1	#	#	#	#	*	*	*	*	#	#	*
2	#	#	#	#	*	*	*	*	#	#	*
3	#	#	#	#	*	*	*	*	#	#	*
4	#	#	*	*	*	*	*	*	#	#	*
5	#	#	#	#	*	*	*	*	#	#	*
6	#	#	A	A	*	*	*	*	#	#	*
7	#	#	#	#	*	*	*	*	#	#	*
8	#	#	#	#	*	*	*	*	#	#	*
9	#	#	#	#	*	*	*	*	#	#	*
10	#	#	#	#	*	*	*	*	#	#	*
11	#	#	#	#	*	*	*	*	#	#	*
12	#	#	#	#	*	*	*	*	#	#	*
13	N/A										
14	A	*	*	*	*	*	*	*	#	#	*
15	#	#	#	#	*	*	*	*	#	#	*
16	N/A										
17	A	*	*	*	*	*	*	*	#	#	*
18	#	A	*	*	*	*	*	*	#	#	*

327. Components of the Mk4/L2A3 Butt Assembly, numbered as in fig 171, showing interchangeability with all other Patchett and Sterling Marks.

# = Mk4/L2A3 part not interchangeable
A = Mk4/L2A3 part could easily be modified to fit
* = Mk4/L2A3 part fully interchangeable
N/A= not applicable.

The Three Series Modifications

The trusty little Sterling sub-machine guns never gave much trouble in service. In fact there were only three series modifications throughout its service life, from 1954 (or thereabouts) to date.

I: Replacing Fixed Foresights with Adjustable Foresights

The first Series Modification originated from the Sterling engineers, at the insistence of the Army Procurement Executive. Dated March 1960, this was to officially remove the remaining fixed foresights from those guns fitted with them and replace them with the adjustable-for-height foresight numbered B3/1005-99-960-0047.

The foresight was retained in place laterally by friction but vertically by a 4BA $\times$ $^{1}/_{16}$″ Allen grubscrew. The modification was classed as priority group 'B', which basically means that when it needs doing, do it!

As a result, thousands of Mk4/L2A3 guns remained in Service with an old-pattern fixed foresight.

II: Arctic Sling Loops and Quick Release Attachment

The second Series Modification came about as a result of a requirement to use the gun under arctic warfare conditions. This instruction detailed the fitting of a loop to the butt plate, No5 rifle fashion, and a corresponding anchor loop and quick release attachment to the top of the gun casing. There was no priority rating for this modification as it was only to be fitted to weapons "… as detailed by the Ministry of Defence".

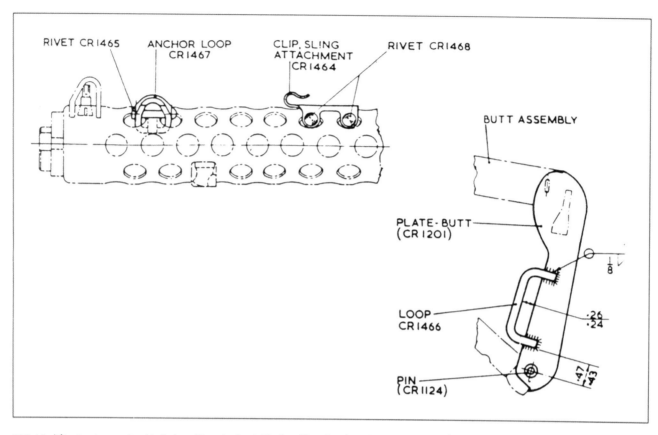

328. Modification Instruction No 2: Installing the Arctic Warfare Sling Brackets. Dimensions in inches.
   This was a little-used and thus quite uncommon modification, only fitted upon instruction from the Ministry of Defence. (MoD Army, REME)

III: Strengthening the Butt Yoke

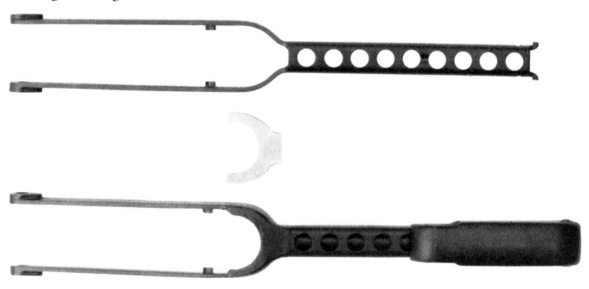

329. Top view of two Mk4/L2A3 butt frames.
   Above: unmodified standard, as originally issued on military guns.
   Centre: Ordnance-supplied strengthening plate. Below: stock with strengthening plate welded in yoke.
   The UK Military were the only users of this most effective feature.
   This modification was the third of only three instigated during the gun's hard 39 years of Service life (from 1956 to 1994). (MoD Army, REME)

The third Series Modification, dated 1972, was the last made to the L2 series in UK Military service. The object was to strengthen the flimsy butt at the area where the butt frame forms the 'U'-shape called the yoke.

A shaped strengthening plate was welded in place. This does the job admirably and does not affect the operation of the gun or the folding butt. However, once this plate is fitted, the butt cannot be folded while the trigger guard is reversed in its arctic position.

Once again, it was priority rating 'B', which required it to be done only when the need arose. It was therefore quite common to see unmodified guns 20 years after the date of this instruction.

James Edmiston in his superb book The Sterling Years implies that this was a Sterling improvement for UK Military guns which differed from commercial guns. In fact, the Military guns were ISSUED with the commercial butts, but were modified in Service later. After this modification came into effect, when the UK Military ordered butts as replacement spares, Ordnance stores supplied the strengthening plates for Sterling to weld in place before finishing the butts. The UK Military were the only users of these strengthened butt frames.

... And Four Miscellaneous Instructions

There were several Miscellaneous Instructions issued for the Sterling, and four deserve mention:

The first is Miscellaneous Instruction number 3, issued in late 1973, which details the conversion of unserviceable L2A3 guns to L49A1 Drill Purpose (DP) specification. Full details of this conversion and the L49A1 gun are given below.

Miscellaneous Instruction number 4 details a repair policy to the usually pre-assembled trigger mechanism, whereby Armourers can totally strip this sealed unit to effect economic repairs.

Repairs to Damaged Magazines

Miscellaneous Instruction number 5 details the repair to damaged magazine lips, thought to be responsible for the majority of misfeeds and subsequent breech explosions.

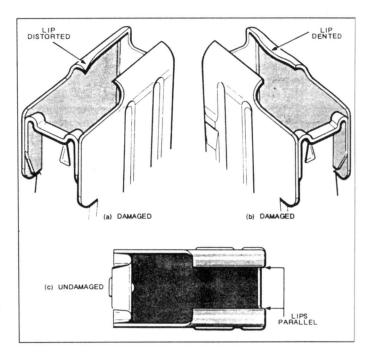

330. Inspection of magazine feed lips. Damaged feed lips were reputed to be responsible for the majority of breech explosions, although mercifully, in Peter Laidler's experience, these were very seldom encountered .
Top row: damaged.
Below: undamaged.

Instruction No 6: Repairing Worn Butt Trunnions

As mentioned in Chapter Seven, Miscellaneous Instruction number 6 details a none-too-successful method of using a compression tool to repair end play on worn butt trunnions, by ring punching the holes to take up this wear. The horrendous butt trunnion compression tool was taught to Armourer apprentices, used once or twice in Service and then promptly forgotten about. A repair to the butt trunnion using this method could only be undertaken once before the butt frame had to be scrapped.

Improvements in Repairing Worn Butt Trunnions

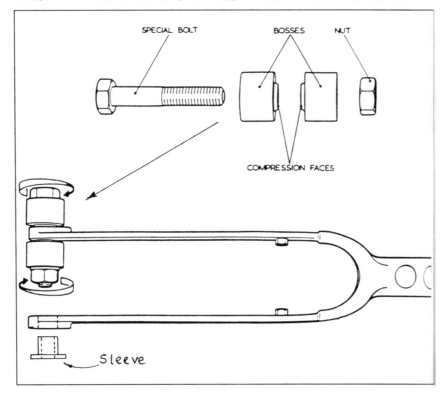

SPECIAL BOLT   BOSSES   NUT

COMPRESSION FACES

Sleeve

331 (right). Two views of the compression tool supplied by REME Technical Branch. Used in conjunction with Miscellaneous Instruction no 6, to eliminate end-to-end play in the butt frame. This repair could only be effected once before the butt frame became unserviceable.

Above: tool in parts form.

Below: tool as fitted to the butt frame. (MoD Army, REME)

When it came to repairing worn butt trunnions, there were a couple of better methods. One was to simply silver solder a washer to the trunnion block on the butt frame. You then reamed this out to size. That solved the end-to-end play. Side play was then cured by filing the thickness of the washers down until the retaining pin held the butt closely to the trunnion on the gun body.

Armourers soon discovered that by silver soldering a washer with a smaller inside diameter onto the lugs, making it off to give the .020″ side play and then drilling out the centre to .310″, any end–play was eliminated. A case of killing two birds with one stone.

Peter Laidler learned an even more successful method from New Zealand Armourers while serving at the Northern Ordnance Depot at Ngaruawahia. New Zealand Armourers would drill the butt frame holes oversize, then sweat (an English term for soft solder) in place brass inserts previously reamed to the size of the casing trunnions. To cure side play, they filed the width of the brass insert to allow the retaining pin to hold the butt close to the gun body. Both methods worked equally well. A departure from the official line but done with the best of intentions while making the best use of resources, AND saving valuable parts.

Of EMERs, AESPs, and VAOS

The above are those modifications and repair instructions listed in the Armourers' bible, the Electrical and Mechanical Engineering Regulations, known to us as simply the 'EMERs' (pronounced eemers, as in reamers without the 'r').

Recently, EMERs have been replaced by Army Equipment Support Publications. Even so, AESPs will be referred to as EMERs for many, many years to come. (The initials AESP don't roll off the tongue as easily as EMER, do they?)

The EMER section dealing with the Mk4/L2A3 is *Small Arms and Machine Guns, E 730-739*. For the Mk5/L34A1, the relevant EMER is E 740-749. Additional equipment relating to the guns can be found within section B3 of the Vocabulary of Army Ordnance Stores (referred to as the VAOS list). As apprentices we were told that this stood for Various Army Odds and Sods, and VAOS is still referred to as the "odds and sods list"!

Theory vs Practice

The small 'Pin, locking, butt retaining pin', (shown in the Mk4/L2A3 parts list as item 19), was a masterpiece of frustration for the Armourer. It was supposed to line up EXACTLY with the corresponding holes in the butt trunnion AND the 'Pin, retaining butt' (Mk4/L2A3 parts list, item 18). It never, or very rarely, did. Most Armourers' shops had a $^1/_{16}''$ drill, brazed to the end of a 7″ length of steel rifle cleaning rod. We could then drill the pins out. Assembly was just as bad! If the hole in the butt trunnions didn't line up EXACTLY with the hole in the butt retaining pin, NOTHING would get the locking pin into place. Once again, we would use the lengthened drill to line-bore the holes.

Another ploy was to just enlarge the hole in the butt retaining pin. This would ensure that the holes lined up, by fair means or foul.

Malayan Army Armourers discarded the thin locking pin and used commercially available 'R'-shaped spring clips, after they had line-bored the holes. If you do chance to see one of these thin locking pins replaced with a split pin, then you can be assured. that this was another ploy used by a frustrated REME Armourer.

However, most features of the Sterling were well thought out. For instance, the extractor, tripping lever, backsight axis and trigger frame pins were all made from .125″ diameter steel bar. It was quite a simple matter to use (as an example) a shortened backsight axis pin as a tripping lever pin, if the correct part was not available. The interchangeable trigger and sear axis pins were both thoughtfully made from .250″ diameter bar in order to reduce wear.

Notes on Barrels in Service

Barrels were extremely tough and long lasting. Barrels that were pitted or showed signs of corrosion but were reasonably bright were perfectly acceptable, providing that the .345″ gauge passed through and the .351″ gauge was rejected. In the event of any doubt, the Armourers would range-test a gun. If it grouped well, then the barrel wear was acceptable.

Range testing usually took place on a Friday morning, when a few guns had gathered together. All the Armourers present would pool their spare cash. Then, overlooking all the usual range procedures and rules, they would have a shooting competition. The winner (normally Peter Smallwood) took the cash and being a Friday, the Sergeant (Gerry Young) would send all off early for the weekend! Being an Armourer certainly had its perks.

Restamping Faint Fazakerley Serial Numbers

Armourers found that Fazakerley guns had the serial numbers (prefixed with UF) electro-pencilled in. This was a very shallow form of engraving and soon became illegible. There was a system operating whereby a new serial number (prefixed by the letters SA-) could be allocated, but we usually identified the correct serial number through the unit War Office Controlled Stores register (the woes Books). We would then stamp the number into the magazine housing, taking care not to dent it. We all had a mandrel to straighten magazine housings. Dented casings could also be straightened, using a suitably sized mandrel.

Guns that were well used would have the sear/sear cradle axis pin hole elongated by the constant hammering of the breech block onto the nose of the sear as the gun resumed the 'cocked and ready' position. This resulted in a rough trigger pull-off, or no pull-off at all in some cases. As described in Chapter Nine, a two-part repair procedure was devised by Diemaco, Inc for the Canadian version of this problem.

If the breech block were not cleaned properly after firing, a ring caused by the mercuric percussion cap compound would form on the breech face. This was deemed acceptable unless it was ringed to the extent that gas escape would occur. In reality, unless it was really bad, it was acceptable.

All-in-all, the Sterling was supremely reliable. In cases where damage to the gun was caused by neglect or misuse we would ask the user to come into the Armourers' shop where we would advise him of the error of his ways. On the other hand, if he came in via the NAAF1 shop with a selection of tea, coffee, milk and sugar, then the matter was quickly forgotten after being discussed over a cup of coffee!

Proving the Casing the Hard Way

As mentioned, during early MkIII production it had been realised that proofing the casing *per se* was not necessary. The strength of the casing has been proven many times since, in action and in accident, some of the latter avoidable.

Peter Laidler witnessed just such an avoidable accident on the range one day, as an impatient corporal was supervising recruits firing the L2A3 for the first time. After a series of misfeeds, a recruit kept his gun facing downrange and put his hand up, as instructed. The NCO took the gun by the pistol grip in his right hand, pulled the trigger and rammed the breechhome with his left thumb, without taking time to discover the ruptured case stuck in the chamber. The breech block duly tried to chamber anew round, and, due to the additional force imparted by the corporal's thumb, immediately fired it while the cartridge was only partially supported within the breech.

A breech explosion occurred, the breech block recoiling faster than the corporal could react His left thumb was broken by the cocking handle, and his left palm was peppered with the sharp remains of the brass case that exploded through the ejection port. The receiver was undamaged.

While the errant instructor was sitting in the Land Rover being patched up by our para-medic prior to being sent to the local hospital, he offered every excuse in the book except his own impatience and recklessness. It was quietly pointed out to him that, if he said nothing, the rest of the Armourers/instructors would say nothing, thereby saving face all round and saving him the customary financial penalty meted out by the Company Commander for causing a negligent discharge.

Of course, there was the question of a crate of beer for the Armourers to be taken into account …

As for the gun, after a quick examination the fault was found. The gun was stripped; cleaned, and used for the rest of the day without another mishap.

Approaching the End: Avoiding 'ZF' (Condemned) Status

Foresight protectors and finger guards were provided to effect repairs, but these, like the rearsight block, had to be replaced with care. Peter Macdonald and 'Tiny' Davidson, both ex-Carlisle apprentices, had a small stock of rearsight housings obtained from Sterling. As required, these were brazed onto needy gun casings. However, if the casing was allowed to get too hot, there was a real danger that it would distort.

Once distorted, the casing would never resume its original shape. The only answer then was to 'ZF the gun. 'ZF' is the REME Armourer's term for "Condemned-to be Reduced to Scrap".

Another fault that would condemn a gun to ZF status was a worn cocking handle slot, which would allow the breech block to rotate in the casing. As a result, the breech block feed horns would foul the ejector, which would result in mis-feeds or misfires. A missing bayonet mounting standard was another fault that was supposed to ZF an otherwise serviceable gun, although we generally ignored this as a minor fault which would not affect the functioning of the gun.

Treating the Silenced Mk5/L34A1 with Respect

The Mk5/L34A1 performed in the same tough and reliable way, but it had to be treated with respect. If the long silencer casing was knocked or dropped, there was a real danger that the hole in the muzzle end-cap would no longer align with the hole in the barrel, with dire results.

REME Armourers had an alignment gauge (locally made to Sterling specifications; fig 363) that would align the bore and the spiral diffuser with the silencer end cap.

Normally, barrels and breech blocks manufactured as spare parts were proofed in specially-made and quite ingenious slave jigs. A barrel or block was quickly slipped into place, proof fired, and removed. The vented Mk5 barrel posed a different problem! This was solved by firing it from a jig covered with a protective sleeve.

Armourer's Tricks for Easier Shipping and Cleaning

One drawback with the Mk5/L34A1 is that there is naturally a buildup of carbon within the interior of the silencer casing. This means that detailed stripping is required after every 1,500 rounds or at six monthly intervals, whichever is sooner. If the carbon deposits are baked on hard, it requires a cold-working, acid paint remover to remove them. Others found that a small bottle of vinegar did the same trick! Armourers soon found that if the parts were first liberally coated with graphite grease 'XG340', then subsequent stripping, cleaning and assembling was a whole lot easier. Assembling the gun was a specialised task, and the Electrical and Mechanical Engineering Regulations EMERs) HAVE to be followed. Over tightening the tie rods can cause the outer casing to move out of line with the path of the barrel and, subsequently, the bullet; although it would take a considerable amount of overtightening for this to occur. For this reason, the long concentricity gauge was employed. If the gauge centred after assembly, then invariably everything was in order.

The REAR tie rod hexagonal nuts are tightened equally to 12 lbs/in, and the FRONT tie rod nuts are tightened equally to 17 .5 lbs/in. It should be emphasised that these torque readings are in POUNDS PER INCH.

Sterling also offered a magnificent Armourers kit (fig 363) which contained all the tools necessary to overhaul the Mk5/L34A1 in a field workshop.

Users were not permitted to strip the silencer unit in order to clean it. Once it was totally gummed up, the user would usually ask one of the arms storemen (who were always on good terms with the Armourers anyway) to bring it to the Armourers shop under some other pretext where we would have the dirty job of stripping it.

Stripping a really badly carbon-fouled gun usually sheared the tie rods, or snapped the tie rod nuts. If you were really unlucky,the tie rod nuts would seize onto the tie rods. Then, regardless of the presence of lock-nuts, the tie rods would unscrew themselves from the brass barrel supporting plate.

Once that happened you really had your hands full, because removal of the spiral diffuser, tie rods and nuts, end cap, extension tube and foresight mount could only be achieved by drilling out the three tie rods through the centre of the 3/16" hexagonal key slot in the end of the tie rod nut, destroying all three nuts and rods in the process!

The Australian Solution: Brass Tie Rod Nuts

Peter Laidler spoke to an Australian RAEME Armourer, John Dudley, about this problem. They had encountered it too, but solved it locally by making the tie rod nuts out of brass. Instead of being tightened (to 17.5 lb/INCH incidentally, which is just over finger tight and a very important torque setting for this gun) with the usual $^3/_{16}$" hexagonal key, their locally-produced nuts are slotted for a screwdriver. John explained that the tie rods didn't seize in the brass barrel supporting plate, so why would they seize within brass nuts? Simple isn't it? Clever boys, these Antipodeans!

332. Two inner silencer assemblies for the Mk5/L34A1.
   Left: fitted with *brass* tie rod nuts.
   Right: fitted with steel tie rod nuts.
   Silencers inevitably became fouled with carbon, making stripping the steel nuts extremely difficult, to the point of having to destroy the three tie rods and their nuts in order to remove them. The solution was fitting tie rod nuts made of brass, to which fouling did not adhere. (MoD Army, REME)

A Few of the Usual Ordnance Snafus

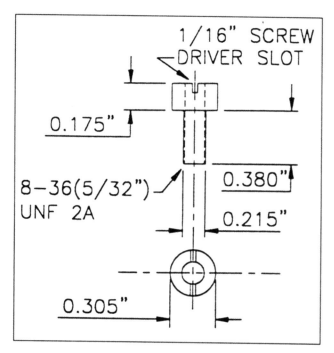

333. Dimensioned drawing of replacement brass Nut, Tie Rod (B3/1005-99-961-4097) for the Mk5/L34A1.

Material: Hard Brass. Thread: 8-36 ($^5/_{32}$") UNF 2A. (Drawing by Peter Laidler)

We know just what the Sterling engineers AND the EMERs said about how to remove the fouled carbon, but Armourers found that the best method was to liberate (a polite army term for steal) a couple of bottles of vinegar from the ration stores, then drop the carbon-fouled parts into the vinegar. After an hour or so they would emerge as bright as buttons, to be rinsed off in water,

dried, and oiled with OX18 or OX52 oil. Assembly was always with a good dose of XG 340 graphite grease.

On one occasion at Tidworth, after a Friday morning Armourers' shooting competition featuring a quantity of captured 9mm ammunition, it was found that a Mk5/L34Al return spring cap would not depress or rotate. Peter Smallwood, another Armourer, discovered that this 'hot' ammunition was even 'hotter' than the reputedly 'very hot' British Service 2Z! The recoil had caused the breech block to hit the return spring cap with such force that it had burred the return spring cap locking ring.

All in all, the Mk5/L34Al behaved admirably, and no one had any cause to complain.

A Few of the Usual Ordnance Snafus

Most spare parts were extremely well made and could be replaced with the minimum of fitting, with the exception of the butt retaining pin! It was not uncommon for Ordnance stores to supply early MkIII/L2A2 spares for Mk4/L2A3 guns. Peter Laidler recalls getting the earlier MkIII/L2A2 pistol grips and return spring caps for Mk4/L2A3 guns. In Malaya during the 1960s, he found that one side of the wooden grips issued for the No5 bayonet were the one-screw-hole variety, while the other side came as the two-screw-hole variety. Recently, a batch turned up as a NO-screw-hole variety!

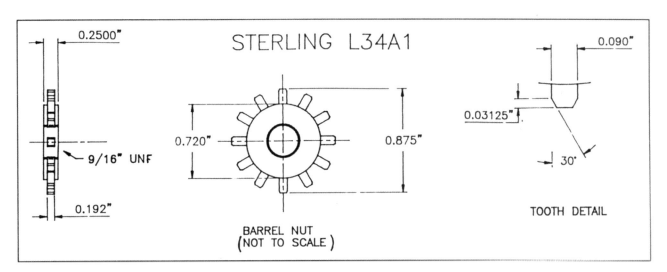

334. Dimensioned drawing of a British variation on the Australian brass tie rod nut idea: a replacement brass Nut, Barrel (B3/1005-99-961-4085) for the Mk5/L34A1 (fig 230, part no 37).

Material: Hard Brass. Thread: $^9/_{16}$"-18 UNF 2B. (Drawing by Peter Laidler)

The Little-Known "DP" Sterling

Gun, Sub-Machine, LA9A1 (Drill Purpose)

Introduction: the Need for Segregated DP Guns for Training

There has always been a need within the Armed Forces for Drill Purpose (DP) guns, the most common in British Service being the Drill Purpose Bren, No4 rifle, and more recently, the L103A1, the DP version of the current 185/SAB0.

A problem arises when serviceable guns are repeatedly used as instructional tools. REME Armourers are constantly pointing out to instructing staff that nothing is more liable to destroy a firearm more quickly than constant dry firing. Add to that the months of repeated stripping, assembling, dry range practice, stripping again, cleaning; and, to cap it all, however well-meaning, the deliberate introduction of faults for the trainees to identify and correct.

(Let That Be) A Lesson

As the Armourer at the 6th Training Battalion, Royal Army Service Corps at Yeovil, Peter Laider recalls:

I remember that the Service IA Bren guns that were used in the teaching classrooms needed constant, ongoing repairs. I even painted onto the sides of two guns "NOT FOR D P", to no avail.

The problem was only solved when the time came for the newly-trained soldiers to live-fire the guns at nearby Mere ranges. I "arranged" with my Armourer colleagues at our parent 27 Command Workshop that there would be no serviceable guns available for use on that day. Could I help out, the training staff asked? Unfortunately, I couldn't; nor could the local TA unit.

Quite soon afterwards Major Frisby, the Officer in charge of the REME detachment, had cause to mention to the Quartermaster of the RASC training unit that the fault was entirely theirs, and that furthermore, the nature of the repairs in some cases-worn body stops, barrel seatings and breech-block faces – could not be attributed to fair wear and tear. Especially not when there were DP guns available from Ordnance stores for the asking!

I wonder if the RASC (later Royal Corps of Transport and now Royal Legistical Corps) Training staff at Yeovil ever realised that it was ME who ended their war of attrition against their own Bren guns!

First DP Sub-Machine Guns: No Uniformity in Conversion

At Regiments where large-scale training is carried out with sub-machine guns, there were Drill Purpose Stens, and it was natural that a Drill Purpose L2A3 should follow.

For many years there was a supply of worn-out guns issued for that purpose. They were converted into Drill Purpose guns with no uniformity.

Standardising the LA9Al DP Conversion

As noted above, Miscellaneous Instruction No 3, issued in late 1973, detailed the conversion of unserviceable L2A3 sub-machine guns to LA9A1 Drill Purpose specification for drill (and weapon training) purposes. This instruction also applied to any L2A3 gun already converted to any previous unapproved pattern for drill purposes.

Previously unconverted guns were only to be converted to LA9A1 specification when specified by the Ministry of Defence, although those already converted to an unapproved pattern could be converted to the LA9A1 specification forthwith.

According to the Instruction, the components that were to be modified were the breech block, the barrel and the body casing. The converted gun should conform to the corresponding service weapon, EXCEPT for minor details that would require reference to gauges. It should be built up as far as possible from unserviceable components, although the degree of unserviceability of these components must not interfere with the normal functioning and handling of the gun.

The LA9A1 loads and functions with drill cartridges, and field strips in the usual manner. However, it is impossible to remove the barrel, and it is impossible to operate the gun with a serviceable, unmodified breech block. The safety and security implications of these requirements are obvious.

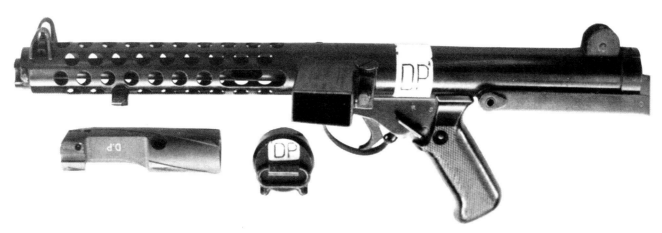

335. Right side view of the front of a 'DP' L49A1, with the casing machined away in front of the magazine housing. The white band and 'DP' marking occur on both sides of the receiver.

Note the extensive modifications to, and markings on, the breech block, and the 'DP' marked return spring cap. Converting the breech block to DP spec was a difficult process, as the material is very hard, and its shape makes it difficult to clamp and hold. (MoD Army, REME)

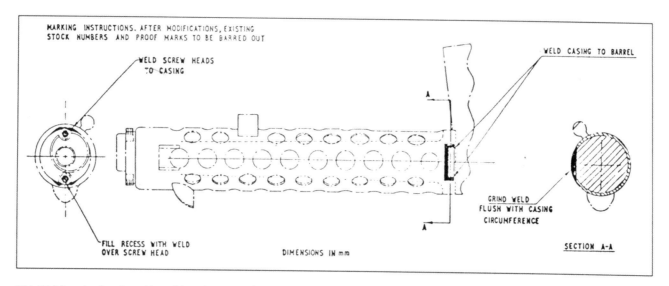

336. Welding the deactivated barrel into the gun casing.

The barrel is plugged and welded in place within the deactivated casing. (MoD Army, REME)

The Final Step: Marking the L49A1

As a final step in the L49A1 conversion the casing was painted with the usual white bands and black 'DP markings, following which all proof and stock marks were barred out, leaving the magazine housing marked: GUN/SUB MACHINE/9mm [L2A3/serial no/NATO code no barred out]/L49A1 D.P.

Drawings that relate to this conversion from L2A3 to L49A1 are shown, not that we expect a rush to convert serviceable guns to DP status. Nonetheless, the L49A1 was a tough little 'gun', and Peter Laidler cannot recall ever having had to carry out a repair due to soldiers training with it.

The L49A1 is yet another in the Sterling series which gave Sterling service.

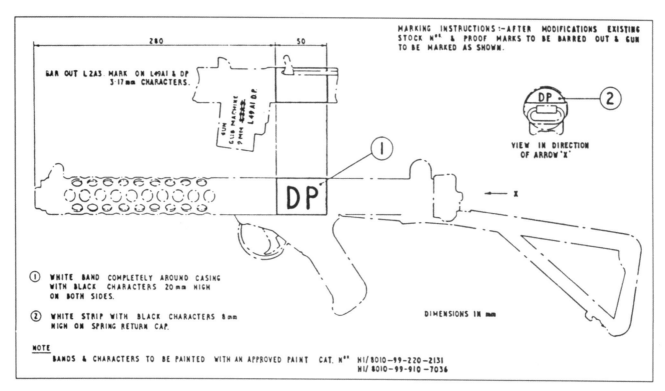

337. The final step in the DP process: the gun is marked with white bands and black characters on both sides of casing (1) and on return spring cap (2), and the erstwhile model markings and serial number are barred out and the gun remarked as shown (above, left). (MoD Army, REME)

L49A1 Interchangeability with the Mk4/L2A3

Due to the fact that the L49A1 is simply a conversion of theMk4/L2A3 gun, then by definition, all parts are fully interchangeable EX r the BARREL, which is welded into place in the L49A1 casing, and the BREECH BLOCK, which in the L49A1 has been rendered totally unserviceable. Modifications to the barrel ensure that a serviceable breech block cannot be made to fit or function.

The 'ZF' (Condemned) Process

On active service, Armourers would reduce unserviceable guns to scrap on-site with a cutting torch, then cut off the magazine housing that contained the gun serial number. This would accompany the necessary paperwork, a form AFG-1043A, to Ordnance stores where a replacement would be issued. In peacetime, the whole gun would be returned to Ordnance stores, where a fate such as that shown above awaited.

338. Truly the unkindest cut. An unserviceable Sterling Mk4/L2A3 is 'ZF'ed: destroyed with the cutting torch and reduced to certified scrap after reaching the end of its remarkable 39-year life.

   Left: the barrel and front of the casing are first cut off.

Right: the magazine housing area with serial number is then cut away, to be handed in as proof of destruction. (MoD REME, BOD Donnington)

Chapter Sixteen

Accessories and Ancillaries

The Bayonet

Settling on the Detachable Bayonet

As discussed in Chapter Four, before the MkII Patchett was adopted as the L2A1 in 1953, much discussion to place as to whether this gun would or would not need provision for a bayonet At length the decision was taken to require a bayonet for the new sub-machine gun. Trials soon established that folding bayonets were prone to inherent weaknesses, and it was decided that the bayonet that would be adopted would be DETACHABLE.

Additionally, the muzzle mounting ring would have to clear the central barrel, not an easy task with a 9mm bore within a 1.5″-diameter gun casing, without a LARGE cross-piece ring.

Fitting the No5 Rife Bayonet

Thus, during 1944, the engineers at Sterling were suddenly faced with having to design another bayonet especially for the Patchett. There was talk at the time that the .303 Service No5 rifle was to be adopted as the standard rifle in the British Army. This talk was pure speculation, and the rifle did not get past the last (or FIRST, depending on one's point of view!) hurdle, BUT, there were a LOT of No5 bayonets in the armouries of the British Army worldwide, and in Ordnance Depots within the UK. Happily, the design specification stated that the bayonet "… should be the type fitted presently to the No5 rifle".

This bayonet was almost made for the Patchett. The late MkI guns COULD be made to accept the No5 bayonet, but it was touch and go. The muzzle ring JUST cleared the barrel. On the MkII/L2A1, the Sterling engineers mounted the bayonet standard about .1″ closer to the barrel casing and moved the .9″ bayonet/muzzle boss the same .1″ in towards the centre line of the casing. This meant that the bayonet muzzle ring could safely clear the bullet path.

339. Two types of No5 rifle bayonet grips.

Above: early (one screw). This was not a success. Once used as a knife, the grips twisted and rotated about the single screw, and cracked.

Below: later (two screw). With the grip attachment problem cured, this bayonet became one of the best and most collectable in the world. (Courtesy Roger Smith)

Touch-and-Go with Wooden Grips

All was fine with the bayonets in use at the time, which were fitted with Tufnol grips. When the time came to fit a Service bayonet to the gun, sightly bulkier wooden grips were the order of the day, and these fouled the casing. A solution was readily found, and from that day a .1″-deep section of metal was machined from the body casing between the bayonet standard and the muzzle, leaving a small flat (fig 362) which JUST clears the wooden grips on the No5 bayonet when fitted. Next time you see one with a bayonet fitted, look to see how touch-and-go it really was!

Commercial Manufacture of the No 5 Bayonet

Supplies of bayonets for use by the UK Ministry of Defence was no problem, they had over 316,000 in stores in the UK and elsewhere. Initially, many of these were supplied to foreign buyers of Sterling guns but in the mid 60's, Sterling had to look to private manufacturers in order to continue supplying bayonets with its guns.

These 'commercial' bayonets were supplied by Hopkinson and Sons, of Sheffield. Sterling made the pommel, screws, catch, spring and nut, and bought in the crossguard from the ex-UK Military contractor of that component. Hopkinson assembled these parts to their fine steel blades. The blades of these bayonets are marked 'STERLING'.

As for the scabbards, Sterling purchased the bodies and mouthpieces from Accles & Pollock, makers of the Sterling SMG casing, and assembled and finished the scabbards themselves.

Sterling issued a one-page brochure on the No5 bayonet, which described the Sterling-made No5 bayonet, as follows:

… Apart from its combat and deterrent uses when it is fitted to the weapon, it is an excellent survival, hunting and general purpose knife.

Length, bayonet and scabbard	*12.5 in*	*31.75cm*
Length, bayonet	*11.6 in*	*28.70cm*
Length, blade	*7.7 in*	*19.55cm*
Length, handle	*3.7 in*	*9.40cm*
Weight, bayonet and scabbard	*1 lb*	*.45kg*
Weight, bayonet	*10.5 oz*	*.30kg*

The introduction of lost-wax casting methods eliminated many machining operations in the manufacture of these bayonets.

340. The bayonet, No5 MkI, as used on the Mk4/L2A3 Sterling SMG. Shown below is the scabbard, No5, which was used with both the No5 bayonet and the L1A3 bayonet, as used on the L1A1 rifle (C1 bayonet on C1 rifle in Canada). (Courtesy Sterling Archives)

Component Parts of the No5 MkI Bayonet and Scabbard

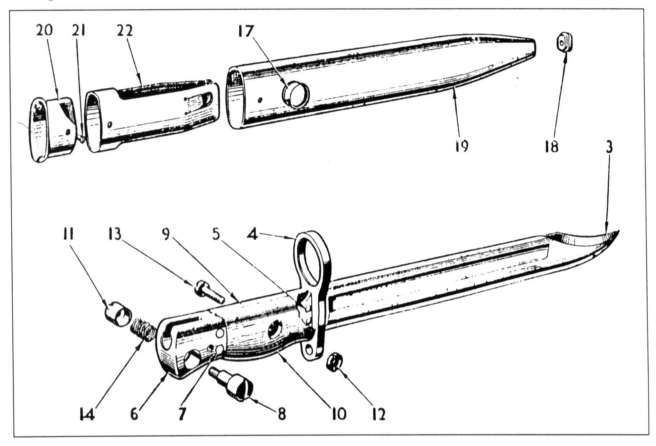

341. From an early (pre-NATO NSN) Illustrated Parts List for the Bayonet and Scabbard, Nk5 MkI as used with the L2A3. The nomenclature is given, below and on the next page.

The bayonet shown is the early pattern with the single grip screw. These single-screw grips (BB-5874 left and 5875 right) were quite common but once the bayonet was used as a knife and twisted, the tops of the wooden grips would split. This was quickly rectified by replacing the single-screw grips with double-screw grips. Alas, the double-hole grips were given the same part numbers as the single-hole grips! A demand for 10 pairs of grips could result in 10 left SINGLE hole grips, and 10 right DOUBLE hole grips, The problem was only rectified once all the single hole grips had been consigned to the bin.

The No5 MkI scabbard was also used with the No7, No9, and L1A1 series of bayonets.

Item	Designation	Part No	No Off
1	Bayonet, No5 MkI	BA5869	1
2	Blade (Assembly)	BB 5870	1
3	Blade	BJ 0091	1
4	Crosspiece	BJ 0092	1
5	Rivet, securing, crosspiece	BJ 0093	2
6	Pommel	BJ 0094	1
7	Rivet, securing, pommel	BJ 0095	2
8	Bolt	BB 5871	1
9	Grip, left	BB 5874	1
10	Grip, right	BB 5875	1
11	Nut, bolt	BB 5872	1

Item	Designation	Part No	No Off
12	Nut, grip	BB 5877	1
13	Screw, grip	BB 5876	1
14	Spring, bolt	BB 5873	1
15	Scabbard, Bayonet, No5 MkI	BA5878	1
16	Body	BB 5879	1
17	Button	BJ 0096	1
18	Tip	BJ 0097	1
19	Tube	BJ 0098	1
20	Mouthpiece	BB 5880	1
21	Screw, instrument head, BA No 6 × ¼ in shorten to 3/16 in	Z2/ZB 11037	1
22	Spring	BB 5881	1

British Military Variations

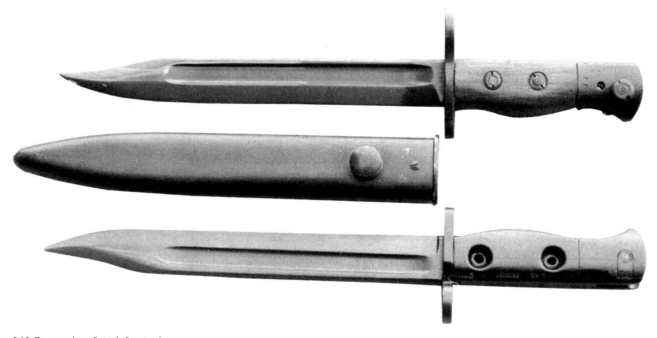

342. Two modern British Service bayonets.
   Above: the Bayonet, No5 MkI, as used with the L2 Sterling SMG.
   Centre: the Scabbard, No5 MkI, common to the No5, No7, No9 and L1A1 bayonet types.
   Below: the Bayonet, L1A3, as used on the L1A1 rifle. Interchangeable with the Canadian C1 bayonet.
   Note the different distances between the screws of the No5 type and the rivets of the L1A3.
   Later Sterling contract bayonets (fig 304) were hybrids using L1A3 blades with metal grips, but with large-ring No5 crosspieces fitted. (MoD Army, REME)

As issued with the L2A3 in the UK Military, bayonets took several different forms. Some were supplied with hard plastic/Paxolin grips rivetted in place while others were hybrids made from L1A3 (L1A1 rifle) bayonet BLADES, fitted with the larger diameter No5 crosspiece and pommel. The latter bayonets can be immediately identified by the cheaper pressed steel grips held in place with hollow 'aerorivets', the distance between the centres of the rivets being different than those of the No5 bayonet with wooden grips and grip screws.

Scabbards were supplied in tube form from Accles and Pollock Ltd and Sterling assembled them with mouthpieces, retaining springs and screws.

With the adoption of the L1A1 rifle and bayonet for UK Military service in 1957, Sterling took the opportunity to supply the UK Military with the necessary scabbards, too! Later, Hopkinson also supplied the UK Ministry of Defence with No5 Bayonets to augment their own diminishing stocks.

A full selection of the variables likely to be encountered can be found in *British and Commonwealth Bayonets* by Skennerton and Richardson.

After 50 years of 'Sterling' service, the No5 bayonet has gone into history as being probably the best looking of all the bayonets ever issued worldwide, highly desired by collectors. Many Armourers kept a couple in their tool boxes as a sort of currency!

If You Need a Bayonet on a Sub-Machine Gun, You Really DO Need a Bayonet!

Most Armourers, and others who have not seen real hand-to-hand, close-quarters fighting, would question the need for a bayonet on a sub-machine gun. However, with the hurried but limited issue of MkI "Troop Trials 101" Patchetts to the King's Shropshire Light Infantry, for combat testing in Korea, when the fighting got tough AND at close quarters, they thanked the designers at Sterling (and Enfield) for the bayonets available to be fitted to their Sterlings and Mk5 Stens. And when most things simply froze up, the Stens and Sterlings carried on working.

The Magazines

From 1942 to 1950, the magazine offered with the Patchett was the standard Sten or Lanchester item. If the Achilles' heel of the Sten was the magazines (and e housing), then there is no point whatsoever in putting the same heel onto a pair of new shoes!

Enough has been written about the Sten magazine to fill several volumes. The Lanchester magazine was even worse. The first six or so bullets were not too difficult to load, the next six were difficult, the next six were thumb-breaking, and the remainder were nigh on impossible.

Two types of magazine loaders were subsequently introduced, which made loading less difficult (note the term "less difficult" rather than "easier"). Filling a Sten magazine, with or without the loader, was never easy, nor could you load one in a hurry. (Mention has already been made of the surprise awaiting anyone determined enough to load 50 rounds into a Lanchester magazine!)

Patchett Improves the Single-Feed Sten Magazine

George Patchett initially set about improving the Sten magazine by developing a platform incorporating a single roller in place of the top step of the existing platform. This failed because as the single roller rotated against the internal side wall of the magazine, it tended to roll the cartridge seated against it in the opposite direction. In turn this cartridge tried to rotate the NEXT cartridge, in the opposite direction. This worked while well with lubricated cartridges, but these with their associated problems of extreme pressure and smoke are not conducive to good small arms design. Still, the roller idea was sound in principle.

George Patchett's next step was to modify the platform-so that both the top and bottom steps were rollers. The problem here was that the mouth of the Sten magazine starts to take on a quite severe taper from .85″ (across the rear edge) to .35″ (feed lips), all within a distance of about .45″. The reason for this taper is to allow the double-stacked cartridges to centralise as they form up in the mouth of the magazine, ready to feed from the single feed position.

A double roller platform, as we now know it, could not operate in this tapered area UNLESS the roller platform was allowed to articulate upon a separate lower platform. Clearly, this posed a whole new series of problems.

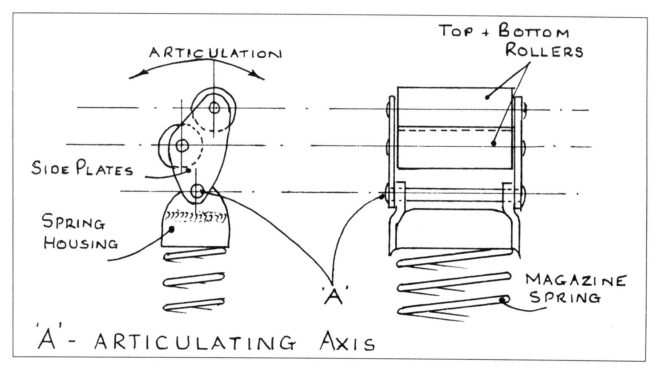

343. A sketch, not to scale, of George Patchett's articulating Sten magazine platform, based on contemporary Ordnance Board Procs.

The Prototype and MkI Patchetts used Sten and Lanchester magazines, the only real option while Britain was at war. As discussed in the text, Patchett found that his first attempt at improving the Sten magazine with a single roller follower was defeated by the restriction of the severe taper of the first ¾" of the single-lipped Sten magazine. He then designed this unique articulating follower, which would find its own position and thus allow the last round to feed. However, the single feed system still proved problematic.

Magazine problems were eliminated once and for all in the MkII Patchett, with its 82° magazine housing and curved 34-round magazine, the subject of two Patchett/Sterling patents (May, 1946 for the feed rollers, fig 88; March, 1952 for the side ribs and round-section magazine spring, fig 96). (Drawing by Peter Laidler)

George patented his roller feed platform system, patent number 615,471 on 6th May, 1946. He eventually abandoned the idea of using the Sten magazine casing altogether, but the roller innovation remained an extremely sound idea indeed.

Designing the Double-Feed Sterling Magazine

Because of the mechanical problems of using an articulated roller platform within the Sten magazine casing, George Patchett, ably assisted in this exercise by Bob Taylor from the Sterling tool room, set about designing the now familiar Sterling magazine.

The first thing they did was to design out the absurd single feed position, in favour of one with a dual feed. This is the method where the next round to be fed into the breech from the magazine is either in the top or bottom of the path-way of the breech block feed horns. Unlike the Sten, whose feed lips must withstand the vertical thrust of the stack of cartridges in a fully-loaded magazine, the dual feed design allows the magazine lips to be made of much thinner material. The dual feed magazines are also much easier to load: much was made in commercial Sterling literature of the advantages of being able to load the 34-round Sterling magazine completely full with only thumb pressure!

George Patchett also incorporated a twin roller platform in place of a conventional pressed steel magazine platform. This reduces friction and assists the feed. These rollers actually only contact the four (two per side) strengthening grooves, rolled into the

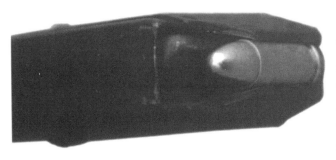

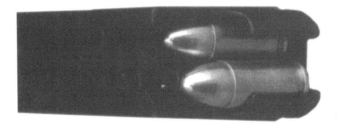

344. A comparison of single and double feed magazines, both shown loaded with Mk2Z ammunition (Sten only 1 round).

Above: the single-feed magazine, the Achilles' heel of the Lanchester, Sten, and MkI Patchett. Note the thick lips, ending in a gap not quite as wide as the cartridge. Filling the magazine to the recommended 28 rounds was virtually impossible without the aid of an accessory magazine loader.

Below: George Patchett's double feed system. The lips are much thinner, because each does not have to withstand the full vertical thrust of the stack of cartridges. They are also wider apart than the width of a cartridge, so full magazines can be loaded easily by hand, simply by laying a fresh cartridge on top of the follower or existing stack of cartridges, and pushing it straight down with the thumb.

sides of the magazine, which follow the curve round. These curvilinear grooves also guide the helical compression magazine spring, so that it cannot distort in its travel up and down the magazine.

George was also wise enough to look at the Sten magazines modified for use with the 9mm Welguns. He saw that these magazines had a small positioning hole in the rear spine. A small peg was located in this hole, which kept the magazines located firmly in place. Not one to be outdone, George soon incorporated a small anti-rattle/locating plate in the rear of his magazine, which in later production Sterling magazines was replaced with a spring (items 16/17, fig 350), which does the same job even better!

Three Different Curved Magazines for Trials

While the very first tool-room handmade examples of the curved magazine were being manufactured, the Sterling company were invited to submit three different magazines for trials. This request clearly took George Patchett by surprise, as was expressed in his letter to the Ordnance Board dated 25th June, 1946, quoted in OB Proc Q4,533 of 16 August, 1946:

We have received your letter of the 17th instant and the writer is surprised to note the proposal of Carrying out a trial of the 'Patchett' Mark II with a 20-round 'Patrol' magazine, a 40-round 'Standard' magazine and a 60-round[!] 'Assault' magazine in comparison with a Service [Sten] magazine as you had informed me that the trials would be comparative trials of several new magazines which were being developed so that they would function under sand and mud conditions.

The 'Patchett' magazines have been developed to meet this requirement and the complete set will be available for trial in about ten days ...

345. Left side closeup of early MkI1 troop trials Patchett, marked "9m/m MIC EX". The serial number has been ground out.

Note the modified magazine fitting: this gun took some sort of special experimental magazine, which has since disappeared without a trace. (MoD Pattern Room collection)

Why the 34-Round Capacity

Quite quickly it was realised that, of the three types requested, only the 40-round magazine was suitable for Service. However, there was a snag. As reported in OB Proc Q 4,644 of 1 October, 1946,

> ... of the three magazines supplied, the 40-round size would appear to be the most suitable for Service trials. It is pointed out, however, that the new basic pouch of the 1944 equipment has an internal depth of 9-¼ inches, which is approximately 1.2 inches less than the 40-round Patchett magazine. Future magazines should, therefore, be shortened accordingly and it is appreciated that this will reduce the capacity by at least 6 rounds.

There it is – the reason why Sterling magazines have a 34-round capacity!

Defending the Hand-Made Prototypes

These early toolroom magazines were hand-made, and although no example appears to exist today, the quality was remarked upon, which caused the Sterling company to write in a letter to the Ordnance Board in March, 1951:

> ... we should record that these magazines have not yet [been] tooled up for and as you are aware, we were in the course of tooling up for the MkI carbine with the [modified] straight magazine.
>
> You are well aware of the difficulties of making, by hand, magazines of our type, which are designed essentially for all parts to come off press tools. The hand made prototypes are seldom as accurate or as satisfactory as the production job.
>
> Thus, while we do not anticipate troubles from the trials, we feel it is only right to inform you that the magazines being used at the present trials are not production magazines.

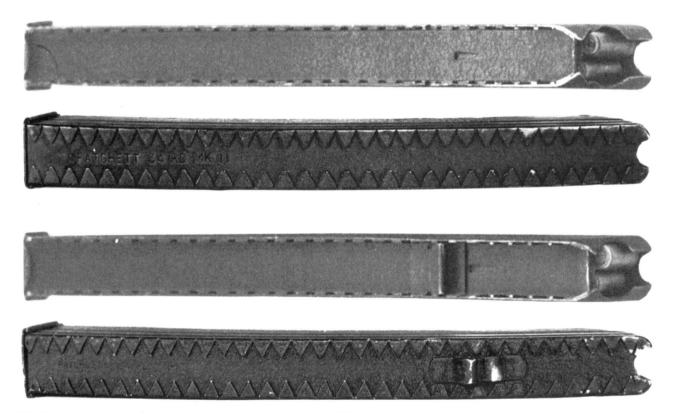

346. Front and rear views of two eary crackle finish magazines for the MkII Patchett. Note the hand-formed and brazed saw-tooth edges, and the roller followers (in front views).
  Above: earliest type known. No stop/positioning plate (front), or anti-rattle/locating plate (rear). Markings read "PATCHETT 34 RD MK II".
  Below: later example, with original stop/positioning plate (front), and anti-rattle/locating plate (rear). Markings read "PATCHETT 34 RD MK2 2". (MoD Pattern Room collection)

Short-Lived Features of Early Magazines: Saw-Tooth Edges and Crackle Paint

The first curved Sterling magazines (fig 93; fig 345) are instantly recognisable as a four-piece construction with a series of saw-tooth flanges on the top and bottom sideplates brazed to the front and rear pieces.

These magazines gave some trouble, but this was of a minor nature and was easily cured by a slight dimensional increase.

Magazines dating from about 1954 onwards are machine-made, spot welded stampings, identified by the familiar scalloped edges.

The first production 9mm Patchett curved magazines caused a certain amount of head scratching. When first used they were fine but after a while, they became loose within the magazine housings.

The problem was investigated and it was found that the thick crackle paint took up a certain amount of horizontal slack when the magazines were new, but once the paint wore off, the magazines became loose. This was easily rectified, and thereafter the magazines were phosphated and smooth-painted: crackle-painted magazines soon became a thing of the past.

The Mystery Explained: Why the Sten Won't Work with Sterling Magazines

During the period of development of the curved magazine in the early fifties, George Patchett was also wise enough to realise that whereas it is one thing to sell the guns WITH magazines, what would be the consequences of a not-so-well-off Government buyer discovering that the superb Sterling magazines also worked in his worn-out Sten guns. Loyalty lying firmly within the covers of one's chequebook, it would be a simple matter to just buy Sterling maga retrofit the Stens, instead of buying new guns AND magazines.

Patchett thus designed his magazine and gun so that whereas a Sten magazine would fit and function in a Sterling gun, the Sterling magazine would NOT fit or function in a Sten. A good sales point, knowing that for several years any newly-purchased Sterlings could operate with existing Sten magazines, but they'd have to come back for the real thing!

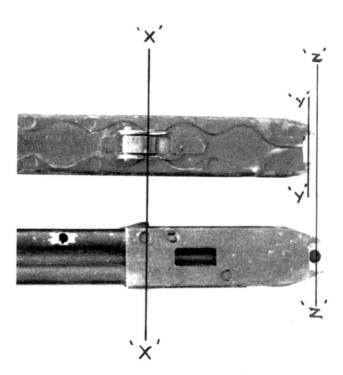

347. Rear view of two SMC magazines, marked to illustrate the reason why a Sterling will work with Sten magazines, but a Sten won't work with Sterling magazines.

  Above: production Mk4/L2A3 SMC, made by Sterling.

  Below: an early 32-round Sten.

  The line 'X' – 'X' indicates the position of both magazines when locked in their respective housings. Line 'Y' – ' Y' shows the feed position of the Sterling, and line 'Z' – 'Z' shows the feed position of the Sten, $^3/_{32}$″ further in. When positioned in the Sterling, the Sten feed position is $^3/_{32}$″ further away, but still reachable by the Sterling's more robust feed horns.

  Not so with the Sterling mag in the Sten, as the Sten feed horns abut the rear of the magazine, preventing the breech block from going forward.

The magazine catch used on the Lanchester is identical to, and interchangeable with, that of the Sterling. Lanchester and Sten magazines are also interchangeable; and Sten (and by definition Lanchester) magazines work fine in the Sterling. Why, then, won't a Sterling magazine work in a Sten?

The answer lies in the shape of the magazine lips. The Sten magazine feeds from a single central position, while the Sterling has a dual feed, and hence feeds from the top or bottom position. The Sten central feed position locates the first round slightly higher in the magazine, and thus closer to the centre line of the breech block, than the corresponding round in the Sterling magazine. To cater for this difference, the Sterling magazine is positioned $^3/_{32}''$ further into the bolt way.

While the Sten magazine fits into the Sterling, albeit $^3/_{32}''$ further away from the centre line of the breech block, the top round in the central feed position remains in line with, and can be pushed forward into the breech, by the more robust feed horns of the Sterling breech block.

This is not the case with the Sten. A Sterling magazine fitted into a Sten intrudes a further $^3/_{32}''$ into the bolt way, and attempting to fire the gun will result in the breech block fouling the rear of the magazine, which prevents it from going forward. If the Sterling magazine were to be withdrawn $^3/_{32}''$ to counteract this, it would still fail to feed, due to the fact that the top round would now be $^3/_{16}''$ out of alignment with the breech block.

There it is, the reason why the Sterling will operate with Sten magazines but the Sten will not operate with Sterling magazines.

Describing the Production Sterling Magazine

The final design emerged as the "Magazine, Sterling, 9mm, 34 Rounds". It was ready for adoption with the MkII/L2A1 Sterling in May, 1953.

The production magazine was 9.6″ long down the rear spine, .9″ deep, and 1.5″ wide, with an 18.5″ radiused curve. The commercial Sterling magazines are immediately recognisable by their corrugated, fabricated method of manufacture. On the rear spine was a spring loaded locating lug which firmly located the magazine in the housing, and eliminated all rattling. The front of the magazine was slightly recessed, showing its corrugated edges and spotwelded construction.

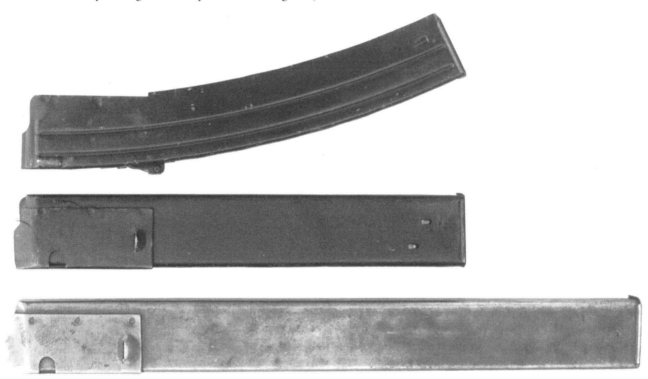

348. Bottom views of three British SMG magazines.
  Above: production 34-round Sterling L1A1, for the Mk4/L2A3. By this time the anti-rattle/locating plate (fig 346) had been redesigned into a small, flat spring, which did the job more effectively. All in all, a VERY successful and reliable magazine.
  Centre: 32-round Sten.
  Below: 50-round Lanchester.

349. Three SMG magazine platforms.
Left: the superb and virtually friction-free Sterling roller platform.
Centre: the single-position Sten platform.
Right: the longer platform for the 50-rd Lanchester magazine.
Most of these appear to have been made from bright stainless steel.

One drawback immediately became apparent. This spot-welded folded magazine had two lengths of sharp material down the front spine. Whatever you did to these front edges, in the bitter cold of Northern Europe or Korea, they always felt sharp. Be that as it may, these magazines were the only ones offered by Sterling.

The tapered magazine base-plates used on the Sterling magazines were VERY similar (but not interchangeable) with those used with the previous STEN and Lanchester magazines. All Sterling-made base plates, even those made for Sten and Lanchester magazines, are recognisable by having· the word "OFF", accompanied by a small directional arrow, stamped thereon. Quite why is a mystery because being tapered, they will only come off one way anyway! Needless to say, those made at UK Government factories did not include the word 'OFF .

Component Parts of the Bayonet, Scabbard, Sling and Magazine

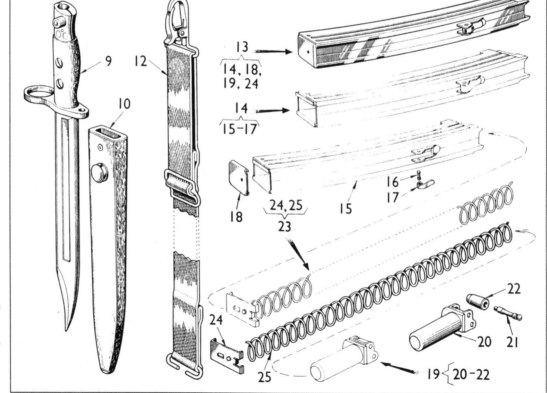

350. From a later (NATO NSN included) Illustrated Parts List for the L2A3 Accessories. From left: Bayonet and Scabbard, Nos MkI; Sling; and Magazine. The nomenclature is given below.
   Compare with fig 341: the bayonet shown here is the later pattern with double grip screws.

Item	NSN	Designation	Part/Dwg No	No Off
9	1005-99-961-7995	Bayonet, No5 MkI	DD(E) 3640	1
10	1005-99-960-0278	Scabbard, bayonet	SM54 A	1
12	1005-99-961-8468	Sling, small arms	CR 119 A	1
13	1005-99-960-0039	Magazine, round	CR 111 A	1
14	1005-99-960-0040	Case, magazine	CR 131 SA	1
15	1005-99-960-2215	Case, magazine	CR 1062	1
16	1005-99-960-2216	Pin, stop, rear	CR 1063	1
17	1005-99-960-2217	Spring, stop, rear	CR 1064	1
18	1005-99-960-2218	Plate, bottom	CR 1065	1
19	1005-99-960-0041	Platform assy	CR 132 SA	1
20	1005-99-960-2219	Platform	CR 1066	1
21	1005-99-960-2220	Pin, axis, roller	CR 1067	2
22	1005-99-960-2221	Roller, platform assy	CR 1068	2
23	1005-99-960-0042	Spring assy, magazine	CR 133 A	1
24	1005-99-960-2222	Plate, retaining	CR 1069	1
25	1005-99-960-2223	Spring, magazine	CR 1070	1

Markings on Sterling-Produced Magazines

The commercial magazines were marked along the rear spine with the wording 'MAGAZINE STERLING 9MM 34RDS' alongside George Patchett's two important patent numbers: 615,471 (roller platform;

9 May, 1946) and 692,768 (curvilinear sidewalls and round-section spring; 6 March, 1952).

The Sterling magazines supplied to the Military were identical in shape and construction but were marked: 'MAGAZINE 9MM L1A1 34 RDS' and 'STERLING-1955' (or whatever year manufactured).

Government Magazine Production

The 'X4E1' Magazine Becomes the 'L1A2'

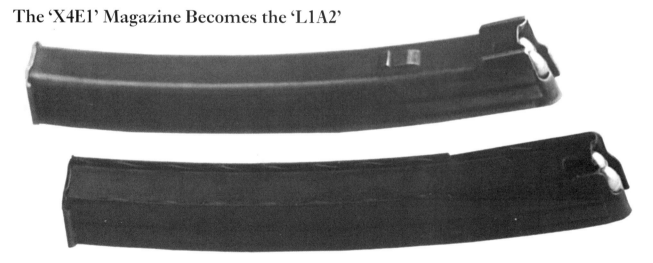

351. Two different philosophies expressed in the manufacture of magazines for the Mk4/L2A3 SMG.
   Above: stamped and electrically welded two-piece UK Government design, called the L1A2. Note the positioning lug, brazed in place, instead of the positioning notches on the front edges of the Sterling.
   Below: four-piece production Sterling design, with scalloped, spot-welded edges and sharp positioning notches on front edges.

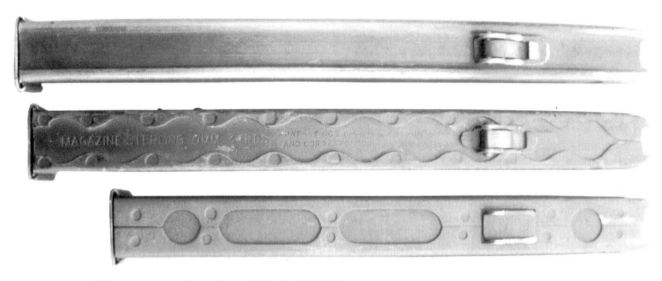

352. Rear views of three magazines, all interchangeable in the Mk4/L2A3.
   Above: 34-round ROF (Fazakerley) L1A2 magazine, which is .2″ longer than the Sterling pattern.
   Centre: 34-round scalloped-edged Sterling L1A1 magazine.
   Below: 30-round Canadian C1 SMG magazine. Note the differences in manufacture.

The Army were not keen on these uncomfortable and expensive Sterling-produced magazines. At the same time the "difficult" (to put it as mildly and diplomatically as one can) labour relations at ROF Fazakerley went a long way to ensure that the Ministry of Defence was not at all keen to have all their production facilities in one basket.

Four contracts were let to supply a "new" MoD design of magazine for the L2A3 SMG, known by the code number X4E1. The production version of the MoD design was known as the "Magazine, L1A2" to distinguish it from the Sterling product.

A total of 1,723,623 L1A2 magazines were contracted for, 227,262 from Mettoy, 309,800 from Rolls Razor with the remaining 1.2 million coming from ROF Fazakerley and Royal Laboratories, Woolwich.

Teething Problems at Rolls Razor

There were teething problems with the first Rolls Razor X4E1 magazines batch-tested in March, 1956. It was established that the magazine locating spring was not properly tempered and this was causing the magazines to be wrongly positioned in the gun. The result was that bullets were being stubbed against the barrel face. The matter was quickly resolved and the next trial batch passed.

353 (right). Markings on Government-produced L1A2 magazines. From top to bottom:
   ROF Fazakerley (Liverpool), 19 58; Mettoy (Walsall), 1958 ; Royal Laboratory (Woolwich), 1958; Rolls Razor (Cricklewood), 1957.

Markings on Government-Produced Magazines

Aside form the makers' identification and year of manufacture markings (fig 353) ; the Government magazines were additionally marked lengthways on the top surface: 'MAGAZINE 9MM L1A2' to indicate the change from the earlier Sterling L1A1 offering.

The Government-Produced L1A2 Magazine: Mysteriously .2″ Longer

L1A2 magazines from ROF Fazakerley, Rolls Razor, Mettoy and Royal Laboratories at Woolwich are immediately identifiable by their wrapped and (almost) invisible electrical seam welded construction, a method that Sterling were loath to imitate.

The sharp leading edges were eliminated, but the virtually friction-free (and patented) roller platform was retained.

The Government-made magazines were 9.8″ long down the rear spine. Quite why there is this .2″ length difference between the Sterling and the MoD pattern is a mystery. Except for the actual casing, the magazines are identical in all other respects, and both use the same internal components.

By definition, the Sterling magazines, having separate front and rear edges, have no rough areas that the magazine platform could possibly rub against; a point forgotten with the introduction of the ROF Radway Green-made magazines for the SABO weapon system that was eventually to replace the Sterling L2 guns in UK Military Service!

Suit for Patent Infringements on Sterling Guns, but NOT on Magazines

While Sterling had successfully sued the UK Government for breech of patent rights over the Fazakerley manufacture of the Mk4 SMG, they did not undertake a similar task in respect of their magazines. The reason might be that, although the Fazakerley, Rolls Razor, Royal Laboratories and Mettoy magazines are similar, they were dissimilar enough to make successful litigation unlikely. However, there is no doubt that George Patchett's

patents were breached by the Government L1A2 magazine production programme.

The Sterling Magazine in Service

Like the trusty Sterling guns, these magazines very rarely cause any concern. Providing that they are reasonably well cared for, they seldom fail. It was quite common to see magazines marked 'STERLING 1955' or 'F56' still in service, indicating their longevity.

The feed lips must be undamaged and parallel. In this regard it has been said that the commercial Sterling 4:-p art magazines were stronger than the 2-part MoD pattern. In Peter Laidler's experience with the guns, from 1964 to 1994, both were equally tough and reliable, with nothing to choose between them. It was common practice to clean the inside of the magazines with the Bren gun magazine cleaning bristle brush, and lightly oil them with the Bren gun gas cylinder mop.

Commercial "Twin Stacked" Magazines

354. Rear view of three Sterling "Twin stacked" magazines. From top: 2 × 10 round; 2 × 15 round; 2 × 34 round.

Sterling "Twin stacked" magazines were introduced along with the Mk7 'Pistols' in 1983. Customers could order any configuration of the available 10, 15 or 34 round magazines, permanently attached together. (MoD Pattern Room collection)

In 1983, along with the introduction of the Mk7 Pistols, Sterling offered both 10- and 15-round capacity magazines as accessories, in addition to the standard 34-round model. The 10- and 15-round magazines were simply shortened 34 round magazines. As these guns were advertised for use in very close-quarters situations and for use by tank and armoured vehicle crews, such magazines were deemed necessary.

Additionally, these magazines were also available "Twin stacked". This "Twin stack" mode simply formalised the age-old tradition started by Commandos and Paratroopers of joining two magazines together, tip-to-toe, with tape. In the case of the Sterling "Twin stack", however, the two magazines were permanently attached to one another.

The Australian F1 SMG and (Sterling) Magazine

After the success of the Owen series of guns with the Commonwealth forces fighting in Malaya and elsewhere within Southeast Asia, the Australians were actively looking for a tough and sturdy replacement for their ageing Owens.

As noted earlier, an Australian representative was present as an observer during the Sub-Machine Gun Steering Committee meetings held between November, 1956 and October, 1959. He was impressed with the results of the UK-Canadian co-operation and the resulting Canadian C1 SMG, although he said that the Australians were still happy with their refurbished Owen guns, for the time being anyway.

After studying a solitary Mk4 gun, bayonet and six magazines, purchased in 1962, the gun the Australians settled on was called "Gun, Sub-Machine, 9mm F1". Once again, this gun utilised the tried-and-tested Owen top feed position, although this time the Australians utilised the Sterling L1A1 and L1A2 magazines, whose reliability with British, New Zealand and Malayan forces operating in the jungle was legendary, thanks to its virtually friction-free internals. Maybe it is time to give recognition to those of the Rhodesian African Rifles, Kenya African Rifles, the Fiji Regiment and the Sarawak Rangers who fought in Malaya with Sterlings, too.

Interchangeability between the British, Malayan and New Zealand troops was also an important factor, and moves were then afoot between Sterling and the Australian Government to license the manufacture of Sterling-type magazines for the F1 SMG at the Australian Small Arms Factory at Lithgow .

These negotiations later bogged down completely, but fate stepped in at the eleventh hour. James Edmiston, owner of Sterling Armament Co at the time, told the authors that during these negotiations, totally unannounced, he went into the Australian High Commission in London, and spoke to the senior Military Attache. Over a few beers, James told him that as staunch allies of Britain, Australia was free to manufacture Sterling magazines at Lithgow free of charge, but on condition that they were not manufactured for sale or redistribution to another country. As the Australians we know would have remarked, "Good on yer mate-you're a good sport, Jim!"

Yes, Sterling knew how to make friends, and as a result the Australians purchased 88 silenced Mk5 guns which they used in Vietnam. The Australians were also true to their word, as an Australian-made 9mm Sterling magazine is extremely unusual outside Australia.

Contrary to reports suggesting otherwise, these Australian-made magazines are fully interchangeable (as complete assemblies) with the British and Canadian versions.

The Slings

This section cannot even begin to cater for the different combinations of carrying slings that have been issued for use on Sterling guns from the mid-1950s to date: surely a complete compendium would range from sisal string in darkest Africa to beautifully embossed leather in the richest Middle-Eastern states where money is NO object. In fact, one country, South Yemen, purchased only quantities of slings from Sterling!

What follows are details on the slings sold by Sterling, and the variations used with Military-service Sterling SMGs by the Governments of the United Kingdom and the Commonwealth.

The Venerable Sten Gun Sling

When the Commonwealth countries (including the United Kingdom and Canada) first purchased supplies of Sterling guns, they had on hand vast stocks of wartime Sten gun slings. These slings were .75″ wide sand or khaki coloured webbing, 50″ long, with a brass adjuster that allowed the sling to be shortened up to half length. The rear end contained a wide metal loop that allowed the sling to be looped through (or around) the butt of the Sten.

The front end contained another loop, but fixed to it and allowed to rotate was a semi-closed coil of tough wire, designed to loop into the barrel jacket of the Sten. On the Sten it worked quite well, because the hole it coiled into was at the end of the barrel jacket. On the Sterling, this was not the case. It had to coil into AND OUT OF a pair of the multiples

of holes within the casing, according to the comfort of the user. In this application, the steel coil wreaked havoc on the protecting phosphate and paint around the casing holes. The Sten sling came with a UK · Military Ordnance supply number of B3/BE-8504.

First Modification

The UK Ministry of Defence soon altered the design of the Sten sling by having the front coiled loop removed and replaced by a spring-loaded, closed brass hook. The sling eye part of the hook was split at the rear to allow the sling to be inserted through it.

This modification formed the basis of what eventually emerged as the standard L2 Sterling sling, and was issued when replacements were required. In fact, these hybrid slings could still be found in armouries as late as 1993.

The Final Version

The final version of the Sterling sling was 60″ long and made from 1″ wide heavy-duty dark green webbing. This sling adopted the best parts of the previously

355. Both ends of four slings used with the UK and Canadian Military Sterlings. From left to right:
1. The original Sten gun sling, with loop and spring-ring.
2. The First Modification of the Sten sling, done for the early trials Patchetts. The loop is now split, and the spring ring has been replaced with spring-loaded brass finger hook (also split to allow webbing to be attached).
3. The final Sterling and UK Military sling, 60″ long and 1″ wide. A most versatile piece of equipment.
4. The Canadian C1 SMG sling.

modified Sten sling, such as the spring-loaded self-closing hook and brass adjuster. The rear end now held an open-ended heavy brass loop. This allowed the user to simply slide that end of the sling through the slingloop on the return spring cap, and then clip the sling into the brass loop without needing to thread it through as per the Sten. This sling was offered with the commercial guns and had a Ministry of Supply number of CR 119A. The same sling was offered to the Ministry of Defence as the "Sling, Small-arms", part number B3/1005-99-961-8468. This was the last Ministry of Defence issue SMG sling.

There was also a short-lived, light grey/blue version of this sling made for use by the Royal Air Force. Its demise was brought about by no less a personage than Sir Derek Rayner, who was brought in to the Ministry of Defence to cut expenditure. And cut it he did, as painlessly as one could while wielding an axe. Sir Derek decided that it was nonsense for

Air Force vehicles to be painted light grey/blue and Army vehicles to be Khaki/deep bronze green, with all the added logistics and expense associated with duplicated procurement agencies. The same principle applied to webbing equipment. Thereafter and to this day, all UK Military vehicle and webbing colours have been standardised to dark green.

These slings were made for Ministry of Defence contracts by Mills Equipment Company (MECo). Those manufactured for Sterling to furnish with export orders were made by Michael Wright and Sons, Quorn Mills, Quorn, Leicestershire. Both patterns are identical.

Because it is an extremely versatile piece of kit, this sling can often be found amongst the extra equipment carried around the waist, in pouches, or in pockets by troops in action. Indeed, this same sling is also favoured by some on the current SABO rifle system.

Enhancing the Sterling

The Singlepoint Sight on the Military Sterling

There was a call in the early 1970s for Sterling guns to be fitted with the commercial red-dot 'Singlepoint' sight. This device, an aiming aid rather than a sight

per se as it cannot be seen through, shows a centred red dot (luminous at night) which the shooter, with both eyes open, projects onto the target. It was reported

356. A typical MkI Patchett Machine Carbine, with butt partially folded. This gun was later used by the MoD as a test bed to mount a Singlepoint sight.

Note (from rear) the cylindrical return spring cap, the alloy metal pistol grip, the early trigger, the 90° magazine housing, and the heavy Lanchester front sight protectors. (MoD Army, RMCS Shrivenham)

that soldiers fighting in terrorist environments were purchasing these sight privately, to fit to their SMGs.

Studies were undertaken by the UK MoD, using an old MkI gun (after all, it was the SIGHT that was on trial and not the gun) to ascertain whether these sights would offer a better chance of 'first-shot-hit'. The Sterling company fitted these sights to Sterling Mk4 guns, KR 55659 being a recorded example.

It was ascertained that the sight did have certain merit at very close ranges. However, after optical tests at the Royal Military College of Science at Shrivenham, it was concluded that, because the central red-dot graticule was fixed in size, it could not be increased or decreased to cater for different ranges.

This was considered a major drawback. Furthermore, if it was (or could be) made adjustable, the instant point-and-shoot benefits would be lost while the user adjusted it!

It was also concluded that the original iron sights were superior for use against fleeting targets in conditions of half-light and poor visibility, just as had been concluded when the Small Arms School Corps team suggested that the distance between the original backsight protectors be increased from .45″ to .55″ during the 1950s trials. As David Howroyd has suggested, in half-light and poor visibility, you don't get a second chance to make a first impression.

357. Sterling worked quite closely with Singlepoint for a time, and experimented with several different mountings of the Singlepoint sight. However, the combination was never marketed by Sterling.

Above: as mounted forward on the casing of a late Mk4/L2A3 SMG.

Below: as mounted forward on the casing of a silenced Mk5/L34A1, using FN-style spring-steel bands. (Courtesy MoD Pattern Room, Nottingham)

Telescopes and Night-Vision Equipment

358. A crackle-finish commercial Sterling Mk4/L2A3 fitted with the Sterling IWS (night sight) mount (fig 235), and mounting an early trigger-activated laser beam projecting device produced by another commercial firm.

Not a Sterling project *per se*, although David Howroyd recalls making up the special sleeve needed to fit between the IWS front ring (intended for the 1¾"-dia casing of the silenced Mlc5) and the 1½"-dia casing of the Mk4. (Courtesy MoD Pattern Room, Nottingham)

359. One problem with the Sterling IWS mount was that when fitted, the buttstock could not be folded and locked. Here a round extension has been added below the muzzle to reposition the butt catch lock.

In a further enhancement, a Mag-Lite has been mounted on the IWS mount and fitted with a special shroud (by QED of Borough Green, Kent) to funnel the beam and absorb dissipating white light.

Here the IWS front ring is sleeved by a special adaptor which surrounds the casing and extends back under the ring. (Courtesy MoD Pattern Room, Nottingham)

Several different night sights were experimentally mounted on the Mk5/L34A1. After 1983, the commercial Sterling Mks was available factory-fitted with the two top-mounted sight rail locating studs, or the Sterling IWS (night sight) mount (fig 235) was used. The UK Military-issue night sight with its NATO (STANAG) specification mounting base required the use of the Sterling IWS (night sight) base.

As noted in Chapter Eight (fig 236), the silenced Mk5/L34 fitted with a night sight makes an extremely potent weapon indeed.

The use of telescopes or night vision equipments on automatic fire was not recommended, due to movement of the graticule caused by the vibration.

Other Tools and Devices

Like every good manufacturer and retailer, the Sterling company lived or died on its commercial success. As with the magazines, bayonets and slings, Sterling would quote a price for and supply almost anything that a buyer requested. Thus they perfected a Sterling 9mm weapons *system*.

Although Sterling would (and did) quote for practically anything, the following list just covers items that relate to the Sterling SMGs.

The Sterling Cleaning Kit

The cleaning kit for the Sterling guns originally comprised W tin box, about the same size as a two-ounce tobacco tin, which contained a small roll of 4″ × 2″ flannelette, a stubby ''brush, cleaning rifle, Mk1'' which we called a 'nook and cranny' brush, the age-old pull through, and a black plastic oil bottle.

Later the tin was replaced with a similar-sized plastic box, conveniently sized to slip into a pocket or ammunition pouch. The 'nook and cranny' brush was never a lot of good, so a cut-down toothbrush usually found its way into the cleaning kit!

The Foresight Tool

We have mentioned the "Tool, foresight cramp", UK Military Ordnance number B3/CR-11GA, each turn of which would move the MPI 2″ at 25 yards. A (large) batch was re-ordered from Hopkinsons of Sheffield in 1985, judging by the number seen recently with the 'HOP-85' logo thereon. Sterling supplied a similar foresight cramp for use on the Mk5/L34A1, but this never found its way into UK Ordnance stores.

360. The UK Military foresight adjustment tool, B3-CR 115A, shown fitted to a Mk4/L2A3.
 This was seldom used, as Armourers could do the same job faster with a small hammer and a brass drift.

This foresight cramp could not be used on the Mk7 'Pistols'.

The Sterling foresight cramp came in kit form with an Allen key to release the blade, and a knurled key to adjust it for height.

Most Armourers could zero the guns without recourse to expensive and intricate tools.

Blank Firing Attachments

Blank Firing Attachments (BFAs) were also offered by Sterling for the Mk4/L2A3 and, by definition, the Mk8 gun too. The Mk4 (and Mk8) BFA fitted over the muzzle port, and was held in place by the barrel retaining screws.

Also offered was a BFA for the Mk7 guns, but only those with 4″ barrels, as the attachment enclosed the end of the barrel and secured onto the barrel nut

361. Top view of the muzzle end of a late MkII/L2A1 Patchett fitted with an experimental BFA.

Note the markings, 'SMG/PATCHETT/9mm L2A1'. (MoD Pattern Room collection)

thread. Sterling also made a BFA for the AR–18 series of rifles and carbines it produced.

The UK and Canadian Militaries utilised different designs of BFA. which were simpler to fit and remove and contained an articulating barrel gas choke (fig 263). These are retained in place by spring clipped round pegs which enter the cooling holes in the body casing.

Blank firing attachments operate by confining and utilising the gases of the (bulletless) explosion within the barrel. A small amount of gas is released through a port in the BFA, and the remainder takes the line of least resistance and pushes back on the fired case, to operate the gun's firing cycle. In the interest of safety, all BFAs come painted with a baked-on coat of bright yellow, hard-wearing, high-temperature enamel.

362. Left side view of a Sterling Mk4/L2A3, with prototype Sterling Blank Firing Attachment (BFA) in place. Note the flat, machined on the casing from the bayonet lug forward, to clear the wooden grips on the No5 MkI bayonet.

Below, left: the prototype Sterling BFA disassembled, showing barrel retaining screws and hollow obturator screws with different-sized apertures.

Below, right: six rounds of 9mm plastic-bullet Blank ammunition.

All BFAs offered for sale were painted with a bright, baked-on, high-temperature yellow enamel. (Courtesy MoD Pattern Room, Nottingham)

The Sterling "Armourers Kit for Silent Gun"

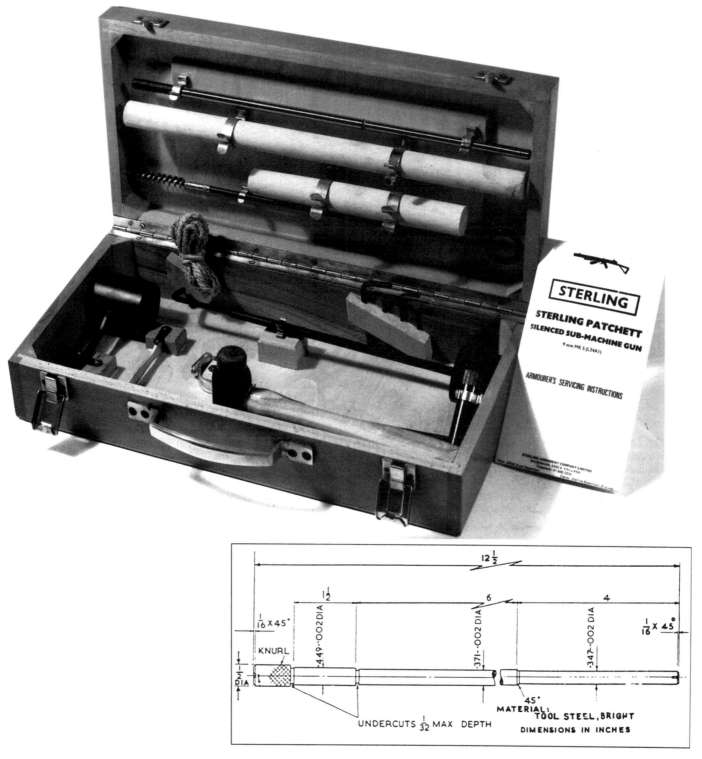

363. The excellent Sterling "Armourers Kit for Silent Gun", as supplied with each commercial Mk5/L34AI. The contents are listed in the text.

Note the special Silencer alignment tool, clipped in the lid, critical to ensure bore concentricity with the silencer end cap. (Courtesy MoD Pattern Room, Nottingham)

Inset, right: drawing of the special Mk5/L34AI Silencer Alignment Tool. UK Army Armourers were given a copy of this drawing, and told to make their own alignment tool! (Drawing by Peter Laidler)

An excellent Armourer's tool kit was supplied for use with the Mk5/L34, called in late Sterling brochures the "Armourers Kit for Silent Gun". It came in a wooden box, about 15″ x 12″ and 4″ deep and contained an explanatory handbook and all the tools necessary to strip and assemble the silenced gun. It also contained a special barrel and silencer alignment gauge, the necessary Allen keys, cleaning rod, brush and pull through, an oil bottle, wooden drifts to remove and re-insert the roll of expanded metal mesh (no easy task without these, Peter Laidler can confirm) and a jubilee clip (fig 224) to hold the mesh in shape while removed; a rawhide mallet, and spring balance to ensure the correct degree of torque when tightening up the silencer casing bolts.

The kit also contained a tub of powdered graphite, although Service Armourers preferred the tubes of 'XG 340' Graphite grease to the powder.

Apart from the usual Armourers' tools, this comprehensive kit was all that was required for the Armourer to overhaul these guns.

The Sterling Arctic Trigger

An arctic trigger adaptor (fig 117) was first designed for use with the MkII Sterling. This adaptor was made to be screwed to the bottom of the pistol grip and an external arm operated the trigger while the user was wearing thick mittens.

A similar arctic trigger adaptor was designed for the Mk4, which screwed to the bottom of th. e pistol grip (trigger guard removed) with a plug that fitted into the hole in the base of the distinctively shaped trigger.

This later arctic trigger adaptor was made redundant by the redesign of the Mk4/L2A3 trigger guard, so that it could be removed and reversed in arctic warfare conditions. The separate Mk4/L2A3 arctic trigger adaptor was thus quietly shelved, and the hole in the base of the trigger was deleted in 1957.

Ammunition

The first and most obvious requirement for any user of Sterling guns is ammunition. Sterling supplied millions of rounds of ammunition, including commercial and NATO-specification BALL, identified by a purple annulus, TRACER with a red bullet tip, and ARMOUR PIERCING with a black and purple tip.

Also available were black plastic-nosed blank, and chromed drill rounds with an inert filling. The latter can further identified by having three red-filled dimples punched into the sides. For Armourers, there were also the solid-brass "Cartridges, Inspectors, Dummy".

Sterling could also supply specially loaded subsonic 9mm ammunition on request.

The (Blank-Firing) Sterling in the Movies

The film industry made regular use of Sterling guns for both commercial and military training films, where the regular yellow BFAs would be out of place. For film industry use, Armourers adapted barrels by threading into the muzzle and screwing an Allen

364. The Sterling Blank Firing barrel. made for film use.
The barrel is threaded internally and a hard steel Allen bolt with a small hole drilled through the centre is inserted. The small hole allowed a realistic flash, while using the remaining gases of the bulletless blank to cycle the action.

bolt into place. The Allen bolt was drilled through centrally to provide a vent. This ensured that while firing blanks a certain amount of propellant and gas would escape through the vent to give the necessary flash and smoke, while the remaining gas would operate the action. Simple isn't it?

In the interests of safety, there is a small shoulder machined onto the head of the Allen bolt. This is to ensure that the Allen bolt is screwed tightly into the barrel first, then the barrel is assembled and locked into the gun casing. This shoulder is now positioned between the muzzle and the gun casing, effectively preventing the Allen screw from unscrewing during firing when it might become a 'real' bullet.

The SMG Tear Gas and Rubber Bullet Discharger

A tear gas/rubber bullet discharger was also designed. This fitted onto the nose of the MkII, MkIII, Mk4/L2A3 and Mk8 guns, and was held in place by means of a securing screw tightened from behind in a hollow, threaded arm which located over the bayonet standard. This was also short-lived as second and subsequent generations of public order equipment became available.

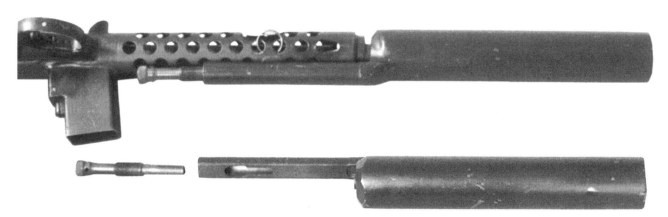

365. Two views of the Tear Gas and Rubber Bullet discharger, first developed for use with the MkII/L2A1 Patchett.
Above: underside view of early MkII Patchett (note the absence of the forward finger guard), with launcher fitted over muzzle and securing screw tightened against bayonet lug.
Below: launcher disassembled showing securing screw and bayonet lug slot in launcher extension. (MoD Army, RMCS Shrivenham)

Two Experimental Sub-Calibre Units

366. Right side view of Sterling Mk4/L2A3 no S 33487 with butt extended, fitted with a .22 conversion 'kit' consisting of a standard-diameter but lightened breech block, and a .22 calibre barrel insert held at the muzzle by a threaded lock nut, itself secured by an Allen key.
Problems with grease buildup from lubricated .22 cartridges contributed to the demise of the .22 conversion programme. (MoD Pattern Room collection)

367. Right side view of Mk4/L2A3 no S 36139 with butt removed, fitted with the second Sterling .22 calibre conversion unit, a semi-permanent device consisting of a reduced diameter breech block and spring, riding in an internal sleeve, and a new, purpose-built .22 calibre barrel.

Note the separate .22 breech block return spring, and the magazine adaptor fitted with curved .22 calibre magazine. (MoD Pattern Room collection)

For indoor training, with an eye on the US market, two guns were experimentally equipped with .22″ sub-calibre kits.

One design, fitted to Mk4/L2A3 no S 33487, was removable by having a sub-calibre barrel and magazine insert. A .22 calibre magazine could then be inserted into the magazine adaptor, and substitution of a special lightweight breech block and return spring completed the package.

Another gun, no S 36139, had the .22 components more or less permanently fitted; they COULD be removed, although it was suggested that the SMG to which this model might be fitted should be considered a dedicated gun.

This design introduced an internal sleeve into the receiver casing, wherein rode a new, reduced-diameter breech block and separate mainspring.

The barrel of this gun was a dedicated .22 calibre component.

Problems Inherent with Sub-Calibre Units

Sadly, both attempts were abandoned. Among the major drawbacks the Sterling engineers encountered when working with .22 rimfire ammunition was that the cartridges were (usually) greased, and this grease quickly built up on and within the working parts of the donor weapon AND the sub-calibre kit.

Once this grease builds up, the .22 cartridges become more difficult to insert into the chamber. Eventually, while being forced by the rim into a REALLY dirty chamber, they have the nasty habit of going off!

Chapter Seventeen
Endgames

Compared with current sub-machine gun manufacturing methods, the Sterling SMG was probably obsolete by about 1975. By then, stamped and fabricated guns were the norm and Sterling was the only company left making high-quality, virtually hand-built guns, while everywhere else, machined components had long been replaced by pressings, folded and wrapped on machines, and brazing had been replaced with quality automatic spot or TIG welding.

Sterling briefly attempted to step through this doorway during the 1960s with the stamped S11, among other designs, but in the marketplace the Mk4 and Mk5 SMGs were left as they were. It isn't cheap to tool-up for an entirely different manufacturing process, and within a company which prided itself on its skilled AND loyal labour force, the inevitable job losses would have had an important effect upon morale.

In later years, Sterling was always dependent upon the last gun sales to finance production of the next batch. In short, by that time the capital needed to invest in new production methods was simply not available.

Hopefully one day, the whole unexpurgated story of the last years of the Sterling Armament Company will be truthfully told, warts and all! In his outspoken book *The Sterling Years* James Edmiston speaks of the mysteriously high price paid by British Aerospace for the languishing shell of the Sterling company in 1988, solely to close it down forever.

And yet, it had emerged during the UK Government/Sterling litigation that ROF Fazakerley L2A3s cost a great deal more to produce than their Sterling-made counterparts. Quite how much more was not disclosed, but Sterling estimated that with the conservative "million pounds or two" spent on tools, machinery, intricate gauges, etc, the whole order could have been undertaken at Dagenham where the machinery and experience were already to hand.

After the closure of ROF Fazakerley, the ROF L2A3 gauges and tooling were purchased by Sterling to help increase Sterling output. In contrast, upon the closure of the Sterling company, all of the gauges and tooling were destroyed, to ensure that the trusty Mk4 series could not emerge from the ashes under a new name with a new owner. The closure of the Sterling Armament Company saw the end of any large- or medium-scale private small-arms manufacture by a UK-based company.

That the Sterling guns were relatively expensive was not in itself a drawback; so are Omega watches, but people still buy them. The problem was, they lasted such a long time! At the time of phaseout in 1994, a British Service L2 made in 1959 was probably (at 36 years) older than three-quarters of the soldiers who had handled it, and at its 1959 contract price of £22.50, it was an extremely GOOD value!

It follows that QUAN1ITY sales of a QUALITY product diminish as the years roll by. Also, it was· difficult to get repeat orders when the armouries of our former allies were being filled with cheap and cheerful Soviet-bloc material, at give-away prices. Many of the unwise sold off their stocks of Sterlings, only to find later, in areal world of hard currency and tough economics, that the new spares and ammunition were still cheerful but NOT cheap!

What Might Have Been Done to Lower Costs

Peter Laidler would have dissected a Canadian C1 SMG and gradually introduced their fabricated and spot-welded methods to Sterling Mk4, 5, 6, 7 and 8 production. Beginning with the return spring cap, continuing with the front and rear finger guards, then the butt trunnion, and so on. These steps would have perpetuated the proud Sterling claim that every part was the same, or certainly interchangeable, from the start of production to the end. The offset No5 bayonet boss on the muzzle and bayonet standard on the casing of the Sterling were costly and time-consuming to manufacture. These would have been ripe for fabrication without detriment, while retaining the No5 bayonet. Not that EVERY large purchaser actually wanted No5 bayonets, or ANY bayonet!

David Howroyd counters that stamping and fabricating techniques were well within the scope of the Sterling company, but the drawings for the L2A3, the Military version of the Mk4, were sealed and as such, deviations were not permitted (although ROF Fazakerley seemed to get away with a few). Friendly governments also wanted the gun to UK Military specification, and the adoption of more fabricated parts for the commercial guns alone would thus have engendered TWO sets of manufacturing procedures, plus attendant assembly convolutions.

Certain relaxations were allowed after consultation but these were few and far between. One that does spring to mind was the use of a casting for the rearsight protectors. Another was the use of pressed steel grips in place of wood on the 'hybrid' bayonet.

Looking Back – Six Years and Counting

Now, in 95, it is six years since the doors of the Sterling Armament works at Rainham Road South, Dagenham, closed for the last time in 1989. The youngest Sterling gun will thus be at least that old and the oldest, discounting the Prototypes, and Trials MkI guns and starting with the MkIIs of 1953, are 42 years old this year. Even the oldest of the most common Mk4s will be at least 39! The manufacture of spare parts also ceased upon closure of the factory. Could this cause a headache later?

At this age, a degree of wear will be inevitable but the quality of materials used, the skills of the designers, assemblers and inspectors and the extremely durable finish has meant that some of the very earliest guns will continue giving service for a long time yet. The Sterling company sales staff are due considerable praise here, for while negotiating sales to military and government buyers, they included a spares package too! Each gun or consignment was sold with

10 magazines and a spare parts holding sufficient for 10 years of use, based upon UK Military spares requirements. After all, they'd had the guns for the longest uninterrupted period. So in THEORY, there should be sufficient spare parts to cater for current user demand for many years to come. We hope that the cross-references we have included as figs 325–327 in Chapter Fifteen will assist users in this respect.

A short story will emphasise the durability of the Sterling. A high-speed ex-Royal Navy launch, subsequently owned by an African Police Force for many years, was returned to its English manufacturers for refurbishment prior to sale to its new Caribbean owner. Down in the bilges, filled with sea-water, filth and mess, after 40 years of service, they found a 1955-vintage MkIII Sterling. Where the Trimite paint and phosphating had broken down in a few places it was rusty with slight pitting, but by no means heavily. It was bathed overnight in a kerosene bath. The next morning it was power-hosed down, cleaned, oiled and test-fired in the afternoon. We think this little anecdote says it all, although quite how the gun got there is one of life's little mysteries: "… just slipped out of me 'ands into the sea, Cap' n …"

The Non-Sterling Sterlings

It was well known by the Sterling staff that some governments purchased guns on the second-hand market and then had them refurbished by several of the companies specialising in this treatment. Some of the more reputable refurbishers would come to Sterling for their spare parts but some, from the shadier end of the market, would use Cawnpore (Indian 1A) spares.

Sterling knew just when this was happening, because even those companies operating at the lower and cheaper end of the scale were forced to buy their springs from Sterling! Foreign springs, especially trigger mechanism springs, simply weren't up to the job. Even Sterling had trouble perfecting the tension and locating recess of the "Spring, Detent Pin" (fig 155 no 10).

Sterling also knew about one of these "specialist" refurbishing outfits who purchased cheap, worn out guns in order to strip them for spares. Well, you get what you pay for!

Two REALLY Non-Sterling "Sterlings"!

The Northern Ireland Copy with Hand-Made Casing

368. Two views of a *circa* 1980 buttless Sterling copy with hand-made casing, using UK Ordnance-issue internal components.

Above: left side view. Note the distinctive front sight guard configuration.

Below: right side view.

This gun was manufactured in Northern Ireland, not by the IRA, who very seldom made their own guns, but by the Ulster Loyalists. (MoD Pattern Room collection)

The Chillean PAF 9mm Parabellum Machine Pistol

369. Right side view of the Chilean PAF Machine Pistoi, with butt extended.

   This late-1980s design is built by the Chilean State Arsenal FAMAE (*Fabricaciones Militares*) in Santiago.

   The compact PAF weighs 2.44kg (5.38 lbs) without magazine and features a barrel 175mm (6.8") in length, with a short recoil compensator at the muzzle end.

   Numerous features mimic those of the Mk4 Sterling, although the barrel attachment system seems more reminiscent of the Mk6! (MoD Pattern Room collection)

370. Top closeup view of the (82°) magazine housing of the Chilean PAF Machine Pistol, showing markings.

   'PAF' stands for *Pistola Ametrelladora* (Machine Pistol) FAMAE.

   Note the reversion to the old Sterling method of butt-welding the housing to the casing! (MoD Pattern Room collection)

A Silent Sterling the Hard Way

There will be instances where those users who possess guns made in limited quantities, with few interchangeable parts, will be forced to improvise. One good example concerned an unnamed South American nation who replaced its ventilated Mks barrels, wh1ch were prone to bulging, with standard Mk4 barrels, machined and threaded to the Mks external specification. (Additionally, this eliminated the need for the expanded metal wrap and the diffuser tube.) To counteract the supersonic 'crack' of the bullets, they developed and manufactured special sub-sonic 9mm ammunition for their modified Mk5s.

The Mk5/L34A1 breech block was lighter than the standard Mk4/L2A3 item, too. Peter Laidler recently weighed about 20 used and new Mk4/L2A3 breech blocks, and found that the weights varied between 460 and 482 grams. This difference in weight would be reflected in variable rates of fire. At the same time, a smaller selection of Mk5/L34A1 breech blocks weighed only varied between 416 and 420 grams. We also established by test-firing that if a Mk4/L2A3 breech block were machined down internally to 416–420g (disregarding the eccentric internal turning, please), then it would function perfectly in a Mk5/L34A1.

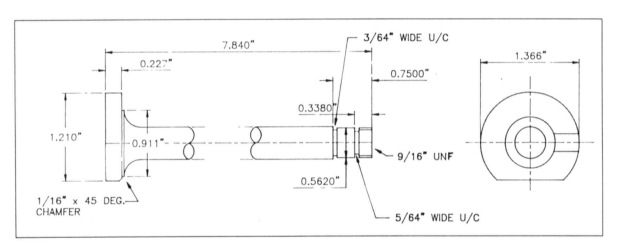

371. Drawing of a standard Mk4/L2A3 SMG barrel converted for use (with sub-sonic ammunition) in the Mk5/L34Als of at least one user nation. Original vented Mk5 barrels, found by many to be prone to bulging, are in any case now scarce and expensive. Once the Mk4 barrel is machined to the above specification, switching the barrels is quite simple, as the modified gun has no need of the Mk5 diffuser tube and expanded metal wrap. (Drawing by Peter Laidler)

Keeping Them Running: a Final Note

Trigger mechanism parts from Mk4 guns can be converted to Mk6, 7 C and 8 specification quite easily by a good bench-fitter or Armourer. Barrels can also be converted to fit.

Magazines are already in relatively short supply and it is highly unlikely that these will be re-manufactured. However, there are large quantities of the UK Military L1A2 magazines, as made by ROF Fazakerley, Royal Laboratories, Mettoy and Rolls Razor, which might eventually be released for sale on the international market.

The stringent changes in firearms legislation in the United States could well affect the import and export of Sterling 34-round magazines to and from there.

Buyers searching for magazines should remember that they were also manufactured in Canada and Australia, as well as India.

Both authors are aware of where stocks of spare parts might be held, and of specialist engineers who might manufacture quantities of spare parts in the future for Government buyers.

Most Commonwealth countries will be putting aside large quantities of Sterling guns and magazines as Mobilisation and War Reserve Stores, and Britain is no exception. Large quantities of SMGs have been refurbished to as-new condition and will remain sealed within Ordnance Stores. Having been caught out in 1939, military planners have no intention of being caught short again!

Chapter Eighteen

Hard Fact

"Jonathan Ferguson, Keeper of Firearms and Artillery at the National Firearms Centre in Leeds, explains that private company owners found it difficult to make a go of small-arms manufacturing which he attributes to a number of factors."

During World War II and the 1950's, says Ferguson, the Royal Small Arms Factory at Enfield relied increasingly upon designers from Czechoslovakia, Poland, and Belgium, who eventually returned home leaving something of a capability gap. Whereas the U.K. excelled in other areas such as aircraft, and vehicle design and manufacture, the private sector for small-arms remained small. "Sterling, Enfield's only real rival in the field, struggled to remain commercially viable," he explains. "Their most successful product was the 1944 vintage Patchett-Sterling sub-machine gun, which lost sales to the German MP5 and Israeli Uzi. Sterling's factory closed in the late 1980's."

But he does not tell the full tale. The Mark 4 version of the Patchett was not formally adopted by the U.K. armed forces until the late 1950's. Sterling was not allowed to compete for ANY small-arms requirements from the MOD as RSAF Enfield was part of that MOD. It was not even a nationalized industry. This was known as the Preferred Source Policy, which effectively ruled out all competition. When RSAF Enfield was finally privatized, Sterling was still not allowed to compete, but that did not prevent Enfield from hawking locally assembled Heckler & Koch's MP5's (a design incidentally as old as the Sterling, but by no means as reliable) around the world using the Defence Attaches and the S.A.S. as salesmen. The S.A.S. and G.S.G.9 are closely associated, hence one of the obscure reasons for adopting the MP5, and presumably to have commonality of equipment.

The Israeli Uzi was a product of Israeli Military Industries. It is worth noting that it is two pounds heavier than the Sterling and not as reliable in extreme conditions, but is compact. It gained ground as a result of a political decision. The Sterling won the trials for its adoption by the (German) Bundeswehr. However, the then German Foreign Minister Franz Josef Strauss pushed for the adoption of the Uzi for the German Armed Forces as it was allowable against war reparations. The order was so large that the Belgian giant F.N. was licensed to produce it.

In the late 1980's, the Sterling Armament Company was bought by British Aerospace who closed it down the same day. British Aerospace at that time already owned Heckler & Koch.

It would be less misleading if the whole truth were to be given.

Ferguson goes on to discuss the SA-80 rifle and how international co-operation with Heckler & Koch made the very poor SA-80 into the L45A1. The actual facts are that the SA-80 was developed at RSAF Enfield using production parts from the Sterling/Armalite AR-18, without any kind of recognition or commercial ethic. It just so happened that RSAF Enfield copied one crucial but relatively innocent looking part wrongly, as is evidenced by the extraordinarily costly remedies that H&K had to build into it to make the gun tolerably reliable.

In an effort to heal the decades long rift between Sterling and the RSAF Enfield, Edmiston had invited the then Director of Enfield, one Stanley Carroll, to visit Dagenham. He was shown around all parts of the operation which was tiny compared to his factory area. However, he observed the special purpose machines developed by Howroyd in conjunction with Messrs. Hodgson & Sanders (specialist machine-tool builders) of Crewe. It was not long after this visit that the prototype SA-80's appeared with those key Sterling/Armalite parts that Frank Waters (the Sterling designer) recognized while at a British Army Equipment Exhibition. It was later discovered that

Enfield had installed many of the same Hodgson & Sanders special machines for the machining of the bolt and bolt carrier of both weapons.

So disgusted was Edmiston at this ungentlemanly conduct that when Carroll was put up for and elected to the Worshipful Company of Gunmakers,

he immediately tendered his resignation. It was only when there was a new clerk to the livery, Colonel Bill Chesshyre who, together with his friend Maurice Robson, then persuaded Edmiston to rejoin after Carroll had died.

Shotgun manufacture: Boxall & Edmiston Ltd.

After his award, James Edmiston decided to return to firearms manufacturing. Simon Trendall, a clever engineer who refurbished all manner of arms for museums, and full of interesting ideas, showed him a small First World War Austrian gun that he was restoring for a museum. Compact and lightweight, if made with modern materials it could be picked up by a couple of squaddies and thrown in the back of a Land Rover, and in 35 mm. could have been very useful in Afghanistan. Edmiston went to the extent of getting a specialist barrel made by one of the real remaining experts left in England. He visited Arthur Smith at his premises near Colchester to order the barrel.

However, in the course of conversation and a general moan about the shortcomings of what remained of gun-making, he suggested that Edmiston should meet one Peter Boxall, and duly arranged a meeting of the two. Boxall had been the works director of Holland & Holland for sixteen years and

had started his life as an apprentice with Jaguar Cars Ltd. He had risen to the post of senior manager and had then been head-hunted to run W&C Scott the Birmingham gun-makers who were in turn taken over by Hollands. The commuting got to such a pitch that after sixteen years, he had set up his own business at home and was making the really difficult parts of guns for the trade. The two decided that there were no new English gun-makers in the last hundred years, and only David Mackay Brown in Scotland, and so the die was cast. They set up making side-by-side shotguns in Shrewsbury, and later built over-and-under guns as well. The constituent parts of the guns were machined to very tight tolerances on brand new computer controlled machine-tools, and were subsequently finished by hand. All the guns were bespoke, finished to the very highest standards, made to special order, and represented quite exceptional value for money.

Back to the military field

Not long after the establishment of the shotgun factory, an opportunity arose for James Edmiston to buy a plant that was making AR-15/M-16 rifles. Sabre Defence Industries had been started by a Briton who saw the value of the .50″ calibre Browning Machine Gun, and had acquired the Ramo plant in Tennessee. He had expanded into the manufacture of the AR-15 and had plants in the USA and in North London at Northolt. The companies had a good reputation for quality, and there was a regular distribution from the British factory into agencies in Europe and beyond. The owner, one Guy Savage had run into problems with the American authorities over

alleged importation of parts into the UK without the requisite authorisation. Edmiston was prepared to buy this as a going concern, but had already been approached by a liquidator who was desperate to sell the plant as quickly as possible as there was finance overdue on the excellent machines which were about to be repossessed. Savage was resentful at the turn of events and tried to be destructive. There were some difficulties with personalities and the police with result that the police would not issue a Registered Firearms Dealer's licence, and as a result, the company was unable to manufacture.

The company had the support of the British Embassy in Santiago where the government arsenal FAMAE wished to collaborate with the new firm, now called Sterling Northolt Ltd, to produce 25,000 for the Chilean Armed Forces. Sterling Northolt were all set to produce the upper and lower receivers complete from aluminium forgings, and the Chileans were to assemble the rest in their plant that had been established by the Swiss to produce an SIG rifle.

The $42,000,000 order was dependent on Sterling Northolt producing 12 prototypes for testing. In spite of the offer of a Section 5 letter from the Home Office to produce prohibited weapons which was dependent upon the Metropolitan Police's licence, the police refused to grant the licence for reasons that are not clear since they are above the law, and do not have to give reasons. There was a further annual requirement for 12,000 semi-automatic AR-15's for Sterling's distributor in the USA which were going to be assembled in Chile. When Britain cries out for exports, the big question remains; why?

After two years the company had to be liquidated, and the major items of plant were purchased by Manroy Engineering, who in turn had been bought by FN of Herstal in Belgium for the setting up of their own FN plant in the USA.

In the two years of its existence Sterling Northolt made some excellent fishing reels with some of the parts and engraving being effected at Boxall & Edmiston Ltd. These were copies of the original Allcocks Aerial Match Centrepin Reel and were the coarse fisherman's dream.

The Cadet Rifle requirement for the MOD is included, as Sterling wished to put forward a "de-gassed" version of the AR-180, and was informed that this was not acceptable. Pictures of the excellent ambidextrous 5.56mm. BSA bolt action are shown.

This rifle was accepted, and six pre-production prototypes were built at huge cost and successfully tested with 10,000 rounds each at Fort Halstead. BSA Guns Ltd. was asked to tender for six thousand guns, and was assured that the tender was to be held in complete confidence. BSA was not awarded the contract, as they were undercut by .50 pence per rifle, by the Royal Small Arms Factory at Enfield, who had submitted a "de-gassed" version of the SA-80. Quite apart from the conditions of the tender, this price was at a figure of c. 25% of the figure originally charged to the British taxpayer for the original version, in short, was nothing short of an utter fudge.

Thus, it was not only Sterling that suffered from state corruption and the body blows dealt to British private enterprise in the field of military small-arms production.

1983 and after

1983 was not a good year for the company as the directors were accused of "gun-running" or to be more precise, contravening Customs & Excise Regulations. The facts, in brief, were that following a British Army Equipment Exhibition at Aldershot where the Ministry of Defence Sales Organisation introduced two Jordanian army officers to the company by the names of General Hilmi Lozi and Colonel Fawzi Bajj, an order was received by the company signed by these gentlemen. The order called for 200 Mark 5 Sterling Patchett Silenced Sub-Machine Guns (L34A1) and came through a third party, namely Major Reginald Dunk. The company following normal procedure applied for and was granted a British Government export licence.

The order was duly packed, addressed to the Jordanian Army stores at Aqaba and delivered for shipment to the Deep Water Terminal at Greenwich.

Co-incidentally at this time, James Edmiston was representing the company aboard an MOD organized floating sales exhibition (Floater) visiting various countries in the Middle East. In Aqaba he met with the same Jordanian officers who enquired after the late delivery of their order. While Edmiston was awaiting details of the progress of the delivery, the news broke in the national press that the consignment had been intercepted by H.M.Customs & Excise as they had reason to believe that the consignment was not bound for Jordan at all, but rather for Iraq which was currently in a state of war with Iran.

Quite apart from the fact that the company was hardly likely to prejudice its future for the sake of a small order, the Customs were hell bent on prosecuting which had serious implications for the company's banking arrangements, and for the whole future of the company and its employees should the manufacturing licence be terminated in the event of a successful prosecution.

Although there was no clear indication whether or not a prosecution would follow, and so in order that the employees' position be protected, Edmiston sold his interests in the company.

It was some two years later that a prosecution followed. Edmiston had to pay the costs of his defence, and since the new owners of the company did not wish for any involvement in it even to the extent of funding their works director, he also covered the costs of David Howroyd who was still their key man.

After four weeks as defendants in a full trial at the Central Criminal Court (the Old Bailey), the (now former) directors were acquitted, although it affected their lives greatly.

However, some nine years later, after other companies including Matrix-Churchill, maker of excellent British machine-tools, had run into difficulties over questions of supplying Iraq with equipment, it appeared that there was an element of governmental involvement, and a public inquiry was ordered by John Major.

Richard Norton-Taylor, the author of *Truth is a Difficult Concept: Inside the Scott Inquiry* !1995),

"The Arms-to-Iraq affair was one of the most seedy, dishonest, buck-passing episodes in the history of modern British government. Had the Matrix-Churchill trial not collapsed (thanks to Geoffrey Robinson QC), and documents ministers wanted to suppress not been disclosed, three men could have been jailed in a miscarriage of justice in which ministers and civil servants would have connived."

Lord Justice Scott's inquiry certainly uncovered some reprehensible conduct by government individuals trying to suitably cover their tracks. Its relevance as far as Edmiston and Howroyd were concerned, was that it revealed collusion between the Foreign and Commonwealth Office and H.M. Customs & Excise in preventing Dunk's witnesses coming to court, and hence Edmiston and Howroyd having to undergo the rigours of a trial and the disposal of the company since Dunk had been forced to plead.

Edmiston's cudgels were taken up by Lawrence Kormornick, Dunk's Mancunian lawyer who had successfully won Dunk compensation for the uncovered governmental misfeasance. Dunk eventually was awarded BPS2M under the Wrongful Conviction Scheme and an ex-gratia scheme for wrongful charge at the discretion of Jack Straw, the Home Secretary. It was this latter scheme that Kormornick fought for and proved serious default by a public authority. Further, it was held by Mr. Justice Henriques giving a judicial review decision, that being in the custody of a court during a trial only, was sufficient requirement to satisfy the scheme. A later Home Secretary, Charles Clarke accepted that there had been serious default by a public authority amounting to a miscarriage of justice in Edmiston's case, but then closed down the scheme. Edmiston, having been accepted into the scheme had to spend the next three years with Kormornick obtaining evidence of past loss to go before the Assessor, Lord Brennan.

Although BPS5M set the record for such compensation, two factors were not nor could not be considered by the assessor. The first was the economic success of selling the Sterling Mark 6 on the US market. To this day, Edmiston receives congratulatory e-mails from the Uzi Owners Club of America which continue to praise the sheer build quality of those little Dagenham made guns, and would have bought considerably more, were it not for the hiatus caused by the prosecution. The second area was compensation for the residential house in Phillimore Place, London W.8., that had to go, having been bought as three flats in 1981 and converted back into one residence comprising eight bedrooms, four reception rooms, and a lift which had to be sold three years later for BPS925,000. Today's value is considerably in excess of BPS15M.

The full account of the saga can be read in James Edmiston's and Lawrence Kormornick's book, The Sterling Redemption, published in 2012 by Pen & Sword Books Ltd.

ANNEX 'G', GUN MARKINGS DECIPHERED.
(See annex 'C' for serial number codes)

Anyone who has looked closely at any firearm, especially those with a Military connection, will have noticed the different markings present. This is equally true with the Sterling. Those shown are representative of those found on UK produced Sterling guns.

Hx	Helix Plastics. Pistol grips
S56, S67, S78	Sterling Armament Co and year of manufacture
F56, F57, F58	ROF Fazakerley and year of manufacture
Ð 56, Ð62	RSAF Enfield and year of manufacture. 'E' within a 'D' is an amalgam of the pre-war 'EFD' logo
∞	Unified thread form within
⋀	UK and Commonwealth government acceptance mark
9 602 153 E 9136	Found on Breech blocks. Indicates coded NATO part number B3-1005-99-960-2153. E 9136 indicates steel batch number
9 602 079	Variation of above, but found on other parts.
CR 1207 N572A	Found on barrels. CR 1207 is Ministry of Supply part number but prefixed by B3 for documentation purposes. N572A is steel batch number
CR 1073	As above, without steel batch number
B3 1005-99-960-2079	Is the full NATO identification number A back-sight could have the following part numbers: CR 1081 (Ministry of Supply number), S4/1/24 (Sterling drawing number), 1005-99-960-2168 (NATO part number) or 9-602-168 (coded NATO number)
H3, H24, H40, H63, H76, H89, H94, J1, J5, J18, J85, K8, K40, K48, K58, K82:	All Fazakerley examiners coded number/mark stamps. There are probably many more in the H, J and K series
S1	The only Sterling examiners mark seen, on top of a Sterling made trigger mechanism frame.

Early UK Military proof mark found on Mk1 and 2 guns. When found on locking ring/flange, this can positively date gun casing

Current UK Military proof mark

Civil London proof house mark. Consists of armed gauntlet carrying scimitar logo. 9mm NATO, 3447 Kg proof pressure, 19.1mm length of chamber with English Proof-1987 mark

Appendix

List of Headings

Bibliography

Books

British and Commonwealth Bayonets by Ian Skennerton and Robert Richardson. Ian D Skennerton (Australia), Greenhill Books (UK), and IDSA Books (USA), 1984

British Small Arms of World War II by Ian Skennerton. Ian D Skennerton (Australia), Greenhill Books (UK), and IDSA Books (USA), 1988

The FAL Rifle (*North American FALs* by R Blake Stevens; *UK & Commonwealth FALs* by R Blake Stevens; *The Metric FAL* by R Blake Stevens and Jean E Van Rutten). Collector Grade Publications Inc, 1993

The Gun that Made the Twenties Roar by William J Helmer. MacMillan, 1969

The Lanchester Legacy by C (Chris) S Clark. Published in three parts by Coventry University Press, 1995

Small Arms of the World (Eleventh Edition) by Edward C Ezell. Stackpole Books, Harrisburg, PA, 1977

The Sterling Years by James Edmiston. Leo Cooper, London, 1992

Textbook of Small-Arms Volumes 1 and 2 (Draft) Royal Military College of Science, Shrivenham, 1953

The World's Submachine Guns Volume I by Thomas B Nelson and Hans B Lockhoven. International Small Arms Publishers, Cologne, 1963

The Sterling Redemption by James Edmiston and Lawrence Kormornick. Pen & Sword Books, 2012.

Military Manuals

Canadian Army EME Manual, Small Arms D 100 *Carbine Machine Patchett 9mm* Issue 1, 27 August, 1955

Canadian Army EME Manual, Small Arms D 110 *Gun, Submachine, 9mm*, C1 Issue 1, 19 December, 1958

Electrical and Mechanical Engineering Regulations (EMERs) *Small Arms and Machine Guns*, Sections E730 and E740. UK Ministry of Defence

Illustrated Parts Catalogue for SMG 9mm L2A3 and L34A1: Ref 12077 and 60122. Director of Ordnance, UK Ministry of Defence

The Lanchester Carbine Manual (*9mm Lanchester Machine Carbine*) Admiralty (Gunnery Branch), 1943

Parts List for Gun, Sub-Machine, 9mm L2A2/Gun, Sub-Machine, 9mm L2A1 Director of Ordnance Services, The War Office, July, 1956

User Handbook and Parts list for Lanchester Machine Carbine Chief Inspector of Naval Ordnance, 1942

User Handbook (Provisional) for Carbine Machine Patchett 9mm EX Inspectorate of Armaments, Woolwich, 1952

User Handbook (Provisional) for Gun, Sub-Machine, 9mm L2A2 Director of Infantry, War Office, 1955

User Handbook for the Gun, Sub-Machine, 9mm L2A3 Director of Infantry, UK Ministry of Defence, 1956 Amendment No 4: *Submachine Gun 9mm L34A1* Quality Assurance Directorate (Weapons), Woolwich, London,1967

Ordnance Board Proceedings

From the UK Military point of view, the tortuous path of the Patchett/Sterling through the years of trials, new specifications, vacillation and indecision is best told in the Proceedings of the Ordnance Board (OB Procs). These preserve the central, running record of all the trials gun orders and/or submissions, the details of all examinations, investigations and trials, and the results thereof.

On 12 January, 1951 the Board remarked in OB Proc Q 6,767 that:

> *… Since 1939, the Board have published nearly 300 Proceeding on the subject of machine carbines and their ammunition. A brief precis of the most important ones concerning the weapons themselves is [reprinted below].*
>
> *The Patchett machine carbines … had shown themselves to be greatly superior to the Sten in previous trials (Procs Nos 30,171 and Q 5,369), had been used in action by Combined Operation troops, and have been recommended as suitable for adoption to replace the Sten (Proc No 30,171) …*

Several of the nearly 300 OB Procs listed hereunder from Appendix I of OB Proc Q6,767 have been quoted and/or excerpted within this book. Not all on the list concern the Patchett, and not all concerning the Patchett are listed; but the list forms an important historical document which makes very informative reading:

Machine Carbines
Summary of Main Proceedings Published Since 1939

Proc No

3,947	1939	Demand from BEF for machine combines. The Board think Thompson 0.38 0inch best immediately available.
4,000	1939	Bren and Seley-Lewis tried from hip. Bren best.
4,055	1940	Schmeisser [MP2BII] tried.
4,450	1940	The Board explain that they recommended the Thompson, which was least desirable on technical grounds, instead of the Suomi, which is the best, because the latter was not likely to be available. The Board are informed of decision to adopt 0.45 inch Thompson to meet immediate needs.
5,157	1940	*Trials arranged with Beretta.*
7,960	1940	*Schmeisser recommended for defence of aerodromes.*
8,189	1940	*Meeting decided to accept Schmeisser for all three Services.*
9,572	1940	*Report on Beretta.*
9,671	1940	*Trial of pilot model Schmeisser made by Sterling Armament Co.*
9,793	1940	*Report on trials of Thompson, Solothum, and Smith & Wesson.*
9,786	1940	*Further trials arranged with British Schmeisser.*
10,117	1941	*Report of above.*
10,310	1941	*Trial Hi-Standard, and Harrington & Richardson MCs.*
10,410	1941	*Simplified Schmeisser designed by CSD (Sten).*
10,411	1941	*Design submitted by Mr Vesley.*
10,672	1941	*Report of trials with CSD's pilot model of simplified Schmeisser – Very satisfactory.*
11,200	1941	*CSD's machine carbine referred to as "Sten" for first time.*
12,331	1941	*Report on endurance trials of drawn tube barrels for Sten.*
12,964	1941	*British Schmeisser referred to as "Lanchester" for first time.*
13,623	1941	*Brief description of Russian MC.*
14,1274	1941	*Trial of production model Stens.*
16,368	1942	*Trial of Sten Mark 3 (Lines Bros).*
16,720	1942	*Redesigned trigger mechanism for [Mk1*] Lanchester approved.*
19,663	1942	*Trials of Sten fitted with bayonet.*
19,930	1942	*Demonstrotion of first Patchett MC.*
19,959	1942	*Special bayonet for Mark 2 Sten approved.*
20,289	1942	*Trials of production model Lanchesters.*
Q930	1943	*Trials of silenced Stens.*
21,622	1943	*DNO turns down drawn tube barrels for Lanchester as outstanding demands for barrels could only be met by conventional manufacture.*
Q 1,062	1943	*Trial of special silenced machine carbines – Silent Sten, Welsilencer, Spare, and shortened Kulikowski.*
22,349	1943	*Comparative trial of various machine carbines (including Patchett) at Pendine.*
23,572	1943	*Report by Hythe Wing SAS on Welgun, Sten Mark 4, and Patchett machine carbines.*
Q 1,377	1943	*Further trials of Silent Sten, Welsilencer, Spare, and shortened Kulikowski machine carbines.*
24,443	1943	*Report on American 0.45 inch/9mm M3 machine carbine.*
Q 1,755	1943	*Comparative trial of Welgun, Patchett, Special Sten, Austen, Owen and Andrews machine carbines at Pendine.*
		The Board considered that not one of the designs rigidly met the specification but the Patchett showed most promise of doing so.
Q 1,798	1944	*General Staff Specification for machine carbine.*
Q 1,799	1944	*Trials arranged with Sten Mark 5.*
Q 1,810	1944	*Trial report of Patchett machine Carbine.*
Q 1,811	1944	*Trial report of American M3.*
Q 1,843	1944	*Detail of Australian Kokoda carbine.*
26,372	1944	*Trial report of Howard Francis carbine.*
Q 1,889	1944	*User trial of silenced Stens.*

Q2,320	1944	*Trial report of Patchett. Further trials arranged.*
30,171	1945	*Trial report of six Patchett carbines. It is reported that user trials of weapons made to special production order have proved satisfactory.*
		The Board note that the weapons meet the amended General Staff Specification and concur with SEE(P) that with regard to accuracy, functioning, endurance and· penetration, the Patchett carbine is suitable for service.
Q3,164	1945	*Mark 6 (silenced) Sten approved.*
Q3,270	1945	*Re-drafted General Staff Specification.*
Q3,685	1945	*Report of visit of Hispano Suiza. They were making Suomi type machine carbine.*
32,346	1945	*Trial report of Smith & Wesson. No further action recommended.*
Q3,946	1945	*Demonstration of Hispano Suiza machine carbine.*
32,769	1945	*Report of trials – Patchett machine carbine functioned correctly with experimental SAP ammunition.*
Q4,353	1946	*Trials arranged with CEAD's machine carbines EM-2, 3 and 6.*
Q4,532	1946	*Proposal for silencing arrangement by Patchett.*
Q4,533	1946	*Further trials arranged with Patchett.*
Q4,644	1946	*Trials arranged with Patchett Mark II.*
Q4,668	1946	*Machine carbine EM-2 withdrawn from trial as it is no better than Mark 5 Sten.*
Q4,702	1946	*Six Patchett Mark II machine carbines ordered.*
Q4,859	1947	*Report on Jürek machine carbine.*
Q4,890	1947	*General Staff policy re silenced weapons.*
Q5,127	1947	*Silent Patchett to continue on low priority.*
Q5,128	1947	*Report of user trials with machine carbine EM-3. Very good report. Machine carbine EM-6 withdrawn from trials.*
Q5,232	1947	*Trials extended to include BSA machine carbine.*
		The Board sum up-Patchett is within specification. BSA may be almost within (the excess weight being offset to some degree by a slower rate of fire which aids handling). Machine carbine EM-3 is outside specification because of weight.
Q5,278	1947	*Trials arranged of Australian experimental model No 1.*
Q5,319	1947	*Report on Viper machine pistol.*
Q5,369	1947	*Trial report of machine carbine EM-3, Patchett, BSA.*
		The Board say that there was little to choose between the machine carbine EM-3 and the Patchett Mark H. The results are not conclusive, as malfunctioning and high rate of fire of the Patchett is easily remedied. They also anticipate that functioning of BSA which was poor, could be much improved.
		Further trials of these three machine carbines arranged.
Q5,545	1948	*Report on further trials of BSA and Patchett.*
		Modified BSA gave best results and the Board said: "As far as can be judged from a single specimen it is a very satisfactory weapon. It complies with the General Staff Specification except that it is 4 oz above the 6 lb limit for weight."
		Machine carbine EM-3 functioned well, except in mud, but is 1¼ lb overweight and exceeds the desired rate of fire of 600 rpm.
		The Patchetts failed in mud and exceeded the rate of fire. The trials suggested that the adjustment of the breech block and return spring weights might be critical. In both the Patchetts tested the return springs were weak.
		Of the three weapons only the BSA was considered fit for troop trials.
		The Board recommended that 100 BSA machine carbines be ordered for troop trials, but owing to the heavy cost of tooling, this was later reduced to six to ensure that no further modifications were required before commencing large scale production.
Q5,721	1948	*Mr Patchett considered that the failure of one of his carbines in the previous trial was due to the ejector fouling the breech block He modified the weapon which was further tested. The conclusions were:*
		a. The modification had no effect on functioning.
		b. The low weight of the return spring was at least partially responsible for the malfunctioning.
		The Board recommended no further action.
Q6,018	1949	*Trials arranged of pilot models of BSA machine carbines.*
Q6,045	1949	*Trial report of Experimental Canadian machine carbine. Though over the specified weight by 1 lb 10 oz, subject to certain proposed modifications it is considered worth further development.*

Q 6,233 1949   *Trial report of pilot BSA machine carbines. Five carbines were tried and none completed the trial. It was considered that faults in manufacture might be partly responsible, but in any case the trigger mechanism required redesign to make it more robust., and to allow easy stripping and assembly. The mechanism of the cocking grip also required redesign to make it more easily removable and so that it would restrain the firer from placing his hand too far forward.*

The machine carbines were returned to the makers for rectification.

Resolving the Cliffhanger

By the sheer accident of timing, the list of OB Procs quoted above from the Appendix of Proc Q 6,767 ends right in the middle of the nail-nibbling hiatus between the first Ordnance Board recommendation of the Patchett Machine Carbine as "suitable for service".(Proc 30,171, 1945, above), and final, official adoption in October, 1953 (Chapter Four).

Sterling Product Literature

Beginning in 1943 and continuing for over forty years, Sterling Engineering Co Ltd and Sterling Armament Co Ltd produced an ever-increasing river of product literature-User Handbooks, Parts Lists, Brochures, Handouts-to support all its military and commercial guns and accessories. Although these are too numerous to list here, relevant quotes and illustrations are included throughout the book. The most valuable Sterling User Handbooks today are the earliest, on the MkI Patchett:

- *Patchett Machine Carbine* undated (summer, 1943) 8-page A4-size mimeograph written by George Patchett himself, with plain cardboard covers
- *Patchett Machine Carbine*, 1943 (autumn, 1943) 16-page 4½" x 8" illustrated green-covered booklet
- *Patchett Machine Carbine* (May, 1948) 22-page 4½" x 8" illustrated green-covered booklet

We have also quoted several excerpts from an undated (circa 1985) three-page press release entitled *Sterling Company Profile*.

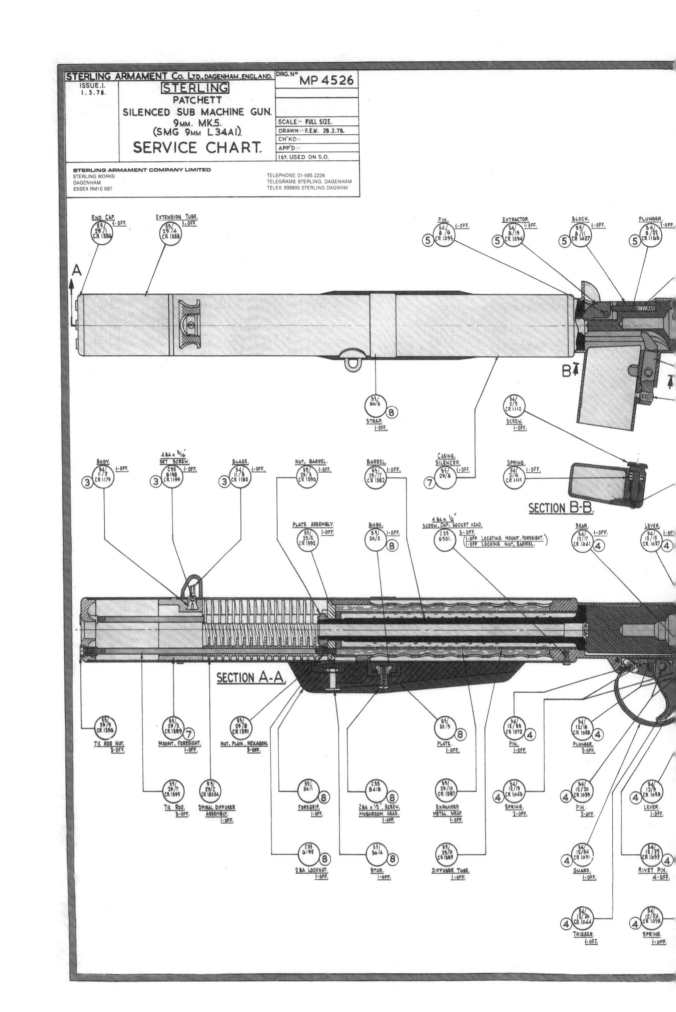

STERLING ARMAMENT Co. LTD., DAGENHAM, ENGLAND.	DRG. Nº MP 4526

STERLING
PATCHETT
SILENCED SUB MACHINE GUN.
9мм. MK.5.
(SMG 9мм L34A1).
SERVICE CHART.

ISSUE. I.
1.3.78.

SCALE :- FULL SIZE.
DRAWN :- F.E.W. 28.2.78.
CH'KD :-
APP'D :-
IST. USED ON S.O.

STERLING ARMAMENT COMPANY LIMITED
STERLING WORKS
DAGENHAM
ESSEX RM10 8ST

TELEPHONE: 01-595 2226
TELEGRAMS: STERLING. DAGENHAM
TELEX: 896895 STERLING DAGNHM

END CAP. 1·OFF. 5 9/29/1 CR 1386

EXTENSION TUBE. 1·OFF. 5 29/4 CR 1388

PIN. 1·OFF. 5 54/8/19 CR 1095

EXTRACTOR. 1·OFF. 5 54/8/19 CR 1094

BLOCK. 1·OFF. 5 55/11 CR 1427

PLUNGER. 5 54/8/22 CR 1168

A

B

STRAP. 1·OFF. 8 55/30/3

SCREW. 1·OFF. 54/2/5 CR 1110

SECTION B-B.

BODY. 1·OFF. 3 54/11/2 CR 1179

4BA x 3/16" SET SCREW. 1·OFF. 3 C55 B198 CR 1398

BLADE. 1·OFF. 3 55/11/3 CR 1180

NUT, BARREL. 1·OFF. 55/29/3 CR 1390

BARREL. 1·OFF. 55/29/17 CR 1382

CASING, SILENCER. 1·OFF. 7 55/29/8

SPRING. 1·OFF. 54/2/6 CR 1411

SEAR. 1·OFF. 54/12/7 CR 1041

LEVER. 1·OFF. 54/12/15 CR 1037

PLATE ASSEMBLY. 1·OFF. 55/29/5 CR 1392

BUSH. 1·OFF. 8 55/30/2

4BA x 1/4" SCREW, CAP, SOCKET HEAD. 3·OFF. C55 B501. 1·OFF LOCATING MOUNT, FORESIGHT. 1·OFF LOCKING NUT, BARREL.

SECTION A-A.

TIE ROD NUT. 3·OFF. 55/29/9 CR 1396

MOUNT, FORESIGHT. 1·OFF. 7 55/29/2 CR 1589

NUT, PLAIN, HEXAGON. 3·OFF. 55/29/3 CR 1391

PLATE. 1·OFF. 8 55/30/9

PIN. 1·OFF. 4 54/12/66 CR 1072

PLUNGER. 2·OFF. 54/12/18 CR 1038

TIE ROD. 3·OFF. 55/29/7 CR 1595

SPIRAL DIFFUSER ASSEMBLY. 1·OFF. 55/29/1 CR 1603A

FOREGRIP. 1·OFF. 8 55/30/1

2BA x 1/2" SCREW, MUSHROOM HEAD. 1·OFF. C55 B41B

EXPANDED METAL WRAP. 2·OFF. 55/29/10 CR 1387

SPRING. 2·OFF. 54/12/19 CR 1048

PIN. 2·OFF. 4 54/12/20 CR 1039

LEVER. 1·OFF. 54/12/5 CR 1058

2BA LOCKNUT. 1·OFF. 8 C55 G192

STUD. 1·OFF. 8 55/30/4

DIFFUSER TUBE. 1·OFF. 55/29/0 CR 1389

GUARD. 1·OFF. 4 54/12/84 CR 1051

RIVET PIN. 4·OFF. 54/12/5 CR 1055

TRIGGER. 1·OFF. 4 54/12/20 CR 1044

SPRING. 54/12/84 CR 1056